'Whenever I find myself at a low ebb spiritually i̶[obscured]̶ and without fail it is there that I find my faith reignited. I am reminded that there is no one in all of history who can compare with Jesus. I find in him the most challenging and comforting person that has ever lived. Therefore I warmly recommend *Knowing You, Jesus*, a devotional resource that draws us back to the Bible, to Jesus, and to his life-changing comfort and challenge.'
Krish Kandiah OBE, founder of Home for Good

'What a brilliant way to get to know Jesus better – spending time each day with his stories and teachings. With depth and insight, Tony Horsfall and crew lead us through a chronological account of the gospels to help us to understand and love Jesus more. Encouraging, powerful, transformative – don't miss this life-changing devotional that enlarges our love for Jesus and helps us become more like him.'
Amy Boucher Pye, retreat leader and author of *Holding onto Hope*

'This is a gentle, leisurely introduction to the gospels, with devotional thoughts from wise and experienced Christians to help the reader see, discover and imitate Jesus. Whether you've read the accounts of his life a hundred times, or are encountering him for the very first time, this book will encourage you to linger in the presence of the greatest person who ever lived.'
Marcus Honeysett, director of Living Leadership, writer and speaker

'This wonderful collection of daily devotions will help you know, love and follow Jesus as you journey through his life in scripture and with prayer. The reflections here will enrich anyone seeking intimacy with God, and would work wonderfully for a home group or a whole church community. Enter in, and be blessed!'
Ruth Bushyager, bishop of Horsham

'Regular reading and engaging with the Bible leads to human flourishing. When we approach the Bible with an open heart and mind it will always lead us to Jesus. Written by six different authors, these devotions have different styles, but they all take us to the gospels, and each reflection holds the possibility of a fresh encounter with him. A year reflecting on the life of Jesus will change you from the inside out.'
Elaine Duncan, chief executive, Scottish Bible Society

'Reading the gospels regularly is crucial if we want to stay near to the real Jesus. *Knowing You, Jesus* is a really helpful guide for doing just that – reflectively, attentively and at a gentle pace. The material is refreshing, relevant and well applied to real life, wherever we are in our relationship with Jesus.'
John and Alison Risbridger, leaders of the leadership and theology training course, Catalyst network of churches

'Nothing is more important for growing more like Christ in life and faith and behaviour, than spending time in his presence. And nothing takes us into the presence of Jesus more than spending time with him in the gospels. This book enables you to do exactly that, and perhaps the best commendation I can give, having read some of it so far, is that I plan to use it myself and benefit from the whole of it.'
Chris Wright, global ambassador, Langham Partnership

'These short reflections are loaded with deep insights and profound practical outworkings to invite Jesus to be the focus of everyday life. The writers encourage us to not only learn more about Jesus (which you will through reading these reflections), but also to get to know, encounter and become more like him. As I have read these reflections, I have sensed my soul slowing down to walk at the pace of Jesus, to choose his way of doing life and to care for those he cares for.'
Ruth Anderson, founder of The Sports Factory, and faith and sports hub coordinator for Scripture Union

'*Knowing You, Jesus* is a wise navigation of the gospel accounts from men and women who know the challenge of walking with Christ and teaching others to do so. They have clearly known the highs and lows of the walk but remain committed to helping you become captivated by the one who has all authority and calls you to make apprentices in his likeness too. Follow their guidance and be inspired.'
Andy Peck, host of *The Leadership Show*, Premier Christian Radio

KNOWING YOU, JESUS

| **365** DEVOTIONAL

With every blessing as you read these pages and discover more of who Jesus is,

Mags/ Tony

following Jesus through the gospels in a year

Tony Horsfall Mags Duggan John Ayrton
Jenny Brown Melinda Hendry Steve Aisthorpe

BRF

BRF

15 The Chambers, Vineyard
Abingdon OX14 3FE
brf.org.uk

Bible Reading Fellowship is a charity (233280)
and company limited by guarantee (301324),
registered in England and Wales

ISBN 978 1 80039 185 7
First published 2023
10 9 8 7 6 5 4 3 2 1 0
All rights reserved

Text © Tony Horsfall, Mags Duggan, John Ayrton, Jenny Brown, Melinda Hendry
and Steve Aisthorpe 2023
This edition © Bible Reading Fellowship 2023
Cover illustrated by Ben Bloxham

The authors assert the moral right to be identified as the authors of this work

Acknowledgements

Unless otherwise stated, scripture quotations are taken from The Holy Bible, New International Version® (Anglicised edition) NIV® Copyright © 1973, 1978, 1984, 2011 by Biblica, Inc. Reproduced with permission of Hodder & Stoughton Limited through PLSclear. All rights reserved worldwide.

See page 404 for a list of other Bible translations quoted in this book.

A catalogue record for this book is available from the British Library

Printed and bound by CPI Group (UK) Ltd, Croydon CR0 4YY

Photocopying for churches

Please report to CLA Church Licence any photocopy you make from this publication. Your church administrator or secretary will know who manages your CLA Church Licence.

The information you need to provide to your CLA Church Licence administrator is as follows:

Title, Author, Publisher and ISBN

If your church doesn't hold a CLA Church Licence, information about obtaining one can be found at **uk.ccli.com**

preface

Do you long to know Jesus more deeply?

Do you want his example and teaching to shape you; to discover what being a follower of Jesus means today?

Well, here is an opportunity for you, an invitation to spend a year reading the gospels slowly and thoughtfully so you can grow in your relationship with Jesus. Whether you have been a Christian for many years or are new to faith, these daily readings will inspire you as you grow in love, knowledge and understanding.

Is this your desire?

If your answer is 'Yes', then read on. The purpose of this book is to make that possible, and those of us who are writing are sharing in that same strong desire with you, opening ourselves up in new ways to the transformative power of the life of Christ.

Knowing You, Jesus is not a commentary. It will not explain every question that arises in the text or comment on everything of note. Neither is it an exposition, carefully explaining every point of interest in the text. It is a devotional guide with an emphasis on spiritual formation. Its purpose is to bring you face-to-face with the life and teaching of Jesus every day for a year, and then to see what happens. If you meet him with openness and honesty, the whole process is likely to be highly transformative.

The inspiration for this approach is a 13th-century prayer from Richard of Chichester (1197–1253), a bishop well known for his godliness and care of the poor. In words that much later became popularised through the musical *Godspell* (could he ever have imagined that?), he expressed his own longing for spiritual growth like this:

> Thanks be to you, my Lord Jesus, for all the benefits you have given me, for all the pains and insults you have borne for me. O most merciful redeemer, friend and brother, of you three things I pray: to see you more clearly, love you more dearly, follow you more nearly, day by day.

Our invitation is for you to make this prayer your own, asking God that as you read and pray you may come to understand Jesus more fully (*see*), be attached to him more deeply (*love*) and apply his teaching to your life more completely (*follow*).

As far as possible we have arranged the life of Christ chronologically, so that we follow his story like a thread through all four gospels, from his birth to his resurrection and ascension. This systematic arranging of the material has been attempted by many but is virtually impossible. It is not an exact science, so bear with us should you regard the chronology of events differently.

As you can imagine, there is a huge amount of material to be included, so some readings will have much more text than comment. Remember that the scripture is always primary. Linger over it, let it speak to you, notice how the Spirit applies it, make your own observations about it. It may also be helpful to compare the different gospel accounts of the same event. Notice, if you can, people and places that are mentioned, when the action takes place and in which period of the life of Christ things happen. Above all, seek to 'read, mark, learn and inwardly digest' the daily portion of scripture, as the Collect says. Respond to any prompts that are given to you in the daily note, perhaps journalling alongside your reading.

To help you interact with the text for yourself, we have included simple guidelines on four of the main ways we may do this – Bible meditation, reading the gospels prayerfully, imaginative reading of a passage and *lectio divina*. Use these at your own discretion, or when prompted by the writer.

As an aid to accountability, why not consider taking this journey in the company of another person or even in a small group? You might meet monthly to share your findings and discoveries, consider any questions that have arisen for you and discuss the practical application of your reading so that this exercise is, above all, transformative. Such a group could meet in person, and therefore be local, or could be online with an international flavour – the possibilities are endless, so use your imagination.

Even better, why not encourage the whole church to be involved? Imagine the impact this could have on a church if the whole congregation were to give themselves intentionally to the task of knowing Jesus more deeply!

So, the adventure awaits. Let's get started.

Your friends

Tony, Mags, John, Jenny, Melinda and Steve

contents

Introduction 9

> **Ways to engage with the Bible: Bible meditation** 10
> Tony Horsfall
>
> **Ways to engage with the Bible: praying the gospels** 11
> Tony Horsfall
>
> **Ways to engage with the Bible: using our imagination in prayer** 12
> Mags Duggan
>
> **Ways to engage with the Bible: *lectio divina*** 13
> Mags Duggan

Beginnings   Days 1–32 15
Tony Horsfall

The first year: the year of inauguration   Days 33–80 49
Mags Duggan

The second year: the year of popularity   Days 81–139 99
John Ayrton

The third year: the year of opposition   Days 140–160 159
Jenny Brown

The last few months   Days 161–195 181
Melinda Hendry

The journey to Jerusalem   Days 196–240 217
Mags Duggan

The last few weeks   Days 241–247 263
Jenny Brown

The last week   Days 248–306 271
Tony Horsfall

Arrest and trial   Days 307–325 341
Jenny Brown and Tony Horsfall

The crucifixion   Days 326–340 361
Steve Aisthorpe

The resurrection and aftermath   Days 341–366 377
Tony Horsfall

List of Bible translations 404

Notes 406

Bibliography 408

About the authors 410

introduction

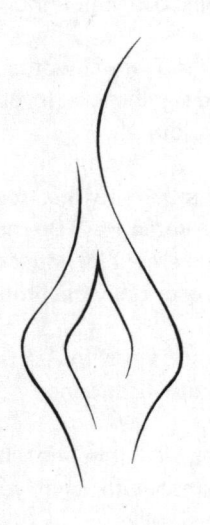

Ways to engage with the Bible: Bible meditation

In Bible meditation, we take a small portion of the word of God and chew it over in our minds, seeking both to understand it and to apply it to our lives in a very personal way. It is a process by which the truth sinks down from our heads into our hearts, and information becomes transformation.

This familiar Hebrew approach to scripture is mentioned in Genesis 24:63; Joshua 1:8; Psalms 1:2–3; 19:14; 104:34; 143:5; and 2 Timothy 2:7. We notice that Mary meditated on the events surrounding the birth of Jesus, she 'treasured up all these things and pondered them in her heart' (Luke 2:19; see also v. 51). Meditation has been likened to a dog chewing a bone, a cow ruminating in the field or a person sucking a sweet.

1. It is helpful to begin by memorising a chosen verse. Repeat the words over and over again to yourself until they are fixed in your mind. Writing it down may help.

2. Next, begin to think about the individual words. Savour each one, asking God to reveal to you their meaning and significance. If you are unsure about the meaning of a word, use a dictionary to help you.

3. Consider then how these words touch your life. How should you respond to them? Do they challenge you to change in some way? Do they contain a promise that you can take hold of? Is there an encouragement for you, or a warning? Seek to apply them to your life. Personalise the verse, especially the pronouns.

4. Turn your thoughts into prayer and worship. Ask God to make this scripture a reality in your life. Thank him for the truth it contains.

5. Live in the light of your meditation. Act in line with the truth you have discovered. Speak in a way that is consistent with what you have learned. Do whatever is necessary to apply the word personally.

It may be helpful to continue meditating on the same scripture for several days, asking the Holy Spirit to reveal its significance and application to you.

Ways to engage with the Bible: praying the gospels

A helpful way to interact with scripture is to turn the words we are reading into prayer, both for ourselves and others. The gospels are steeped in both prayer and teaching about prayer, so we can pick up on this as we are reading and use it to stimulate our own prayer life. The example of Jesus, who continually withdrew in order to pray, is especially motivating.

1. Read scripture as a dialogue between yourself and God. Turn your thoughts into prayer. Have a conversation with God as you read. Allow your prayers to be formed and shaped by what you are reading.

2. Pray the Lord's Prayer, the basic pattern for prayer as taught by Jesus. (See Matthew 6:9–13; Luke 11:1–4.)

3. Pray the promises. Notice when Jesus makes a promise and make it your own. Personalise it, put your name there and remind him in prayer of what he has said. For example, based on Matthew 11:28, you could pray:

Lord, you say here that if we are weary and burdened we may come to you, and you will give us rest. So this day, Lord, I come just as I am. Yes, weary because of all that I have been doing, rushing here and there, trying to achieve so much. And burdened, too, carrying so much responsibility, with so many people looking to me for help and advice. To be honest, Lord, I am exhausted. So I come and lay my burdens down at your feet and allow you to refresh my soul this day. Amen.

4. Pray the stories. Look for examples to follow or avoid. Let them inspire you to ask for greater faith, to avoid certain temptations, to stand fast during trials or persevere under persecution, and so on.

5. Pray the prayers of Jesus, making them your own. See, for example, Matthew 26:39–42; Luke 22:31–32; John 11:41–42; 17:1–26.

6. Listen and respond to any commands to pray, or instructions about prayer, and put them into practice – for example, Matthew 5:44; 6:6; 9:38.

7. Use any prompts to prayer that are given to you in the daily notes.

Ways to engage with the Bible: using our imagination in prayer

Jesus constantly painted pictures with words. He drew his audience into his stories with vivid descriptions of mountains moving into the sea, of thorn bushes bearing figs and briers bearing grapes, of sons covered in pig muck and fathers who picked up their skirts and ran down the road, flinging their arms around their smelly son! Jesus graphically described people and places to fire the imagination of his hearers, inviting them to enter into the scene he was describing.

The parables of Jesus brilliantly lend themselves to this kind of reading – but so do other events in the gospels. When we engage with a Bible passage by building up a picture in our minds, we have the opportunity to enter into the events of the gospels, which are as relevant and life-changing today as they were 2,000 years ago. Our aim is to become as present as possible to what is happening in the passage we are reading, allowing ourselves to enter the scene and letting God speak through what we find, trusting his Spirit to lead us into all truth (John 14:17; 16:13).

Steps into reading and prayer

- Begin by asking the Holy Spirit to guide your thoughts, imagination and prayer.
- Read the Bible passage through several times until it becomes familiar.
- Then, explore the scene in your mind. You may find the following approaches helpful:
  - What can you see/hear/taste/smell? For example, what is the weather like? Windy? Still? Sunny? What about smells – animals, humans, grass, flowers, dust? What can you hear – wind, donkeys braying, waves hitting a boat, shouting, shuffling?
  - Next, imagine yourself as one of the participants in the scene. Who are you, where are you? Where is Jesus? What is he doing? Do you have any interaction with him – or are you a bystander?
- Gently sit with the passage and simply allow it to unfold in your mind.
- Take time to respond to the Lord in prayer over what you have seen/heard/felt.
- What do you sense Jesus is inviting you to be, or to do? Simply to sit in silent wonder is a response!
- Note down anything particular that struck you or seemed important. You may wish to come back to this in a subsequent prayer time.

Ways to engage with the Bible: *lectio divina*

In reading the scriptures, how we read is as important as what we read. One ancient prayer practice helps us move from an analytical, informational approach to a more formational and relational one and is called *lectio divina* or spiritual reading. Rather than reading the Bible, we allow the Bible to read us and address us by name.

There are four basic moves to this practice: read; reflect; respond; rest.

We prepare by quietening ourselves, acknowledging God's presence with us and surrendering our hearts to God so that we can listen expectantly to what he wants to say to us from his word.

- *Read*. First, we read a short passage of scripture – just a few verses are enough. It helps to read aloud and slowly, so that we are not just glancing at the words with our eyes, but really hearing and noticing them, tasting and savouring them. As we read, we are listening, watching for whatever individual word or phrase seems to stand out and grab our attention, or in some way to be given to us. We ask, 'What do you want to say to me today, Lord?'

- *Reflect*. Next, staying with the word or phrase that we sense God has given to us as we have read, we reflect on it, perhaps asking, 'Why this word? What was it about this word that touched my heart? How does it speak to my life right now?' Take your time here, there is no rush to accomplish anything; simply reflect.

- *Respond*. We have listened and reflected, now is the time to respond in prayer and by action. What seems appropriate – praise and thanksgiving? Confession or an expression of sorrow or lament? A moment of surrender, giving yourself to God again in trust and faith? Taking the first step in obedience? Whatever has been stirred up in us by our reading, we bring to God, honestly and openly, in prayer.

- *Rest*. Finally, after we have said all we want or need to say, we rest in God's loving presence. So often after our Bible reading, we rush into our days, but the practice of *lectio divina* invites us to pause and to rest awhile in God's presence before moving off.

beginnings

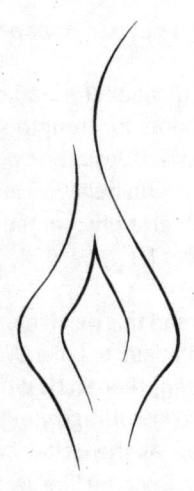

TONY HORSFALL

Day 1

Why write a book?

LUKE 1:1–4

Many have undertaken to draw up an account of the things that have been fulfilled among us, just as they were handed down to us by those who from the first were eye witnesses and servants of the word. With this in mind, since I myself have carefully investigated everything from the beginning, I too decided to write an orderly account for you, most excellent Theophilus, so that you may know the certainty of the things you have been taught.

As an author I am often asked, 'How did you get into writing?' Well, I had always wanted to write, even as a schoolboy, and dreamed of being a sports journalist, but that never materialised. Instead, I followed the path I felt God had for me, serving overseas as a missionary and then as a pastor of a local church in my home country. Eventually, when I felt I had something worth saying, I put pen to paper and my writing career began.

Luke is thought to have been a medical doctor and companion of the apostle Paul. His motivation in writing is clear – he wants to strengthen the faith of his friend Theophilus, and so has researched the whole story of Jesus and presented it in an organised way that would be easy for a Gentile to follow and believe. He may have gathered some material from Mary the mother of Jesus, and certainly seemed to have enjoyed writing – he is also responsible for the book of Acts (Acts 1:1).

I wonder why you have decided to read this particular book? Those of us who are writing are doing so because we have a similar aim to Luke. We want to strengthen the faith of our readers, even as our own faith is strengthened by writing and reflecting on the amazing story of Jesus. Above all, we want to encourage you to let the story impact your life and change you as you read day-by-day. As the writer and priest Henri Nouwen said: 'The whole message of the gospel is this: Become like Jesus.'[1]

> *Lord, as I begin this journey with Jesus, open my eyes to see his beauty and glory, and help me to become more like him in my thoughts and actions. Give me perseverance as I read and grace to stay the course. Amen.*

TH

Day 2

The genealogy of Jesus (1)

MATTHEW 1:1–6

This is the genealogy of Jesus the Messiah the son of David, the son of Abraham: Abraham was the father of Isaac, Isaac the father of Jacob, Jacob the father of Judah and his brothers, Judah the father of Perez and Zerah, whose mother was Tamar, Perez the father of Hezron, Hezron the father of Ram, Ram the father of Amminadab, Amminadab the father of Nahshon, Nahshon the father of Salmon, Salmon the father of Boaz, whose mother was Rahab, Boaz the father of Obed, whose mother was Ruth, Obed the father of Jesse, and Jesse the father of King David.

Have you done any research into your family tree? I have, and it is fascinating to discover more about where I came from and the people who are part of my ancestry, mostly humble, working-class people.

Matthew begins his gospel with a long genealogy tracing the ancestors of Jesus, but not simply for the purpose of family history. Matthew writes to convince Jewish readers that Jesus is the long-awaited Messiah. To achieve this, he has first to establish Jesus' credentials – that Jesus is descended not only from King David (and therefore is the son of David), but also from Abraham, the father of all who believe.

As you read this list of hard-to-pronounce names, and wonder who they all are, try to sense what Matthew is doing – connecting Jesus to the very beginning of Israel's history and making him the fulfilment of all the promises that God gave to father Abraham, and to that other great figure, King David. The plans and purposes of God have been worked out over many centuries. Despite many ups and downs and failures among God's chosen people, the river of blessing kept flowing, culminating in the arrival of Jesus. All the hopes of Israel's history are gathered up into his birth, and Matthew is laying a foundation of understanding so we can appreciate this.

History may not be your strong point, but if you remember that history is simply 'his story' you may appreciate it all so much more. And the amazing thing is that as a follower of Jesus you are now part of this sacred history.

> Lord, you know who I am and where I am from. Thank you for including even me in your eternal purpose.

TH

Day 3

The genealogy of Jesus (2)

MATTHEW 1:6-11

David was the father of Solomon, whose mother had been Uriah's wife, Solomon the father of Rehoboam, Rehoboam the father of Abijah, Abijah the father of Asa, Asa the father of Jehoshaphat, Jehoshaphat the father of Jehoram, Jehoram the father of Uzziah, Uzziah the father of Jotham, Jotham the father of Ahaz, Ahaz the father of Hezekiah, Hezekiah the father of Manasseh, Manasseh the father of Amon, Amon the father of Josiah, and Josiah the father of Jeconiah and his brothers at the time of the exile to Babylon.

A popular British TV programme charts the ancestry of various celebrities. Called *Who Do You Think You Are?*, it uses experts to dig out the stories behind the facts and make forgotten people come alive, both heroes and villains, often to the surprise of those who are the subject of the documentary.

As we look at this list of names here, we will be familiar with some, for they are heroes, prominent in Israel's history: David, the man after God's own heart, slayer of Goliath and their champion against the Philistines; Solomon, builder of the temple; Jehoshaphat, who led their armies into battle with songs of praise; Uzziah, whose wise and prosperous reign brought peace and stability; Hezekiah and Josiah, who both purified the temple and brought spiritual renewal.

Some, however, were villains, like Jehoram, who passed away to no one's regret; Ahaz, who was pointedly not buried alongside the other kings; and Manasseh, who did evil in the sight of God. Yet they are included in the genealogy of the Messiah, and not airbrushed out. This says to me that grace is greater than our sin and shortcomings, and the purpose of God is stronger than human failure and weakness.

This I find greatly encouraging. My own spiritual history is mixed, with moments of high achievement and times of abject failure and demoralising folly. You probably feel much the same when you chart the course of your journey with God. Yet God not only forgives us when we repent but weaves our mistakes and sin into his overall good purpose for us.

> *Take a moment to review your spiritual history. What have been the highs? And the lows? Hand both over to God, knowing that his love for you is undiminished and his gracious purpose for you undefeatable.*

TH

Day 4

The genealogy of Jesus (3)

MATTHEW 1:12–17

After the exile to Babylon: Jeconiah was the father of Shealtiel, Shealtiel the father of Zerubbabel, Zerubbabel the father of Abihud, Abihud the father of Eliakim, Eliakim the father of Azor, Azor the father of Zadok, Zadok the father of Akim, Akim the father of Elihud, Elihud the father of Eleazar, Eleazar the father of Matthan, Matthan the father of Jacob, and Jacob the father of Joseph, the husband of Mary, and Mary was the mother of Jesus who is called the Messiah. Thus there were fourteen generations in all from Abraham to David, fourteen from David to the exile to Babylon, and fourteen from the exile to the Messiah.

Are you an organised person? Do you like structure and order in your life? Do you do things in a methodical, logical way? I think Matthew certainly did. As a former tax collector (Matthew 9:9) he probably liked things to add up, to make sure his accounts tallied at the end of the day. His approach to the genealogy of Jesus demonstrates this tendency towards an orderly mind.

Matthew divides the history of Israel neatly into three time periods, each of 14 generations. He is not so much concerned with historical accuracy as the shape of that history and where that history is going – in this case, flowing towards the birth of Jesus, the long-awaited Messiah. This ordering of history suggests planning and forethought, that God was in fact shaping world events in preparation for the coming of the Saviour.

It is interesting to see how Joseph finds a place in the bigger story of Israel as a descendant of King David. This will be an important factor in where Jesus will be born and his connection with the line of David.

Mary too is mentioned, the fifth woman named by Matthew, and the one who would be the mother of the Messiah. Her love for Joseph was no accident; it brought her too into David's line, another indication of the planning of God. Nothing it seems is happening by chance.

> *I hope you find great comfort from knowing that God's purpose is being worked out in history, that he 'works out everything in conformity with the purpose of his will' (Ephesians 1:11) and that this applies to the events of your life as well. Take a moment to ponder the implications of this.*

TH

Day 5

Zechariah the priest

LUKE 1:5–10

Jerusalem, the temple
In the time of Herod king of Judea there was a priest named Zechariah, who belonged to the priestly division of Abijah; his wife Elizabeth was also a descendant of Aaron. Both of them were righteous in the sight of God, observing all the Lord's commands and decrees blamelessly. But they were childless because Elizabeth was not able to conceive, and they were both very old. Once when Zechariah's division was on duty and he was serving as priest before God, he was chosen by lot, according to the custom of the priesthood, to go into the temple of the Lord and burn incense. And when the time for the burning of incense came, all the assembled worshippers were praying outside.

Some days are 'red letter' days, aren't they – days that stand out and stay long in the memory; days when the extraordinary seems to burst into the ordinary.

Luke writes about a special day in the life of a humble priest named Zechariah, a once-in-a-lifetime occasion when he was chosen to serve in the temple in Jerusalem. Imagine his excitement as he prepared for his big day, perhaps a little nervous in case he makes a mistake. Did he sleep well the night before or did he toss and turn?

Yet despite his obvious joy there remained buried in his heart a deep sorrow, a sadness shared with his wife Elizabeth, for they had been unable to have children. Only those who have longed for children yet been unable to conceive know the depth of this pain. Even the faithful obedience of this godly couple did not immunise them against the pains of life, but they did not rail against God. Instead, they got on with life as best they could, surrendering their broken dreams to the God they worshipped and served.

What are we to do with our disappointments? We must face the pain of unanswered prayer and unfulfilled longing in whatever form it takes, shed our tears and taste the grief, and yet not get stuck there. The challenge is to offer our pain to God and trust in his goodness no matter how we feel, and then, like this godly couple, choose to get on with life even if the pain is always there, somewhere.

▌ *Are you disappointed with God? Tell him about it, and give your pain to him.*

TH

Day 6

John's birth foretold

LUKE 1:11-18

Jerusalem, the temple
Then an angel of the Lord appeared to him, standing at the right side of the altar of incense. When Zechariah saw him, he was startled and was gripped with fear. But the angel said to him: 'Do not be afraid, Zechariah; your prayer has been heard. Your wife Elizabeth will bear you a son, and you are to call him John. He will be a joy and delight to you, and many will rejoice because of his birth, for he will be great in the sight of the Lord. He is never to take wine or other fermented drink, and he will be filled with the Holy Spirit even before he is born. He will bring back many of the people of Israel to the Lord their God. And he will go on before the Lord, in the spirit and power of Elijah, to turn the hearts of the parents to their children and the disobedient to the wisdom of the righteous – to make ready a people prepared for the Lord.' Zechariah asked the angel, 'How can I be sure of this? I am an old man and my wife is well on in years.'

Zechariah's day got even better, for the God of great surprises had something special in mind for this faithful couple.

First, the appearance of an angel, an event so unusual and awe-inspiring as to startle and terrify this humble country priest. No doubt he expected to feel the presence of God in the temple, but not as tangibly as this!

Then the message that all those tearful prayers had not gone unnoticed in heaven, but had been saved up for the right moment, and that moment had just arrived when it most seemed impossible. Zechariah and Elizabeth were to have a child after all, despite their advanced years. I expect Zechariah struggled to take that in, to believe that such a thing were possible.

But there is more. The son to be born will have a special part to play in the purpose of God, and will become an instrument whom God will use to bring many back to himself, preparing the hearts of all for a special visitation.

No wonder Zechariah struggled to accept all this. Sometimes the goodness of God is simply too good to comprehend.

> *When has God surprised you? How have you experienced the goodness of God?*

TH

Day 7

Silence and seclusion

LUKE 1:19–25

Jerusalem, the temple
The angel said to him, 'I am Gabriel. I stand in the presence of God, and I have been sent to speak to you and to tell you this good news. And now you will be silent and not able to speak until the day this happens, because you did not believe my words, which will come true at their appointed time.' Meanwhile, the people were waiting for Zechariah and wondering why he stayed so long in the temple. When he came out, he could not speak to them. They realised he had seen a vision in the temple, for he kept making signs to them but remained unable to speak. When his time of service was completed, he returned home. After this his wife Elizabeth became pregnant and for five months remained in seclusion. 'The Lord has done this for me,' she said. 'In these days he has shown his favour and taken away my disgrace among the people.'

I don't regard Zechariah's imposed silence as a punishment, rather as a discipline at the hand of God. Punishment suggests we have done something wrong; discipline implies that we have something to learn. Zechariah needed to be trained further in the ways of God, to be schooled in the life of faith, and that is a normal part of the growth process in our walk with God.

His time of silence gave him space to ponder what had happened that day in the temple, and even Gabriel's censure brings with it an important lesson – that whatever God says will come to pass when the time is right. That is how faith works, as the book of Hebrews reminds us: 'Now faith is confidence in what we hope for and assurance about what we do not see' (Hebrews 11:1). Over time Zechariah came to see that, even though it appeared impossible, the word of God would prove to be true, and his faith was strengthened.

Elizabeth seems to have found it all much easier, rejoicing in the favour of God upon her life and the removal of her cultural disgrace. Yet even she hides away as she awaits the fulfilment of God's word.

> *What has God been teaching you about the life of faith? When have you found it difficult to believe his promises to you? How are you growing in faith?*

TH

Day 8

The angel and Mary

LUKE 1:26–33

Nazareth
In the sixth month of Elizabeth's pregnancy, God sent the angel Gabriel to Nazareth, a town in Galilee, to a virgin pledged to be married to a man named Joseph, a descendant of David. The virgin's name was Mary. The angel went to her and said, 'Greetings, you who are highly favoured! The Lord is with you.' Mary was greatly troubled at his words and wondered what kind of greeting this might be. But the angel said to her, 'Do not be afraid, Mary, you have found favour with God. You will conceive and give birth to a son, and you are to call him Jesus. He will be great and will be called the Son of the Most High. The Lord God will give him the throne of his father David, and he will reign over Jacob's descendants for ever; his kingdom will never end.'

I came to faith as a 14-year-old boy, hearing the gospel preached in the village chapel where I grew up. I knew almost at once that God had a plan for my life. We should never underestimate the ability of God to use young people in his purposes.

Many scholars suggest that Mary would have been a teenage girl when the angel appeared to her. She was not chosen at random, for her faith and willingness to obey were already known to God. She was designated to be the one to give birth to the Saviour of the world, and despite some initial fear, she accepted this staggering assignment.

This is the first mention we have of the name of Jesus and the purpose of his coming. He will be Mary's son and yet people will recognise his divine origins as Son of the Most High. He will come in fulfilment of the promises made to King David that one from his line will establish a new kingdom, the kingdom of God (2 Samuel 7:11–14).

Whether we are young or old, the privilege of being caught up into the purposes of God is open to all. What is required is that, like Mary, we show a willingness to offer ourselves totally to God for whatever purpose he has for us. This may seem daunting, but God says to us as well, 'Do not be afraid.' Those whom God calls, he also enables.

▎ *Ponder this: 'You have found favour with God' (v. 30).*

TH

Day 9

Mary's submission

LUKE 1:34-38

Nazareth
'How will this be,' Mary asked the angel, 'since I am a virgin?' The angel answered, 'The Holy Spirit will come on you, and the power of the Most High will overshadow you. So the holy one to be born will be called the Son of God. Even Elizabeth your relative is going to have a child in her old age, and she who was said to be unable to conceive is in her sixth month. For no word from God will ever fail.' 'I am the Lord's servant,' Mary answered. 'May your word to me be fulfilled.' Then the angel left her.

Not long after my conversion I came across *Prayers of Life* by Michel Quoist.[2] One of his prayers is entitled 'Help me to say "Yes"', and it contains this profound truth – that God needs our 'Yes' even as he needed Mary's 'Yes' to come to earth. This understanding that joyful surrender to the will of God is at the heart of discipleship has never left me and even today, many decades later, it remains one of my guiding principles.

There may have been a naiveté to Mary's youthful response, yet it was one of courage and faith and built upon some reassurances from the angel Gabriel. First, it is the power of the Holy Spirit that will make this miraculous thing come about. Then, the testimony of her aged cousin Elizabeth to a similar visitation from God will add credence to what God appears to be doing. Finally, there is the angelic guarantee that if God says something, it will definitely come to pass. Here are solid reasons on which faith and obedience can rest.

Mary's response is one of surrender to God's will, despite the enormity of the call and the potential repercussions. Such surrender shows her love for God and her awareness of God's love for her. In that security, she dares to give herself completely. God does not force us to do his will, but gently invites us to trust him and to follow his leading.

> Take time today to meditate on Mary's words, 'I am the Lord's servant. May your word to me be fulfilled' (v. 38). Put yourself in her shoes. What does surrender mean to you? What is God asking you to do?

TH

Day 10

Mary visits Elizabeth

LUKE 1:39-45

Hill country of Judea
At that time Mary got ready and hurried to a town in the hill country of Judea, where she entered Zechariah's home and greeted Elizabeth. When Elizabeth heard Mary's greeting, the baby leaped in her womb, and Elizabeth was filled with the Holy Spirit. In a loud voice she exclaimed: 'Blessed are you among women, and blessed is the child you will bear! But why am I so favoured, that the mother of my Lord should come to me? As soon as the sound of your greeting reached my ears, the baby in my womb leaped for joy. Blessed is she who has believed that the Lord would fulfil his promises to her!'

Where would be a safe place for you? Where would you go to find peace and quiet and time to think? And if you were in need, who would be a safe person to whom you could unburden yourself? Who would you trust with your most important secrets?

For Mary, at this important juncture in her life, there was only one place to go, and one person she wanted to be with. She fled (notice the word 'hurried') to the remote hill country of Judea away from the scrutiny of life in Nazareth. She ran to her cousin Elizabeth, a mother-like figure to her and someone she knew would welcome her with open arms.

This special relationship illustrates the importance of building close, supportive friendships so that when we are in trouble, need help and guidance or an encouraging word, we know where to turn. Some would call this mentoring, a relationship where one helps another to recognise the work of God in their life.

Elizabeth's encouragement is more than platitudes or well-wishing. Under the inspiration of the Spirit, she speaks a word from God that lifts Mary's heart and fortifies her for the days ahead. How wonderful to be the mouthpiece of God, to receive a word in season to strengthen and sustain a weary one (Isaiah 50:4). How wise to know when to seek counsel and help from an experienced friend or mentor.

> *Thank God today for those who have been a place of refuge for you. Let them know you appreciate their support. How might you in turn be a safe person to someone else? Who do you know who needs encouragement right now?*

TH

Day 11

Mary glorifies God

LUKE 1:46–56

Elizabeth's house
And Mary said: 'My soul glorifies the Lord and my spirit rejoices in God my Saviour, for he has been mindful of the humble state of his servant. From now on all generations will call me blessed, for the Mighty One has done great things for me – holy is his name. His mercy extends to those who fear him, from generation to generation. He has performed mighty deeds with his arm; he has scattered those who are proud in their inmost thoughts. He has brought down rulers from their thrones but has lifted up the humble. He has filled the hungry with good things but has sent the rich away empty. He has helped his servant Israel, remembering to be merciful to Abraham and his descendants forever, just as he promised our ancestors.' Mary stayed with Elizabeth for about three months and then returned home.

In the safety and security of Elizabeth's home, Mary's soul found a refuge and her faith began to grow. Stepping back for a while enabled her to gain a sense of perspective and allow the truth of what the angel Gabriel had said to sink into her heart and captivate her mind.

The three months with Elizabeth were like a retreat for the young mother-to-be, and the loving attention of her cousin guided her through the early days of pregnancy. They had much to share about the staggering things that God was doing in their lives, things which most people could never understand. Such is the value of spiritual friendship.

Mary's song of praise, often called the Magnificat, reveals her developing understanding of who God is. She sees that God is mindful of her, giving loving attention to her despite her lowly background. She knows that he is merciful, showing kindness especially to the poor. He is powerful, deposing proud, earthly rulers and exalting the humble. He is faithful, and through the child to be born fulfilling ancient promises to Israel and the patriarch Abraham. Such a God is worthy of our praise.

> Why not meditate on these words: 'the Mighty One has done great things for me' (v. 49). What makes you rejoice in God today? You may like to write your own version of the Magnificat – what are you learning about who God is? In what ways has he blessed your life?

TH

Day 12

His name is John

LUKE 1:57–66

Hill country of Judea
When it was time for Elizabeth to have her baby, she gave birth to a son. Her neighbours and relatives heard that the Lord had shown her great mercy, and they shared her joy. On the eighth day they came to circumcise the child, and they were going to name him after his father Zechariah, but his mother spoke up and said, 'No! He is to be called John.' They said to her, 'There is no one among your relatives who has that name.' Then they made signs to his father, to find out what he would like to name the child. He asked for a writing tablet, and to everyone's astonishment he wrote, 'His name is John.' Immediately his mouth was opened and his tongue set free, and he began to speak, praising God. All the neighbours were filled with awe, and throughout the hill country of Judea people were talking about all these things. Everyone who heard this wondered about it, asking, 'What then is this child going to be?' For the Lord's hand was with him.

For some parents, choosing the name of a new baby is a difficult task. Do they go for a name that is currently popular or one with family connections? Do they choose a name with meaning or simply one that sounds right? Often cultural factors play a part, and there can be pressure from well-meaning relatives and friends in the decision-making.

Zechariah may have faltered in his faith but is resolute now in his obedience. His time of silence and seclusion have clarified his thinking and, although there is external pressure to conform to the expectation of others, he does not waver. 'His name is John' may be a simple statement, but on such small acts of obedience to God much depends. Happily, Zechariah and Elizabeth are agreed on this important detail. Immediately Zechariah's tongue is released, and praise begins to flow from his mouth.

It is easy to allow popular opinion to push us off course when it comes to obeying God. We need the strength to say 'No' sometimes, otherwise we can find ourselves compromising on important principles. We do not say 'No' to be awkward, but in order to say 'Yes' to God.

> *When may you need to swim against the tide? Remember, the majority are not always right.*

TH

Day 13

Zechariah's praise

LUKE 1:67–75

Hill country of Judea
His father Zechariah was filled with the Holy Spirit and prophesied: 'Praise be to the Lord, the God of Israel, because he has come to his people and redeemed them. He has raised up a horn of salvation for us in the house of his servant David (as he said through his holy prophets of long ago), salvation from our enemies and from the hand of all who hate us – to show mercy to our ancestors and to remember his holy covenant, the oath he swore to our father Abraham: to rescue us from the hand of our enemies, and to enable us to serve him without fear in holiness and righteousness before him all our days.'

The unusual events surrounding the birth and naming of John have stirred up a feeling in the community that something is happening, that God is on the move. There is an excitement and a buzz of expectation.

Zechariah's act of obedience has released not only his tongue but his spirit and opened him up to the influence of the Holy Spirit. His God-given words reveal exactly what is going on. Long-held hopes for a visitation from God are about to be fulfilled.

The first part of his prophecy speaks not of his own child, but that of Mary. The time has come for the promises given to Israel, and to Abraham in particular, to come to pass. Zechariah is enabled to see the bigger picture of God's great plan of salvation and redemption, the outworking of his covenant with Abraham. A new day is about to dawn when God's people will be free from their enemies and enabled to serve him in holiness and righteousness.

It is helpful to remember that our lives are lived in the context of the outworking of God's plans for the world. This stops us becoming narrow-minded or blinkered in our approach to life. What happens to us matters, but it is not the whole story. We are part of something far bigger and are being carried along on the stream of God's eternal purpose.

It is tempting sometimes to think that the world is out of control, that events happen randomly, and that evil has the ascendency, but that is not so. Behind all the upheavals, God remains in charge, and his purpose unstoppable.

> *How can you focus on the bigger picture?*

TH

Day 14

Zechariah's prophecy

LUKE 1:76–80

Hill country of Judea
'And you, my child, will be called a prophet of the Most High; for you will go on before the Lord to prepare the way for him, to give his people the knowledge of salvation through the forgiveness of their sins, because of the tender mercy of our God, by which the rising sun will come to us from heaven to shine on those living in darkness and in the shadow of death, to guide our feet into the path of peace.' And the child grew and became strong in spirit; and he lived in the wilderness until he appeared publicly to Israel.

Most parents cherish dreams for their children and do their best to help them reach their full potential. I often look at my grandchildren and wonder, 'What will they become? Where will life take them?'

In the second part of his prophecy, Zechariah is given insight by the Spirit into the God-given destiny that awaits the baby named John. No doubt he had pondered the words of the angel, how the boy would develop spiritually and operate in the spirit and power of Elijah (Luke 1:14–18). Now he receives from God his own insight into the child's future.

John will have a particular role to play as the purposes of God for Israel reach a crescendo – he will have the honour to prepare the way for the visitation of God. His calling will be to awaken people to the merciful offer of salvation through forgiveness, and to the dawning of the new day when God's sunrise will lighten the darkness. The birth of Jesus will not happen in a vacuum. His arrival will be anticipated, and Zechariah's son will pave the way.

There is never any hurry with God. The infant John will grow and develop like other children, being especially sensitive to God from an early age. He will find solitude in the desert, learning to hear God's voice, and bide his time until the moment comes for him to begin his work of preparing the way. Public ministry is often preceded by long years of private preparation.

> *What calling do you sense God has given to you? How has he prepared you for this? How did your childhood shape and fashion you? Perhaps he is preparing you even now for something that is still to come.*

TH

Day 15

Joseph's predicament

MATTHEW 1:18-21

Nazareth

This is how the birth of Jesus the Messiah came about: his mother Mary was pledged to be married to Joseph, but before they came together, she was found to be pregnant through the Holy Spirit. Because Joseph her husband was faithful to the law, and yet did not want to expose her to public disgrace, he had in mind to divorce her quietly. But after he had considered this, an angel of the Lord appeared to him in a dream and said, 'Joseph son of David, do not be afraid to take Mary home as your wife, because what is conceived in her is from the Holy Spirit. She will give birth to a son, and you are to give him the name Jesus, because he will save his people from their sins.'

Matthew immediately identifies for his readers Jesus as the Messiah, the one sent by God to be the fulfilment of the ancient promises, and through whom the kingdom of God will come to earth. We are left in no doubt about his true identity, although for Joseph it is not so straightforward.

The news that Mary was pregnant threw Joseph into a quandary, probably the greatest dilemma of his life. He knew Mary to be honourable and God-fearing, yet she was with child, and not by him. He also knew that the law was clear about her apparent misbehaviour, yet his love for her cried out for a merciful response – a private parting rather than public disgrace. Fortunately, Joseph was not hasty in his decision and did not respond out of anger. He considered carefully what he should do. His measured approach prevented him from making a big mistake.

God knew the dilemma that Joseph was in and spoke to him so he could understand what was happening and that the child had been conceived miraculously through the agency of the Spirit. Like Zechariah's son, this child will also have a divine mission, to save his people from their sins.

> *How do you make your decisions? Are you impetuous and reactive, or measured and careful in your approach? Can you think back to a moment of dilemma in your own life? How was it resolved? What did you learn from that experience? Pray for anyone you know currently having to make big decisions.*

TH

Day 16

Joseph's obedience

MATTHEW 1:22-25

Nazareth
All this took place to fulfil what the Lord had said through the prophet: 'The virgin will conceive and give birth to a son, and they will call him Immanuel' (which means 'God with us'). When Joseph woke up, he did what the angel of the Lord had commanded him and took Mary home as his wife. But he did not consummate their marriage until she gave birth to a son. And he gave him the name Jesus.

Matthew writes mainly for a Jewish audience, to convince them that Jesus is the promised Messiah. It is important for him to show that in the birth of Jesus, scripture is being fulfilled. This would give validity to the claim that Jesus is the one sent from God.

The promise that Matthew turns our attention to is from the prophet Isaiah (7:14) which is being fulfilled in three specific ways: (1) a virgin will conceive – and Mary was a virgin; (2) she will give birth to a son – and Mary's child will be a boy; and (3) he will be called Immanuel, meaning 'God with us' – and the child born to Mary will be God in human form.

This prophecy is what we see coming to pass in the birth of Jesus. It is a confirmation of the true identity of Jesus, and Matthew's readers would get the point he is making.

Joseph is convinced by the angel's words and acts in costly obedience, knowing his actions will be misconstrued by many, yet courageously deciding to stand by Mary and welcome her into his home. When the baby is born, he gives him the name Jesus, as directed, the name that means 'Saviour' and describes so fully his mission in the world.

We have already seen Mary's obedience, and then that of Zechariah and Elizabeth. Now Joseph is called to walk a similar path, choosing to follow God's way even if it is misunderstood by others and does not lead to a comfortable life. Living life before God will often require us to walk the path of costly obedience, but that is the way of blessing and the way by which God's purposes are fulfilled in the world.

> *When did you realise the importance of obedience in discipleship? Has obedience been costly for you? Why not take time to offer yourself to God again, even though you know what it costs?*

TH

Day 17

Jesus is born

LUKE 2:1-7

Bethlehem
In those days Caesar Augustus issued a decree that a census should be taken of the entire Roman world. (This was the first census that took place while Quirinius was governor of Syria.) And everyone went to their own town to register. So Joseph also went up from the town of Nazareth in Galilee to Judea, to Bethlehem the town of David, because he belonged to the house and line of David. He went there to register with Mary, who was pledged to be married to him and was expecting a child. While they were there, the time came for the baby to be born, and she gave birth to her firstborn, a son. She wrapped him in cloths and placed him in a manger, because there was no guest room available for them.

Things don't always go according to plan, do they? We have an idea of how things will work out, but often circumstances refuse to cooperate, and we find ourselves in Plan B. Perhaps Mary and Joseph felt that way as news of the forthcoming census filtered through to them. They expected the baby to be born in Nazareth. They didn't expect to welcome God's Son to makeshift accommodation far away in Bethlehem.

Yet all this was in the plan and purpose of God. The census was called at the whim of Caesar Augustus, far away in Rome, but unwittingly he is the means by which God arranges for the birth to take place in King David's hometown. The Messiah was to be the Son of David, and other prophecy specified the place of his birth as Bethlehem (Micah 5:2).

This supernatural ordering of events is called the providence of God, and if we look carefully we can see the guiding hand of God at work in our own lives as he coordinates events and circumstances so that his plans for us are fulfilled. This truth is a great source of strength to God's people, for when we feel things are not going according to our plan, we can trust that a higher plan is at work and that God knows what he is doing.

> *Think back over your life. When have you seen the providence of God at work? How does this truth give you confidence for the future?*

TH

Day 18

The shepherds

LUKE 2:8–12

Bethlehem
And there were shepherds living out in the fields nearby, keeping watch over their flocks at night. An angel of the Lord appeared to them, and the glory of the Lord shone around them, and they were terrified. But the angel said to them, 'Do not be afraid. I bring you good news that will cause great joy for all the people. Today in the town of David a Saviour has been born to you; he is the Messiah, the Lord. This will be a sign to you: you will find a baby wrapped in cloths and lying in a manger.'

I often marvel at the way ordinary people unexpectedly find themselves caught up in extraordinary events and for a few short moments become the centre of media attention. They just happen to be present when something newsworthy happens, and their eyewitness account becomes front-page news.

These humble shepherds had no idea that they would be the first to herald the birth of the Saviour. Working class, and disregarded by others, they are the ones surrounded by God's glory and chosen to visit the newly born Messiah. To them is given the startling news that they will find him not in a palace, but in a lowly manger. No fanfare of trumpets or guard of honour for his arrival, only a group of noisy, dishevelled shepherds. Humble visitors for a humble king.

Henri Nouwen comments: 'The way of God is the way of weakness. The great news of the gospel is precisely that God became small and vulnerable, and hence bore fruit among us... Jesus brought us new life in ultimate vulnerability. He came to us as a small child, dependent on the care and protection of others.'[3]

What this means is that God delights to take us in our weakness and use us for his glory. He chooses those that are weak in the world to shame the strong, and those who are considered foolish to shame the wise (1 Corinthians 1:27). Since this is true, our weakness is not a liability but an asset.

> *Jesus, Lord of glory, I pause to worship you in your humility. I thank you for your welcome and acceptance, unworthy as I am. Fill me with the joy of the shepherds and use me – even me – for your glory.*

TH

Day 19

Angel hosts

LUKE 2:13-15

Bethlehem
Suddenly a great company of the heavenly host appeared with the angel, praising God and saying, 'Glory to God in the highest heaven, and on earth peace to those on whom his favour rests.' When the angels had left them and gone into heaven, the shepherds said to one another, 'Let's go to Bethlehem and see this thing that has happened, which the Lord has told us about.'

One of my ambitions is to see the Northern Lights (*aurora borealis*). This celestial phenomenon includes waves of bright, multicoloured lights dancing in the sky. Sky watchers often describe it as like seeing angels.

Angelic activity is prominent in the lead-up to the birth of Jesus but becomes concentrated at the time of the actual birth. The armies of heaven are marshalled to herald his arrival and declare his glory when earth itself is oblivious to what is taking place.

Angels exist to do God's will, and to worship him day and night. Something of that immense glory spills over into the night sky on the hills outside lowly Bethlehem, treating the lowly shepherds to a heavenly choral performance. It must have taken their breath away, as well as their fear. It is a performance that brings heaven and earth together, glory and peace intermingling.

Such special events do not last forever, though. The shepherds have to decide what to do next in response to what they have seen and heard. Their decision is unanimous – they will go and see the child. This is always the way in the spiritual life. God reveals himself and speaks to us, but then we are required to respond – to act in faith and step out in obedience. Only then can we move into the purpose of God for us and receive the blessing he has in store.

> *Why not use your imagination to enter into this story? Try to picture the glory of this angelic visitation. Imagine yourself there as one of the shepherds or an anonymous bystander. What do you see? What do you hear? How do you feel? How will you respond?*

TH

Day 20

Mary ponders

LUKE 2:16-20

Bethlehem
So they hurried off and found Mary and Joseph, and the baby, who was lying in the manger. When they had seen him, they spread the word concerning what had been told them about this child, and all who heard it were amazed at what the shepherds said to them. But Mary treasured up all these things and pondered them in her heart. The shepherds returned, glorifying and praising God for all the things they had heard and seen, which were just as they had been told.

The writer of Ecclesiastes says that there is a time to speak and a time to be silent (Ecclesiastes 3:7). For the shepherds, this is a moment to excitedly share the good news that they have been given; for Mary, it is a time to quietly ponder the significance of what she has been told.

These unskilled, blue-collar workers become the first evangelists of the gospel. First, they verify that what the angel said was true. Before their eyes they saw the Christ-child, tiny and vulnerable, resting in the manger. It was just as they had been told and so, second, they do not hesitate to spread the word about the child – who he is and why he has come. They speak with conviction and assurance about something they know to be true, and their testimony is convincing.

Here is vital aspect of how we absorb truth. We do so by sharing what we know with others, verbalising what we understand and passing on the insights that we have received. This not only does good to those who hear us but solidifies the truth within us. Joy leads to witness and thanksgiving.

Mary's response is to choose silence and to reflect on what has been said, a second way by which we receive spiritual truth. Meditating on the word of God enables us to internalise the truth, which in turn transforms us. The shepherds confirm what she has already been told and strengthen her faith that her son is indeed the promised Messiah. She treasures these things in her heart, realising that these are important truths to keep and not forget. Then she ponders them – prayerfully meditating on their meaning and significance, and turning her meditation into thanksgiving.

> Lord, show me when to speak out from the depths of my heart, and when to be silent and thoughtful.

TH

Day 21

Jesus consecrated

LUKE 2:21–24

Jerusalem, the temple
On the eighth day, when it was time to circumcise the child, he was named Jesus, the name the angel had given him before he was conceived. When the time came for the purification rites required by the Law of Moses, Joseph and Mary took him to Jerusalem to present him to the Lord (as it is written in the Law of the Lord, 'Every firstborn male is to be consecrated to the Lord'), and to offer a sacrifice in keeping with what is said in the Law of the Lord: 'a pair of doves or two young pigeons'.

Most parents put a lot of effort into preparing for the arrival of a new baby. They get the room ready, buy clothes and equipment, find a suitable cot and pushchair, and so on. They perhaps attend classes and learn how to look after a baby, how to change nappies and how to give a feed. Seldom do they consider the spiritual aspect of the child's welfare as Mary and Joseph did.

It is natural for this godly couple to honour God by offering the child back to him. The word 'present' means literally to place at the disposal of someone (in this case God). It is to make a present of the boy, and all his potential, to God. This was in keeping with the law about every firstborn son (see Exodus 13:2, 12).

Then, for Mary's own cleansing, they make an offering in the temple, not of a lamb but that prescribed for the poorest people, a pair of doves and two young pigeons. She may have given birth to the Son of God, but Mary is still inclined to follow the Old Testament legislation and do what is required by the law. In this way Paul can say that Jesus was 'born of a woman, born under the law, to redeem those under the law, that we might receive adoption to sonship' (Galatians 4:4–5).

Notice the word 'consecrated' (v. 23). It means to be set apart for a holy purpose. As far as the parents are concerned, their desire is for the boy to follow God. The day will come when he makes his own choice to set himself apart for his mission.

> *How has your own childhood helped or hindered you in your spiritual growth? Bring your thoughts and feelings to God.*

TH

Day 22

Simeon

LUKE 2:25-32

Jerusalem, the temple
Now there was a man in Jerusalem called Simeon, who was righteous and devout. He was waiting for the consolation of Israel, and the Holy Spirit was on him. It had been revealed to him by the Holy Spirit that he would not die before he had seen the Lord's Messiah. Moved by the Spirit, he went into the temple courts. When the parents brought in the child Jesus to do for him what the custom of the Law required, Simeon took him in his arms and praised God, saying: 'Sovereign Lord, as you have promised, you may now dismiss your servant in peace. For my eyes have seen your salvation, which you have prepared in the sight of all nations: a light for revelation to the Gentiles, and the glory of your people Israel.'

Many people fear that as they grow older their best days will be behind them. Simeon is no prisoner to such fears. He is carried along by the promise of God to him, conscious that his work is not yet finished. Here is a man who lives under the inspiration of the Spirit despite his age.

The Spirit is on Simeon and has created in him a holy expectation for the 'consolation of Israel', that is the fulfilment of all God's ancient promises to his chosen people. He is part of a remnant who had not lost hope, patiently waiting for God to act.

Further, the Spirit had revealed to him that he would one day see the promised Messiah for himself, and this prospect gave meaning to his life and fuelled his faith even as he grew older.

Then one day, the Spirit, whose prompting he recognised so well, moves Simeon to enter the temple, and there he sees the young family. Here is an encounter orchestrated by God and he intuitively knows that this is indeed the Christ-child.

Immediately the Spirit speaks through him a powerful declaration to all those around that here is the child through whom salvation will come, who will bring light to the Gentiles and glory to Israel. This is intergenerational ministry at its best.

> *What fears do you have about growing old? How does Simeon's story inspire you? What do you know of the Spirit's working in your life? Be open today to any way in which he may want to use you.*

TH

Day 23

Simeon prophesies

LUKE 2:33-35

Jerusalem, the temple
The child's father and mother marvelled at what was said about him. Then Simeon blessed them and said to Mary, his mother: 'This child is destined to cause the falling and rising of many in Israel, and to be a sign that will be spoken against, so that the thoughts of many hearts will be revealed. And a sword will pierce your own soul too.'

The theme of 'discovering your destiny' is a common one nowadays in inspirational talks to young people. Usually, this sort of destiny involves becoming rich and famous, and while that may happen to a few, it often leaves many disappointed and feeling like a failure.

Under the inspiration of the Spirit the aged Simeon now speaks of the God-given destiny of the child Jesus. Yes, this will be magnificently positive because he will bring salvation to Jew and Gentile alike, but there is a darker side to it, as Simeon goes on to declare. Here is an early indication that the Messiah will be a suffering Messiah. His work will only be accomplished at great personal cost. Mary and Joseph need to be aware of this.

First, he will be a divisive figure. Some will be drawn to him, others will turn away. Some will love him, others hate him. He will be the making of some, and the breaking of others. He will not be universally popular.

Then, he will be controversial, 'a figure misunderstood and contradicted' (v. 34, MSG). People's opinions will be divided about him; his forthrightness will upset many.

Finally, he will reveal what is in the hearts of people. His presence will shine light into the darkness. People will not be able to pretend or hide any more.

All this will mean that his parents (particularly Mary) will feel the sharp pain of seeing him suffer and be rejected. The cross is not spoken of specifically, but the violent rejection foretold here will lead to his death. This is a theme we will see developing from the start of his ministry to its climax at Calvary. The shadow of the cross is upon the child's life from his earliest days.

> Remember that being faithful to God may not always bring us earthly approval. Pray now for the courage to fulfil your calling no matter how hard that may be.

TH

Day 24

Anna's testimony

LUKE 2:36–38

Jerusalem, the temple
There was also a prophet, Anna, the daughter of Penuel, of the tribe of Asher. She was very old; she had lived with her husband seven years after her marriage, and then was a widow until she was eighty-four. She never left the temple but worshipped night and day, fasting and praying. Coming up to them at that very moment, she gave thanks to God and spoke about the child to all who were looking forward to the redemption of Jerusalem.

'What use am I now?' That is often the heart-cry of older people as they advance in years and decline in ability, but Anna's story shines a light on this false thinking. Both Simeon and Anna remind us that we can bear fruit for God even in old age (Psalm 92:12–15).

In the planning of God, the arrival of the newborn babe is greeted by two of his elderly servants. Anna had known times of deep suffering, being widowed at a young age and having lived alone for most of her life. We have no idea of the circumstances yet can surmise that her husband's death may have been a tragedy. She bore this pain courageously, allowing it to draw her closer to God while refusing to become bitter.

As she reached the end of her life, most of her time was given to prayer and worship. The ministry of older people in intercession and attentiveness to God is not to be underestimated; it forms the bedrock of faith in many churches where younger people are more active but more time scarce.

Perhaps the crowning moment of Anna's long life came when, prompted by God, she entered the temple at just the moment Simeon was blessing the child. She had long been used to receiving and passing on the word of God to others, and her spirit is stirred by what she sees. From the well of longing within her for a visitation from God, she speaks prophetically to those around confirming Simeon's attestation that this child is indeed the promised Saviour.

The testimony of two witnesses – Simeon and Anna – regarding the child's identity must have greatly strengthened the faith of Mary and Joseph.

> What do you learn from the example of Anna about facing suffering? What does her story teach about faith in later life?

TH

Day 25

Jesus the child

LUKE 2:39-40

Nazareth
When Joseph and Mary had done everything required by the Law of the Lord, they returned to Galilee to their own town of Nazareth. And the child grew and became strong; he was filled with wisdom, and the grace of God was on him.

It is difficult to reconcile Luke's chronology with that of Matthew. Here Luke suggests that following their temple visit the family returned home to Nazareth. Matthew, however, includes the visit of the magi (wise men) and the flight into Egypt before they return to Nazareth. Perhaps on this occasion they simply returned to collect their belongings, and then went back to Bethlehem.

What stands out to us now is that Jesus, even as the Son of God, was subject to all the normal stages of human growth and development. He would have gone through phases such as learning to walk, to speak, to dress himself and so on. His parents would have delighted in every new achievement, and especially to see that he was a strong and healthy boy.

Although some apocryphal sources describe the child Jesus doing amazing things (like making real birds from clay), the only thing that stood out as far as Luke is concerned was that he was filled with wisdom. This would have come across in the way he spoke and discussed matters, as if he had an old head on young shoulders.

Most importantly, we are told that the grace of God was on him, suggesting he was spiritually aware from a young age and that the love of God was very real to him. Again, people would have noticed his spiritual responsiveness and soundness of character.

These insights remind us that Jesus was fully human, taking our flesh and blood and sharing in our humanity. It was necessary for him to be like us in every way so that he could understand the human condition and later become a sympathetic high priest (Hebrews 2:14-18). They also reveal the humility of God. In choosing to be born in this way, as a baby, and then grow as a child, God became dependent upon human beings, needing Mary and Joseph to care for him, teach him and protect him.

> Lord, I love your vulnerability, your willingness to stoop so low to save us. Help me to accept the limitations of my own humanity.

TH

Day 26

The magi arrive

MATTHEW 2:1–6

Bethlehem
After Jesus was born in Bethlehem in Judea, during the time of King Herod, Magi from the east came to Jerusalem and asked, 'Where is the one who has been born king of the Jews? We saw his star when it rose and have come to worship him.' When King Herod heard this he was disturbed, and all Jerusalem with him. When he had called together all the people's chief priests and teachers of the law, he asked them where the Messiah was to be born. 'In Bethlehem in Judea,' they replied, 'for this is what the prophet has written: "But you, Bethlehem, in the land of Judah, are by no means least among the rulers of Judah; for out of you will come a ruler who will shepherd my people Israel."'

God has a thousand ways by which he can speak to us, some of them surprising. Who would have thought that God would use stargazing and astrology to gain the attention of some Gentile scholars far away from Jerusalem? But he did.

The appearance of a large and previously unknown star in the night sky triggered in their minds the belief that a new king had been born, which they associated with the Jewish nation. Being spiritually minded, they felt compelled to witness this royal birth and set off on a long and dangerous journey to Jerusalem, the obvious place to search for a king.

King Herod's disturbance is due to the possibility of a rival. His research revealed something even more alarming. An ancient prophecy from the prophet Micah (5:2) foretold that a king would be born in the obscure town of Bethlehem. Could the prophecy about a shepherd ruler possibly be coming true?

Both the magi and King Herod begin a search for the newborn king, but for very different reasons. The magi, with a sense of the transcendent in their hearts, want to worship him. Herod, an insecure and jealous ruler, seeks only to destroy a rival. Already Simeon's prophecy is being fulfilled. Some will love the Christ-child, others will hate him. This will be the pattern of his life.

> *What first awakened you to the reality of spiritual things? How did your journey towards Jesus begin? Has God spoken to you in any surprising ways? How has your journey continued?*

TH

Day 27

They worship Jesus

MATTHEW 2:7-12

Bethlehem
Then Herod called the Magi secretly and found out from them the exact time the star had appeared. He sent them to Bethlehem and said, 'Go and search carefully for the child. As soon as you find him, report to me, so that I too may go and worship him.' After they had heard the king, they went on their way, and the star they had seen when it rose went ahead of them until it stopped over the place where the child was. When they saw the star, they were overjoyed. On coming to the house, they saw the child with his mother Mary, and they bowed down and worshipped him. Then they opened their treasures and presented him with gifts of gold, frankincense and myrrh. And having been warned in a dream not to go back to Herod, they returned to their country by another route.

God not only has many ways by which he can speak to us, but many ways by which he guides our steps. The magi are sincere in their desire to find the newborn king. Openness of heart is a key factor in discovering spiritual truth – as God says in Jeremiah: 'You will seek me and find me when you seek me with all your heart' (Jeremiah 29:13).

Guided by Micah's ancient prophecy (Micah 5:2), they head for Bethlehem. The star keeps on moving and leads them onwards not to a manger, but to a house where the young family are settled for a while. How would they have found the place without the star? God will always lead us if we want to follow his way.

Entering the house, these foreign nobles gladly bow the knee to the infant Jesus and willingly open their treasures before him. This is a wonderful picture of true worship – the offering of all that we are, and all that we have, to King Jesus. The coming of the Saviour, born in such a humble way and identifying himself with us so fully, demands from us a similar response of adoration and self-giving love.

▌ *Lord, guide my steps; lead me to know you more, and to worship you with my whole being.*

TH

Day 28

The flight to Egypt

MATTHEW 2:13–15

Egypt
When they had gone, an angel of the Lord appeared to Joseph in a dream. 'Get up,' he said, 'take the child and his mother and escape to Egypt. Stay there until I tell you, for Herod is going to search for the child to kill him.' So he got up, took the child and his mother during the night and left for Egypt, where he stayed until the death of Herod. And so was fulfilled what the Lord had said through the prophet: 'Out of Egypt I called my son.'

For a second time God speaks to Joseph in a dream, warning him of the threat from the enraged King Herod and directing him to find refuge in the land of Egypt. This must have been a frightening experience for the young family, and a massive step to take on the basis of nothing more than a dream. Obedience and faith combine, however, and with great courage Joseph leads his family to a place of safety.

Behind the jealous rage of an insecure ruler, we must see the scheming of the powers of darkness. Already Satan fears the birth of the promised Messiah and seeks the child's destruction. Herod is easily manipulated into serving the prince of darkness, such is his thirst for unrivalled power.

So it is that Mary and Joseph, with the child Jesus, find themselves as refugees in a foreign land, a plight shared by millions of people even today. How encouraging it is to know that Jesus understands what it is to flee because of persecution, be made homeless and live at the mercy of strangers. God is not aloof from our sufferings, not immune to the cries of the needy.

Notice one more strand. Matthew, keen to link current events to Old Testament prophecy, sees an immediate connection with an obscure sentence in the book of Hosea: 'Out of Egypt I called my son.' It is in the providence of God that Joseph and family find themselves in Egypt, and in his goodness that they return to their homeland. Even the unexpected and unwanted movements of our lives are under his control. It is God who rules, not a crazy dictator.

> *Lord, make me sensitive to your leading. Grant me the assurance that all my movements are within the boundaries of your care.*

TH

Day 29

The slaying of the children

MATTHEW 2:16-18

Bethlehem
When Herod realised that he had been outwitted by the Magi, he was furious, and he gave orders to kill all the boys in Bethlehem and its vicinity who were two years old and under, in accordance with the time he had learned from the Magi. Then what was said through the prophet Jeremiah was fulfilled: 'A voice is heard in Ramah, weeping and great mourning, Rachel weeping for her children and refusing to be comforted, because they are no more.'

No narcissistic ruler with a public image to protect can stand to be outsmarted. The failure of the magi to return and report to him, and the embarrassment of his being unable to find the newborn king, triggers Herod's paranoia and propels him into the wicked crime of infanticide. We are not sure how many boys would have been murdered. Estimates vary from a dozen to a few thousand. Either way, this calculated cruelty is a shocking crime and abuse of power.

We may wonder how this can happen in a world where God is in control, but he rules without taking away our free will. In world spoilt by sin, wicked people still perpetrate their crimes, which is why the belief in a day of judgement is so comforting. Evil may appear to triumph but, in the end, justice will be meted out, even if not in this life.

Matthew links this terrible event with the atrocious killing of children during the downfall of Jerusalem and the exile into Babylon. Rachel, a matriarchal figure in Israel's history, represents all women who mourn for lost children (Jeremiah 31:15). It is never wrong to cry and weep in the face of tragedy. It is a natural response to bereavement and loss. Tears bring their own healing. Injustice needs to be acknowledged, and the pain of trauma released.

Sadly, so many centuries on and with so much progress in the world, children still suffer through war, famine, exploitation and other evils. Perhaps like Rachel, we should cry for those who suffer now.

> *Pause to be still before God. Bring to mind the suffering of children worldwide. Pray for innocent victims, and for the parents who shed unstoppable tears. Ask that evil rulers will be defeated, and for justice to triumph. Be aware, too, of your own pain. Do you need to talk with someone, like a counsellor?*

TH

Day 30

They return to Galilee

MATTHEW 2:19–23

Nazareth
After Herod died, an angel of the Lord appeared in a dream to Joseph in Egypt and said, 'Get up, take the child and his mother and go to the land of Israel, for those who were trying to take the child's life are dead.' So he got up, took the child and his mother and went to the land of Israel. But when he heard that Archelaus was reigning in Judea in place of his father Herod, he was afraid to go there. Having been warned in a dream, he withdrew to the district of Galilee, and he went and lived in a town called Nazareth. So was fulfilled what was said through the prophets, that he would be called a Nazarene.

'How did you sleep?' is a common greeting first thing in the morning. Perhaps Mary was a little nervous to ask Joseph this question in case he replied again, 'Well, actually, I had a dream...'

Joseph was a man whose spirit was sensitive to God and who could discern the divine voice through his dreams. It is certainly one way by which God communicates with us, and I have experienced it myself on a handful of occasions. Each time the dream has been vivid and memorable and accompanied by a clear word of direction or encouragement. Psychologist David Benner writes: 'Dreams are most useful in spiritual growth when we prayerfully listen to them rather than seek to interpret them. We should receive them as gifts from God, asking him for what he wishes to draw our attention to through them.'[4]

Just as they had gone down to Egypt under the guidance of God, now some years later the little family set off for their homeland. They settle at first in Judea, but then a second warning and a sense of unease causes them to head further north and back to their hometown of Nazareth. The circle is at last complete; Mary and Joseph are now back to where it all began.

The psalmist says, 'The Lord directs the steps of the godly. He delights in every detail of their lives' (Psalm 37:23, NLT). This is the principle we see clearly in the movements of Mary and Joseph.

Lord, direct my steps and teach me your ways. Grant me discernment.

TH

Day 31

The boy Jesus at the temple

LUKE 2:41–50

Jerusalem
Every year Jesus' parents went to Jerusalem for the Festival of the Passover. When he was twelve years old, they went up to the festival, according to the custom. After the festival was over, while his parents were returning home, the boy Jesus stayed behind in Jerusalem, but they were unaware of it. Thinking he was in their company, they travelled on for a day. Then they began looking for him among their relatives and friends. When they did not find him, they went back to Jerusalem to look for him. After three days they found him in the temple courts, sitting among the teachers, listening to them and asking them questions. Everyone who heard him was amazed at his understanding and his answers. When his parents saw him, they were astonished. His mother said to him, 'Son, why have you treated us like this? Your father and I have been anxiously searching for you.' 'Why were you searching for me?' he asked. 'Didn't you know I had to be in my Father's house?' But they did not understand what he was saying to them.

The early years of Jesus' childhood are shrouded in silence. After the return from Egypt, we hear nothing about his boyhood. No doubt life settled into a pattern of ordinary living, with Joseph working as a carpenter, Mary caring for her family and Jesus learning and playing, doing the things that boys of his age enjoy doing. This is a reassuring thought for it blesses the ordinariness of family life and values the mundaneness of much of life.

The trip to Jerusalem was a very special occasion, a coming-of-age milestone in the life of Jesus. The incident in the temple provides a confirmatory lesson for his parents that Jesus is no ordinary child. He is marching to a different drumbeat, that of his heavenly Father. Sometimes this will mean he chooses a different path to the one expected. He is still young and subject to their care, but the day will come when they need to let him go to follow the calling on his life. He will often astonish and perplex them. Not only must he be in the Father's house (v. 49), he must also be about the Father's business.

> *Think about yourself, aged twelve. What sense of God did you have? How has life developed since then?*

TH

Day 32

Growing in favour

LUKE 2:51–52

Nazareth
Then he went down to Nazareth with them and was obedient to them. But his mother treasured all these things in her heart. And Jesus grew in wisdom and stature, and in favour with God and man.

This summary statement encapsulates what life was like for Jesus for the next 18 years. His teenage years and his growing into a man are passed over without comment, leaving us full of unanswered questions. Yet the silence speaks loudly of the preparation for ministry taking place within him, reminding us that God is prepared to spend a lot of time in forming and shaping us in the secret place.

Jesus became *submissive*. He learned to be obedient to his parents, even though he was aware of his identity as God's Son. This willingness to place oneself under the direction of another is a primary quality in preparing us for leadership. We cannot lead others safely unless we are willing to be led. How do I practise submission?

Jesus embraced *hiddenness*. Henri Nouwen comments: 'In our time, with such emphasis on visibility, the hidden life of Jesus is of special importance for a deeper understanding of our lives in the Spirit.'[5] Much contemporary Christian ministry involves a media profile, a public platform and a polished image. Do I covet the limelight or am I content in the background?

Jesus accepted *obscurity*. Nazareth was by any standards a backwater, yet he buried himself in the life of a Galilean village, accepting the ordinariness of daily life and eschewing fame. Do I crave only the spectacular or am I comfortable with the everyday?

Jesus developed *patience*. It took time for him to grow into manhood, to learn about life and understand people. His awareness of God developed, too, as did his understanding of scripture. Am I willing to wait for God's timing or am I impatient to get going?

Nazareth was not only his home, but also his training ground, his place of preparation and soul formation. Mary watches on with love and amazement, pondering in her heart the work of God in the life of her son.

Lord, have your way in me. Make me into the person you want me to be.

TH

the first year:
the year of inauguration

MAGS DUGGAN

Day 33

The messenger has arrived

MARK 1:1–3 (*MATTHEW 3:1–3; LUKE 3:3–6*)

By the River Jordan
The beginning of the good news about Jesus the Messiah, the Son of God, as it is written in Isaiah the prophet: 'I will send my messenger ahead of you, who will prepare your way' – 'a voice of one calling in the wilderness, "Prepare the way for the Lord, make straight paths for him."'

Sometimes the very best news doesn't need an abundance of words to communicate the wonder, the excitement, the sheer joy of it: 'He got the job!' 'She said yes!' 'The baby's here!' Short phrases, simple words, cradling a wealth of meaning.

Mark's gospel may be the shortest of the gospels and focused very much on the actions of Jesus, but its opening words punch well above their weight in theological depth. With no preamble, Mark announces the best, most life-changing news we could ever hope to hear: God has broken into human history in an unprecedented way through the person of Jesus.

And then Mark layers title after glorious title on Jesus: he is the Messiah, the one anointed by God to be our Saviour and King. He is the Son of God, equal with God, one with God. He is the Lord, translated from the Hebrew, 'Yahweh,' the ever-present God, who comforts, forgives and restores his people (Isaiah 40:1–3).

This is the explosive good news that Mark proclaims in this opening sentence. It's as though Mark built a frame out of the names and titles of Jesus and wants us to understand that everything we hear from this point on has to be understood in the light of this framework. This is our God. He has come.

> *Lord Jesus, help me to see that my life and all that is in it are framed by the wonder of all that you are as my Saviour, my King, my Lord. Help me this day to see who you are, and who you are for me.*

MD

Day 34

John the Baptist: the promise of God fulfilled

MARK 1:4–8 (MATTHEW 3:4–6, 11; LUKE 3:3, 15–16)

By the River Jordan
And so John the Baptist appeared in the wilderness, preaching a baptism of repentance for the forgiveness of sins. The whole Judean countryside and all the people of Jerusalem went out to him. Confessing their sins, they were baptised by him in the River Jordan. John wore clothing made of camel's hair, with a leather belt round his waist, and he ate locusts and wild honey. And this was his message: 'After me comes the one more powerful than I, the straps of whose sandals I am not worthy to stoop down and untie. I baptise you with water, but he will baptise you with the Holy Spirit.'

My five-year-old goddaughter has just discovered the term 'pinkie promise' and with it the idea that when you make a promise, it's really important that you keep it.

God is the ultimate promise-keeper. It had been 800 years since Isaiah's prophecy that one day God would send a messenger to prepare his people for the arrival of their king. The people of God had waited so long for the fulfilment of that promise, but now at last that longed-for day had arrived. Mark spotlights the appearance of John with the simple words, 'And so...' There in the wilderness was the living embodiment of the faithfulness of God to his promises. John's spectacular appearance in the wilderness was clear evidence that God was returning to redeem and restore his people to himself.

Years before, another prophet, Habakkuk, had been encouraged to wait for God's promises to be fulfilled: 'If it seems slow, do not despair, for these things will surely come to pass' (Habakkuk 2:3, TLB).

I wonder if we sometimes despair that God will ever fulfil the promises we believe he's given us personally. May John's appearance in the wilderness inspire hope in us that God will keep his promise to us – however long we have to wait.

> *Faithful God, thank you that you always keep your promises. Today, I'm trusting you for _____. Renew hope in me. Give me grace to trust. Let me know you more fully, even here. Amen.*

MD

Day 35

John's preaching

LUKE 3:7-9 (MATTHEW 3:7-10)

By the River Jordan
John said to the crowds coming out to be baptised by him, 'You brood of vipers! Who warned you to flee from the coming wrath? Produce fruit in keeping with repentance. And do not begin to say to yourselves, "We have Abraham as our father." For I tell you that out of these stones God can raise up children for Abraham. The axe has been laid to the root of the trees, and every tree that does not produce good fruit will be cut down and thrown into the fire.'

I think John and my grandmother would have understood each other well: 'If I had a sixpence for every time you said sorry, I'd be a millionaire by now.' I heard those words often when I was growing up. I was quick to acknowledge and apologise for wrongdoing, but nothing in my behaviour changed, and it's that incongruity that John is addressing here in these blunt words.

Genuine repentance leads to a change of behaviour. If there is no change in behaviour, there has been no genuine repentance, however heartfelt or sincere the remorse over our sin may be. John is clear that the length of time we've been in a relationship with God doesn't excuse us from this need for ongoing change as we recognise our sin, turn away from it and act in ways consistent with what we know of the character of Jesus. In fact, Tim Keller suggests that 'pervasive, all-of-life repentance is the best sign that we are growing deeply and rapidly into the character of Jesus'.[6] A lifestyle of repentance is the pathway to a deepening likeness to Jesus – and that is 'good fruit,' and good news.

> *As you reflect on this passage, is the Lord touching an area of your life where you know that words of repentance are no longer enough – there needs to be action that leads to change? Bring that area and your desire for change to him now in prayer.*

MD

Day 36

What should we do then?

LUKE 3:10–14

By the River Jordan
'What should we do then?' the crowd asked. John answered, 'Anyone who has two shirts should share with the one who has none, and anyone who has food should do the same.' Even tax collectors came to be baptised. 'Teacher,' they asked, 'what should we do?' 'Don't collect any more than you are required to,' he told them. Then some soldiers asked him, 'And what should we do?' He replied, 'Don't extort money and don't accuse people falsely – be content with your pay.'

'And you, what would you do for love?' Not a question asked by John the Baptist, but by actress Natalie Portman in an advert for a famous perfume brand. Her defiant question follows a series of short dramatic clips, in which, for example, she jumps off the end of a jetty. Very heroic! And all done for love. Apparently.

The crowds who listened to John as he challenged them to 'produce fruit in keeping with repentance' (Luke 3:8) responded with a very pragmatic question: 'What should we do then?' (v. 10). John's response made it clear that genuine repentance is to be lived out in the everyday practices of life: be generous, be fair in how you treat people, be kind in how you exercise the influence you have. Basically, love your neighbour as you love yourself.

His counsel to them seems very ordinary, mundane; no mention of anything explicitly religious, such as fasting or temple sacrifices. And nothing heroic at all. But challenging. John seems to be encouraging his hearers to take advantage of the many opportunities they had 'to love their neighbour' in the contexts in which they lived, in whatever role they found themselves, in whatever ways the needs they encountered demanded of them. His response to their question clearly reflects his conviction that, although repentance may *begin* with a heartfelt acknowledgement of the many ways in which we have failed to love God, it's lived out in the practical ways we love and care for one another.

| *Perhaps today you might want to ask the Lord to help you to recognise the different ways, however unheroic, you can respond to the needs of the people who are around you.*

MD

Day 37

A case of mistaken identity

LUKE 3:15–18 (JOHN 1:19–28; MARK 1:7–8; MATTHEW 3:11)

The people were waiting expectantly and were all wondering in their hearts if John might possibly be the Messiah. John answered them all, 'I baptise you with water. But one who is more powerful than I will come, the straps of whose sandals I am not worthy to untie. He will baptise you with the Holy Spirit and fire. His winnowing fork is in his hand to clear his threshing-floor and to gather the wheat into his barn, but he will burn up the chaff with unquenchable fire.' And with many other words John exhorted the people and proclaimed the good news to them.

He was running to catch the train when he crashed into the boy holding the box. The jigsaw pieces went everywhere – and the man went nowhere. He just bent down and began putting the pieces back into the box. Finally, as he finished, the boy quietly asked, 'Mister, are you Jesus?'

I heard this story years ago – and I've never forgotten it. How incredibly wonderful to be mistaken for Jesus – unless you're John the Baptist, who quickly moved to correct that view. John had made such an impact through his preaching and his lifestyle that it wasn't surprising that people wondered if he might be the Messiah, but his response was to point them to Jesus.

John didn't downplay his own ministry, he just acknowledged that Jesus' ministry would be so much greater. John knew that neither his preaching nor his baptising – as powerful as it was – could actually empower a life to be changed – only the baptism of Jesus could do that. His would be a baptism of the Holy Spirit and of fire – the breath and power of God to transform a life from the inside out. John couldn't do what only Jesus could do – but *he did what he could*. His actions prepared people's hearts for the arrival of their Saviour.

I wonder about my own life: is there anything about my life that draws people to ask questions about Jesus? Anything about how I live my life that prepares their hearts to experience for themselves the life that Jesus came to give?

> *A blessing to take into today: may you be one in whom others encounter Jesus, the living God. Amen.*

MD

Day 38

John the witness

JOHN 1:6-9 (ESV)

There was a man sent from God, whose name was John. He came as a witness, to bear witness about the light, that all might believe through him. He was not the light, but came to bear witness about the light. The true light, which enlightens everyone, was coming into the world.

The other gospel accounts describe John as 'the Baptist', but throughout John's gospel, John is described as the 'witness'. I'm not a Greek scholar, so I was fascinated to discover that our English word 'witness' comes from the Greek word *martureo*, from which we get our word 'martyr' – someone who dies for their belief or conviction. The connection is obvious – especially in John's case, because his role as witness eventually led to his role as a martyr at the hands of a weak and foolish ruler (Matthew 14:1–12).

John died because of his witness to Jesus, and I wonder about my own witness. I may not die *because* I'm a witness to Jesus, but is there anything in my life that I need to die to in order *to be* a witness?

Are there ways of speaking and acting which I need to die to because they don't reveal the character of Jesus in me – his grace, his kindness, his patient love? Do I need to die in some way to the ways I spend my money or time or resources because those ways don't reflect Jesus' wisdom or generosity or values? Do I need to die to fear? The fear of losing friends or reputation, respect or affection among people I care about, if I witness to who Jesus is, to who he is to me? Or do I fear that even if I wanted to be a witness, I know I have so far to go in knowing and loving and becoming like Jesus that I'm disqualified from saying a word before I even begin?

> *It's encouraging that the role of a witness is to just speak the truth about what they know, what they have seen and heard and experienced for themselves. No more. No less. This we can do. Even today we might have the opportunity to 'do a John' – to be a witness to the wonder of who Jesus is and the wonder of who he is for us. May it be so.*

MD

Day 39

John's witness

JOHN 1:19-27

Bethany on the other side of the Jordan
Now this was John's testimony when the Jewish leaders in Jerusalem sent priests and Levites to ask him who he was. He did not fail to confess, but confessed freely, 'I am not the Messiah.' They asked him, 'Then who are you? Are you Elijah?' He said, 'I am not.' 'Are you the Prophet?' He answered, 'No.' Finally they said, 'Who are you?'... John replied in the words of Isaiah the prophet, 'I am the voice of one calling in the wilderness, "Make straight the way for the Lord."' Now the Pharisees who had been sent questioned him, 'Why then do you baptise if you are not the Messiah, nor Elijah, nor the Prophet?' 'I baptise with water,' John replied, 'but among you stands one you do not know. He is the one who comes after me, the straps of whose sandals I am not worthy to untie.'

In the early 1950s a new term appeared in the field of psychology: 'messiah complex'. We may recognise it as a term that refers to a person who believes they are responsible for saving or rescuing others, whatever the cost to themselves. John had no such complex!

We've already seen that John clearly knew who he was and what he had been sent to do (John 1:6–8). Here in these words John makes it abundantly clear, yet again, who he is not: 'I am not the Messiah' (v. 20).

When we are faced with great need, obvious distress, brokenness in all its heartbreaking manifestations, it can be so easy to slip into Jesus' shoes, to assume the role of Messiah in someone else's life. Out of real concern we may try to be for them what only Jesus can be, to do for them what only Jesus can do. There may be times in our lives when the most helpful thing we can do for someone is to repeat to ourselves, 'I am not the Messiah; Jesus is,' and go from there.

> Lord Jesus, help me to recognise when I may be stepping into your shoes in someone else's life. Give me grace to step back and to point them to you, so that they can know that you are with them and will be for them all that they need.

MD

Day 40

The Lamb of God

JOHN 1:29–31

Bethany on the other side of the Jordan
The next day John saw Jesus coming towards him and said, 'Look, the Lamb of God, who takes away the sin of the world! This is the one I meant when I said, "A man who comes after me has surpassed me because he was before me." I myself did not know him, but the reason I came baptising with water was that he might be revealed to Israel.'

I say 'lamb', you say… 'Spring'? 'Sunday roast'? 'Mint sauce'? For the Jews of John's day, the word 'lamb' would trigger only one association: sacrifice. The words 'lamb' and 'sacrifice' were inextricably connected in the Jewish mind. Their faith was steeped in the sacrificial blood of lambs – the Passover lamb of Exodus 12; the unblemished lamb led to the slaughter of Isaiah 53; the lamb of the daily sacrifices; the guilt offerings for sin – all the way back to Abraham's reference to a lamb in Genesis 22. The death of a pure, innocent lamb was the price paid for the forgiveness of their sins, for the restoration of their relationship with God, for life itself.

But here, in a moment of breathtaking prophetic revelation, John recognises Jesus as *the* Lamb of God – the sacrifice foreshadowed in the death of every other lamb which had come before. The death of this lamb would remove the guilt and the punishment not just of Israel's sins, but the sin of the whole world.

This was a radical statement, but John seems to recognise that through the sacrifice of this lamb, the boundaries of the kingdom of God would stretch way beyond the borders of Israel. The Lamb of God would take away *the sin of the world*, because the love of God embraced all of that world (John 3:16).

So John shouts out '*Ide*' – See! Look! Behold! – as he saw Jesus coming towards him. He wanted everyone to recognise Jesus for who he truly was, to recognise that this man walking in their midst was God's own costly sacrifice, his own, dearest lamb.

> *Father, help me today to recognise the presence of Jesus in my day just as John recognised him. Grace me with a sense of awe and wonder, of deep thankfulness that Jesus sacrificed his life – for me.*

MD

Day 41

The baptism of Jesus

MATTHEW 3:13-17 (MARK 1:9-11; LUKE 3:21-22)

The River Jordan
Then Jesus came from Galilee to the Jordan to be baptised by John. But John tried to deter him, saying, 'I need to be baptised by you, and do you come to me?' Jesus replied, 'Let it be so now; it is proper for us to do this to fulfil all righteousness.' Then John consented. As soon as Jesus was baptised, he went up out of the water. At that moment heaven was opened, and he saw the Spirit of God descending like a dove and alighting on him. And a voice from heaven said, 'This is my Son, whom I love; with him I am well pleased.'

When Joan Osborne's song 'One of Us' was released, it offended some Christians who felt that identifying God with a 'slob' or 'stranger' somehow diminished God's glory. And yet, in his birth, Jesus became 'one of us', human. In his baptism that day, Jesus clearly identified with the reality of our humanity – with our messed up, lost and guilty human selves.

John's baptism was for repentant sinners – but Jesus had nothing to repent of and nothing to confess, so why be baptised? A clue may be found in Jesus' answer to John's objection: it was 'to fulfil all righteousness'. Jesus' answer is a reference to Deuteronomy 6:25: 'If we are careful to obey all this law... that will be our righteousness.' What the children of Israel completely failed to do, Jesus would do; he would be perfectly obedient to his Father. His baptism was a public declaration of that obedience.

The response from heaven was immediate – the Holy Spirit came and settled on him, and the words of his Father drenched him in love, approval and pride.

As we trust in Jesus, we discover that his perfect obedience has becomes ours; *we* are the beloved, *we* are the ones who bring pride and joy to our Father's heart. This means there is nothing more we could ever do to be more accepted and acceptable, loved and delighted in. Jesus has done it all.

> *Father, today I surrender to you my efforts to earn your love and approval. Help me to accept your joy and delight in me, to embrace your love and acceptance of me. Amen.*

MD

Day 42

John's testimony

JOHN 1:32-34

Bethany on the other side of the Jordan
Then John gave this testimony: 'I saw the Spirit come down from heaven as a dove and remain on him. And I myself did not know him, but the one who sent me to baptise with water told me, "The man on whom you see the Spirit come down and remain is the one who will baptise with the Holy Spirit." I have seen and I testify that this is God's Chosen One.'

The psalmist encourages us to, 'Keep your eyes open for God, watch for his works; be alert for signs of his presence' (Psalm 105:4, MSG). This is exactly what we see John doing in this passage. So much of John's gospel is about seeing and believing – and here we see the pattern reversed: John the Baptist believed God's word to him – and then saw that word fulfilled; he experienced the truth of it for himself. John's experience was the result of an intentional watchfulness. Among all the hundreds who came to him to be baptised, John was watching for that one man on whom the Spirit would descend. So much depended on a steady watchfulness, even in the midst of so many possible distractions.

There may be times when we wonder why it is that we rarely see God at work in or through our lives. There may be times when we sense that God has spoken to us specifically about an area of our lives, or about a situation that is a concern to us, but there is no real expectation that God will get involved, that he will actually fulfil that word in our lives. So we don't keep watch, we are not 'alert for signs of his presence,' and sadly, our lack of intentional watchfulness may cause us to miss the wonder of seeing the fulfilment of God's word to us, of realising God's purposes for us.

Perhaps we could pause here for a moment: do you sense that God has spoken to you recently about a specific situation or circumstance in your life? Pray for the grace to be watchful and attentive for how God may be wanting to fulfil that word in your life, and ask for wisdom to know how best to respond.

MD

The first year: the year of inauguration

Day 43

A test of trust

MATTHEW 4:1-4 (MARK 1:12-13; LUKE 4:1-4)

Judean desert
Then Jesus was led by the Spirit into the wilderness to be tempted by the devil. After fasting for forty days and forty nights, he was hungry. The tempter came to him and said, 'If you are the Son of God, tell these stones to become bread.' Jesus answered, 'It is written: "Man shall not live on bread alone, but on every word that comes from the mouth of God."'

'Will you trust me?' Have you ever been asked this question? I wonder how you responded. So much of our response is determined by who is asking, what we know of them and our past experience of their trustworthiness. Trust is too precious a commodity to be given to just anyone.

In the wilderness, just as for God's children centuries before, Jesus' trust in God's heart and God's word would be tested to the limit. After weeks without food, Jesus was famished. And it's at this point that we witness the first of Jesus' recorded encounters with the devil,[7] who knew exactly when Jesus would be at his weakest – and vulnerable to temptation. The devil spoke the truth: since Jesus was the Son of God (the 'if' here is not about doubt; it carries the meaning 'since'), he had the wherewithal to act independently of his Father in order to satisfy a legitimate need. He could do this. But Jesus pushed back with a greater truth – he quoted from Deuteronomy 8:3, where God reminded his children that when they were hungry, he had provided manna in the wilderness. He had proved they could trust him to care for them. In his baptism, Jesus had heard his Father's words of love – and he trusted them. At a time of acute need, the devil was tempting Jesus to turn away from trusting his Father and to trust instead in his own resources, his own strength and abilities to satisfy his needs.

And I wonder if, in our own moments of gnawing hunger for whatever we believe will satisfy our needs, we don't face that same temptation?

> *Father, in those moments when I am weak and vulnerable and feel the tug of temptation, help me to trust your love for me – to trust that you know me and that you know my needs, and that you are with me and will care for me.*

MD

Day 44

The second test in the wilderness

MATTHEW 4:5-7 (*LUKE 4:9-12*)

Judean desert
Then the devil took him to the holy city and set him on the highest point of the temple. 'If you are the Son of God,' he said, 'throw yourself down. For it is written: "He will command his angels concerning you, and they will lift you up in their hands, so that you will not strike your foot against a stone." Jesus answered him, 'It is also written: "Do not put the Lord your God to the test."'

When the children of Israel in their trek through the desert came to a place called Rephidim, they demanded proof that God was still with them. Their circumstances were so challenging that they questioned God's presence with them, his care for them. Moses' response was clear: 'Do not put the Lord your God to the test' (see Exodus 17:1-7).

When Jesus was tempted to deliberately place himself in circumstances which would test God's word and God's care of him, he rebuffed the devil with the same words. For most of us, we are rarely, if ever, tempted to deliberately place ourselves in harm's way to prove God's care of us; the stuff of our ordinary lives is challenging enough.

There are times when our circumstances are so hard, when our relationships, our jobs, our finances, our health – are so overwhelmingly pressured that we wonder if God has actually forgotten about us – and if he hasn't, then why isn't he doing something about it? We can live as spiritual yo-yos: doubting God's care for us when things are hard, affirming his love for us when things are easier. Up and down, up and down; our circumstances, not God's word, become the benchmark against which we judge God's character. In such trying times our only recourse is to draw from the truth of God's word; not an isolated verse, but the whole teaching of scripture, as Jesus did here. In that trying moment, Jesus had exactly what we have in our own temptations: God's word and God's Spirit. And they were enough.

> *What temptation are you facing at the moment? Jesus has already faced the full force of that temptation – and he is with you in it. Take a deep breath and trust him with it now.*

MD

Day 45

A test of timing

MATTHEW 4:8-10 (*LUKE 4:5-8*)

Judean desert
Again, the devil took him to a very high mountain and showed him all the kingdoms of the world and their splendour. 'All this I will give you,' he said, 'if you will bow down and worship me.' Jesus said to him, 'Away from me, Satan! For it is written: "Worship the Lord your God, and serve him only."'

Waiting is hard, isn't it? Continuing to trust God as we wait for him to fulfil his promises, to unfold his purposes for our lives can be challenging. It can be tempting to take matters into our own hands, to make things happen, to rush ahead.

This final temptation faced by Jesus has to do with trusting God's timing. The devil is offering to give Jesus something which he had already been promised by God! At his baptism, when Jesus heard the words 'You are my beloved Son', he would have recalled those words as coming from Psalm 2, a messianic psalm in which God's Son is promised all the kingdoms of the earth. Jesus recognised those words as God's words *to him* – and he understood what they meant.

The temptation facing him now was to short-circuit the waiting process. It seemed so innocuous – no waiting needed; he could take what was already his. The promise had already been given; the whole world would one day be his. The temptation was to turn from trusting God's timing and to pursue a course of action by which he would end up acting independently of God.

And again, Jesus resisted the temptation with the word of God, words taken from Deuteronomy 6:13. On his lips, they were an affirmation of his wholehearted commitment to God, a declaration that there was nothing more important to him than his relationship with his Father.

> *What are you waiting for? Trusting for? Perhaps you sense that God has promised you something, but it's so slow in coming and the temptation to make it happen is so real. Pause for a moment... Ask... for the grace to wait... to trust... to hold on to hope.*

MD

Day 46

Great expectations

MARK 1:14–15 (*MATTHEW 4:12–17; LUKE 4:14–15*)

Galilee
After John was put in prison, Jesus went into Galilee, proclaiming the good news of God. 'The time has come,' he said. 'The kingdom of God has come near. Repent and believe the good news!' [8]

When I was six, I asked Father Christmas for a car – red, with pedals, a steering wheel and a horn. What I got was a set of Matchbox cars and a garage. It was my first experience of disappointed expectations.

In this proclamation of good news, Jesus was arousing all sorts of expectations. The kingdom of God had come! The reign of God had been inaugurated! Finally, after centuries of waiting, the Messiah had come! But not as expected. As they watched Jesus' life, people would discover that life in the kingdom of God would look like grace and mercy and compassion for all. It would look like celebration and healing and forgiveness. It would be a safe place for the broken and the bruised, the battered and the beggared (Luke 4:18–19). But where was the power, the might, the dominion that everyone was expecting and had been waiting for so long?

To understand the character of the kingdom of God would demand a change in their thinking – the true meaning of the word – *metanoia*, translated here as 'repent'. It would also demand trust. For many who listened and who watched the unfolding of *this* kingdom, it was too much, too little, not enough – and it would end in death – of dreams and hopes – and of Jesus himself.

Many of us have felt disappointed with God. Our expectations of what our lives should look like haven't been fulfilled, perhaps. Prayers have not been answered as expected, hopes have been dashed, dreams broken beyond repair. And still, through it all, Jesus invites us to trust that God *is* sovereign in our lives, our world. Jesus taught us to pray, 'Your kingdom come' (Matthew 6:10) – and every time we breathe those words we declare our trust in the God who works in unexpected ways to fulfil his purposes in our lives, and in our world.

> Father, may your kingdom come. Today, I invite you to rule over the circumstances of my life with your grace and mercy, your compassionate wisdom and your love.

MD

Day 47

John's disciples follow Jesus

JOHN 1:35-39

Bethany on the other side of the Jordan
The next day John was there again with two of his disciples. When he saw Jesus passing by, he said, 'Look, the Lamb of God!' When the two disciples heard him say this, they followed Jesus. Turning round, Jesus saw them following and asked, 'What do you want?' They said, 'Rabbi' (which means 'Teacher'), 'where are you staying?' 'Come,' he replied, 'and you will see.' So they went and saw where he was staying, and they spent that day with him. It was about four in the afternoon.

Ayeka – the very first recorded word of God in the Bible. It means 'Where are you?' and is addressed to Adam and Eve, who were hiding after eating the forbidden fruit. The question is not about location – God already knows that. He is asking about their hearts: what is going on inside you?

The first recorded words of Jesus in John's gospel are also a question: 'What do you want?' Or 'What are you looking for?' And again, they are words which address the heart. Jesus has seen the disciples following him – and he takes the initiative to draw them out. John's disciples have a clear answer – 'Where are you staying?' It was a bold, and vulnerable, response. This wasn't about an address; it was an expression of desire – 'Can we be where you are? Can we spend time with you?' Jesus completely understood their meaning and his 'Come and see' was an invitation to enter into a relationship with him. It was the beginning of something which would change their lives.

I wonder how we would answer Jesus' question? Those early disciples opened their hearts to Jesus. They didn't hide what they really wanted, but took the risk to tell him exactly what it was they wanted. And he responded.

Hear Jesus ask you, 'What do you want? What are the desires of your heart today? What are you looking for?' How will you answer – honestly, vulnerably, trustingly?

MD

Day 48

Jesus meets Simon Peter

JOHN 1:40-42

Bethany on the other side of the Jordan
Andrew, Simon Peter's brother, was one of the two who heard what John had said and who had followed Jesus. The first thing Andrew did was to find his brother Simon and tell him, 'We have found the Messiah' (that is, the Christ). And he brought him to Jesus. Jesus looked at him and said, 'You are Simon son of John. You will be called Cephas' (which, when translated, is Peter).

'Every block of stone has a statue inside it, and it is the task of the sculptor to discover it. I saw the angel in the marble and carved until I set him free.' Perhaps you recognise these words of Michelangelo; they speak of the power of vision, of transformation, of skill.

Michelangelo's insight into the work of the sculptor came to mind when I read Jesus' words to Simon Peter. Jesus saw the commanding leader buried deep within this impetuous, impulsive disciple, who is mentioned more than 100 times in the gospels – more than any other disciple. No other disciple spoke as much – or as often – and yet in this first encounter with Jesus, he is completely silent. I wonder if Simon, whose name means 'one who hears', was stunned into silence as he heard Jesus' words of confidence in who he would become.

In the years that followed, Jesus would chip away to reveal the man embedded in the marble of his stubbornness, self-sufficiency and arrogance. There would be no instant transformation, just the slow and steady work of a master sculptor, revealing his vision, his love, his confidence in the life of this most unlikely candidate for the eventual leadership of the church.

And I look at my own life – at the slow transformation into the Christlikeness that Paul tells me I'm purposed for by God (Romans 8:29). So much needed chipping away at what hides and limits and distorts what could be seen of him in my life. In his hands, circumstances become tools of transformation; difficulties, the chisel which shapes character, *his* character, in me.

> Lord Jesus, you see me, you know me; all that I am and all that I would ever hope to be. Help me to trust you and your vision and purposes for my life. Help me to surrender to your work in my life. Amen.

MD

Day 49

Growing the ministry

JOHN 1:43-46

Bethany on the other side of the Jordan
The next day Jesus Jesus decided to leave for Galilee. Finding Philip, he said to him, 'Follow me'... Philip found Nathanael and told him, 'We have found the one Moses wrote about in the Law, and about whom the prophets also wrote – Jesus of Nazareth, the son of Joseph.' 'Nazareth! Can anything good come from there?' Nathanael asked. 'Come and see,' said Philip.

The TV show *Keeping Faith* became a surprise hit in the UK, not because the pundits rated the show with brilliant reviews (which they did), but because viewers stumbled across this remarkable Welsh thriller, loved it and passed their experience of it on to others, who also then passed it on. It spread by word of mouth.

This is what we see happening here and throughout John's gospel. Beginning with the witness of John the Baptist, we see one person telling another about their experience of Jesus. There are no big evangelistic meetings, no big personalities, just one ordinary person telling another who they've discovered Jesus to be. It's clear that none of those early disciples completely understood who Jesus was; there was ignorance and doubt and scepticism. But as they spent time with Jesus, they grew to know him better, to believe he was their Saviour, and that led them to want others to know him too.

We don't have to understand every nuance of our faith to tell someone about Jesus; we just need to know him for ourselves, to spend time with him so that our personal experience of him is real and growing. And then, when the time is right, we can introduce our friends to the Jesus we know and love.

I watched all three seasons of *Keeping Faith* and raved about it to anyone who hadn't yet discovered it! I'd like to rave about Jesus in the same way – naturally, easily, to speak from my heart with excitement, conviction and joy, to share in such a way that others may find – and keep – faith in Jesus.

> *Father, today, give me grace to naturally speak about the Jesus who I am learning to know and love. Let my words flow from a heart touched by the wonder of who Jesus is and a longing that others would know him too.*

MD

Day 50

Calling the first disciples

MATTHEW 4:18–22 (MARK 1:16–20)

Sea of Galilee
As Jesus was walking beside the Sea of Galilee, he saw two brothers, Simon called Peter and his brother Andrew. They were casting a net into the lake, for they were fishermen. 'Come, follow me,' Jesus said, 'and I will send you out to fish for people.' At once they left their nets and followed him. Going on from there, he saw two other brothers, James son of Zebedee and his brother John. They were in a boat with their father Zebedee, preparing their nets. Jesus called them, and immediately they left the boat and their father and followed him.

Throughout our lives we make choices, decisions which in some instances change the whole course of our lives. We can rarely predict with any certainty where our choices may take us, but we make them. And the moment we do, consequences are set in motion, just as they were for these first disciples.

They were fishermen – ordinary, hard-working men, with families to support, taxes to pay, homes and boats that needed maintaining. And yet Jesus unapologetically interrupts the everydayness of their lives with an invitation which would lead them into places they could hardly have imagined. He calls them to leave behind the lives they know so well in exchange for a new friendship, a new purpose. Jesus is calling them to trust him, to follow him, to join him in the costly work of bringing the presence of the kingdom of God into their communities, their families, their world. Their decision to follow him would turn their lives upside down. Eventually, their witness would turn the whole *world* upside down – and in time, our worlds too. On that day, they could never have imagined what the consequences would be of responding to Jesus' call. But they made their choice – and the rest is history. Literally.

> *Lord Jesus, you step into the ordinary everydayness of my life and invite me to trust you, to follow you in that very place. Help me to recognise your voice, and just as these early disciples did, give me grace to let go of any 'nets' that may hold me back from responding to you. Use me, even today, to bring your presence into the places in my world that need you. Amen.*

MD

Day 51

Ministry in Galilee

MATTHEW 4:23–25 (MARK 1:39)

Galilee
Jesus went throughout Galilee, teaching in their synagogues, proclaiming the good news of the kingdom, and healing every disease and illness among the people. News about him spread all over Syria, and people brought to him all who were ill with various diseases, those suffering severe pain, the demon-possessed, those having seizures, and the paralysed; and he healed them. Large crowds from Galilee, the Decapolis, Jerusalem, Judea and the region across the Jordan followed him.

Until recently I doubt any of us were too familiar with the term 'social distancing', but over recent years we have become all too familiar with that term and all it implies. Social distancing was practised in Jesus' day too! Jews kept social distance from 'defiling' Gentiles, and ritually clean Jews distanced themselves from those who would be considered unclean by virtue of physical or mental disease or handicap. No one wanted to be infected – either physically or spiritually. And yet in these few sentences, Matthew paints a picture of the ministry of Jesus in which this ancient practice of social distancing seems to have been blown apart.

To begin with, although Jesus' ministry at this time is based in Galilee – a cultural, ethnic and religious melting pot – his fame had spread way beyond Galilee. The inevitable happened: people brought to him the sick and afflicted, and great crowds started following him. Can you imagine the crowds? Think Wembley. Think Cheltenham Racecourse. Think of all those places in which thousands of unsuspecting people mingled together, and walked away infected with Covid.

At that time, these sports fans didn't know any better, but Jesus knew exactly what he was doing as the crowds milled around him. He was completely aware of their 'uncleanness' – and he welcomed them all, taught them, healed them, proclaiming in word and deed that the kingdom of God had arrived – for them. *All* of them.

His acceptance was total, his message uncompromising, his love all inclusive.

> What about us? Can we welcome into our prayers today someone we might normally try to avoid – for whatever reason? Who comes to mind?

MD

Day 52

At a wedding in Cana

JOHN 2:1-12

Cana in Galilee
On the third day a wedding took place at Cana in Galilee. Jesus' mother was there, and Jesus and his disciples had also been invited to the wedding. When the wine was gone, Jesus' mother said to him, 'They have no more wine.' 'Woman, why do you involve me?' Jesus replied. 'My hour has not yet come.' His mother said to the servants, 'Do whatever he tells you.' Nearby stood six stone water jars, the kind used by the Jews for ceremonial washing, each holding from eighty to a hundred and twenty litres. Jesus said to the servants, 'Fill the jars with water'; so they filled them to the brim. Then he told them, 'Now draw some out and take it to the master of the banquet.' They did so, and the master of the banquet tasted the water that had been turned into wine. He did not realise where it had come from, though the servants who had drawn the water knew. Then he called the bridegroom aside and said, 'Everyone brings out the choice wine first and then the cheaper wine after the guests have had too much to drink; but you have saved the best till now.' What Jesus did here in Cana of Galilee was the first of the signs through which he revealed his glory; and his disciples believed in him. After this he went down to Capernaum with his mother and brothers and his disciples. There they stayed for a few days.

Acknowledging God's gift, the psalmist sang, 'You give us wine that makes happy hearts' (Psalm 104:15, NCV). But what happens when the wine runs out? It's a simple statement: 'They have no more wine.'

There may be days in our lives when we might echo these same stark words: 'I have no more wine. I have nothing left which brings joy or comfort or hope. The wine of my life has run out, my glass is empty, my mouth is dry; my hoarded resources are no longer adequate for the demands of my days, my life.' But Mary came to Jesus – and that changed everything.

> Pause to reflect on the following statement and what it might mean for your life in those days when you feel that you 'have no more wine': 'The miracle happens, the glory is seen, when the wine runs out.'[9]

MD

Day 53

Clearing the temple

JOHN 2:13–22

Jerusalem
When it was almost time for the Jewish Passover, Jesus went up to Jerusalem. In the temple courts he found people selling cattle, sheep and doves, and others sitting at tables exchanging money. So he made a whip out of cords, and drove all from the temple courts, both sheep and cattle; he scattered the coins of the money-changers and overturned their tables. To those who sold doves he said, 'Get these out of here! Stop turning my Father's house into a market!' His disciples remembered that it is written: 'Zeal for your house will consume me.' The Jews then responded to him, 'What sign can you show us to prove your authority to do all this?' Jesus answered them, 'Destroy this temple, and I will raise it again in three days.' They replied, 'It has taken forty-six years to build this temple, and you are going to raise it in three days?' But the temple he had spoken of was his body. After he was raised from the dead, his disciples recalled what he had said. Then they believed the scripture and the words that Jesus had spoken. [10]

I wonder what makes you angry, *really* angry? And what happens when you get that angry? In our reading, Jesus is angry – with the righteous, holy anger of a son who comes home to his father's house only to discover that corrupt men have moved in and taken over.

In what follows, Jesus does more than upend tables. His actions point to an upending of the whole sacrificial system which had been entrenched in Jewish life for centuries. He is giving notice of the temple's demise.

When questioned about his authority to cause such a disruption, Jesus' defence was that he was the true temple, the real meeting place of heaven and earth, of God and man. God's presence would no longer be accessed through costly sacrificial offering, but freely, through the one standing before them in the flesh and blood and blazing righteousness of Jesus. No wonder they crucified him.

> Father, as I draw near to you, help me to recognise those places in my life where I am unhelpfully entrenched in patterns of believing or behaving which block my experience of your life in me, which block the expression of your life through me. Amen.

MD

Day 54

A different agenda

JOHN 2:23–25

Jerusalem
Now while he was in Jerusalem at the Passover Festival, many people saw the signs he was performing and believed in his name. But Jesus would not entrust himself to them, for he knew all people. He did not need any testimony about mankind, for he knew what was in each person.

If it talks like a duck and walks like a duck and looks like a duck – it's probably a duck! It's a reasonable conclusion, isn't it? Many of the people who saw the miracles which Jesus performed during those Passover days in Jerusalem also came to a conclusion – the Messiah had come! They would have known Isaiah's prophecy which declared that when the Messiah came the blind would see, the deaf would hear, the lame would dance and the mute sing for joy (Isaiah 35:5–6). These things were happening there, in their midst. Surely, the Messiah had finally come. They believed in him.

So why didn't Jesus entrust himself to them? John tells us that Jesus knew what was in them. He knew that the moment he entrusted himself to them, they would declare him Messiah and expect him to do what they believed the Messiah should do: proclaim himself king, rid Israel of the Romans and set up a restored kingdom of Israel.

Jesus had a different agenda. He hadn't come to re-establish the kingdom of Israel, but to inaugurate the kingdom of God. His miracles were *signs* (Greek *semeion*) – not an end in themselves, but a means of directing attention to the character and purposes of the God whose love for them was incarnate in Jesus' every word and action.[11] It was a love which would ultimately be demonstrated in giving his Son for them (John 3:16), the last and final sacrifice which would open the door wide into fulness of life (John 10:10).

But all that was to come. This was not the time to take on the mantle of Messiah, however popular that would be. That day would eventually come. But this was not that day.

> *When God's agenda for our lives and our world seems to differ widely from our agenda, it is an invitation to trust – to trust that God is working out his purposes in and through our lives in ways that are yet to be revealed, but will be. Hold on to that hope; hold on.*

MD

Day 55

A night-time encounter

JOHN 3:1–8

Jerusalem

Now there was a Pharisee, a man named Nicodemus who was a member of the Jewish ruling council. He came to Jesus at night and said, 'Rabbi, we know that you are a teacher who has come from God. For no one could perform the signs you are doing if God were not with him.' Jesus replied, 'Very truly I tell you, no one can see the kingdom of God unless they are born again.' 'How can someone be born when they are old?' Nicodemus asked. 'Surely they cannot enter a second time into their mother's womb to be born!' Jesus answered, 'Very truly I tell you, no one can enter the kingdom of God unless they are born of water and the Spirit. Flesh gives birth to flesh, but the Spirit gives birth to spirit. You should not be surprised at my saying, "You must be born again." The wind blows wherever it pleases. You hear its sound, but you cannot tell where it comes from or where it is going. So it is with everyone born of the Spirit.'

Sometimes I look in the mirror and see Nicodemus looking back at me. I see Nicodemus whenever I think that my relationship with God is determined by how much Bible study I do, or the influence I may have in Christian circles, or how hard I work in caring for others. But the truth is that my life in Christ began with a Spirit-graced birth and is nurtured through glad responsiveness to that same gloriously unpredictable Spirit.

That night, Jesus told an incredulous Nicodemus that to even see the kingdom of God, he needed to begin again; he had to experience what could not be book-learned, to receive what could not be achieved. To enter the kingdom of God, he would need to accept new life from the Spirit of God.

You see, for all his learning, Nicodemus was in the dark about a profound spiritual truth: 'Flesh gives birth to flesh, but the Spirit gives birth to spirit' (v. 6). Only the Spirit of God can accomplish a work of God. Whatever needs to be born in me, whatever needs to change, happens through the work of the Spirit of God; not my flesh – however well-intentioned.

Who do you see when you look in the mirror?

MD

Day 56

Jesus teaches Nicodemus

JOHN 3:9–15

Jerusalem
How can this be?' Nicodemus asked. 'You are Israel's teacher,' said Jesus, 'and do you not understand these things? Very truly I tell you, we speak of what we know, and we testify to what we have seen, but still you people do not accept our testimony. I have spoken to you of earthly things and you do not believe; how then will you believe if I speak of heavenly things? No one has ever gone into heaven except the one who came from heaven – the Son of Man. Just as Moses lifted up the snake in the wilderness, so the Son of Man must be lifted up, that everyone who believes may have eternal life in him.'

During the pandemic, we saw it almost daily. As they gave the latest update, representatives of the World Health Organisation sat in front of the organisation's flag, and there, front and centre, was the most widely recognised symbol of medicine and health care in the world – an image of a snake coiled around a pole. Rooted in classical mythology, this symbol also connects with a historical reference that Jesus points to in his conversation with Nicodemus that night.

Jesus takes Nicodemus back to Numbers 21:4–9, to the day when the children of Israel were bitten by poisonous snakes, sent by God as punishment for their grumbling. They would be healed only when they looked in faith at the remedy God had provided – a bronze serpent lifted up on a pole.

Jesus clearly equates the serpent on the pole with his own death on the cross. Lifted up on the cross, Jesus would take on all our sin – and God's judgement of it. In this place the scriptures are fulfilled where: 'Mercy and truth meet together. Righteousness and peace kiss each other' (Psalm 85:10, EHV).

Jesus' message to Nicodemus that night was 'Believe – and live.' That's his message to us today.

> Every day Jesus invites us to trust his love and his forgiveness – and to go out and live – healed and free. It's a glorious invitation – for Nicodemus then, and for us today. It really is.

MD

Day 57

Comment by John

JOHN 3:16-21

Jerusalem
For God so loved the world that he gave his one and only Son, that whoever believes in him shall not perish but have eternal life. For God did not send his Son into the world to condemn the world, but to save the world through him. Whoever believes in him is not condemned, but whoever does not believe stands condemned already because they have not believed in the name of God's one and only Son. This is the verdict: light has come into the world, but people loved darkness instead of light because their deeds were evil. Everyone who does evil hates the light, and will not come into the light for fear that their deeds will be exposed. But whoever lives by the truth comes into the light, so that it may be seen plainly that what they have done has been done in the sight of God.

Today is an opportunity to engage with what will be a familiar passage to many of us through the practice of *lectio divina* or spiritual reading. The guidelines for this practice are found on page 13. In summary, the four moves of *lectio divina* are read, reflect, respond, rest.

> *May you know the Lord more clearly, be drawn to love him more dearly, and be enabled to follow him more nearly, as you encounter him through his word to you today.*

MD

Day 58

Conflict, competition and letting go

JOHN 3:22–26

Judean countryside and Aenon near Salim
After this, Jesus and his disciples went out into the Judean countryside, where he spent some time with them, and baptised. Now John also was baptising at Aenon near Salim, because there was plenty of water, and people were coming and being baptised. (This was before John was put in prison.) An argument developed between some of John's disciples and a certain Jew over the matter of ceremonial washing. They came to John and said to him, 'Rabbi, that man who was with you on the other side of the Jordan – the one you testified about – look, he is baptising, and everyone is going to him.'

If we've heard them once, we've probably heard them a thousand times: 'Let it go! Let it go!'[12] My goddaughter belts out Elsa's words as she twirls around, flinging out her arms in exuberant abandon. Letting go seems so gloriously easy.

But it's not, as the reaction of John's disciples reminds us here. John's gospel is the only one which describes the overlapping ministries of Jesus and John the Baptist in Judea – an overlap which seems to present some challenges for John's disciples. Leaving the religious and political hotbed that was Jerusalem, Jesus had taken his disciples into the Judean countryside, and during that time his disciples baptised a growing number of people.

John 4:2 explains that Jesus didn't baptise, only his disciples did. But John's disciples nevertheless interpreted what was happening as competition. John was their rabbi – their teacher. They would be proud to be his disciples, learning from him and sharing his life and message. His ministry had been so significant. And now? Jesus seemed to be usurping John's place, drawing more crowds than John. Little wonder, then, that they were reactive, defensive, perhaps even resentful and jealous.

They seem to have missed the whole point of John's ministry, which was to prepare the way for the Messiah. It seems that John had become more important to them than his message. But the Messiah *had* come; it was now time to let go of John and follow Jesus. It was time to move on.

> I wonder what we may need to let go of today in order to know and follow Jesus more wholeheartedly. What relationships or roles, attitudes or perspectives? What might be our first step in doing that?

MD

Day 59

The surrendered man

JOHN 3:27–30

Aenon

To this John replied, 'A person can receive only what is given them from heaven. You yourselves can testify that I said, "I am not the Messiah but am sent ahead of him." The bride belongs to the bridegroom. The friend who attends the bridegroom waits and listens for him, and is full of joy when he hears the bridegroom's voice. That joy is mine, and it is now complete. He must become greater; I must become less.'

Every Sunday, as our vicar receives the offering plate, he recites a prayer based on 1 Chronicles 29:14: 'Lord, everything we have has come from you and of your own do we give you.' I always find it a moving moment in the service – a chance to pause and remember that my whole life, not just my money, is a gift from God, to be offered back to him with great thankfulness.

In contrast to the agitated, fractious tone of his disciples in the words which precede this passage, John's response is redolent of a heart which is surrendered, at peace and confident in the knowledge that everything he had in his life – including his successful ministry – had been given to him by God. Because of this confidence, John could step out of the limelight, joyfully acknowledging himself best man to Jesus' bridegroom.

John had been the 'voice crying in the wilderness'. It was a time-limited role until the voice of the bridegroom was clearly heard in the land. Once that voice was heard, John's part was over. John knew that his calling and his message were an entrustment from God with one objective – that Jesus be introduced to Israel as her Messiah. Once that was done, he was done. There was no bitterness, no arguing, no complaining from John. His voice was no longer needed. As was the custom for the best man in those days, he had brought bride and groom together; there was nothing left for him to do.

From John we learn that there can be no letting go, no stepping back, no moving on without this deep conviction that everything we have – our opportunities, success, recognition, influence, resources – all come from God.

> Father, I ask for a heart that is surrendered to you. Fulfil your purposes in my life and through my life. For your glory's sake.

MD

Day 60

Reflection by John (apostle)

JOHN 3:31-36

The one who comes from above is above all; the one who is from the earth belongs to the earth, and speaks as one from the earth. The one who comes from heaven is above all. He testifies to what he has seen and heard, but no one accepts his testimony. Whoever has accepted it has certified that God is truthful. For the one whom God has sent speaks the words of God, for God gives the Spirit without limit. The Father loves the Son and has placed everything in his hands. Whoever believes in the Son has eternal life, but whoever rejects the Son will not see life, for God's wrath remains on them.

'The body of Christ, broken for you.' We hear the words, we taste the bread, we move on. And behind the words lies the love of a Father for his Son; the love of a Redeemer for a world gone awry.

Sonship is a key theme in the gospel of John: like a fine gold thread, the word 'Son' weaves its way throughout this gospel. John writes of the 'Son of God', the 'Son of Man' and sometimes just 'the Son'. As a son, Jesus calls God 'the Father' or 'my Father' around 107 times and refers to himself as 'the Son of God' or simply 'the Son' in context with 'the Father' around 30 times.

And here, amid all the reasons which John piles up to support the Baptist's assertion that Jesus must increase, we find this sudden switch of words from 'God' to 'Father', and a glimpse into the relationship between Jesus and his Father. Jesus is the Son who is loved by his Father. Love expresses itself in giving, generously, to the beloved one. John tells us that the Father loves the Son so much that he has given him *everything*.

Such a love makes the words of John 3:16 even more staggering: 'God so loved the world that he *gave*…' The Father gave this Son, whom he so dearly loved, that we would know his love for *us*, know life in all its fulness through faith in him.

> The Father loves the Son. Feel the weight of those words. Know the truth they carry of the depth of the Father's love for you. And worship.

MD

Day 61

Jesus arrives in Samaria

JOHN 4:1-6

Sychar in Samaria
Now Jesus learned that the Pharisees had heard that he was gaining and baptising more disciples than John – although in fact it was not Jesus who baptised, but his disciples. So he left Judea and went back once more to Galilee. Now he had to go through Samaria. So he came to a town in Samaria called Sychar, near the plot of ground Jacob had given to his son Joseph. Jacob's well was there, and Jesus, tired as he was from the journey, sat down by the well. It was about noon.

Samaritans are good – aren't they? We're probably all familiar with the parable of the good Samaritan, but we perhaps don't fully appreciate the staggering irony of a Samaritan being the star of the story, because as far as Jews were concerned there were no good Samaritans.

The animosity between Samaritans and Jews was centuries-long and deep-rooted. Jews considered Samaritans to be heretical half-breeds, racially and religiously compromised. They loathed each other and had as little as possible to do with each other. A righteous Jew would be considered ritually contaminated by any contact with a Samaritan, so although Samaria was directly between Judea and Galilee and the quickest way would be to go straight through it, many God-fearing Jews would take the extra three days to go east across the Jordan to avoid Samaria.

Which raises the question, why Jesus would choose this route? We can't be certain, but one thing is clear, his very presence in Samaria that day is evidence that Jesus has no regard for barriers in any shape or form. Weary from the journey, resting by the well, Jesus is perfectly placed and ready for an encounter which will change not only one woman's life, but also the lives of an entire community. Jesus has come to town – and nothing will ever be the same again.

Where is your Samaria? Perhaps one way to find out is to ask yourself who you try to avoid the most – and why? Whose values, beliefs and lifestyle are so different from yours that you would rather go out of your way than sit down with them?

> Surrender that person and those differences to the Lord now, trusting him to lead you more deeply into his heart for them.

MD

Day 62

Jesus crosses boundaries in Samaria

JOHN 4:7–15

Sychar in Samaria
When a Samaritan woman came to draw water, Jesus said to her, 'Will you give me a drink?' (His disciples had gone into the town to buy food.) The Samaritan woman said to him, 'You are a Jew and I am a Samaritan woman. How can you ask me for a drink?' (For Jews do not associate with Samaritans.) Jesus answered her, 'If you knew the gift of God and who it is that asks you for a drink, you would have asked him and he would have given you living water.' 'Sir,' the woman said, 'you have nothing to draw with and the well is deep. Where can you get this living water? Are you greater than our father Jacob, who gave us the well and drank from it himself, as did also his sons and his livestock?' Jesus answered, 'Everyone who drinks this water will be thirsty again, but whoever drinks the water I give them will never thirst. Indeed, the water I give them will become in them a spring of water welling up to eternal life.' The woman said to him, 'Sir, give me this water so that I won't get thirsty and have to keep coming here to draw water.'

They talked; across the divides of race and religion and culture and gender. They talked of water – of wells and springs – and all the while, Jesus is drawing this thirsty woman towards the source of living water – towards life, towards himself. She may not have fully understood what Jesus was offering but she believed he could give it to her – so she asks for whatever will bring an end to her thirst and the constant effort needed to satisfy it.

> *For a moment, picture Jesus, sitting alone by the well, waiting – for you to be with him. He sees you as he saw her that day. What thirsts will you open to him? What words do you need to hear from him?*

MD

Day 63

Jesus reveals his identity for the first time

JOHN 4:16-26

Sychar in Samaria

He told her, 'Go, call your husband and come back.' 'I have no husband,' she replied. Jesus said to her, 'You are right when you say you have no husband. The fact is, you have had five husbands, and the man you now have is not your husband. What you have just said is quite true.' 'Sir,' the woman said, 'I can see that you are a prophet. Our ancestors worshipped on this mountain, but you Jews claim that the place where we must worship is in Jerusalem.' 'Woman,' Jesus replied, 'believe me, a time is coming when you will worship the Father neither on this mountain nor in Jerusalem. You Samaritans worship what you do not know; we worship what we do know, for salvation is from the Jews. Yet a time is coming and has now come when the true worshippers will worship the Father in the Spirit and in truth, for they are the kind of worshippers the Father seeks. God is spirit, and his worshippers must worship in the Spirit and in truth.' The woman said, 'I know that Messiah' (called Christ) 'is coming. When he comes, he will explain everything to us.' Then Jesus declared, 'I, the one speaking to you – I am he.'

'This Is Me!' It's one of the most captivating songs in the film, but Jesus is not 'the Greatest Showman' – he is far more that that! In this profoundly honest and theologically significant conversation, for the first time ever Jesus self-identifies as the Messiah – and the revelation is to this woman who has trusted him with the truth of her life and with her questions. His response is to trust *her* with the truth of *his* life and with this astounding disclosure of who he is.

His grace and acceptance of her gradually turned her suspicions to trust, her defensive antagonism to vulnerability. Throughout their conversation, Jesus has honoured this woman, treating her questions with respect and dignity, drawing her into a deepening awareness of her need of him, into understanding more clearly who he is for her.

> *Perhaps you could use these prayer prompts, as a guide for your own response to Jesus today:*
> *Lord, my thirsts draw me into…*
> *I know that you…*
> *I trust you now to…*
> *Thank you for…*

MD

Day 64

Confused disciples and a woman's testimony

JOHN 4:27-33

Sychar in Samaria
Just then his disciples returned and were surprised to find him talking with a woman. But no one asked, 'What do you want?' or 'Why are you talking with her?' Then, leaving her water jar, the woman went back to the town and said to the people, 'Come, see a man who told me everything I've ever done. Could this be the Messiah?' They came out of the town and made their way towards him. Meanwhile his disciples urged him, 'Rabbi, eat something.' But he said to them, 'I have food to eat that you know nothing about.' Then his disciples said to each other, 'Could someone have brought him food?'

Questions matter. I wonder what would have happened if Jesus' disciples had actually asked this woman what she wanted or had asked Jesus why he was talking with her? What would they have learned? What did they miss by not asking?

They were understandably shocked that Jesus was talking with a woman, because the convention against talking to any woman in public – including your wife – was inviolable for a law-abiding Jewish man. Yet they don't ask Jesus why he would so lightly cast such a convention aside. Who was she that that he would do that for her? Risk his reputation for her? So many unasked questions.

While they address him as 'Rabbi' and ask questions about who brought him lunch, back in town this woman is telling everyone that she might have met the Messiah. She is bold, but not arrogant. She knows that the testimony of a woman is not trusted – so instead she poses a question: 'Could this be the Messiah?' It was probably the most important question she'd ever asked – and one which had the most life-changing impact on her community as they streamed out to see this possible Messiah for themselves.

Our questions may carry seeds of transformation in their pockets. What fresh questions are we asking about who Jesus is and who Jesus is for us? About who Jesus is inviting me to be and what he may be inviting me to do? About how I can open up my life, my faith, in ways that cause others to want to know him?

> *This woman kept asking Jesus questions – and Jesus kept answering – all the way to faith. Where are your questions?*

MD

Day 65

The harvest is already here

JOHN 4:34–38

Sychar in Samaria
'My food,' said Jesus, 'is to do the will of him who sent me and to finish his work. Don't you have a saying, "It's still four months until harvest"? I tell you, open your eyes and look at the fields! They are ripe for harvest. Even now the one who reaps draws a wage and harvests a crop for eternal life, so that the sower and the reaper may be glad together. Thus the saying "One sows and another reaps" is true. I sent you to reap what you have not worked for. Others have done the hard work, and you have reaped the benefits of their labour.'

I live in Gloucestershire, which is a predominantly rural county, and over the years I've become very aware of the changing agricultural seasons, particularly the excitement – and the work – surrounding harvest time. It's so obvious that for there to be a harvest someone has to sow and someone has to reap – and on the smaller farms, it's often the same person. But he's not alone. He works with family and friends and any willing hands. Communities pitch in to help each other until the work is done.

Jesus is drawing on farming language here to teach his disciples more about their role as 'sent' ones. They will reap the rewards of the hard work of generations of men and women, of centuries of sowing gone before by prophets and more recently by John the Baptist. They are stepping into deep-furrowed ways. He is teaching them about the need to work together, to appreciate and build on the work done by others, and to understand the deep satisfaction that comes from fulfilling the will and the purposes of God.

As the people from the village stream out towards them, Jesus draws his disciples' attention to what must not be missed – the harvest is not a future event; it's now! It's ripe and it's ready. And they have a part to play in bringing it in, just as we do when we respond to the Lord's promptings in our own lives.

> Where is your harvest field? Where has God placed you to sow or to reap? Who are you partnering with? And what are you expecting from God's presence with you in that place?

MD

Day 66

The impact of a testimony

JOHN 4:39–42

Sychar in Samaria
Many of the Samaritans from that town believed in him because of the woman's testimony, 'He told me everything I've ever done.' So when the Samaritans came to him, they urged him to stay with them, and he stayed two days. And because of his words many more became believers. They said to the woman, 'We no longer believe just because of what you said; now we have heard for ourselves, and we know that this man really is the Saviour of the world.'

Despite how she's been portrayed by some commentators, John makes it very clear that in a culture where a woman's word is rarely believed, *this* woman's word is trusted. Many in that village came to faith in Christ because of her word. It was a great beginning to their journey of faith – but it didn't end there.

After being with Jesus for just two days, their faith became more personal; it became a first-hand experience. Over that brief time, their understanding of Jesus had blossomed. Initially believing him to be the Messiah, the one who had come to be the Saviour of his people Israel, they now boldly declared him to be the Saviour of the whole world. These Samaritans had grasped what so few of Jesus' orthodox Jewish hearers had understood: the wideness of God's mercy, God's generous welcome, God's expansive acceptance of all who come to Jesus in trusting faith, regardless of who they are, where they've come from, what their past may have been. All are welcome, all are included in God's kingdom.

This courageous Samaritan woman is a great model for our own ventures in sharing our faith in Christ. We don't need a spectacular testimony or impressive words – we just need to speak the truth about who we've discovered Jesus to be. As we share our experience of him, as honestly, clearly and humbly as we can, we can trust God to use us to draw others into their own encounter with him.

> Lord Jesus, even today, give me an opportunity to share with someone something of my life with you. Give me grace to share wisely and humbly who you are to me, what you've done in my life. For your glory's sake.

MD

Day 67

Healing the official's son

JOHN 4:46–54

Cana in Galilee
Once more he visited Cana in Galilee, where he had turned the water into wine. And there was a certain royal official whose son lay ill at Capernaum. When this man heard that Jesus had arrived in Galilee from Judea, he went to him and begged him to come and heal his son, who was close to death. 'Unless you people see signs and wonders,' Jesus told him, 'you will never believe.' The royal official said, 'Sir, come down before my child dies.' 'Go,' Jesus replied, 'your son will live.' The man took Jesus at his word and departed. While he was still on the way, his servants met him with the news that his boy was living. When he enquired as to the time when his son got better, they said to him, 'Yesterday, at one in the afternoon, the fever left him.' Then the father realised that this was the exact time at which Jesus had said to him, 'Your son will live.' So he and his whole household believed. This was the second sign Jesus performed after coming from Judea to Galilee.

When this desperate father came to Jesus to plead for the life of his boy, he begged Jesus to make the 20-mile journey with him back to Capernaum to heal his son. He probably couldn't imagine a better outcome than that. This father had faith Jesus could heal his son, but understandably believed that Jesus needed to be present to do that, so on that basis, asked Jesus to come home with him. It was a reasonable request, but made in ignorance of the limitless scope of Jesus' power and authority.

Jesus pushed the father's faith even further that day, by asking him to believe his word. To go home, alone, with nothing but Jesus' word for company. And he did.

> *Lord Jesus, I come to you so often with my needs – and then tell you how you should meet them. Forgive me for not trusting your wise kindness, your limitless understanding and power. Help me to grow in simply entrusting my needs to you and leaving you to sort it out your way.*

MD

Day 68

Jesus' inaugural speech

LUKE 4:16–21

Nazareth

He went to Nazareth, where he had been brought up, and on the Sabbath day he went into the synagogue, as was his custom. He stood up to read, and the scroll of the prophet Isaiah was handed to him. Unrolling it, he found the place where it is written: 'The Spirit of the Lord is on me, because he has anointed me to proclaim good news to the poor. He has sent me to proclaim freedom for the prisoners and recovery of sight for the blind, to set the oppressed free, to proclaim the year of the Lord's favour.' Then he rolled up the scroll, gave it back to the attendant and sat down. The eyes of everyone in the synagogue were fastened on him. He began by saying to them, 'Today this scripture is fulfilled in your hearing.'

In 2022 Britain celebrated the Queen's platinum jubilee. It was a joyous celebration in the midst of economic and social challenges – a chance to catch our collective national breath and to hope for better days ahead.

In his reading from Isaiah 61, Jesus referenced another jubilee year in the phrase 'the year of the Lord's favour'. Every seven years Israel celebrated a sabbatical year in which the land lay fallow and people rested. The 'jubilee' was the sabbatical of sabbaticals! Scholar N.T. Wright says: 'Seven times seven years producing a great celebration of release, forgiveness and rescue from all that has crippled human life.'[13] Isaiah places the phrase in the context of the ministry of the Messiah, a ministry to all who were beggared, broken, bound, blind and bruised – the literal meaning of Jesus' words. In the synagogue that day, Jesus declared that *he* was the anointed one; this would be *his* ministry.

Centuries before, a broken, barren and soul-bruised woman called Hannah declared that God 'puts poor people on their feet again; he rekindles burned-out lives with fresh hope, restoring dignity and respect to their lives' (1 Samuel 2:8, MSG). *This* is exactly what Jesus was promising to do that day in Nazareth. *This* is what he is doing today – still.

> Lord Jesus, I name before you all those places in my life where I am broken and bound, blind and beggared and bruised… Heal me. Release me. Restore me. Give me hope.

MD

Day 69

The scandal of grace

LUKE 4:22–30

Nazareth
All spoke well of him and were amazed at the gracious words that came from his lips. 'Isn't this Joseph's son?' they asked. Jesus said to them, 'Surely you will quote this proverb to me: "Physician, heal yourself!" And you will tell me, "Do here in your hometown what we have heard that you did in Capernaum." Truly I tell you… no prophet is accepted in his hometown. I assure you that there were many widows in Israel in Elijah's time, when the sky was shut for three and a half years and there was a severe famine throughout the land. Yet Elijah was not sent to any of them, but to a widow in Zarephath in the region of Sidon. And there were many in Israel with leprosy in the time of Elisha the prophet, yet not one of them was cleansed – only Naaman the Syrian.' All the people in the synagogue were furious when they heard this. They got up, drove him out of the town, and took him to the brow of the hill on which the town was built, in order to throw him off the cliff. But he walked right through the crowd and went on his way.

He was doing so well. They were so impressed with him. And then he ruined it. In a moment, surprise had turned to shock, admiration to loathing. They were ready to kill him. Why?

It seems they'd believed that 'the day of the Lord's favour' was exclusively for them, the chosen ones. And they were wrong. Jesus pointedly reminded them of a God who was expansive in his grace, inclusive in his favour, a God whose love and mercy went beyond all national and cultural boundaries.

It's challenging, isn't it, when we are presented with a new perspective on who God is or how God works, or when the settled understanding of our faith is shaken by new insights? These Nazarenes didn't respond well, but I wonder what my own response would have been in the synagogue that day? Would I have been overwhelmed with awe or incensed by the scandal of grace? So easy to judge them; so painful to see myself in them.

> Lord Jesus, give me a heart to rejoice in your generous grace wherever it's displayed.

MD

Day 70

Healing in the synagogue

LUKE 4:31–37 (NKJV) (MARK 1:21–28)

Capernaum
Then he went down to Capernaum, a city of Galilee, and was teaching them on the Sabbaths. And they were astonished at his teaching, for his word was with authority. Now in the synagogue there was a man who had a spirit of an unclean demon. And he cried out with a loud voice, saying, 'Let us alone! What have we to do with you, Jesus of Nazareth? Did you come to destroy us? I know who you are – the Holy One of God!' But Jesus rebuked him, saying, 'Be quiet, and come out of him!' And when the demon had thrown him in their midst, it came out of him and did not hurt him. Then they were all amazed and spoke among themselves, saying, 'What a word this is! For with authority and power he commands the unclean spirits, and they come out.' And the report about him went out into every place in the surrounding region.

'Sticks and stones may break my bones but words will never hurt me.'

Really? Words have immense power. To hurt. To heal. Jesus' words were words of transformation and healing for all who heard and obeyed them – including the demon-possessed.

The moment Jesus spoke, the demon screamed out in recognition of Jesus, provoked perhaps by the profound difference he encountered between the words of Jesus and the words he was accustomed to hearing in that synagogue, because Jesus 'taught… as one who had authority, not as the teachers of the law' (Mark 1:22). The fight was on. It was a short one. The demon lost.

The apostle John would later write that Jesus had come to destroy the works of the devil (1 John 3:8), and that is exactly what he is doing here – confronting evil with nothing but a word of rebuke. No elaborate healing ritual, no long prayers, just the unadorned authority of his word.

> Lord Jesus, let me never lose the wonder of your word and its power to transform my life. Thank you that, as I surrender to you, your word can heal me, free me, transform me into all you long for me to be.

MD

Day 71

Healings

MARK 1:29-34 (MATTHEW 8:14-17; LUKE 4:38-41)

Capernaum
As soon as they left the synagogue, they went with James and John to the home of Simon and Andrew. Simon's mother-in-law was in bed with a fever, and they immediately told Jesus about her. So he went to her, took her hand and helped her up. The fever left her and she began to wait on them. That evening after sunset the people brought to Jesus all who were ill and demon-possessed. The whole town gathered at the door, and Jesus healed many who had various diseases. He also drove out many demons, but he would not let the demons speak because they knew who he was.

We learn so much about the nature, power and expansive grace of the reign of God through the lens of this healing of Simon's mother-in-law. Jesus had earlier announced the arrival of the reign of God (Mark 1:15), and in this healing we catch a glimpse of that reign and its impact on ordinary life.

It's significant that the first person to be healed in Mark's gospel is a woman; Mark seems to be deliberately spotlighting the trajectory of Jesus' ministry here. As a woman, she might be considered among the least in that society – but without any hesitation, Jesus heals her. When God reigns, *everyone* is noticed, *every* life matters. Brushing aside the purity laws which dictated that a man may not touch a woman who is not his wife, Jesus takes her hand and helps her up. When God reigns, compassion trumps rules.

It was her calling and her honour to show hospitality to guests in her home. By healing her, Jesus restored her dignity, her place in the community and her role in life. When God reigns, our lives have meaning, our gifts and contribution have a place. She serves them. She isn't healed so that she can serve; she serves because she is healed. There's a huge difference. When God reigns, there is free and joyful service of one another.

Later that evening, Jesus would do for many what he did for Simon's mother-in-law: healing, releasing, restoring dignity, honour, purpose and meaning with his touch, his word and his compassion-driven power.

> And me? Where do I need to experience the reign of God in my life? 'Lord, reign in me, today.'

MD

Day 72

A solitary place

MARK 1:35–39 (*LUKE 4:42–44*)

Capernaum
Very early in the morning, while it was still dark, Jesus got up, left the house and went off to a solitary place, where he prayed. Simon and his companions went to look for him, and when they found him, they exclaimed: 'Everyone is looking for you!' Jesus replied, 'Let us go somewhere else – to the nearby villages – so that I can preach there also. That is why I have come.' So he travelled throughout Galilee, preaching in their synagogues and driving out demons.

Jesus is constantly doing the unexpected. After an immensely successful day of ministry, his disciples naturally expected a repeat performance of the day before. And yet Jesus walks away. He walks away from the needs of people who would have had their lives transformed by an encounter with him – with just a word, a touch from him. How could he just pack up his power and walk away?

Perhaps the most obvious answer is that in those early morning quiet moments with his Father he heard what he was to do next. Jesus would later tell his disciples, 'I do nothing on my own initiative, but I speak just what the Father taught me' (John 8:28, NET).

Throughout the gospel accounts, we see Jesus consistently take time out of a challengingly full and demanding life to be alone with his Father. His example suggests that, unless we also take the time to withdraw, we can be in danger of living our lives on autopilot – just doing the next thing, and the next… And in the process, we might be missing out on learning what God wants us to be and to do.

Ruth Haley Barton writes that in such times of withdrawal we have the opportunity to 'attend to what is real in our own lives – celebrate the joys, grieve the losses, shed tears, sit with the questions, feel our anger, attend to our loneliness – and allow God to be with us in those places'.[14]

In the coming days, when do you think you can press the pause button on your life for a while, just to be with Jesus?

MD

Day 73

The call of the first disciples

LUKE 5:1-11 (MATTHEW 4:18-22; MARK 1:16-20)

Sea of Galilee
One day as Jesus was standing by the Lake of Gennesaret, the people were crowding round him and listening to the word of God. He saw at the water's edge two boats, left there by the fishermen, who were washing their nets. He got into one of the boats, the one belonging to Simon, and asked him to put out a little from the shore. Then he sat down and taught the people from the boat. When he had finished speaking, he said to Simon, 'Put out into deep water, and let down the nets for a catch.' Simon answered, 'Master, we've worked hard all night and haven't caught anything. But because you say so, I will let down the nets.' When they had done so, they caught such a large number of fish that their nets began to break. So they signalled to their partners in the other boat to come and help them, and they came and filled both boats so full that they began to sink. When Simon Peter saw this, he fell at Jesus' knees and said, 'Go away from me, Lord; I am a sinful man!' For he and all his companions were astonished at the catch of fish they had taken, and so were James and John, the sons of Zebedee, Simon's partners. Then Jesus said to Simon, 'Don't be afraid; from now on you will fish for people.' So they pulled their boats up on shore, left everything and followed him.

Perhaps you know the weariness of having poured yourself out, of having worked your heart and mind and body to the bone – and… nothing. Nothing to show for your effort, nothing to show for all that you have done, all you have given, all you have prayed for, hoped for and trusted for. You have nothing left to give.

And you're asked for more… by Jesus, who is calling you to something greater than you can imagine. You're asked to go deeper, to go further – to draw on strength and grace and resilience you never even knew you had.

You're invited to follow him.

> *Where are those places – relationships, circumstances, situations in your life – where you sense Jesus may be asking you to let down nets of grace and love and forgiveness and patience and… Bring those places to him in prayer now.*

MD

Day 74

Healing a leper

LUKE 5:12-16 (*MATTHEW 8:1-4; MARK 1:40-45*)

One of the towns
While Jesus was in one of the towns, a man came along who was covered with leprosy. When he saw Jesus, he fell with his face to the ground and begged him, 'Lord, if you are willing, you can make me clean.' Jesus reached out his hand and touched the man. 'I am willing,' he said. 'Be clean!' And immediately the leprosy left him. Then Jesus ordered him, 'Don't tell anyone, but go, show yourself to the priest and offer the sacrifices that Moses commanded for your cleansing, as a testimony to them.' Yet the news about him spread all the more, so that crowds of people came to hear him and to be healed of their illnesses. But Jesus often withdrew to lonely places and prayed.

The courage of the man! A leper would be flogged if he came within six feet of another person. And yet he risks that flogging to come within touching distance of Jesus – who unflinchingly reaches out his hand to touch this brave and desperate man.

Whatever it was he'd heard about Jesus, it was enough for him to risk leaving his lonely place outside the town to plead with the one he hoped might be willing to help him. He wanted more than healing from Jesus; he asked to be clean – *katharizo* – which means not only being cleansed from defilement and disease but also purified from guilt and sin. That one word, 'clean', held all his hope, all his longing.

And Jesus immediately responded.

This dear man could have stood at a distance, silently cradling the hope in his heart, watching Jesus move among the crowds, too scared to move forward. And nothing would have changed. But he came to Jesus – in all his bedraggled neediness – and poured out his heart. And *everything* changed.

> *Lord Jesus, thank you that there is nothing in my life that is too messy, too shameful, too awful to bring to you. Thank you that you look at me through eyes of deepest knowledge, deepest compassion, complete understanding. Lord of all kindness, grace me now with the courage of this leper as I bring to you those things in my life which need your cleansing touch. Touch me. Free me. Change me.*

MD

Day 75

Healing the paralysed man

LUKE 5:17–26 (MATTHEW 9:1–8; MARK 2:1–12)

Capernaum
One day Jesus was teaching, and Pharisees and teachers of the law were sitting there. They had come from every village of Galilee and from Judea and Jerusalem. And the power of the Lord was with Jesus to heal those who were ill. Some men came carrying a paralysed man on a mat and tried to take him into the house to lay him before Jesus. When they could not find a way to do this because of the crowd, they went up on the roof and lowered him on his mat through the tiles into the middle of the crowd, right in front of Jesus. When Jesus saw their faith, he said, 'Friend, your sins are forgiven.' The Pharisees and the teachers of the law began thinking to themselves, 'Who is this fellow who speaks blasphemy? Who can forgive sins but God alone?' Jesus knew what they were thinking and asked, 'Why are you thinking these things in your hearts? Which is easier: to say, "Your sins are forgiven," or to say, "Get up and walk"? But I want you to know that the Son of Man has authority on earth to forgive sins.' So he said to the paralysed man, 'I tell you, get up, take your mat and go home.' Immediately he stood up in front of them, took what he had been lying on and went home praising God. Everyone was amazed and gave praise to God. They were filled with awe and said, 'We have seen remarkable things today.'

Every one of us knows someone who is paralysed.

Paralysed by guilt, fear, anxiety, disappointment, addictive patterns of behaviour and the corrosive effects of sin on soul and body.

And like the faith-filled friends in our narrative, we also know the Jesus who, with lavish grace, forgives and heals and restores; who does 'remarkable things'.

Without the concern and efforts of his friends, this paralysed man would never have encountered Jesus' transforming power. What they did for him took courage and faith – and some creativity in overcoming the obstacles in their way. But they did it.

> Who in your life needs to experience Jesus' forgiveness, his healing? Who needs to encounter Jesus in a new way? Hold that person before Jesus in prayer now, trusting he will lead you into the part you can play in their healing, freedom and transformation.

MD

Day 76

The calling of Levi

LUKE 5:27–32 (NRSV; *MATTHEW 9:9–13; MARK 2:13–17)*

Capernaum
After this he went out and saw a tax collector named Levi sitting at the tax-collection station, and he said to him, 'Follow me.' And he got up, left everything, and followed him. Then Levi gave a great banquet for him in his house, and there was a large crowd of tax collectors and others reclining at the table with them. The Pharisees and their scribes were complaining to his disciples, saying, 'Why do you eat and drink with tax collectors and sinners?' Jesus answered them, 'Those who are well have no need of a physician but those who are sick; I have come to call not the righteous but sinners to repentance.'

Have you ever felt like an outsider? Within your family or among your friends, at work – or in church?

If you have, then you will understand something of Levi's life, because during this time in Israel, Levi (also known as Matthew) would have been the quintessential outsider.

As a tax collector for the occupying Roman forces, he would have been hated and despised by other Jews as a traitor, a collaborator and a thief. Tax collectors grew rich by charging their fellow Jews with taxes that went above and beyond what Rome required. They grew enormously wealthy, but they paid a high price for their corruption.

One scholar writes that tax collectors were excluded from the synagogue, could not tithe to the temple and would not be called on as a witness in a trial.[15] They were considered on a par with prostitutes, robbers and the worst of sinners. They were social pariahs whose only friends were people just like them.

And yet Jesus called Levi to be his disciple, proving then and now, that no one is beyond the reach of his love, grace, mercy and acceptance. In defence of this calling, Jesus made it abundantly clear that the Matthews of this world were the very ones he had come for; the soul-sick ones who needed the healing and liberating touch of his compassion on their lives. Jesus drew this outsider *inside* his growing circle of disciples, *inside* his friendship, *inside* his kingdom purposes.

> Picture an 'outsider' in your family, your work setting, your neighbourhood. Now pray for ways to draw them into the love and grace and transforming acceptance of Jesus.

MD

Day 77

Of old clothes and old wineskins

LUKE 5:33–39 (MATTHEW 9:14–17; MARK 2:18–22)

Capernaum
They said to him, 'John's disciples often fast and pray, and so do the disciples of the Pharisees, but yours go on eating and drinking.' Jesus answered, 'Can you make the friends of the bridegroom fast while he is with them? But the time will come when the bridegroom will be taken from them; in those days they will fast.' He told them this parable: 'No one tears a piece out of a new garment to patch an old one. Otherwise, they will have torn the new garment, and the patch from the new will not match the old. And no one pours new wine into old wineskins. Otherwise, the new wine will burst the skins; the wine will run out and the wineskins will be ruined. No, new wine must be poured into new wineskins. And no one after drinking old wine wants the new, for they say, "The old is better."'

How do you feel about change? Are you someone who wholeheartedly embraces change, someone who is a little more cautious, or someone who actively resists change until it's forced upon you?

In this passage, Jesus is inviting his questioners to be open to new ways of being and doing. As they compare Jesus' disciples with those of John or the Pharisees, they have questions about his disciples, and by implication, about Jesus.

The lives of the Pharisees were visibly holy: Mondays and Thursdays were fast days. Always. Inviolate. Prayer was made promptly at noon, three o'clock and six o'clock no matter where they were or what they were doing. In contrast, Jesus seems to be going against tradition and custom and not behaving like any rabbi they know. But Jesus is inaugurating a new kingdom, characterised by grace, by wedding-day joyfulness and generosity.

This kingdom's life will demand new and expansive ways of thinking and living. It will demand change. It may mean leaving some old ways behind, even if they've worked well in the past. It will mean being stretched in new ways in order to fully receive what God may want to give.

> *Lord Jesus, where in my life are you inviting me to embrace something new? Help me not to be resistant or hardened; release my grip on whatever old 'wine skin' I may be clinging to. Keep me open to whatever you want to do in my life.*

MD

Day 78

Questions about the sabbath

LUKE 6:1-5 (*MATTHEW 12:1-8; MARK 2:23-28*)

Galilee
One Sabbath Jesus was going through the cornfields, and his disciples began to pick some ears of corn, rub them in their hands and eat the grain. Some of the Pharisees asked, 'Why are you doing what is unlawful on the Sabbath?' Jesus answered them, 'Have you never read what David did when he and his companions were hungry? He entered the house of God, and taking the consecrated bread, he ate what is lawful only for priests to eat. And he also gave some to his companions.' Then Jesus said to them, 'The Son of Man is Lord of the Sabbath.'

Some of us would have made great Pharisees! We are the guardians of tradition, inveterate rule-keepers, and judge and jury in any infraction of rules we consider inviolable. Others of us are less encumbered by rules. Through this interaction with the Pharisees, Jesus addresses us both.

Mired in rules, the sabbath had effectively lost its original intent, which was to provide God's people with a day in which they could acknowledge their created humanity. The sabbath guarded their legitimate need for rest, for refreshment, and for renewing and nurturing their relationship with God and others.

But in an effort to preserve this law, Jewish lawmakers had developed a set of guidelines for what could and could not be done on the sabbath. They had developed a list of 39 main tasks that could not be performed on the sabbath, which included harvesting, threshing, winnowing grain and preparing food – all of which the disciples are technically doing here.

In his response to the Pharisees, Jesus is not seeking to denigrate the sabbath law – which was as important as the commands not to kill, lie or steal – but he is challenging *the traditions* which had grown around it. In directing their attention to David's situation (found in 1 Samuel 21), Jesus is anchoring the sabbath law in the needs of people. Mark records a phrase Luke omits: 'The Sabbath was made for man, not man for the Sabbath' (Mark 2:27). In declaring himself 'Lord of the Sabbath' here, Jesus is asserting his unrivalled authority over the sabbath and its practices.

> *As you consider your own sabbath practices, is there anything you want to change to bring them more in line with God's intent for that time?*

MD

The first year: the year of inauguration

Day 79

The law of love

LUKE 6:6-11 (MATTHEW 12:9-14; MARK 3:1-6)

Galilee
On another Sabbath he went into the synagogue and was teaching, and a man was there whose right hand was shrivelled. The Pharisees and the teachers of the law were looking for a reason to accuse Jesus, so they watched him closely to see if he would heal on the Sabbath. But Jesus knew what they were thinking and said to the man with the shrivelled hand, 'Get up and stand in front of everyone.' So he got up and stood there. Then Jesus said to them, 'I ask you, which is lawful on the Sabbath: to do good or to do evil, to save life or to destroy it?' He looked round at them all, and then said to the man, 'Stretch out your hand.' He did so, and his hand was completely restored. But the Pharisees and the teachers of the law were furious and began to discuss with one another what they might do to Jesus.

'What's love got to do with it?' Tina Turner raises a valid question. The answer is: 'Everything' – especially when it applies to the sabbath.

This passage is not primarily about keeping the sabbath law. It's about love – the complete fulfilment of the law (Romans 13:8). The greatest commandment is to love – first, the Lord, and then everyone else. But the heavy blanket of tradition placed on to the sabbath law had starved this commandment of oxygen, leaving death by legalism in its place.

Jesus' question to the Pharisees was rhetorical; of course, it's lawful to do good and not harm on the sabbath. Underlying the question, however, is the implication that *not* acting in the face of need actually dishonours the sabbath as greatly as any act does, because the sabbath was intended to be life-giving, not life-denying.

This man's healing demonstrated that when love encounters need, and acts, the grace of God is made visible and the sabbath is truly honoured. The Pharisees didn't see it that way as their incensed reaction demonstrated; they put commitment to their traditions above the command to love and, in the process, dishonoured the sabbath.

> *Father, deliver me from self-righteousness, from a calculating response in the face of need. Give me grace to grasp the depths of your love and the willingness and wisdom to share it with all you bring my way.*

MD

Day 80

At the lake – as a follower or as a disciple?

MARK 3:7-12

Galilee
Jesus withdrew with his disciples to the lake, and a large crowd from Galilee followed. When they heard all he was doing, many people came to him from Judea, Jerusalem, Idumea, and the regions across the Jordan and around Tyre and Sidon. Because of the crowd he told his disciples to have a small boat ready for him, to keep the people from crowding him. For he had healed many, so that those with diseases were pushing forward to touch him. Whenever the impure spirits saw him, they fell down before him and cried out, 'You are the Son of God.' But he gave them strict orders not to tell others about him.

Are you a follower or a disciple? We often use the terms interchangeably, don't we, but in this passage Mark seems to hint at a distinction between these two words which is worth unpacking.

Picture the scene: Jesus has left the city of Capernaum and the growing opposition of the religious establishment there (Mark 3:6) and has headed to the relative safety of Lake Galilee. With him are his disciples – *mathetes* – those who were committed to learning from him and following him as their teacher. But then, Mark tells us, a large crowd from Galilee *followed*. They are joined by thousands more who pour in from far and near. These crowds are driven to Jesus by their desperate needs – which he powerfully meets – with just a touch, a word.

Now picture something else: the crowds have finally gone home, the dust has settled and, in the quiet, Jesus talks with his disciples – as any good rabbi would – about what they'd learned that day. Perhaps they talked about who he was, about the kingdom of God, about compassion and the exercise of power and authority. For starters.

And I wonder – at the end of the day, where are we? Are we with those who, having had their prayers answered, their needs met, walk away satisfied and contented – until the next lot of needs draw them back to Jesus? Or are we those who linger with Jesus, who listen to his words, who learn from him, who stay close?

I wonder, are we followers or are we disciples?

▌ *Bring your reflection to the Lord in prayer.*

MD

the second year:
the year of popularity

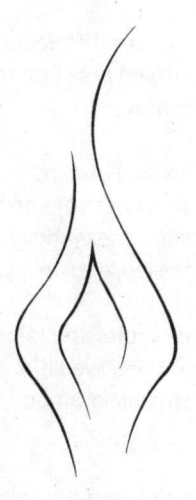

JOHN AYRTON

Day 81

Living by royal appointment

MARK 3:13–19 (*LUKE 6:12–16*)

Galilee
Jesus went up on a mountainside and called to him those he wanted, and they came to him. He appointed twelve that they might be with him and that he might send them out to preach and to have authority to drive out demons. These are the twelve he appointed: Simon (to whom he gave the name Peter); James son of Zebedee and his brother John (to them he gave the name Boanerges, which means 'sons of thunder'), Andrew, Philip, Bartholomew, Matthew, Thomas, James son of Alphaeus, Thaddaeus, Simon the Zealot and Judas Iscariot, who betrayed him.

Many people have been around Jesus for some time now, for all kinds of reasons. From this crowd of people, Jesus wants twelve, to be with him, to come closer, to learn and to follow. Faced with massive needs and seeds of opposition, Jesus is moved to share his life and work with this group of disciples. What he starts, they continue; he will 'send them out'.

Luke reports Jesus praying all night about this decision, for these people. Filled with his Father's love for them and with a burning heart for the mission to be shared with them, Jesus' priority is for them to be with him.

Can you remember when you sensed God inviting you to come closer to him for the first time? Vague interest, background awareness or knowing about him just wasn't enough. Maybe, like me, you began to know that he wants you most to be with him, drawn into the Father's loving purpose to a place close to Jesus. He still wants us there.

Jesus knew these disciples with their faults and failures; the list starts with Simon, who denied him, and ends with Judas, who betrayed him. And then there's those two volcanic brothers, James and John, who Jesus nicknamed 'sons of thunder', along with Simon the terrorist (Zealot).

> *Sit for a while and enjoy the truth that you are called to be with Jesus. He really wants you with him; from there he sends you into today! He is with us in the whole of life. We're sent with his authority – the gift of his presence – making the difference in our words and actions.*

JA

Day 82

The blessing of a Jesus-shaped life

MATTHEW 5:1–12 (*LUKE 6:17–49*)

Mountainside
Now when Jesus saw the crowds, he went up on a mountainside and sat down. His disciples came to him, and he began to teach them. He said: 'Blessed are the poor in spirit, for theirs is the kingdom of heaven. Blessed are those who mourn, for they will be comforted. Blessed are the meek, for they will inherit the earth. Blessed are those who hunger and thirst for righteousness, for they will be filled. Blessed are the merciful, for they will be shown mercy. Blessed are the pure in heart, for they will see God. Blessed are the peacemakers, for they will be called children of God. Blessed are those who are persecuted because of righteousness, for theirs is the kingdom of heaven. Blessed are you when people insult you, persecute you and falsely say all kinds of evil against you because of me. Rejoice and be glad, because great is your reward in heaven, for in the same way they persecuted the prophets who before you.'

Jesus is popular; crowds are experiencing God's power (Luke 6:17–19). But Jesus gathers the disciples around him showing us what it is to really be blessed.

Blessed people know they are empty, with nothing left; they know tears; they are meek. Living with Jesus starts here. It's built upon what we are with him, not what we get from him. Blessed people look like Jesus and are like this because of their relationship with him. We may well suffer because of that connection. We are with him as we follow.

Being blessed like this means living in hope. Jesus says we *will* be comforted; we *will* be filled as we hunger for righteousness in our lives and in the world; we *will* know mercy; we *will* see God.

Disciples are blessed by being part of the kingdom of heaven (vv. 3, 10). We are with Jesus now in the kingdom. His loving rule is a process of growth in our lives that will be completed when we see him face to face. Loving Jesus and living with him today means we have that kingdom, we're in that kingdom, and it's moving us forward to something unimaginably glorious.

> Father, thank you that your best for me is to be like Jesus. Please bring forward Jesus' promises of what will be into my experience. Thank you that your kingdom is mine for today, tomorrow and forever.

Day 83

Making a difference

MATTHEW 5:13-16

Mountainside
'You are the salt of the earth. But if the salt loses its saltiness, how can it be made salty again? It is no longer good for anything, except to be thrown out and trampled underfoot. You are the light of the world. A town built on a hill cannot be hidden. Neither do people light a lamp and put it under a bowl. Instead, they put it on its stand, and it gives light to everyone in the house. In the same way, let your light shine before others, that they may see your good deeds and glorify your Father in heaven.'

Jesus continues to focus on what we *are* as disciples, showing us why it matters so much.

Disciples are like salt, which is only useful if it adds flavour to the food it's mixed with. Living with Jesus is very different from the ways of this world, and from how we were outside the kingdom. Jesus wants us to live his way because just as salt acts on what it touches, so our lives are to affect the people we know and the situations we're in.

Being what we are is lived out for the long haul. Without it, we lose our difference and become good for nothing, like tasteless salt.

Jesus goes on to explain that we are also light. Paul later puts it: 'You were once darkness, but now you are light in the Lord' (Ephesians 5:8). Jesus pictures a purpose for this, reminding those listening of a town on a hill. At night a hilltop town is seen from far away, because light from homes, buildings or streets alive with people make it visible. Meanwhile inside, an individual light is meant to be seen by 'everyone in the house' (v. 15).

I love this picture. Like a town on the hill, lights together in one place make a big impact, drawing people from miles around. As we follow Jesus, we're not just lights shining on our own but in community, shining together so that other people glorify our Father. They see where our light comes from and can be drawn to that for themselves.

> *Jesus says we shine by doing good deeds. What could they be for you? How could the 'Blessed are' statements flavour your life today? Look out for ways you can shine with others in doing good deeds where you are today.*

JA

Day 84

Following Jesus in the big story

MATTHEW 5:17–20

Mountainside

'Do not think that I have come to abolish the Law or the Prophets; I have not come to abolish them but to fulfil them. For truly I tell you, until heaven and earth disappear, not the smallest letter, not the least stroke of a pen, will by any means disappear from the Law until everything is accomplished. Therefore anyone who sets aside one of the least of these commands and teaches others accordingly will be called least in the kingdom of heaven, but whoever practises and teaches these commands will be called great in the kingdom of heaven. For I tell you that unless your righteousness surpasses that of the Pharisees and the teachers of the law, you will certainly not enter the kingdom of heaven.'

Jesus wants his followers to grasp the reason he came – to fulfil the Old Testament (the 'Law and the Prophets'). These powerful writings reveal what God is like and his purpose for us. They signpost God's sweeping activity in our world from creation to new creation. Jesus says it's all heading towards being accomplished through him.

Think of one of those airport moving walkways. You might step on to it some way into its long journey but once there, you are part of where it's come from as well as where it's going, moving steadily forwards. Being in the kingdom with Jesus is like that. The scriptures promised God's king (Messiah) coming to put right everything that's broken. From the first day of his ministry, Jesus showed himself to be that king and invited people to be with him, living under his reign. The opportunity is still there for us.

When we trust and follow him, we are with him in the kingdom of heaven. We're on the moving walkway, in the movement of God's word. The religious elites had reduced this to a list of rules and ways to behave. But Jesus says the kingdom of heaven brings much more, a better way – a righteousness that surpasses religion and rules, a righteousness that comes from a changed heart. Next, he will go on to show how this works.

> *Father, I want to live with Jesus today, knowing that in the kingdom I am now part of the movement of all that you will accomplish through him. Fill me with your Spirit to live this way today.*

Day 85

Rage and relationships

MATTHEW 5:21–26

Mountainside
'You have heard that it was said to the people long ago, "You shall not murder, and anyone who murders will be subject to judgment." But I tell you that anyone who is angry with a brother or sister will be subject to judgment. Again, anyone who says to a brother or sister, "Raca," is answerable to the court. And anyone who says, "You fool!" will be in danger of the fire of hell. Therefore, if you are offering your gift at the altar and there remember that your brother or sister has something against you, leave your gift there in front of the altar. First go and be reconciled to them; then come and offer your gift. Settle matters quickly with your adversary who is taking you to court. Do it while you are still together on the way, or your adversary may hand you over to the judge, and the judge may hand you over to the officer, and you may be thrown into prison. Truly I tell you, you will not get out until you have paid the last penny.'

Jesus promises that those with him in the kingdom will know God at work in their lives in a way that surpasses the way of the Pharisees. Quite a possibility!

How does this happen? By listening to what Jesus says about God's way to live. Jesus has a better way to fulfil the law: not 'You have heard it said,' but 'I tell you.'

Think about murder. People not only kill each other; anger in their hearts erupts in abusive words. A brother or sister is labelled 'a fool'. Anger, like the fire of Gehenna burning Jerusalem's rubbish, destroys relationships. Avoiding murder is not good enough. Something internal must change.

So what do we do? We put our relationships with others in the same space as our relationship with God. We don't worship until we have been reconciled. And when something goes wrong, we work to be right with each other as soon as we possibly can.

This is Jesus' way, and it starts with a change in our hearts. Without this, the cost of broken relationships can leave us spiritually bankrupt.

> *Reflect and thank God for Jesus' better way. Is there anyone you should reconcile with? How can you start that process?*

JA

Day 86

The pure in heart

MATTHEW 5:27–32

Mountainside

'You have heard that it was said, "You shall not commit adultery." But I tell you that anyone who looks at a woman lustfully has already committed adultery with her in his heart. If your right eye causes you to stumble, gouge it out and throw it away. It is better for you to lose one part of your body than for your whole body to be thrown into hell. And if your right hand causes you to stumble, cut it off and throw it away. It is better for you to lose one part of your body than for your whole body to go into hell. It has been said, "Anyone who divorces his wife must give her a certificate of divorce." But I tell you that anyone who divorces his wife, except for sexual immorality, makes her the victim of adultery, and anyone who marries a divorced woman commits adultery.'

Jesus' amazing promise won't go away. His disciples' righteousness will surpass that of the Pharisees. The Pharisees made being righteous into a religious art form, but Jesus has a different way, a better way for those with him in the kingdom. His way starts somewhere else – not in outward rule-keeping or good living, but in the heart. Jesus-followers don't just avoid murder or violence. They deal with the root – an angry heart.

Jesus takes the same approach with sexual purity. It's more than remaining faithful before and within marriage. Jesus points out that when we lust after someone else then, 'in our heart', adultery has happened.

Pure hearts belong to those blessed in the kingdom, and such people hunger for righteousness. In a society filled with pornography and a media saturated with sexual images, we are to be careful about what we look at and how. With God's help, we can choose to avoid actions that lead our hearts astray. Jesus uses shocking pictures prompting us to make wise choices (rather than surgery!) that lead to radical changes in our behaviour or lifestyle.

Righteousness-hungry hearts move us to value and honour one another in our relationships. There is no quick-and-easy divorce. Marriage covenants are only ended when they have been truly broken.

> Need a heart check? Use Psalm 51:10 as a meditative prayer (see page 10): 'Create in me a clean heart, O God, and renew a right spirit within me' (ESV).

JA

Day 87

Enough said

MATTHEW 5:33–37

Mountainside
'Again, you have heard that it was said to the people long ago, "Do not break your oath, but fulfil to the Lord the oaths you have made." But I tell you, do not swear an oath at all: either by heaven, for it is God's throne; or by the earth, for it is his footstool; or by Jerusalem, for it is the city of the Great King. And do not swear by your head, for you cannot make even one hair white or black. All you need to say is simply "Yes," or "No"; anything beyond this comes from the evil one.'

Jesus continues to unpack his vision that with the kingdom of heaven growing in our lives, we know a righteousness way beyond tick-box religious behaviour. The Pharisees said you could show how strongly you feel about something, or prove how truthful you are being, by swearing an oath by anything except God's name.

Against this background, Jesus challenges us about how we use words. He shows us a better way for his kingdom people. We don't need to add anything to prove the point; our language does not need to be super-strong to show how truthful we are.

Another time Jesus said, 'The mouth speaks what the heart is full of' (Matthew 12:34). What comes out of our mouths reveals what's going on in our hearts. Think about that for a moment. I am personally disturbed by this. My words reveal what's brewing in my heart, and what I say when stressed, frustrated or limited by others (or myself) is often not good. How about you?

It seems that in this section (Matthew 5:13 onwards), Jesus is colouring in the picture he drew of being really blessed. Meek people are blessed, he said. Someone described meekness as 'strength under control', a willingness to let go of my way, my will and my rights. There is nothing to prove, and we need no forceful language to get our way or ensure our points are heard, just words truthfully spoken. The alternative approach opens us up to something very dark, so Jesus warns us about this.

> *Heavenly Father, I want my words today to come from a heart that's changing to be more like Jesus. Fill me today with the Holy Spirit and grow that fruit of gentleness and self-control in me as I walk with Jesus today.*

JA

Day 88

Not taking revenge

MATTHEW 5:38-42

Mountainside
'You have heard that it was said, "Eye for eye, and tooth for tooth." But I tell you, do not resist an evil person. If anyone slaps you on the right cheek, turn to them the other cheek also. And if anyone wants to sue you and take your shirt, hand over your coat as well. If anyone forces you to go one mile, go with them two miles. Give to the one who asks you, and do not turn away from the one who wants to borrow from you.'

Those with Jesus on the mountainside that day knew only one way to be righteous. Keep the rules demanded by the religious elites. Jesus continues to point us to his new, better, joyously heart-led way.

The old way limited the revenge you could take. If someone knocks out your tooth, you don't knock off their head. Jesus takes a fresh approach. If I'm personally faced with a threat, with exploitation or with being harshly taken for granted, he invites me to respond by not personally retaliating. At the time, a Roman soldier could demand you go a mile with him to help with his stuff. Jesus says that his disciples should offer to go two. A new kind of righteousness played out on the dusty roads of everyday life. It's a radically different approach.

What kind of people would we be if we responded this way to those who mistreat us? Look at Jesus' words about our way with such people in this new life. Turn towards them, be willing to give, go with them further, don't turn away from them.

Does this mean we let abuse go unchecked, or ignore injustice and human rights violations? Jesus isn't talking about how states defend themselves or protect their citizens. Rather, it's a way I can choose to live as an individual follower in my everyday life. I don't have to demand my rights or defend my pride (more likely to be hurt in my Western context than my cheek)! It doesn't mean that I empty my bank account to help all the people in my city who ask me, but it does mean that I can't simply shut my heart to people in need.

> This is the way Jesus lived and died. He is the source of this surpassing righteousness – we worship him today.

JA

Day 89

Family likeness

MATTHEW 5:43-48

Mountainside
'You have heard that it was said, "Love your neighbour and hate your enemy." But I tell you, love your enemies and pray for those who persecute you, that you may be children of your Father in heaven. He causes his sun to rise on the evil and the good, and sends rain on the righteous and the unrighteous. If you love those who love you, what reward will you get? Are not even the tax collectors doing that? And if you greet only your own people, what are you doing more than others? Do not even pagans do that? Be perfect, therefore, as your heavenly Father is perfect.'

Jesus ends his tour of traditional ways to live a good life by showing us that loving our neighbour while hating our enemies is not enough. There's another, better way. But how can we honestly do that? Are we to be more scrupulous than the Pharisees?

For us, there's something completely new: the Father-factor. We have a Father in heaven – we are his children and share his life and his nature. Something new is happening – we're living out his likeness. Jesus invites us as children of our Father to live his way.

Our heavenly Father is good. His love is expressed to all through his gifts of sun and rain, shared indiscriminately. He loves all, not just those who love him back. To be like him, our hearts must be enlarged and our capacity to love vastly increased.

So we're not trying to be super-religious but simply imitating our Father. Our life with Jesus in the kingdom of heaven is one of growing to be more like him, letting the family likeness shape and transform us. The word 'perfect' here does not mean to be sinless, but rather 'mature' or 'fully grown'. It reminds us that spiritual growth happens gradually, and we change little by little into his likeness. The only limit on our living his way is our hunger to grow towards his example.

Everything our Father does is poured-out love. He has loved and welcomed us when we were enemies. From that, his love flows out of us for our enemies. It starts in our prayers, even for those who persecute us.

> *Lord, to live like this is impossible unless you live in us, and through us. Enlarge my heart, increase my love.*

JA

Day 90

Knowing the Father changes everything

MATTHEW 6:1-4

Mountainside
'Be careful not to practise your righteousness in front of others to be seen by them. If you do, you will have no reward from your Father in heaven. So when you give to the needy, do not announce it with trumpets, as the hypocrites do in the synagogues and on the streets, to be honoured by others. Truly I tell you, they have received their reward in full. But when you give to the needy, do not let your left hand know what your right hand is doing, so that your giving may be in secret. Then your Father, who sees what is done in secret, will reward you.'

At the heart of our experience as disciples is the most astonishing privilege that changes everything about us. We have a Father in heaven. Everything we do can be done under the protection, care and presence of the Father. We are called to live generously, as he is generous. How we live is influenced by his active involvement with us. All that need matter to us is that he sees what we do and is part of it. He loves to be involved with us, and he rewards us.

Jesus lived this way himself and invites us to walk that way with him. To be loved and accepted by our Father frees us so that whether anyone sees what we do for others doesn't matter at all. We want to know that he knows, and that gives us the joy of walking and working with him. There is a reward that no one else knows about.

What if today you cultivate the awareness that he sees in secret? You could review the day in the light of this promise that he will be with you in secret. The ancient discipline of Examen helps us do just that. We reflect on the day, pausing to ask the Holy Spirit to help us to become aware of times in the day when we knew God with us, and times when we were less aware. We then ask him to help us know the difference, and why.

Why not try that at the end of this day? Thank God for his remembered presence, ask for forgiveness when you've missed him, or grieved him, and then commit yourself to him for sleep and the day tomorrow.

JA

Day 91

Prayer at the heart

MATTHEW 6:5-15

Mountainside
'And when you pray, do not be like the hypocrites, for they love to pray standing in the synagogues and on the street corners to be seen by others. Truly I tell you, they have received their reward in full. But when you pray, go into your room, close the door and pray to your Father, who is unseen. Then your Father, who sees what is done in secret, will reward you. And when you pray, do not keep on babbling like pagans, for they think they will be heard because of their many words. Do not be like them, for your Father knows what you need before you ask him. This, then, is how you should pray: "Our Father in heaven, hallowed be your name, your kingdom come, your will be done, on earth as it is in heaven. Give us today our daily bread. And forgive us our debts, as we also have forgiven our debtors. And lead us not into temptation, but deliver us from the evil one." For if you forgive other people when they sin against you, your heavenly Father will also forgive you. But if you do not forgive others their sins, your Father will not forgive your sins.'

Jesus' straightforward words about prayer are roughly in the middle of this talk to his disciples on the mountainside, and it's at the heart of what he is promising us. Our Father sees what we do – nobody else matters. Our Father knows what we need, so to receive from him we don't need to impress him with many words! This means that the foundation of all I really need for this life in the kingdom is to be with my heavenly Father. Prayer is at the heart of this life.

How am I doing in living that kind of prayer-based life?

> Jesus tells us what prayer looks like in the prayer example he gave. Imagine you knew nothing else about God other than what is here in this prayer that Jesus taught us. Slowly go over each line and pause to consider – what is this God like, what do you learn about him? How can he be involved in your life? What does he expect from you? What does he promise you? Then respond in worship and trust.

JA

Day 92

Fasting: an audience of one

MATTHEW 6:16–18

Mountainside
'When you fast, do not look sombre as the hypocrites do, for they disfigure their faces to show others they are fasting. Truly I tell you, they have received their reward in full. But when you fast, put oil on your head and wash your face, so that it will not be obvious to others that you are fasting, but only to your Father, who is unseen; and your Father, who sees what is done in secret, will reward you.'

Throughout his message on the mountain, Jesus has shown us how life in the kingdom of heaven touches the inner world of our hearts and the outer world of our everyday lived experience. As a disciple, I may well find myself aware that I'm empty unless God fills me, and hungry for righteousness, battling with desires towards a pure heart. This is my inner world.

Of course, it's not just my inner world that's touched by the kingdom of heaven. Following Jesus, I might find myself with two sore cheeks (or at least a bruised ego), my feet might be tired from the extra mile I've walked and I may have fewer shirts than I had before!

But fasting is entirely about my inner life. Quite literally. It's basically to do with what goes into my stomach for a while! The picture Jesus paints of the religious elites behaving as they do when they give and pray is amusing and grotesque. When they fasted, they took it to another level; they made themselves look terrible, presumably so that people could ask them what was wrong. This gave them a chance to impress others with their wonderfully committed fasting! Jesus calls these people hypocrites. The word means mask-wearers and was used of actors in the Greek/Roman world who wore masks on stage.

As with giving, praying and anything else we do to please and honour God, we want to be doing it for an audience of one – our heavenly Father who sees and rewards us.

> *Would I live to serve God if the only person who saw my life was him? Is there anything I do to honour him that nobody else sees? Could I serve him as my life unfolds today like he is the only one watching, and what might the reward be?*

JA

Day 93

Treasure in heaven

MATTHEW 6:19–24

Mountainside
'Do not store up for yourselves treasures on earth, where moths and vermin destroy, and where thieves break in and steal. But store up for yourselves treasures in heaven, where moths and vermin do not destroy, and where thieves do not break in and steal. For where your treasure is, there your heart will be also. The eye is the lamp of the body. If your eyes are healthy, your whole body will be full of light. But if your eyes are unhealthy, your whole body will be full of darkness. If then the light within you is darkness, how great is that darkness! No one can serve two masters. Either you will hate the one and love the other, or you will be devoted to the one and despise the other. You cannot serve both God and Money.'

Jesus teaches us that our Father in heaven sees and rewards us. These rewards are not just for the future, we can know them here and now as we live in the kingdom of heaven.

But we're also living in this world where there are treasures to pursue, although they can be eaten away or taken from us. It's like a little parable. As always, the clue to understanding it comes right at the end. Our hearts tend to follow our treasure, what we most value. Is it the stuff of this world that my heart loves most – or the Father's rewards as I turn to him?

Likewise, the eyes are the lamp of the body. Am I going to fix my gaze, my affection, on the light or on other things on offer? My answer to that question either floods my whole being with light or leaves me groping in the darkness.

Jesus' final parable is about who we give our hearts to. This isn't a picture of employment, nor of slavery, either then or now. It is about devotion. *Lord of the Rings* fans might think of the way the hobbit Samwise Gamgee serves his master Frodo on their great quest, willingly out of love and devotion.

Notice the idea that money (mammon) is itself a spiritual power that can enslave us. Materialism is a form of idolatry.

> *I can choose who I serve, who gets my heart. Jesus says it's God or money. Where will your heart go today?*

JA

Day 94

Do not worry

MATTHEW 6:25-34

Mountainside
'Therefore, I tell you, do not worry about your life, what you will eat or drink; or about your body, what you will wear. Is not life more than food, and the body more than clothes? Look at the birds of the air; they do not sow or reap or store away in barns, and yet your heavenly Father feeds them. Are you not much more valuable than they? Can any one of you by worrying add a single hour to your life? And why do you worry about clothes? See how the flowers of the field grow. They do not labour or spin. Yet I tell you that not even Solomon in all his splendour was dressed like one of these. If that is how God clothes the grass of the field, which is here today and tomorrow is thrown into the fire, will he not much more clothe you – you of little faith? So do not worry, saying, "What shall we eat?" or "What shall we drink?" or "What shall we wear?" For the pagans run after all these things, and your heavenly Father knows that you need them. But seek first his kingdom and his righteousness, and all these things will be given to you as well. Therefore do not worry about tomorrow, for tomorrow will worry about itself. Each day has enough trouble of its own.'

What kind of person was Jesus? Notice how he sees the Father working all around him. How did this affect his state of mind? Tom Wright suggests these verses give us more than a clue:

> He wasn't always looking ahead anxiously, making the present moment count only because of what might come next. No: he seems to have had the skill of living totally in the present, giving attention totally to the present task, celebrating the goodness of God here and now. If that's not a recipe for happiness, I don't know what is.[16]

Jesus says this Father is my Father. A Father who provides for his creation, a Father who knows what I need, who gives me a kingdom and righteousness to seek so I don't need to frantically run after everything else. Here's a way of living one day at a time in my Father's presence and goodness even when there is trouble.

▌ *Father, today I want to live this way with Jesus.*

JA

Day 95

Beyond judging

MATTHEW 7:1-6

Mountainside
'Do not judge, or you too will be judged. For in the same way as you judge others, you will be judged, and with the measure you use, it will be measured to you. Why do you look at the speck of sawdust in your brother's eye and pay no attention to the plank in your own eye? How can you say to your brother, "Let me take the speck out of your eye," when all the time there is a plank in your own eye? You hypocrite, first take the plank out of your own eye, and then you will see clearly to remove the speck from your brother's eye. Do not give dogs what is sacred; do not throw your pearls to pigs. If you do, they may trample them under their feet, and turn and tear you to pieces.'

Jesus takes us again into our lived experience of everyday relationships with others – brothers or sisters who share our little worlds in his new community. It's easy for us to start judging them – comparing them with what we think they should be like and despising them for their failings.

Jesus then tells a joke. Here's someone with a huge lump of wood in their eye trying to get close enough to another person to help with the tiny piece of sawdust in their eye! It's ridiculous to shake our heads at the flaws of others while missing our own. It's particularly stupid because the way we look at others will be the way we're looked at ourselves, ultimately by God.

Several times in his message, Jesus has encouraged us to be like our Father. It's here again in a different form. If God has given me a full measure of his grace, then I give that to others. Then it comes back to me, and I share it again, in a cycle of grace.

We need to share this grace together, excited by the value of the goodness of God we have experienced. If we don't, then we will find we are like dogs who cannot grasp what's sacred or pigs who value swill but reject costly pearls.

> *Lord, thank you for your grace towards me, I want to show that same grace to others. I pray that today my heart will be alive to your grace with no room for judgemental thoughts towards others.*

JA

Day 96

Ask, seek, knock

MATTHEW 7:7–12

Mountainside
'Ask and it will be given to you; seek and you will find; knock and the door will be opened to you. For everyone who asks receives; the one who seeks finds; and to the one who knocks, the door will be opened. Which of you, if your son asks for bread, will give him a stone? Or if he asks for a fish, will give him a snake? If you, then, though you are evil, know how to give good gifts to your children, how much more will your Father in heaven give good gifts to those who ask him! So in everything, do to others what you would have them do to you, for this sums up the Law and the Prophets.'

Life with Jesus in the kingdom of heaven isn't easy. Times come upon us when we don't have what we need. Have you ever felt like that? There are times, too, when we seem to have lost something – we used to have it, but now it's gone. Maybe we've lost our way completely. Is that happening to you or someone you care about? Then there are areas in our circumstances or inner lives where we seem to be up against something that won't move, and we are stuck. Is that where you are?

Jesus reminds us that at these times we need to hold on to the truth that we have a Father in heaven. Everyone listening to Jesus knew that any half-decent parent wants to give their children good gifts. When the children are hungry, parents want to give them good food, not rocks or deadly reptiles!

We are to keep asking our Father for what we need, keep looking to find what we've lost, and keep knocking on the closed door until it opens. We do this because our Father gives good gifts when we ask him. We need to persist in prayer, asking for the things we need until we receive them. God is not a reluctant giver, but persistence reveals our genuine desire.

> Read through the passage slowly and prayerfully, in the way of *lectio divina* (see page 13). What stands out for you? What does God highlight to you today?

Day 97

Choices: the narrow and wide gates

MATTHEW 7:13-14

Mountainside
'Enter through the narrow gate. For wide is the gate and broad is the road that leads to destruction, and many enter through it. But small is the gate and narrow the road that leads to life, and only a few find it.'

Jesus often seems to ask us to choose one course of action, or a way of seeing life, as opposed to another. It is not surprising. Our lives are powerfully shaped by the choices we make. Here Jesus gives us the starkest of choices.

He shows us two gates and two roads leading to two places. One road takes us towards destruction and the other leads towards life. One choice is obvious, easy and popular – many simply drift through the wide gate and are on their way with plenty of company. The other choice is not so obvious, leads to difficulty and is less popular – few want to go that way and it can be lonely, but it leads to life.

Let's consider our own choices. In the many decisions I make each day, do I simply take the easy way, the most popular and culturally acceptable path, or do I look for the road Jesus gives me to walk, even though it may be difficult, costly and countercultural?

The picture of many people following the crowd towards destruction is chilling. Even so, Jesus is also telling us that there is a gate to take us on a different road, that leads to life. 'I am the gate', Jesus said, and again, 'I am the way' (John 10:7; 14:6). There is no need for anyone to be lost.

If you and I are on the way to life, then others can be too. Our choices can be shared with others who may come with us. Destruction is not inevitable, but if people are to come through the gate and walk the way of Jesus, they need to know about it. We are to be signposts to a different, more fulfilling path.

> *Pray for those close to you who have yet to join the road that leads to life. Thank God for the life you have found in Jesus. Pray for his help in the choices you face today and for an opportunity to tell someone about the way.*

JA

Day 98

Choices: true and false prophets

MATTHEW 7:15-20

Mountainside
'Watch out for false prophets. They come to you in sheep's clothing, but inwardly they are ferocious wolves. By their fruit you will recognise them. Do people pick grapes from thorn-bushes, or figs from thistles? Likewise, every good tree bears good fruit, but a bad tree bears bad fruit. A good tree cannot bear bad fruit, and a bad tree cannot bear good fruit. Every tree that does not bear good fruit is cut down and thrown into the fire. Thus, by their fruit you will recognise them.'

Who we listen to on the 'Jesus road' really matters if we're to make good choices. There are plenty of people around with opinions, ideas and words to share. Some even claim to speak from God. It was so then and little has changed now. Jesus warns of 'pseudo prophets' offering to teach us. In a day of worldwide social media channels and innumerable internet websites, false teachers are ten-a-penny.

Jesus tells us to search behind the words they generate or the ideas they offer us because it's possible that those who look like Jesus-followers are wearing a disguise to hide a harmful intention. What do we do? How can we figure out who we should listen to?

Jesus says we must look for the kind of fruit they are producing. Do we see Jesus in them? Do the people who follow them become more like Jesus because of what they are learning? Good trees will produce good fruit, hearts made pure by God growing within us the qualities of the blessed life we saw at the beginning of his talk on the hillside (Matthew 5:3-11). Are these teachers honest, full of integrity? Do they demonstrate the fruit of the Spirit – love, joy, peace, patience, kindness, faithfulness, meekness and self-control (Galatians 5:22-23)? Do they exalt Christ or themselves?

The gift of discernment is the ability to distinguish the true from the false, the genuine from the imitation. It has never been more needed. Don't allow yourself to be hoodwinked by smooth talking, apparently successful teachers who present themselves well but peddle a false gospel. Ask God to protect you so you make wise choices.

> Lord, I don't want to make bad choices as I listen to others. Please grant me wisdom and discernment.

JA

Day 99

Choices: true and false disciples

MATTHEW 7:21-23

Mountainside
'Not everyone who says to me, "Lord, Lord," will enter the kingdom of heaven, but only the one who does the will of my Father who is in heaven. Many will say to me on that day, "Lord, Lord, did we not prophesy in your name and in your name drive out demons and in your name perform many miracles?" Then I will tell them plainly, "I never knew you. Away from me, you evildoers!"'

Jesus turns from the words we might hear from 'pseudo prophets' to the words that might come out of our own mouths.

We can say the right things, calling him 'Lord'. We can be really passionate in what we say, repeating his name, 'Lord, Lord', to show how sincere we are. We may even be people that do amazing and spectacular things, even the miraculous, and yet miss what really matters most to Jesus. We may even miss the way into the kingdom.

It's a shocking picture. Jesus has put it that way to stop us in our tracks and get us thinking.

It seems to me that we find ourselves again being faced with the question: what is of greatest value to Jesus? Is it fine sounding, correct and passionate words? Is it powerful signs and wonders that impress him, as they do others? No. What matters to Jesus is our obedience. It is the hunger to do what God wants me to do that delights him, whether spectacular or barely noticeable to anyone else. It is the fact that not only do we call him Lord, but we do what he says.

What stands on the final day, 'that day' as Jesus calls it, is a relationship. Jesus says that the key issue is whether we're known by him. If we're with him on the road, knowing his Father and doing his will, then there's no way he cannot know us – we share the same Father.

Are pleasing the Father, following the Lord Jesus and wanting to know him better as the Spirit takes me forward more important to me than what I do and say?

> *Pause to worship Jesus as Lord. Praise him for the Father you share because you have been adopted into his family. Be ready for whatever he wants you to say and do.*

JA

Day 100

Choices: two ways to build

MATTHEW 7:24–29

Mountainside
'Therefore everyone who hears these words of mine and puts them into practice is like a wise man who built his house on the rock. The rain came down, the streams rose, and the winds blew and beat against that house; yet it did not fall, because it had its foundation on the rock. But everyone who hears these words of mine and does not put them into practice is like a foolish man who built his house on sand. The rain came down, the streams rose, and the winds blew and beat against that house, and it fell with a great crash.' When Jesus had finished saying these things, the crowds were amazed at his teaching, because he taught as one who had authority, and not as their teachers of the law.

Jesus brings his message to an end with another story, and another choice. We meet two people – one is wise, the other foolish.

Wisdom was important to the Jewish people. They had a whole section of their scriptures devoted to wisdom literature, like the book of Proverbs. In their thinking, wisdom pointed to living in the right way with God and others so that society reflected his rule and became a better place to be.

Many people today want to live well with themselves and others, knowing wholeness and well-being. It's a good aspiration and not far from the Bible's vision of a wise way of life.

The way of wisdom is found in hearing the words of Jesus and putting them into practice. Not just knowing what he says, but doing it. This is to build on the rock. Both men in Jesus' story hear his words; both build houses, but only one has a house by the end. The wise man does what Jesus says, and so his house stays standing. The foolish man ignores his teaching, and his house (that is, his life) collapses under pressure.

> As we leave the sermon on the mount, ask God to remind you of anything that you thought you should do because of what Jesus says. Ask him to give you a way to be different, seek him for anything you need to find as you put Jesus words into practice and knock on the door for the opportunity to live the Jesus way more distinctly.

JA

Day 101

A leper healed

MATTHEW 8:1-4 (MARK 1:40-45; LUKE 5:12-16)

Foot of the mountain
When Jesus came down from the mountainside, large crowds followed him. A man with leprosy came and knelt before him and said, 'Lord, if you are willing, you can make me clean.' Jesus reached out his hand and touched the man. 'I am willing,' he said. 'Be clean!' Immediately he was cleansed of his leprosy. Then Jesus said to him, 'See that you don't tell anyone. But go, show yourself to the priest and offer the gift Moses commanded, as a testimony to them.'

Jesus and the disciples leave the hillside for the road again. The crowd is never far away but Jesus focuses on the individuals he encounters. First, there's a man with leprosy.

'Leprosy' was a catch-all word for any kind of serious skin disorder. This was a world without antibiotics, sterile dressings or even clean water for bathing. People with these conditions suffered greatly. On top of this, the Jewish law declared them unclean, insisting they stay away from the rest of the community. So they ended up alone or in small groups trying somehow to survive.

Think for a while about how the man must have felt about himself. His head was full of thoughts about being dirty, wanting more than anything else to be clean, to have his life back. What did he think about Jesus? He kneels before him – is this worship or just his desperation? He's certain that Jesus could cleanse him; his only doubt is whether Jesus was willing to help. It all comes out in a plain statement: 'If you're willing, you can make me clean' (v. 2).

Jesus reaches out to touch the man. How does he feel as he's touched? When had he last been touched with care by someone who wasn't as 'dirty' as he was? Jesus' touch on his skin says it all, but in case he's missed it, Jesus tells him that he is willing and declares him clean. Jesus releases his grip, and the skin is pure again.

Jesus sends the man off to see the priest to verify his healing, and honour God with an offering so he can rejoin the community. His relationship with God and with others matters more to Jesus than the miracle of his pure skin.

> 'The blood of Jesus, his Son, purifies us from all sin' (1 John 1:7). Acknowledge your sin, feel Jesus' touch, hear his words: 'I am willing. Be clean.'

JA

Day 102

An outsider's faith

MATTHEW 8:5–13 (*LUKE 7:1–10*)

Capernaum
When Jesus had entered Capernaum, a centurion came to him, asking for help. 'Lord,' he said, 'my servant lies at home paralysed, suffering terribly.' Jesus said to him, 'Shall I come and heal him?' The centurion replied, 'Lord, I do not deserve to have you come under my roof. But just say the word, and my servant will be healed. For I myself am a man under authority, with soldiers under me. I tell this one, "Go," and he goes; and that one, "Come," and he comes. I say to my servant, "Do this," and he does it.' When Jesus heard this, he was amazed and said to those following him, 'Truly I tell you, I have not found anyone in Israel with such great faith. I say to you that many will come from the east and the west, and will take their places at the feast with Abraham, Isaac and Jacob in the kingdom of heaven. But the subjects of the kingdom will be thrown outside, into the darkness, where there will be weeping and gnashing of teeth.' Then Jesus said to the centurion, 'Go! Let it be done just as you believed it would.' And his servant was healed at that moment.

In Capernaum, another man comes to Jesus. An officer in the Roman army, as a non-Jew he too is an outsider. His villa would have been 'unclean' to Jews and strictly off limits. He asks Jesus for help because his servant is suddenly paralysed, 'suffering terribly' (v. 6). Jesus offers to go and heal him.

The centurion declines the visit, sure that Jesus can say the word and the servant will be healed. He recognises that he and Jesus have something in common. The soldier can issue commands because of the authority of Rome behind him. He believes Jesus has a greater authority behind him, so can simply give an order to an illness and it will be gone!

This faith from the outsider amazes Jesus. It's a sign of many more like him who will be with him in the Messiah's kingdom banquet. Tragically, those thinking they have a right to be there could be the real outsiders in the end.

> Lord, today I want to be able to see people who are open to you. Help me to be your ambassador to those who know they need your help, whoever they are.

JA

Day 103

Raising of a widow's son

LUKE 7:11-17

Nain
Soon afterwards, Jesus went to a town called Nain, and his disciples and a large crowd went along with him. As he approached the town gate, a dead person was being carried out – the only son of his mother, and she was a widow. And a large crowd from the town was with her. When the Lord saw her, his heart went out to her and he said, 'Don't cry.' Then he went up and touched the bier they were carrying him on, and the bearers stood still. He said, 'Young man, I say to you, get up!' The dead man sat up and began to talk, and Jesus gave him back to his mother. They were all filled with awe and praised God. 'A great prophet has appeared among us,' they said. 'God has come to help his people.' This news about Jesus spread throughout Judea and the surrounding country.

You could explore this in prayer – stepping into the story and praying imaginatively. See page 12.

Two crowds converge around the entrance to a small town in Galilee. One is with Jesus, arriving on the road with his disciples and many others along 'for the ride'. The other crowd moves steadily in the opposite direction, filling the air with the noisy grief of a Middle Eastern funeral procession following the body carried on a bier.

One woman stands out from the rest. She's dressed in widow's clothes, surrounded, yet alone, because her only son has now been taken from her. She faces desolation and poverty without a husband or other family to support her. Jesus steps in and does something.

We see so much of Jesus here – his heart of compassion for the woman in her need, the comfort he gives her, the identification with the tragedy, touching the bier. This is a shocking act; nobody would opt to do that as they'd become ritually unclean. This stops the procession in its tracks. Then comes the power of his word along with his tender care as he gives the woman back her only son.

This is what it looks like when God comes to help people. It's Jesus bringing life, God revealing his power and glory. No wonder the news about Jesus spread far and wide!

> 'God… uses us to spread the aroma of the knowledge of him everywhere' (2 Corinthians 2:14).

JA

Day 104

John the Baptist's questions

LUKE 7:18–23 (MATTHEW 11:2–6)

Galilee region
John's disciples told him about all these things. Calling two of them, he sent them to the Lord to ask, 'Are you the one who is to come, or should we expect someone else?' When the men came to Jesus, they said, 'John the Baptist sent us to you to ask, "Are you the one who is to come, or should we expect someone else?"' At that very time Jesus cured many who had diseases, illnesses and evil spirits, and gave sight to many who were blind. So he replied to the messengers, 'Go back and report to John what you have seen and heard: the blind receive sight, the lame walk, those who have leprosy are cleansed, the deaf hear, the dead are raised, and the good news is proclaimed to the poor. Blessed is anyone who does not stumble on account of me.'

Even John the Baptist faced doubts. Although he fearlessly spoke truth to power in God's name, he is now locked up in Herod's prison. John spent years telling thousands of people of the awesome way God's promised one would come to them with axe in hand and judgement fire to follow.

News of what Jesus is doing reaches John in prison; there's awe for sure, but not from fiery judgement. All people are talking about is God's rescue and help. John has big questions: is Jesus really the one he was expecting, the one God promised, the one he preached, or is the wait still on?

John's followers come and spend time with Jesus, and he sends them back with a message for John. It lists all they've seen in a way deliberately echoing Isaiah's description of the promised Messiah (Isaiah 29:18; 35:6; 61:1). Jesus shows John that he knows what he's doing. God's blessing is on John, even in his struggles. He can trust Jesus.

Like John, I can be disappointed because I don't see Jesus working in the way I expect. Sometimes too, the promises I know are there come with a timescale I don't understand. As we bring him these deep concerns, we know this doesn't lose us God's blessing; rather we can trust him with our questions, doubts and fears.

> Is there a question you would like to ask Jesus, as John did? Put it into a sentence and leave it with him in prayer.

JA

Day 105

Jesus' view of John the Baptist

LUKE 7:24-35 (MATTHEW 11:7-19)

Galilee region
After John's messengers left, Jesus began to speak to the crowd about John: 'What did you go out into the wilderness to see? A reed swayed by the wind? If not, what did you go out to see? A man dressed in fine clothes? No, those who wear expensive clothes and indulge in luxury are in palaces. But what did you go out to see? A prophet? Yes, I tell you, and more than a prophet. This is the one about whom it is written: "I will send my messenger ahead of you, who will prepare your way before you." I tell you, among those born of women there is no one greater than John; yet the one who is least in the kingdom of God is greater than he.' (All the people, even the tax collectors, when they heard Jesus' words, acknowledged that God's way was right, because they had been baptised by John. But the Pharisees and the experts in the law rejected God's purpose for themselves, because they had not been baptised by John.) Jesus went on to say, 'To what, then, can I compare the people of this generation? What are they like? They are like children sitting in the market-place and calling out to each other: "We played the pipe for you, and you did not dance; we sang a dirge, and you did not cry." For John the Baptist came neither eating bread nor drinking wine, and you say, "He has a demon." The Son of Man came eating and drinking, and you say, "Here is a glutton and a drunkard, a friend of tax collectors and sinners." But wisdom is proved right by all her children.'

John was hugely popular. Now he has gone, Jesus reminds the crowd that above all John was a prophet, and more. He was the messenger going before the Lord promised by Malachi and Isaiah. He had the greatest privilege of any of his era. But now that Jesus has arrived with the kingdom of heaven, a new era has begun.

Jesus and John divided the crowd, being loved or hated. Every generation must make a choice about who they believe. By trusting in Jesus, we are aligned with that new kingdom. That may not be the popular choice, but it is the wise one.

> *Where are you placing your allegiance?*

JA

Day 106

Unrepentant cities

MATTHEW 11:20-24 (LUKE 10:13-15)

Around Galilee
Then Jesus began to denounce the towns in which most of his miracles had been performed, because they did not repent. 'Woe to you, Chorazin! Woe to you, Bethsaida! For if the miracles that were performed in you had been performed in Tyre and Sidon, they would have repented long ago in sackcloth and ashes. But I tell you, it will be more bearable for Tyre and Sidon on the day of judgment than for you. And you, Capernaum, will you be lifted to the heavens? No, you will go down to Hades. For if the miracles that were performed in you had been performed in Sodom, it would have remained to this day. But I tell you that it will be more bearable for Sodom on the day of judgment than for you.'

People in the towns around Galilee had seen many miracles, yet Jesus sees no difference in them. 'Repent' is an important word; the idea of change is at the heart of it. These towns had seen so much but with little change, even though many of their people were no longer sick or disabled because Jesus had healed them.

Everyone must have known someone who had been blessed by him, but nothing deep had happened in their lives and communities. People were just as they'd always been; these towns were just the same – except the wait to see a doctor was shorter!

This leads Jesus to bring a terrible warning. He compares these towns, full of people he loves, with cities like Tyre, Sidon and Sodom. Everyone knew about how these cities were judged by God, their scriptures told them so. Jesus warns them that they had seen so much more of God's power around Galilee, yet were rejecting him as God's king.

Jesus warns of consequences from ignoring or rejecting him. He's not threatening them with terrible things if they don't repent. It's rather that if you're needing rescue and refuse the only rescuer, then there's no way out. As someone put it: 'Only the rejection of forgiveness is unforgivable'!

> Lord, you speak truth even when it's hard to hear. Please show me areas in me or my life that need to change in the light of your word.

JA

Day 107

Rest for the weary

MATTHEW 11:25–30 (*LUKE 10:21–22*)

Around Galilee
At that time Jesus said, 'I praise you, Father, Lord of heaven and earth, because you have hidden these things from the wise and learned, and revealed them to little children. Yes, Father, for this is what you were pleased to do. All things have been committed to me by my Father. No one knows the Son except the Father, and no one knows the Father except the Son and those to whom the Son chooses to reveal him. Come to me, all you who are weary and burdened, and I will give you rest. Take my yoke upon you and learn from me, for I am gentle and humble in heart, and you will find rest for your souls. For my yoke is easy and my burden is light.'

Jesus goes right on from his terrible warning to open his heart in prayer. He overflows in praise because stubborn refusal to repent is not the end of the story. The Lord of heaven and earth is moving, revealing to the least likely people what is hidden from those who think they are wise.

What is being revealed is that the relationship between the Father and Son can be shared by people to whom the Son (Jesus) reveals it. Jesus' joy comes from being in this close relationship with his Father, something only experienced in the community of God. Then comes the bombshell! Jesus will draw others into that same relationship as he reveals it to us.

Is this for a selective group of people on the inside track? Immediately Jesus welcomes anyone and everyone who will come to him. Our only qualification: to be weary and burdened, to need the rest he offers us and be willing to take the yoke he gives us. We learn from him and walk with him.

Yokes were used to put oxen to work side-by-side, but also for individuals to carry things easily. In my younger days, rucksacks were supported by a metal frame that could be detached from the bag. The yoke in Jesus' day worked like that, a wooden frame to help you carry things more easily.

Jesus pictures our life with him as rest from trusting ourselves and anything else but him, learning from him, easily carrying what he gives us.

> Is this what your Christian lives look like? Is it characterised by rest?

Day 108

The Pharisee and the sinful woman

LUKE 7:36-50

Unnamed city
When one of the Pharisees invited Jesus to have dinner with him, he went to the Pharisee's house and reclined at the table. A woman in that town who lived a sinful life learned that Jesus was eating at the Pharisee's house, so she came there with an alabaster jar of perfume. As she stood behind him at his feet weeping, she began to wet his feet with her tears. Then she wiped them with her hair, kissed them and poured perfume on them. When the Pharisee who had invited him saw this, he said to himself, 'If this man were a prophet, he would know who is touching him and what kind of woman she is – that she is a sinner.' Jesus answered him, 'Simon, I have something to tell you.' 'Tell me, teacher,' he said. 'Two people owed money to a certain money-lender. One owed him five hundred denarii, and the other fifty. Neither of them had the money to pay him back, so he forgave the debts of both. Now which of them will love him more?' Simon replied, 'I suppose the one who had the bigger debt forgiven.' 'You have judged correctly,' Jesus said. Then he turned towards the woman and said to Simon, 'Do you see this woman? I came into your house. You did not give me any water for my feet, but she wet my feet with her tears and wiped them with her hair. You did not give me a kiss, but this woman, from the time I entered, has not stopped kissing my feet. You did not put oil on my head, but she has poured perfume on my feet. Therefore, I tell you, her many sins have been forgiven – as her great love has shown. But whoever has been forgiven little loves little.' Then Jesus said to her, 'Your sins are forgiven.' The other guests began to say among themselves, 'Who is this who even forgives sins?' Jesus said to the woman, 'Your faith has saved you; go in peace.'[17]

You could enjoy this account using imaginative prayer as described on page 12. Jesus declares her sins are forgiven; she's been saved by her faith.

What can this woman teach me about loving Jesus? Where does this love come from, what does it look like? Spend some time watching what she does, learn how to worship from her example.

JA

Day 109

The twelve and the women

LUKE 8:1-3

Region of Galilee
After this, Jesus travelled about from one town and village to another, proclaiming the good news of the kingdom of God. The Twelve were with him, and also some women who had been cured of evil spirits and diseases: Mary (called Magdalene) from whom seven demons had come out; Joanna the wife of Chuza, the manager of Herod's household; Susanna; and many others. These women were helping to support them out of their own means.

With his popularity growing, Jesus sets off on tours around the towns and villages of Galilee and beyond, sharing the good news of the arrival of the kingdom of God. With him are 'the Twelve', particular disciples he appointed as apostles, and other disciples too. We're told that in the group were a number of women who travelled with them.

Just like the other disciples, they were a diverse group. Some were wealthy and helped to cover the expenses. One is married to a very prominent government official; another has been rescued from a life dominated by evil spirits. All of them had experienced Jesus transforming their lives.

Like the woman at the meal, they were showing their appreciation and love for Jesus by doing something for him. For them it was the obvious thing to do. The 'sinful woman' made a one-off lavish gesture of love; these women show their appreciation in longer-term commitment. Who's to say that the 'many others' mentioned did not include the grateful ex-prostitute?

Here we get a taste of how Jesus lived and worked. His attitude to women was scandalously different to the culture around. Jewish rabbis would have never allowed women to travel with them like this, and one of their writers (Ben Sirach) strongly urged men never to allow women to support them financially. But Jesus is different – he is willing to welcome the help and involvement of others in his mission. He delights to receive from others, affirming who they are and what they can give.

> If I am thankful for the rescue and welcome Jesus has given me, then I can express that by sharing my resources so that others can know him. If my life is Jesus-shaped, then I too need to be willing to let others help me as I join in with the diverse community that make up his disciples.

Day 110

Parable of the sower

MATTHEW 13:1-9 (MARK 4:1-9; LUKE 8:4-8)

House by the lake in Galilee
That same day Jesus went out of the house and sat by the lake. Such large crowds gathered around him that he got into a boat and sat in it, while all the people stood on the shore. Then he told them many things in parables, saying: 'A farmer went out to sow his seed. As he was scattering the seed, some fell along the path, and the birds came and ate it up. Some fell on rocky places, where it did not have much soil. It sprang up quickly, because the soil was shallow. But when the sun came up, the plants were scorched, and they withered because they had no root. Other seed fell among thorns, which grew up and choked the plants. Still other seed fell on good soil, where it produced a crop – a hundred, sixty or thirty times what was sown. Whoever has ears, let them hear.'

Jesus' popularity is growing through this second year of his ministry such that he has to take action to accommodate 'such large' crowds. He uses the natural auditoriums formed by the little bays around Galilee, teaching from a boat just off the shore so that the crowd on the beach and the gently sloping areas behind it can hear perfectly.

Jesus does something else, he starts telling them parables, memorable stories that leave you thinking about what he has said. The point of this is also so we can hear – or miss it altogether.

Of the many stories Jesus shared that morning, we have just one. As people walked home later, what were they thinking about? What does he mean by the challenge he throws out to be the kind of person who can 'hear'?

The story tells us about growing crops in that area; having the seed land on the ground isn't necessarily enough. There's a lot going on to work against it growing at all, let alone bearing a harvest. What if listening to Jesus is like that?

It's hard to realise that seeds don't always produce a harvest. Can Jesus' words really be heard but not go further than the surface of our minds, or remain with us for no longer than the moment they're in our ears?

▍ *Pray for 'ears to hear' Jesus in every part of your life today.*

Day 111

Why parables?

MATTHEW 13:10–17 (*MARK 4:10–12; LUKE 8:9–11*)

House by the lake in Galilee
The disciples came to him and asked, 'Why do you speak to the people in parables?' He replied, 'Because the knowledge of the secrets of the kingdom of heaven has been given to you, but not to them. Whoever has will be given more, and they will have an abundance. Whoever does not have, even what they have will be taken from them. This is why I speak to them in parables: Though seeing, they do not see; though hearing, they do not hear or understand. In them is fulfilled the prophecy of Isaiah: "You will be ever hearing but never understanding; you will be ever seeing but never perceiving. For this people's heart has become calloused; they hardly hear with their ears, and they have closed their eyes. Otherwise they might see with their eyes, hear with their ears, understand with their hearts and turn, and I would heal them." But blessed are your eyes because they see, and your ears because they hear. For truly I tell you, many prophets and righteous people longed to see what you see but did not see it, and to hear what you hear but did not hear it.'

The disciples ask Jesus why he's teaching in this puzzling way. His answer draws a dividing line that runs through humanity. Some people want to hear and understand; they're open to God's word. Others do not; they simply don't want what Jesus is offering. The parables help those who want to know to understand more, and those who don't want what Jesus offers to miss it with no worries.

Jesus says many people in his day, and ours, just don't want to really see, so they close their eyes or shut their ears because they don't want to turn towards him for salvation. They would rather carry on their own way. This is what Isaiah the prophet faced in his time, and people haven't changed much over the centuries.

But Isaiah promised that some would see and some would turn. He prophesied that God would send a servant to bring this about. Jesus reminds the disciples that they have seen and are blessed – God has enabled their eyes to be opened. He is the promised servant, and he still offers the word to those who want to hear.

▎ *Meditate on the last two sentences Jesus speaks here (vv. 16–17, see page 10).*

JA

Day 112

The sower explained

MATTHEW 13:18–23 (*MARK 4:13–20; LUKE 8:11–15*)

House by the lake in Galilee
'Listen then to what the parable of the sower means: when anyone hears the message about the kingdom and does not understand it, the evil one comes and snatches away what was sown in their heart. This is the seed sown along the path. The seed falling on rocky ground refers to someone who hears the word and at once receives it with joy. But since they have no root, they last only a short time. When trouble or persecution comes because of the word, they quickly fall away. The seed falling among the thorns refers to someone who hears the word, but the worries of this life and the deceitfulness of wealth choke the word, making it unfruitful. But the seed falling on good soil refers to someone who hears the word and understands it. This is the one who produces a crop, yielding a hundred, sixty or thirty times what was sown.'

Jesus explains the puzzle to them. The message about the kingdom, or 'the word', is what we hear – look at how many times he mentions 'the word' here. This word brings us to life; 'we are born by the word', it is planted in us (1 Peter 1:23; James 1:21).

However, this is not a straightforward process, the word can be threatened in our lives. An evil one wants to snatch it away from our hearts. Or we can start enthusiastically with Jesus and his kingdom word, but when trouble or opposition comes then what has been growing dies.

Then it is possible for what God does in our lives to be choked, just as young plants can be overwhelmed by weeds, starving them of light or crucial nutrients. Jesus warns that difficult circumstances, life's worries or money and its deceptive promises can choke God's word in our lives.

The good news is that Jesus' word about the kingdom of God, how he can reign in our lives, can enter our hearts as we understand it. A crop grows in our lives producing good fruit and more word-seed to share with others who see it.

> *Heavenly Father, I want my life to be fruitful. Help me to recognise those areas in my life where your word to me can be threatened by other things. Fill me with your Spirit and make me a fruitful follower of Jesus today.*

JA

Day 113

Lamp on a stand

MARK 4:21–25 (LUKE 8:16-18)

By the lake in Galilee
He said to them, 'Do you bring in a lamp to put it under a bowl or a bed? Instead, don't you put it on its stand? For whatever is hidden is meant to be disclosed, and whatever is concealed is meant to be brought out into the open. If anyone has ears to hear, let them hear.' 'Consider carefully what you hear,' he continued. 'With the measure you use, it will be measured to you – and even more. Whoever has will be given more; whoever does not have, even what they have will be taken from them.'

The way Jesus wraps the truth up in stories and puzzles might be leaving the disciples, and us, thinking that somehow God wants to keep this good news to himself. It seems like the truth is being hidden. Is this what God is doing? The sad fact that people can't and won't see, along with our ideas of what God could do if he really chose to, may leave us wondering whether God really wants people, outside of a chosen few, to know about him at all?

If that's what we're thinking, Jesus' next parable helps us find an answer. The whole point of something giving light is that it's meant to be seen, like the lamp that's placed where its light can be appreciated. The big concept behind the parables, and everything else about Jesus, is that the truth about God is brought into the open. It's available for anyone to know. The scriptures tell us that creation reveals the Creator to us. The big story since Genesis is that God has spoken and acted in history, revealing himself, and Jesus came as God's last word to humankind.

Jesus makes it clear that we do have a real choice about how and what we hear, or if we listen at all. We can 'consider it carefully'. Something is given to us as we respond to what God says, and what we receive grows and multiplies once we start.

> *The apostle Paul testified of being sent by Jesus to people 'to open their eyes and turn them from darkness to light, and from the power of Satan to God, so that they may receive forgiveness of sins' (Acts 26:18). Pray that God will use you and your Christian community in the same way.*

JA

Day 114

Growing seed

MARK 4:26–29

By the lake in Galilee
He also said, 'This is what the kingdom of God is like. A man scatters seed on the ground. Night and day, whether he sleeps or gets up, the seed sprouts and grows, though he does not know how. All by itself the soil produces corn – first the stalk, then the ear, then the full grain in the ear. As soon as the corn is ripe, he puts the sickle to it, because the harvest has come.'

The disciples have been with Jesus for over a year now. He is drawing them into the kingdom of God, a new way of life under God's loving rule with Jesus as their promised king. We see them as Jesus explains the stories he is telling the crowds, watch them on the road with him as they learn how he meets people in great need and discover what it means to trust him in the midst of challenges.

When we read the gospels we are in the stream of generations of Jesus-followers to whom he told the apostles to teach to observe all that he had commanded them (Matthew 28:20). He has a vision of each generation of disciples learning to keep his commands and then continuing to make new disciples, sharing with others.

There is much for us to grasp and learn as we travel along with Jesus and those first disciples in the gospels, and here Jesus tells us stories about what the kingdom of God is like.[18]

What do we learn of the kingdom from these stories? Here the farmer sows the seed and then must leave it to grow. How it grows is a mystery to him. He cannot do much about it once he has finished planting. There is life in the seed, and it just happens. It is a natural process that will inevitably be completed. At the right time harvest will come and he can reap.

> *Reflect on your life as a planter in the kingdom. What can you learn from this parable? Offer to God those areas where the wait seems long. Praise him that the whole process is entirely in his hands and ask for grace to trust in this. Pray for eyes to see where the shoots are beginning to appear in the kingdom-field of your life and service.*

JA

Day 115

Parable of the weeds

MATTHEW 13:24-30

House by the lake in Galilee
Jesus told them another parable: 'The kingdom of heaven is like a man who sowed good seed in his field. But while everyone was sleeping, his enemy came and sowed weeds among the wheat, and went away. When the wheat sprouted and formed ears, then the weeds also appeared. The owner's servants came to him and said, "Sir, didn't you sow good seed in your field? Where then did the weeds come from?" "An enemy did this," he replied. The servants asked him, "Do you want us to go and pull them up?" "No," he answered, "because while you are pulling the weeds, you may uproot the wheat with them. Let both grow together until the harvest. At that time I will tell the harvesters: first collect the weeds and tie them in bundles to be burned; then gather the wheat and bring it into my barn."'

Jesus tells another story about a man who sows seed in his field. This time it's not quite as straightforward; there's a big surprise coming. As the crops begin to grow, the workers see that it's not what they planted – a weed is growing. It's probably darnel, it looks like wheat to begin with, but as it grows the difference becomes obvious. The problem with darnel is that its 'grain' is poisonous; it was an offence in Roman law to plant darnel as an act of revenge.

The servants talk to the owner about their confusion and disappointment, suggesting a solution they've come up with. The owner has a better idea and a bigger long-term plan. They trust him with his answer, obediently waiting for his time to act so that the wheat will be safe and the weeds will be dealt with.

As planters in the kingdom, we can be surprised and disappointed. Sometimes things don't turn out as we expected or what we're doing is opposed by 'an enemy'. What can we do then? We can ask the owner – the Lord – about it, bringing our concerns to him in prayer, listening to his response and learning to trust him that the final victory is certain.

> *Are there areas in your life or service where although you've been obedient, you are disappointed, feeling opposed? Name them before the Lord, asking for his perspective, trusting him for the final outcome.*

JA

Day 116

Mustard seed and yeast

MATTHEW 13:31–35 (*MARK 4:30–34*)

By the lake in Galilee
He told them another parable: 'The kingdom of heaven is like a mustard seed, which a man took and planted in his field. Though it is the smallest of all seeds, yet when it grows, it is the largest of garden plants and becomes a tree, so that the birds come and perch in its branches.' He told them still another parable: 'The kingdom of heaven is like yeast that a woman took and mixed into about thirty kilograms of flour until it worked all through the dough.' Jesus spoke all these things to the crowd in parables; he did not say anything to them without using a parable. So was fulfilled what was spoken through the prophet: 'I will open my mouth in parables, I will utter things hidden since the creation of the world.'

Jesus tells us more about what the kingdom of heaven is like. There are two pictures, and both talk about spectacular growth. The black mustard plant has small seeds used in cooking and could grow to over five metres high. It was well known for its record-breaking growth from the small seed to the high shrub.

Women would keep old bread on one side to mix with water to make a starter for their next batch, rather as sourdough enthusiasts do today. In Jesus' story, the woman uses her starter-leaven to go into a dough that is made from about 30 kg of flour. That's enough bread for 100 people.

The kingdom of heaven is able to grow from very small beginnings to something that is almost indescribably large. The picture of the mustard tree hosting the birds of the air suggests images in Daniel of an empire made up of other nations. Isaiah saw a time when all nations would come into God's community, symbolised by Jerusalem. Revelation speaks of an uncountable host of people from every people-group worshipping together:

> Before me was a great multitude that no one could count, from every nation, tribe, people and language, standing before the throne and before the Lamb... And they cried out in a loud voice: 'Salvation belongs to our God, who sits on the throne, and to the Lamb.'
> REVELATION 7:9–10

Meditate on this vision of the kingdom, of which you are a part. Let hope arise within you for what will be. May your heart be thrilled by the song we will one day sing together.

Day 117

Parable of the weeds explained

MATTHEW 13:36-43

House by the lake in Galilee
Then he left the crowd and went into the house. His disciples came to him and said, 'Explain to us the parable of the weeds in the field.' He answered, 'The one who sowed the good seed is the Son of Man. The field is the world, and the good seed stands for the people of the kingdom. The weeds are the people of the evil one, and the enemy who sows them is the devil. The harvest is the end of the age, and the harvesters are angels. As the weeds are pulled up and burned in the fire, so it will be at the end of the age. The Son of Man will send out his angels, and they will weed out of his kingdom everything that causes sin and all who do evil. They will throw them into the blazing furnace, where there will be weeping and gnashing of teeth. Then the righteous will shine like the sun in the kingdom of their Father. Whoever has ears, let them hear.'

Away from the crowds, the disciples ask Jesus to explain the parable about the weeds. Jesus' explanation emphasises the ending of his story. Most people expected the Messiah to come with one powerful act of rescue and judgement, sweeping away those outside of his kingdom. For many, the Romans were prime candidates for destruction, and some were enthusiastic to start the process right away!

This left some puzzled about Jesus' timescale – this could have been what caused John the Baptist to wobble in his trust in Jesus as the promised king. The story helps us to understand and live in the 'waiting period' and makes it crystal clear that he will one day complete the job of ridding creation of all that has spoiled it, weeding it out of his kingdom.

This is not an easy picture to look at, but this is where we all stand before God 'rescues us from the kingdom of darkness and transfers us into the kingdom of the Son he loves' (see Colossians 1:13). Jesus focuses our attention on how the people he calls 'righteous' will shine like the blazing sun in the kingdom of their Father. Once again, we're reminded that our Father has a glorious future awaiting us.

> *What will it mean for you today to shine like the sun with kingdom light?*

JA

Day 118

Treasure, pearls and the net

MATTHEW 13:44–50

House by the lake in Galilee
'The kingdom of heaven is like treasure hidden in a field. When a man found it, he hid it again, and then in his joy went and sold all he had and bought that field. Again, the kingdom of heaven is like a merchant looking for fine pearls. When he found one of great value, he went away and sold everything he had and bought it. Once again, the kingdom of heaven is like a net that was let down into the lake and caught all kinds of fish. When it was full, the fishermen pulled it up on the shore. Then they sat down and collected the good fish in baskets, but threw the bad away. This is how it will be at the end of the age. The angels will come and separate the wicked from the righteous and throw them into the blazing furnace, where there will be weeping and gnashing of teeth.'

Do you remember the joy of finding the kingdom for the first time, that point when you discovered a personal relationship with God? For me that was over 50 years ago, but even now as I stop and remember I can still feel the scary excitement of realising Jesus and his kingdom was available to me. He had been *around* my life. At that point I knew he could be *in* my life.

These parables describe someone finding the kingdom. They capture the joy of discovering something so precious it's worth having whatever the cost, like coming across buried treasure. Or it could be finding what you have always been searching for, like the merchant who sells his entire stock to buy the pearl he long dreamt about owning. The best thing that can ever happen to someone is to find the kingdom and invest their life in it.

The other story shows us that it's not just an individual matter. The scope of the kingdom is vast, like a trawler-net able to catch everything in its path. However, sadly, not everyone who could be part of it, will be in the end. Those who refuse to be with Jesus will ultimately have their own way.

> *Think back to that time when you found the kingdom. Review your journey so far and thank God for his faithfulness. What has it cost you? Has it been worth it?*

JA

Day 119

After understanding, what?

MATTHEW 13:51–52

House by the lake in Galilee
'Have you understood all these things?' Jesus asked. 'Yes,' they replied. He said to them, 'Therefore every teacher of the law who has become a disciple in the kingdom of heaven is like the owner of a house who brings out of his storeroom new treasures as well as old.'

The disciples have been listening to Jesus' stories, asking questions and talking about it with him when the crowds were not there. No doubt they have been thinking it over, as well as discussing and arguing with each other about it. Now Jesus asks them whether they have understood it and they are able to tell him that, yes, they do understand. They probably still have many questions, but they've grasped enough to be able to give a positive answer to his question.

What now? Because they understand, Jesus tells them one more story. It's about someone who is blessed with a house and enough good stuff to warrant a storeroom. The story begins with 'therefore' so it must be connected to the disciples' new understanding. In the story, the man, or woman, with good things in their storeroom brings them out. Others are given the chance to enjoy their treasure. They do that with older items people know about and new objects they have not seen before.

Now they understand, the disciples are to be like the teachers of the law (scribes), but these disciple-teachers are passionate for others to know about the kingdom, not the law! They share from their treasure (what they have been taught and experienced) so that others can learn and grow.

Only Matthew has this story. Later in his gospel, he will record how Jesus tells his people to be disciples who make disciples (28:19–20). That is for us too; now that we understand, the treasure of the kingdom cannot stay inside our storerooms. We bring it out for others to enjoy.

Jesus makes it plain that living in the kingdom is being a disciple (v. 52). Following Jesus is how we live under God's rule. What does that mean for you?

> *Pray for people you know or may meet today. Ask for opportunities to bring out new, fresh treasure for them along with what they may already know.*

Day 120

A kingdom divided

MARK 3:20–30

Galilee
Then Jesus entered a house, and again a crowd gathered, so that he and his disciples were not even able to eat. When his family heard about this, they went to take charge of him, for they said, 'He is out of his mind.' And the teachers of the law who came down from Jerusalem said, 'He is possessed by Beelzebul! By the prince of demons he is driving out demons.' So Jesus called them over to him and began to speak to them in parables: 'How can Satan drive out Satan? If a kingdom is divided against itself, that kingdom cannot stand. If a house is divided against itself, that house cannot stand. And if Satan opposes himself and is divided, he cannot stand; his end has come. In fact, no one can enter a strong man's house without first tying him up. Then he can plunder the strong man's house. Truly I tell you, people can be forgiven all their sins and every slander they utter, but whoever blasphemes against the Holy Spirit will never be forgiven; they are guilty of an eternal sin.' He said this because they were saying, 'He has an impure spirit.'

Life for Jesus is impossibly busy. The crowd invade the home he is visiting, leaving no time or space to eat. His family, thinking it has all become too much for him, come to 'take charge of him' (v. 21).

The religious experts from Jerusalem have a darker explanation. Jesus is tapping into evil powers. The kingdom he preaches is real and powerful, but they are convinced it comes from a very bad place.

Jesus agrees that Satan is being opposed and driven out, and a strong man tied-up. Wherever Jesus is, hundreds of people are experiencing deliverance; but if that is true, how can Jesus be opposing evil with its own power? No, he operates by the power of God, and to attribute his work to Satan is to blaspheme against the Holy Spirit, the source of his power.

To turn away from what Jesus brings by the Holy Spirit, slandering him by saying his work is evil is to commit a sin which, by its very obstinacy, cannot be forgiven. However, if we repent even of such an attitude, we can pray 'deliver us from evil' and know that he will.

> Remember today, Jesus is stronger than Satan.

JA

Day 121

Another family

MATTHEW 12:46–50 (MARK 3:31–35; LUKE 8:19–21)

> Galilee
> *While Jesus was still talking to the crowd, his mother and brothers stood outside, wanting to speak to him. Someone told him, 'Your mother and brothers are standing outside, wanting to speak to you.' He replied to him, 'Who is my mother, and who are my brothers?' Pointing to his disciples, he said, 'Here are my mother and my brothers. For whoever does the will of my Father in heaven is my brother and sister and mother.'*

Still in that crowded house, we're reminded that Jesus' mother and brothers had come to get him away, fearing he was out of his mind! Joseph, his father, is not mentioned in the gospels throughout Jesus' ministry, so it's likely that Mary is now a widow. Jesus has answered the criticism from the religious elites and is now talking again to the crowd. Someone interrupts to tell him his family are outside. They want to speak to Jesus but can't get in!

Since he was at least twelve years old, Jesus had lived with an awareness that his relationship with his Father, God, took priority in his life. Remember how Jesus' worried parents heard the son they'd lost in Jerusalem ask them: 'Why were you searching for me? Didn't you know I had to be in my Father's house' (Luke 2:49).

Here Jesus goes even further. The relationship he enjoys with his Father can be shared; people who 'do the will of my Father in heaven' (v. 50), he says, become a new family with him. Jesus is not rejecting his family here. Remember how, as he was dying, Jesus asked John to be a son to Mary. Family still matters, but in following Jesus we have a heavenly Father who will never fail us and an older brother who will never be ashamed of us.

The heart of kingdom discipleship is made clear by Jesus, and it is very simple. Following him is about seeking and doing the Father's will, nothing more and nothing less. This is the DNA that all true children of God have in common. It is what makes us family.

> Meditate and pray into this truth from Hebrews 2:11: 'Both the one who makes people holy and those who are made holy are of the same family. So Jesus is not ashamed to call them brothers and sisters.'

Day 122

Following Jesus into the storm

MATTHEW 8:18, 23-27 (MARK 4:35-41; LUKE 8:22-25)

> Sea of Galilee
> *When Jesus saw the crowd around him, he gave orders to cross to the other side of the lake… Then he got into the boat and his disciples followed him. Suddenly a furious storm came up on the lake, so that the waves swept over the boat. But Jesus was sleeping. The disciples went and woke him, saying, 'Lord, save us! We're going to drown!' He replied, 'You of little faith, why are you so afraid?' Then he got up and rebuked the winds and the waves, and it was completely calm. The men were amazed and asked, 'What kind of man is this? Even the winds and the waves obey him!'*

Jesus decides to cross the lake of Galilee to escape the crowds. With him are the disciples, maybe happy that they can get across the lake, away from the pressures. If so, they were in for a big shock.

Before long, a storm has blown up that even the experienced fishermen among them knew could be fatal. Jesus was asleep, so they wake him. They need him to save them, because it looks certain they are going to drown. As he wakes, Jesus is surprised they are so overcome with fear. Why was it, that as the sky got darker and the wind grew stronger, their faith dwindled to almost nothing?

Jesus rebukes the storm – other gospels suggest he used a phrase for calling a dog to behave. Immediately there is calm. The disciples are left with a question: what kind of man can command winds and waves to obey him? The rules of physics are suspended at Jesus' word as the immense natural energy of the storm is muzzled in an instant.

We can all face sudden, unexpected crises that can overwhelm us with fear. Here, when the disciples ask for his help, Jesus seems to be shocked that it has got to this stage before they are willing to trust him. Trusting him can be a constant factor before, during and after crises, and we need to learn to live that way. Jesus' authority over everything is constant; he is faithful and he is trustworthy. Faith comes in living in the light of who he is, trusting him through every storm that comes our way.

> *What storms are you facing? How can you apply what you know about Jesus to bring calm to your soul?*

JA

Day 123

Jesus' authority in the spiritual world

MATTHEW 8:28–34 (*MARK 5:1–20; LUKE 8:26–39*)

> **The land of the Gadarenes**
> *When he arrived at the other side in the region of the Gadarenes, two demon-possessed men coming from the tombs met him. They were so violent that no one could pass that way. 'What do you want with us, Son of God?' they shouted. 'Have you come here to torture us before the appointed time?' Some distance from them a large herd of pigs was feeding. The demons begged Jesus, 'If you drive us out, send us into the herd of pigs.' He said to them, 'Go!' So they came out and went into the pigs, and the whole herd rushed down the steep bank into the lake and died in the water. Those tending the pigs ran off, went into the town and reported all this, including what had happened to the demon-possessed men. Then the whole town went out to meet Jesus. And when they saw him, they pleaded with him to leave their region.*

Jesus and the disciples cross the lake, arriving on the southern side. Immediately they are accosted by two terrifying men. Both were demon-possessed, their lives tormented by dark forces that left them with a violent hatred of anyone else. The locals stayed away from them, knowing any incursion on to their territory would end violently.

The other gospels focus on one of these men. It could be that only one remained with Jesus after his healing, the other having decided differently.

The demonic powers accept Jesus' authority as the coming king. They know he will eventually deal with everything evil. In effect they are saying, 'You've come early!' They beg to be sent into the herd of pigs feeding nearby. Jesus says one word and the men are free and the demons homeless. The spooked pigs stampede into the lake and drown.

The whole community come to meet Jesus. Here is God's king, who delivers suffering people from evil, makes their area safe again and restores two men to their lives and families. Yet the people see all that Jesus can do but not want him in their lives or communities. The community pleads with Jesus, just like the demons, to let them stay as they are.

> Lord, thank you for your authority over evil, and the freedom you give people, even to reject you. Help me to live trusting you in this uncomfortable paradox.

JA

Day 124

Woman healed, girl raised

MATTHEW 9:18–26 (MARK 5:21–43; LUKE 8:40–56)

Capernaum
While he was saying this, a synagogue leader came and knelt before him and said, 'My daughter has just died. But come and put your hand on her, and she will live.' Jesus got up and went with him, and so did his disciples. Just then a woman who had been subject to bleeding for twelve years came up behind him and touched the edge of his cloak. She said to herself, 'If I only touch his cloak, I will be healed.' Jesus turned and saw her. 'Take heart, daughter,' he said, 'your faith has healed you.' And the woman was healed at that moment. When Jesus entered the synagogue leader's house and saw the noisy crowd and people playing pipes, he said, 'Go away. The girl is not dead but asleep.' But they laughed at him. After the crowd had been put outside, he went in and took the girl by the hand, and she got up. News of this spread through all that region.

Jesus and the disciples have gone back across the lake and are probably in Capernaum when they are met by a man pleading for help. His daughter has been very sick and has just died, but he is convinced Jesus can restore her life with a touch of his hand.

On the way they meet a woman who is experiencing a kind of living death. Prolonged menstrual bleeding has ruined her life for twelve years. She is 'unclean' under Jewish law, unable to worship and effectively banned from sharing food or hospitable spaces. She touches Jesus' cloak believing that this will heal her. Notice that Jesus 'turned and saw her' (v. 22). He calls her 'daughter', assuring her that her faith (her trust in him) has brought healing. Her sickness has gone; she will never be the same.

We see Jesus' personal care for the synagogue leader's family too. Jesus dismisses the professional mourners and their band and, with her parents looking on, he wakes the girl up. His authority over death is seen as he gently takes her hand.

Jewish law said impurity could be spread by touch. How different it is with Jesus. Touched by the woman, his purity heals her, and when he holds the hand of a dead girl, his life restores her.

| Lord, touch my life today. You know my need. Your power is the same now as it was then.

JA

Day 125

Two healings

MATTHEW 9:27–34

Outside Capernaum
As Jesus went on from there, two blind men followed him, calling out, 'Have mercy on us, Son of David!' When he had gone indoors, the blind men came to him, and he asked them, 'Do you believe that I am able to do this?' 'Yes, Lord,' they replied. Then he touched their eyes and said, 'According to your faith let it be done to you'; and their sight was restored. Jesus warned them sternly, 'See that no one knows about this.' But they went out and spread the news about him all over that region. While they were going out, a man who was demon-possessed and could not talk was brought to Jesus. And when the demon was driven out, the man who had been mute spoke. The crowd was amazed and said, 'Nothing like this has ever been seen in Israel.' But the Pharisees said, 'It is by the prince of demons that he drives out demons.'

During the miracles we've been witnessing, Matthew speaks of many being brought to Jesus, 'and he drove out the spirits with a word and healed all who were ill'. This, the gospel says, fulfilled Isaiah's prophecy of the coming servant-king who 'took up our infirmities and bore our diseases' (Matthew 8:16–17, quoting Isaiah 53:4).

Once again, we see the servant-king in action doing just that. The blind men are not healed on first contact in front of the crowds. Rather, Jesus wants them to come to the house, to be prompted by him to believe in him for themselves. Faith flows through so many of these encounters, and this is no different. New Testament scholar R.T. France says, 'Faith is shown to be a practical confidence in the power of Jesus.'[19]

Along with this, we see Jesus' power and authority to release people from the power of evil, like the man who was silent in his spiritual darkness, unable to express faith or anything else. This healing amazes the crowd and anticipates what Jesus will do as the king on the cross when he disarmed the powers of evil and 'rescued us from the dominion of darkness and brought us into the kingdom of the Son' (Colossians 1:13).

> How are you demonstrating your faith in Jesus with practical confidence? How are you applying what you believe to the challenges of everyday life?

JA

Day 126

The compassionate ministry

MATTHEW 9:35–38 (*MARK 6:34; LUKE 10:2*)

Towns and villages
Jesus went through all the towns and villages, teaching in their synagogues, proclaiming the good news of the kingdom and healing every disease and illness. When he saw the crowds, he had compassion on them, because they were harassed and helpless, like sheep without a shepherd. Then he said to his disciples, 'The harvest is plentiful but the workers are few. Ask the Lord of the harvest, therefore, to send out workers into his harvest field.'

Jesus carries on using the amazing opportunities this time of popularity has given him. Synagogue congregations are hanging on his every word and, every day, people were coming to him, discovering that the kingdom he spoke about really was good news for everyone.

This must have been exciting and challenging, but it was his compassion that energised him. Where did that come from? He saw people in a particular way; as he looked at them, he saw them as sheep wandering without a shepherd, vulnerable to all the dangers and difficulties of a broken world, powerless to do anything about it.

He shares this way of seeing with his disciples. He must have. How else would Matthew have known what was going on in Jesus' heart? As a disciple, I can learn to see people in my world as Jesus sees them, and this creates space in my heart for his compassion.

Disciples are also given something to do in response to what we see when we look with his eyes. It's a simple first step; we pray. We don't start to respond, regarding ourselves and our activities as the answer. We begin in dialogue with the Lord of the harvest. We bring what we have seen and understand of the need to the only one who can really change anything, and ask him to send out workers. Of course, we need to be open to the possibility of being one of them!

Compassion is more than sympathy or pity. It is a deep-seated (literally, in the bowels) emotion of love and concern expressed in practical ways.

> Father, please give me eyes to see people as Jesus sees them. Open my heart, Lord, to your compassion and make me aware of your harvest. Send harvest workers wherever they are needed and help me to live today, open to being sent by you.

JA

Day 127

A prophet without honour

MATTHEW 13:54–58 (MARK 6:1–6)

Nazareth
Coming to his home town, he began teaching the people in their synagogue, and they were amazed. 'Where did this man get this wisdom and these miraculous powers?' they asked. 'Isn't this the carpenter's son? Isn't his mother's name Mary, and aren't his brothers James, Joseph, Simon and Judas? Aren't all his sisters with us? Where then did this man get all these things?' And they took offence at him. But Jesus said to them, 'A prophet is not without honour except in his own town and in his own home.' And he did not do many miracles there because of their lack of faith.

Jesus' travels bring him back to his hometown, Nazareth, perhaps to the relief of his worried family. Here, just like everywhere else, Jesus is given the guest preacher slot in the synagogue on the sabbath.

The people are amazed, but it's not really what he says or does that grabs them. They're buzzing from the shock that the man saying and doing these things was the boy who grew up 'round here'. They simply can't get past this, and soon amazement turns to hostility. They're not going to take this from someone who, just a few years ago, repaired their houses.

Jesus knew suffering and hurt throughout his life. What must it have been like for him to be rejected by those he knew best and had loved the longest?

After all we've seen of his spectacular ministry in this season, it comes as a shock, perhaps a wake-up call, for us to see Jesus here, limited by the unbelief, or lack of faith, of the people around him. As far as we can tell, this is one of the last times Jesus will teach in a synagogue. His popularity will not last much longer, and yet Jesus is able to live with these limitations.

Jesus faced rejection just as we do. He knew the disappointment too of meagre results and a lack of response. As our great high priest (Hebrews 4:15–16), he can sympathise with us and give us grace to move forward in resilient obedience, even when we are hurt by those closest to us.

> When have you felt the sting of rejection or the pain of disappointment? Bring your woundedness to Jesus for him to heal. He knows and understands. He does not condemn.

JA

Day 128

Sent by Jesus

MATTHEW 10:1-10 (MARK 6:7-13; LUKE 9:1-6)

Jesus called his twelve disciples to him and gave them authority to drive out impure spirits and to heal every disease and illness. These are the names of the twelve apostles: first, Simon (who is called Peter) and his brother Andrew; James son of Zebedee, and his brother John; Philip and Bartholomew; Thomas and Matthew the tax collector; James son of Alphaeus, and Thaddaeus; Simon the Zealot and Judas Iscariot, who betrayed him. These twelve Jesus sent out with the following instructions: 'Do not go among the Gentiles or enter any town of the Samaritans. Go rather to the lost sheep of Israel. As you go, proclaim this message: "The kingdom of heaven has come near." Heal those who are ill, raise the dead, cleanse those who have leprosy, drive out demons. Freely you have received; freely give. Do not get any gold or silver or copper to take with you in your belts – no bag for the journey or extra shirt or sandals or a staff, for the worker is worth his keep.'

Previously Jesus told the disciples to ask the Lord of the harvest to send out workers and now they are being sent themselves. They've even got a special title – 'apostles', meaning sent ones.

They must only go to Jewish people at this stage, who they already know are lost sheep – shepherdless and vulnerable. In other places it's clear that non-Jews will be part of his kingdom, but at this stage the scope is limited.

The disciples are given authority by Jesus to do all that he has been doing. They are like official representatives of his kingdom with the same message that the kingdom of heaven is near. People can receive all that Jesus gives them, freely.

They proclaim the kingdom in words and actions, demonstrating Jesus' authority over evil, death and sickness. How they do it authenticates the truth they share; they give away what Jesus offers, never asking for money in return. In return, in this culture, the disciples receive hospitality and enough to eat. They are welcomed for his sake.

> *Can we learn to follow Jesus this way? It's different since the resurrection, but there is a continuity too. We still go, offering Jesus' kingdom-works freely, relying upon his Holy Spirit-given authority, speaking and acting in ways that show the kingdom of heaven is near. How might that look for you?*

JA

Day 129

Sent to people

MATTHEW 10:11-20

'Whatever town or village you enter, search there for some worthy person and stay at their house until you leave. As you enter the home, give it your greeting. If the home is deserving, let your peace rest on it; if it is not, let your peace return to you. If anyone will not welcome you or listen to your words, leave that home or town and shake the dust off your feet. Truly I tell you, it will be more bearable for Sodom and Gomorrah on the day of judgment than for that town. I am sending you out like sheep among wolves. Therefore be as shrewd as snakes and as innocent as doves. Be on your guard; you will be handed over to the local councils and be flogged in the synagogues. On my account you will be brought before governors and kings as witnesses to them and to the Gentiles. But when they arrest you, do not worry about what to say or how to say it. At that time you will be given what to say, for it will not be you speaking, but the Spirit of your Father speaking through you.'

The disciples are being sent to people. They're going to towns and villages, taking the kingdom to people in their homes. Jesus is open about how some people won't receive them, though some will.

His comments about witnessing before ruling authorities and Gentiles makes it clear that this mission briefing is not just for the twelve on their trip. It's for all disciples, including us. Listening in, we hear Jesus briefing us as we're sent into our world.

Jesus knows all about how tough it can be. He's intentionally sending us like sheep among wolves, so we trust him as we go and are wise in what we do. We don't need to worry about what we will say, because the Father will speak through us, by the Spirit. It's all happening because of Jesus, 'on account' of him.

We go with the presence of God and the authority of Jesus. We carry with us good news of the kingdom that brings peace. Disciples sent by Jesus can change the atmosphere of lives, homes and communities as we go with his peace. This great gift rests upon those who receive it.

How can I share his peace today? How can I bless those I meet?

JA

Day 130

Sent: persecution and hope

MATTHEW 10:21–31

'Brother will betray brother to death, and a father his child; children will rebel against their parents and have them put to death. You will be hated by everyone because of me, but the one who stands firm to the end will be saved. When you are persecuted in one place, flee to another. Truly I tell you, you will not finish going through the towns of Israel before the Son of Man comes. The student is not above the teacher, nor a servant above his master. It is enough for students to be like their teachers, and servants like their masters. If the head of the house has been called Beelzebul, how much more the members of his household! So do not be afraid of them, for there is nothing concealed that will not be disclosed, or hidden that will not be made known. What I tell you in the dark, speak in the daylight; what is whispered in your ear, proclaim from the roofs. Do not be afraid of those who kill the body but cannot kill the soul. Rather, be afraid of the One who can destroy both soul and body in hell. Are not two sparrows sold for a penny? Yet not one of them will fall to the ground outside your Father's care. And even the very hairs of your head are all numbered. So don't be afraid; you are worth more than many sparrows.'

Jesus' mission briefing includes the possibility of persecution, even to the point where family loyalties are smashed. His words are for all disciples, and they fuel our prayers for those suffering now.

Persecution happens because we're inseparably linked to Jesus, as his students and servants. We're members of his household, his extended family. Persecution is time-limited, ending when 'the Son of Man comes' (v. 23). Whether Jesus means his ascension, his second coming or taking us to be with him when we die, it will end.

Jesus mentions being afraid four times, showing us that fear can find perspective. Fear needn't grow wild, overwhelming our hearts; instead, we can look up to the day when God will reveal his glorious kingdom to everyone, destroying evil and sin forever. Meanwhile, our heavenly Father cares for us in every detail of our lives.

> *What opposition or suffering are you facing on account of Jesus? How do you find strength to stay strong?*

Day 131

Sent: Jesus at the centre

MATTHEW 10:32-39

'Whoever acknowledges me before others, I will also acknowledge before my Father in heaven. But whoever disowns me before others, I will disown before my Father in heaven. Do not suppose that I have come to bring peace to the earth. I did not come to bring peace, but a sword. For I have come to turn "a man against his father, a daughter against her mother, a daughter-in-law against her mother-in-law – a man's enemies will be the members of his own household." Anyone who loves their father or mother more than me is not worthy of me; anyone who loves their son or daughter more than me is not worthy of me. Whoever does not take up their cross and follow me is not worthy of me. Whoever finds their life will lose it, and whoever loses their life for my sake will find it.'

Jesus brings us back to the reason we're sent by him at all, whatever might happen as a result. Disciples go because he is the king, who brings his loving lordship into our lives. He enables us to know God as our Father in heaven. Disciples know these realities and reflect them in our lives before others, acknowledging Jesus as our Lord. He does the same for us before his Father in heaven.

Beginning this new way of living, we step into a place where he is our Lord, with the first place in our lives. If our families, or anything else, competes with Jesus for first place then there will be a conflict of loyalties and our ability to follow him may be compromised.

As we follow him as 'sent followers', then our love for him must be front and centre of who we are and how we live. We take up a cross, like someone on the way to crucifixion, giving up our right to direct our lives, following Jesus who took that same path and walks with us. We follow in his steps and paradoxically, as we lose our life, we find real life with him.

These are challenging words. How do they impact you as you read? What does it mean for you to take up your cross and follow Jesus? Only a deep appreciation of what Jesus has done for us can motivate us to place him at the centre of our lives.

JA

Day 132

Sent: privilege and rewards

MATTHEW 10:40–11:1

> 'Anyone who welcomes you welcomes me, and anyone who welcomes me welcomes the one who sent me. Whoever welcomes a prophet as a prophet will receive a prophet's reward, and whoever welcomes a righteous person as a righteous person will receive a righteous person's reward. And if anyone gives even a cup of cold water to one of these little ones who is my disciple, truly I tell you, that person will certainly not lose their reward. After Jesus had finished instructing his twelve disciples, he went on from there to teach and preach in the towns of Galilee.

The scope of Jesus' mission briefing has been wide, touching on the lives of Jesus-followers far beyond the towns and villages the twelve will soon visit. What they've learned will stay with them for years to come as they find themselves in the situations Jesus has prepared them for.

It will soon be time for them to go, so Jesus leaves them with a key truth to take with them. They are part of something bigger than they could have imagined. As they go, sent by Jesus, somehow he is with them. And not just in a personal, reassuring way, but there for others. Those in the villages who receive the disciples are receiving Jesus, and as they are receiving Jesus, they're receiving God.

Sent disciples carry the presence of God with them. The kingdom really is coming near as ordinary, everyday, flawed disciples show up. These sent people go as givers, bringing God's blessing to those who will receive them. They're coming with good news; rewards are on offer!

Traditionally you were rewarded in receiving a prophet or righteous person by what they were able to share with you by their great talk or righteous goodness. With the disciples there's nothing like that. Just to let them in and give them a cup of water is enough to bring a reward. They're not special, but they are disciples of Jesus bringing the kingdom close. Who wouldn't want to be sent by Jesus? As you go, remember who you are and who you represent.

> Lord, I pray for joy in knowing that the kingdom of the living God comes near to people when I show up as a sent disciple. Open my eyes to any opportunity to bring something from you to someone who will receive it today.

JA

Day 133

The death of John the Baptist

MATTHEW 14:1–12 (MARK 6:14–29; LUKE 9:7–9)

At that time Herod the tetrarch heard the reports about Jesus, and he said to his attendants, 'This is John the Baptist; he has risen from the dead! That is why miraculous powers are at work in him.' Now Herod had arrested John and bound him and put him in prison because of Herodias, his brother Philip's wife, for John had been saying to him: 'It is not lawful for you to have her.' Herod wanted to kill John, but he was afraid of the people, because they considered John a prophet. On Herod's birthday the daughter of Herodias danced for the guests and pleased Herod so much that he promised with an oath to give her whatever she asked. Prompted by her mother, she said, 'Give me here on a dish the head of John the Baptist.' The king was distressed, but because of his oaths and his dinner guests, he ordered that her request be granted and had John beheaded in the prison. His head was brought in on a dish and given to the girl, who carried it to her mother. John's disciples came and took his body and buried it. Then they went and told Jesus.

The disciples' mission activity adds to Jesus' fame. Herod, the local Roman puppet-ruler of Galilee, finds out and wonders whether Jesus is John come back from the dead. There is an echo here (more explicit in the other gospels) of Jesus' mission briefing warning them that following him could be dangerous and costly.

It was for John. He fearlessly spoke out about sin and God's holiness, telling everyone to be ready to meet the soon-coming Messiah. Clearly, he was more than willing to speak truth to power, and ended up incarcerated in Herod's jail.

The account of John's end is tragic and awful to read. It seems so pointless; a weak, drunken despot, lusting with his friends after his teenage 'stepdaughter', revelling in his power to promise anything. This leads to the greatest man who ever lived (according to Jesus), losing his life so terribly.

How do we live with this kind of pointless tragedy? What can I do when I just about believe God is sovereign and good in my head, but it's hard to find in my heart?

> *All I can do is what John's disciples did. Go to Jesus and tell him about it.*

JA

Day 134

Healing at Bethesda (1)

JOHN 5:1-9

Jerusalem
Some time later, Jesus went up to Jerusalem for one of the Jewish festivals. Now there is in Jerusalem near the Sheep Gate a pool, which in Aramaic is called Bethesda and which is surrounded by five covered colonnades. Here a great number of disabled people used to lie – the blind, the lame, the paralysed. One who was there had been an invalid for thirty-eight years. When Jesus saw him lying there and learned that he had been in this condition for a long time, he asked him, 'Do you want to get well?' 'Sir,' the invalid replied, 'I have no one to help me into the pool when the water is stirred. While I am trying to get in, someone else goes down ahead of me.' Then Jesus said to him, 'Get up! Pick up your mat and walk.' At once the man was cured; he picked up his mat and walked.

Jesus is in Jerusalem for one of the Jewish religious festivals, as required by the law of Moses. John takes us with Jesus on these festival visits, as the coming clash with the Jewish religious elite develops.

The pool of Bethesda was a magnet for people in need of healing. There was a strong belief that when its waters started bubbling, there was healing for the person who could get into the pool. Jesus picks his way through the crowd of people languishing around the pool, stopping with one man for a chat. In conversation he learns that the man had been disabled for 38 years and had been getting himself along to the pool with his limited mobility for decades.

Jesus asks the man if he wants to be made well. He answers, 'I can't because of my mobility issue.' At that point he's certain that healing is only possible by getting into the water when it is stirred, which is impossible because he's not mobile enough to make it. It's a vicious circle; his problem is preventing him from getting to the answer. Jesus breaks the circle with a powerful word; the man gets up and walks.

> *Are you trapped in a vicious circle, where you struggle to find a way forward, but can't because you have decided where the answer lies and can't get there? Hear Jesus' question: 'Do you want to be...?' Ask him for his way of dealing with the difficulty.*

JA

The second year: the year of popularity

Day 135

Healing at Bethesda (2)

JOHN 5:9-15

Jerusalem
The day on which this took place was a Sabbath, and so the Jewish leaders said to the man who had been healed, 'It is the Sabbath; the law forbids you to carry your mat.' But he replied, 'The man who made me well said to me, "Pick up your mat and walk."' So they asked him, 'Who is this fellow who told you to pick it up and walk?' The man who was healed had no idea who it was, for Jesus had slipped away into the crowd that was there. Later Jesus found him at the temple and said to him, 'See, you are well again. Stop sinning or something worse may happen to you.' The man went away and told the Jewish leaders that it was Jesus who had made him well.

Keeping the sabbath was very important to the Jewish religious elite at this time. It was a sure way of knowing if people were honouring God because you could see what they did and how well they kept to the rules. Because it happened each week, out in public, you could easily check.

Some of these religious leaders come across the man Jesus healed, walking along carrying his mat. They're not bothered about the miracle, but they are outraged that the man is carrying his mat on the sabbath. He responds to their challenge by 'blaming' the one who made him well, which in their view is even worse, because someone else has ordered him to break the sabbath, leading him astray.

The ex-disabled man doesn't know who Jesus is and can't tell them who it was. He was simply a stranger. This all changes when Jesus finds him in the temple, somewhere he'd not been for a lifetime because of his disability. Jesus suggests that the man, like the religious leaders, was also missing the main point. He encourages him not to leave it at being healed, but to go on to turn from sin, to care as much for his relationship with God as he does about his physical healing.

> *Lord, I pray that I won't miss the point about what you do for me and others. Thank you that when I do, you come and find me to bring me closer to you. Show me where I need healing, and also where I need to stop sinning.*

JA

Day 136

The Son and the Father

JOHN 5:16-23

Jerusalem
So, because Jesus was doing these things on the Sabbath, the Jewish leaders began to persecute him. In his defence Jesus said to them, 'My Father is always at his work to this very day, and I too am working.' For this reason they tried all the more to kill him; not only was he breaking the Sabbath, but he was even calling God his own Father, making himself equal with God. Jesus gave them this answer: 'Very truly I tell you, the Son can do nothing by himself; he can do only what he sees his Father doing, because whatever the Father does the Son also does. For the Father loves the Son and shows him all he does. Yes, and he will show him even greater works than these, so that you will be amazed. For just as the Father raises the dead and gives them life, even so the Son gives life to whom he is pleased to give it. Moreover, the Father judges no one, but has entrusted all judgment to the Son, that all may honour the Son just as they honour the Father. Whoever does not honour the Son does not honour the Father, who sent him.'

Continuing his stay in Jerusalem, Jesus' sabbath activity leads to pressure from the religious leaders. He tells them that his sabbath-healing follows God's work, which never stops. He calls God 'my Father', which enrages them. In talking this way about God and saying he is working like God, they hear him claiming to be equal with God, which is blasphemy.

Jesus answers this with a description of his relationship with his Father, calling himself the Son. He is not another God, but working together with the Father, following the Father in his work. They're together in love; the Father loves the Son and shows him all he does, they delight to honour one another. They're together in an eternal process of revealing amazing works, and they're giving life together. The Father entrusts final judgement to the Son. His will be the last word.

> Meditate on this: 'the Son can do nothing by himself; he can only do what he sees the Father doing' (v. 19). Even Jesus lived in dependency upon God, sensing what the Father was doing, and then responding. How might that become a pattern for your life with God?

JA

Day 137

Jesus: the word of life

JOHN 5:24–30

Jerusalem

'Very truly I tell you, whoever hears my word and believes him who sent me has eternal life and will not be judged but has crossed over from death to life. Very truly I tell you, a time is coming and has now come when the dead will hear the voice of the Son of God and those who hear will live. For as the Father has life in himself, so he has granted the Son also to have life in himself. And he has given him authority to judge because he is the Son of Man. Do not be amazed at this, for a time is coming when all who are in their graves will hear his voice and come out – those who have done what is good will rise to live, and those who have done what is evil will rise to be condemned. By myself I can do nothing; I judge only as I hear, and my judgment is just, for I seek not to please myself but him who sent me.'

Jesus defends himself to hostile religious leaders who want to kill him. Yet he's offering them the opportunity to cross from death to life, to not be judged on the day when the whole process is entrusted to Jesus, but instead receive eternal life beginning now. This is for anyone who takes his words seriously and trusts themselves to the God who sent him. It's a remarkable offer.

Jesus calls himself 'the Son'. Now he makes it plainer; he means the 'Son of God'. He reminds them that he is also the Son of Man, a figure in the Old Testament prophecy of Daniel who approaches God and is given authority to reign over everything forever (Daniel 7:13). The meaning was usually hidden, but with the talk about authority and judgement, the religious leaders could not miss it. Jesus says the dead will hear his voice at the final resurrection.

Jesus depends upon the Father in everything, only wanting to please him. This was the key to his life, and it is the key to the life of discipleship.

> Follow yesterday's meditation by considering this: 'By myself I can do nothing… I seek not to please myself but him who sent me' (v. 30). How does it add to your understanding of how we are to live our life in God?

JA

Day 138

The testimony about Jesus

JOHN 5:31–40

Jerusalem
'If I testify about myself, my testimony is not true. There is another who testifies in my favour, and I know that his testimony about me is true. You have sent to John and he has testified to the truth. Not that I accept human testimony; but I mention it that you may be saved. John was a lamp that burned and gave light, and you chose for a time to enjoy his light. I have testimony weightier than that of John. For the works that the Father has given me to finish – the very works that I am doing – testify that the Father has sent me. And the Father who sent me has himself testified concerning me. You have never heard his voice nor seen his form, nor does his word dwell in you, for you do not believe the one he sent. You study the Scriptures diligently because you think that in them you have eternal life. These are the very Scriptures that testify about me, yet you refuse to come to me to have life.'

Jesus shows his critics such grace, being willing to discount his own testimony because of their scepticism. As the Son, he doesn't need authentication from human beings but is happy to accept it, so that his enemies 'may be saved' even though there is murder in their hearts.

Jesus presents the testimony of witnesses to back up his claims to be the Son. John the Baptist preached about the coming Messiah, and thousands accepted his word. The religious leaders went to hear him and chose to accept what John said at first. Then there are his 'works', the miracles Jesus did publicly; they too are evidence of his unique status. They were then and still are today.

There is also the testimony of God speaking. Jesus is talking about the Old Testament scriptures that these leaders loved so much. They believed that they could find eternal life by careful study, but will not believe in the one God is testifying about in the scriptures, that is, Jesus. He wants them to come to him for the life he offers, but they refuse.

| 'John was a lamp that burned and gave light' (v. 35). How can your life, words and actions bear testimony to Jesus? People may choose not to believe, but we can still shine brightly.

JA

The second year: the year of popularity

Day 139

Refusal to believe

JOHN 5:41–47

Jerusalem
'I do not accept glory from human beings, but I know you. I know that you do not have the love of God in your hearts. I have come in my Father's name, and you do not accept me; but if someone else comes in his own name, you will accept him. How can you believe since you accept glory from one another but do not seek the glory that comes from the only God? But do not think I will accuse you before the Father. Your accuser is Moses, on whom your hopes are set. If you believed Moses, you would believe me, for he wrote about me. But since you do not believe what he wrote, how are you going to believe what I say?'

Why is it that some people refuse to believe? It's a heart problem. Jesus shows them that the one thing God required of his people – to love him with all their hearts – is missing. In the hearts of these religious leaders, God's love has been displaced by something that mattered more to them, the glory they can receive from other people.

This has left them unwilling and unable to see God's glory, in the person of Jesus, standing in front of them in God's name. Yet they're more than willing to accept just about anyone else who can impress them with their own smart ideas, capabilities or promises.

Jesus would have every right to condemn them to judgement but will not do so – still he wants them to be saved. He points them to Moses, their favourite Old Testament hero, whose writings they loved to study. It seems to me that Jesus is telling them to look again at Moses, because there they might find a way to believe in him. I wonder if any of them went and did that? We do know that some of this group became Jesus' followers later, though many continued in their unbelief.

> *Meditate on this: 'You do not have the love of God in your hearts' (v. 42). Pray for anyone you know who seems to be refusing to believe. Pray that they may be open to look again at what they think they know and become open-hearted to the love of God in Jesus. Pray that they may see this in what you do and say as you live alongside them.*

JA

the third year:
the year of opposition

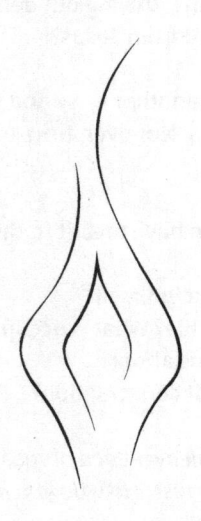

JENNY BROWN

Day 140

The twelve return

MARK 6:30-32 (*LUKE 9:10-11*)

Galilee
The apostles gathered round Jesus and reported to him all they had done and taught. Then, because so many people were coming and going that they did not even have a chance to eat, he said to them, 'Come with me by yourselves to a quiet place and get some rest.' So they went away by themselves in a boat to a solitary place.

You might like to refer to page 12 as we use our imagination to engage with today's passage.

The disciples had been commissioned by Jesus, given his authority and sent out in pairs to act in his name. It was their first ministry experience without Jesus alongside them. Imagine the scene as the apostles returned to Jesus from their village ministry trips. After all they had done – teaching, healing, driving out demons – how do you think they felt? What do you sense they might want from Jesus?

However, they get caught up into another busy and demanding setting, where people are coming and going to see Jesus. Not even time to eat! How might they have felt at this point in the story?

What, then, would Jesus' invitation have meant to them?

Re-read the passage thinking about yourself:
- What has been going on in your life? What is occupying your time, your energy? What is on your mind to talk with Jesus about?
- What is getting in the way of that conversation?

Hear Jesus' invitation to you. Mull over each phrase: 'Come with me... by yourselves... to a quiet place... and get some rest.' How do you feel as you hear his invitation? How do you want to respond?

JB

Day 141

Feeding the 5,000

MATTHEW 14:13-21 (MARK 6:33-44; LUKE 9:12-17; JOHN 6:1-14)

Galilee
When Jesus heard what had happened, he withdrew by boat privately to a solitary place. Hearing of this, the crowds followed him on foot from the towns. When Jesus landed and saw a large crowd, he had compassion on them and healed those who were ill. As evening approached, the disciples came to him and said, 'This is a remote place, and it's already getting late. Send the crowds away, so that they can go to the villages and buy themselves some food.' Jesus replied, 'They do not need to go away. You give them something to eat.' 'We have here only five loaves of bread and two fish,' they answered. 'Bring them here to me,' he said. And he told the people to sit down on the grass. Taking the five loaves and the two fish and looking up to heaven, he gave thanks and broke the loaves. Then he gave them to the disciples, and the disciples gave them to the people. They all ate and were satisfied, and the disciples picked up twelve basketfuls of broken pieces that were left over. The number of those who ate was about five thousand men, besides women and children.

Perhaps you can identify with that feeling of being overwhelmed by the needs of others. You know you can't do enough to help: you just don't have the resources. Out of that concern, your instinct is to push people away to find their needs met elsewhere.

Jesus, however, doesn't see your inadequacy as you do. He invites you to identify what you *do* have and give it to him.

It's costly as you surrender it, placing it in his hands. But as you do, he appreciates your gift, giving thanks to the Father for it. Now he breaks it – making it ready to be used for his purposes.

As he hands it back to you, it is now both yours and his. And he commissions you to partner with him in compassion for those in need.

Instead of being pushed away, they are invited to sit, eat and be satisfied. What you considered inadequate is used by God to bring abundant blessing.

> What needs of others, near or far, are concerning you? Ask the Lord to help you identify what you might give to him. Where is he drawing you further into partnership with himself?

Day 142

Jesus walks on water

MATTHEW 14:22-33 (MARK 6:45-52; JOHN 6:15-21)

Lake of Galilee
Immediately Jesus made the disciples get into the boat and go on ahead of him to the other side, while he dismissed the crowd. After he had dismissed them, he went up on a mountainside by himself to pray. Later that night, he was there alone, and the boat was already a considerable distance from land, buffeted by the waves because the wind was against it. Shortly before dawn Jesus went out to them, walking on the lake. When the disciples saw him walking on the lake, they were terrified. 'It's a ghost,' they said, and cried out in fear. But Jesus immediately said to them: 'Take courage! It is I. Don't be afraid.' 'Lord, if it's you,' Peter replied, 'tell me to come to you on the water.' 'Come,' he said. Then Peter got down out of the boat, walked on the water and came towards Jesus. But when he saw the wind, he was afraid and, beginning to sink, cried out, 'Lord, save me!' Immediately Jesus reached out his hand and caught him. 'You of little faith,' he said, 'why did you doubt?' And when they climbed into the boat, the wind died down. Then those who were in the boat worshipped him, saying, 'Truly you are the Son of God.'

Just like Peter, our experience of the Christian life is that faith mingles with doubt. We see what Jesus is doing and want to join in, but as we get involved our attention is drawn to the challenges, and our focus on Jesus himself drops. We begin to doubt and falter.

What should we do? Rather than give up, or condemn ourselves, we fix our gaze on Jesus again, hear his words of encouragement and keep walking with him. Even if it seems a bit crazy at times!

> *Lord, amid the buffeting of life, help me to recognise your presence, not as an added threat, but as my source of courage; help me to look not at the surrounding storm, but at you; and help me to discern your invitation, to take steps of faith to do with you what seems impossible to me. I worship you, my Saviour and my God.*

JB

Day 143

Many are healed

MATTHEW 14:34–36 (MARK 6:53–56; JOHN 6:22–27)

Gennesaret, western side of the Sea of Galilee
When they had crossed over, they landed at Gennesaret. And when the men of that place recognised Jesus, they sent word to all the surrounding country. People brought all who were ill to him and begged him to let those who were ill just touch the edge of his cloak, and all who touched it were healed.

I used to live and work in central London, and almost every day I walked past Broadcasting House, home of the BBC. While my colleagues often came into the office excitedly reporting which celebrity they had seen that morning, I never did. I never recognised anyone of note! Perhaps that was because I didn't read the right magazines or register who played in the latest films. Or perhaps I'm just not very observant!

The men of Gennesaret recognised Jesus. He was becoming a bit of a celebrity. News about his miracles of feeding and healing were spreading, and as it did more crowds were drawn in.

Was it just his face they recognised, or were they beginning to recognise him as the one spoken of and promised through their scriptures? At the beginning of his ministry, just up the road in Nazareth, Jesus had applied Isaiah's prophecy to himself (Luke 4:16–21, quoting Isaiah 61:1–2). In response to John's question about who he was, Jesus had pointed to his preaching and healing miracles as fulfilment of the scriptures (e.g. Isaiah 35:5–6). What Jesus says and does points to who he is. Who can recognise him?

Who do we see when we look at Jesus? Is he just a historical figure? Or do we recognise him as the one who is alive and active today? Are we attentive to him, noticing his activity in us, through us and around us? Do we recognise him in the words and actions of others?

> *Look out for him today. Be observant. See if you can recognise him.*

Day 144

Jesus, the bread of life

JOHN 6:28–35

The synagogue in Capernaum
Then they asked him, 'What must we do to do the works God requires?' Jesus answered, 'The work of God is this: to believe in the one he has sent.' So they asked him, 'What sign then will you give that we may see it and believe you? What will you do? Our ancestors ate the manna in the wilderness; as it is written: "He gave them bread from heaven to eat."' Jesus said to them, 'Very truly I tell you, it is not Moses who has given you the bread from heaven, but it is my Father who gives you the true bread from heaven. For the bread of God is the bread that comes down from heaven and gives life to the world.' 'Sir,' they said, 'always give us this bread.' Then Jesus declared, 'I am the bread of life. Whoever comes to me will never go hungry, and whoever believes in me will never be thirsty.'

At the smell of fresh bread, something inside of me goes 'Mmm'. It invokes a sense of welcome, warmth and satisfaction. It is inviting. It draws me in. No wonder supermarkets pipe the bakery air to the front door: it kindles desire!

The crowd had not only smelled but also tasted the bread. They'd experienced the miraculous feeding. They came looking for Jesus, wanting more. Like us, perhaps, their focus was on what they should *do*. Jesus' reply, however, was about *who* to *trust*, what to *desire*.

'I am the bread of life.' Echoing the 'I am' of God's self-revelation to Moses, Jesus presents himself as both the ultimate reality and the one who sustains and nourishes life, who satisfies. He is the one to hunger for. As David Ford says: 'The reality of Jesus and what he gives is to be desired above all.'[20]

> *Reflect on Jesus as the bread of your life. Where have you 'tasted' Jesus as you've trusted him in your life? How does that experience kindle your desire for more of him? What does it mean for you to desire him above all?*

JB

Day 145

The Father's will

JOHN 6:35-40

The synagogue in Capernaum
Then Jesus declared, 'I am the bread of life. Whoever comes to me will never go hungry, and whoever believes in me will never be thirsty. But as I told you, you have seen me and still you do not believe. All those the Father gives me will come to me, and whoever comes to me I will never drive away. For I have come down from heaven not to do my will but to do the will of him who sent me. And this is the will of him who sent me, that I shall lose none of all those he has given me, but raise them up at the last day. For my Father's will is that everyone who looks to the Son and believes in him shall have eternal life, and I will raise them up at the last day.'

Yesterday we thought about our desire for Jesus. Today we begin to realise that he desires us! And his desire is in line with the Father's desire.

We may have many questions about what God's will is for our life, but here is a clarity that undergirds everything else. His desire is that we come to the Son, and, trusting in him, begin to enjoy his life lived in us, being held safe by him until resurrection day. The Father has sent the Son for this purpose. David Ford comments: 'Jesus' ministry is fundamentally one of attraction, drawing people to himself.'[21]

There is an openness to the invitation of Jesus: notice the words of inclusion.

There is security in the acceptance of that invitation: notice the words of promise.

Rather than get anxious about what we do not know, we do well to focus on what God has made clear.

> *Spend some time hearing these words as God's desire for you. How do you want to respond to him?*

Day 146

Grumbling

JOHN 6:41–51

The synagogue in Capernaum
At this the Jews there began to grumble about him because he said, 'I am the bread that came down from heaven.' They said, 'Is this not Jesus, the son of Joseph, whose father and mother we know? How can he now say, "I came down from heaven"?' 'Stop grumbling among yourselves,' Jesus answered. 'No one can come to me unless the Father who sent me draws them, and I will raise them up at the last day. It is written in the Prophets: "They will all be taught by God." Everyone who has heard the Father and learned from him comes to me. No one has seen the Father except the one who is from God; only he has seen the Father. Very truly I tell you, the one who believes has eternal life. I am the bread of life. Your ancestors ate the manna in the wilderness, yet they died. But here is the bread that comes down from heaven, which anyone may eat and not die. I am the living bread that came down from heaven. Whoever eats this bread will live for ever. This bread is my flesh, which I will give for the life of the world.'

Grumbling can be rooted in wrong expectations. The Jews grumbled because they struggled to match the Jesus they thought they knew with the Jesus being revealed to them. Their image of him held them back from receiving all he had for them. The gift he offered far surpassed any expectations they had of what this local boy could give them.

When my image of Jesus is limited, my expectations of his impact in my life are far too small. Then life feels like a grind, and I start to grumble. But Jesus is 'life itself' from heaven, and his offer of 'eternal life' is not just existence beyond death. As Tom Wright explains, it is 'sharing the inner life of Jesus'.[22] This is far more exciting and transformative than I have yet experienced!

Over the last weeks or months, where has your image of Jesus been challenged? How is the Jesus being revealed to you different to the one you thought you knew? How does this impact your expectations?

> Lord Jesus, expand my view of you, and enable me to participate more fully in the abundant life you wish to share with me.

JB

Day 147

Eat my flesh, drink my blood

JOHN 6:52-59

The synagogue in Capernaum
Then the Jews began to argue sharply among themselves, 'How can this man give us his flesh to eat?' Jesus said to them, 'Very truly I tell you, unless you eat the flesh of the Son of Man and drink his blood, you have no life in you. Whoever eats my flesh and drinks my blood has eternal life, and I will raise them up at the last day. For my flesh is real food and my blood is real drink. Whoever eats my flesh and drinks my blood remains in me, and I in them. Just as the living Father sent me and I live because of the Father, so the one who feeds on me will live because of me. This is the bread that came down from heaven. Your ancestors ate manna and died, but whoever feeds on this bread will live for ever.' He said this while teaching in the synagogue in Capernaum.

Well, this is a strange invitation: 'Eat my flesh, drink my blood'! The Jews listening were not the last ones to argue over these words as they tried to understand, but it is a very powerful image if we think about it.

No matter how good it looks on the plate, food can only nourish and sustain us if we eat it. Then, when we take it into our body, the very molecules of the food become incorporated into our own bodies. What was on the plate becomes our bones, muscles, blood cells, without which we would not be alive.

So, in a similar way, Jesus invites us not just to admire him, but to 'eat' him, to allow his life to become incorporated with our life as his Spirit indwells us. As Mags Duggan puts it, he is not offering just 'an improved, reformed, upgraded version of our present lives, but a dynamically transformed life'. Jesus is 'bursting with the creative, nurturing, dynamic, compassionate, loving life of God'.[23] To have such life living within us and through us is what it is to *truly* live.

What word would you choose to describe the change you'd like the life of Jesus to bring to your life? You may want to invite Jesus to live his life in you and through you, and to bring that transformation.

| *When you eat today, you might use it as a reminder of your prayer.*

Day 148

A hard teaching

JOHN 6:60-65

Capernaum
On hearing it, many of his disciples said, 'This is a hard teaching. Who can accept it?' Aware that his disciples were grumbling about this, Jesus said to them, 'Does this offend you? Then what if you see the Son of Man ascend to where he was before! The Spirit gives life; the flesh counts for nothing. The words I have spoken to you – they are full of the Spirit and life. Yet there are some of you who do not believe.' For Jesus had known from the beginning which of them did not believe and who would betray him. He went on to say, 'This is why I told you that no one can come to me unless the Father has enabled them.'

As we read the gospels, perhaps, if we're honest, we too sometimes find Jesus' words hard to accept.

For the disciples in Capernaum, what Jesus had been saying required them to radically rethink who he was and what he was doing. The one they knew as Mary and Joseph's son was claiming to be sent from God and be the source of life. That was shocking, hard to accept! But they needed to understand that Jesus is as 'at home' in heaven as he is on earth. If he is only of earthly flesh, his claims and teachings would be irrelevant and powerless, but because his human body was indwelt by the very Spirit of God, his words have the power to bring life to those who receive them.

Like those disciples before us, sometimes we feel shocked, even offended, by what Jesus said or did. Our familiar image of him gets disturbed when we read some gospel passages. Will we shy away from them, afraid of losing the Jesus we have become accustomed to? Or will we stay in them with him, even when we initially feel uncomfortable, in order to get to know him better? While we cannot grasp who he *fully* is, we can seek to know him as he *truly* is.

Paul wrote, 'I consider everything a loss because of the surpassing worth of knowing Christ Jesus my Lord... I want to know Christ' (Philippians 3:8, 10). We can join in his prayer, 'asking that the God of our Lord Jesus Christ, the glorious Father, may give you the Spirit of wisdom and revelation, so that you may know him better' (Ephesians 1:17).

JB

Day 149

Many turn back

JOHN 6:66–71

Galilee
From this time many of his disciples turned back and no longer followed him. 'You do not want to leave too, do you?' Jesus asked the Twelve. Simon Peter answered him, 'Lord, to whom shall we go? You have the words of eternal life. We have come to believe and to know that you are the Holy One of God.' Then Jesus replied, 'Have I not chosen you, the Twelve? Yet one of you is a devil!' (He meant Judas, the son of Simon Iscariot, who, though one of the Twelve, was later to betray him.)

Have you ever felt like giving up on being a follower of Jesus? I've had my moments. Perhaps most of us have. I expect our reasons are many and varied.

This was a turning point in Jesus' ministry. Up until then, crowds had followed him. Now, many decided to turn back. It seems his teaching was too hard for them to take. There were too many implications. Jesus gave no room for mere admiration or theoretical interest in his teaching. Following him is not about consenting to a new concept. It's much bigger than that. It has implications for our whole being and our whole life. His 'words of eternal life' are not abstract ideas, but an invitation to relationship. Life hinges on receiving the person of Jesus, not just his teachings.

We have a great advantage over those early disciples: we know the end of the story and have the whole Bible as explanation of it. What would you want to say to those who had followed Jesus, but were now considering turning away from him?

And what about yourself? If you've had times of turning back, what were your reasons? (Maybe you're hovering at such a moment now.) What might Peter want to say to you? And Jesus, what is he saying to you?

> *'Have I not chosen you?' Yes, we choose to follow Jesus, but undergirding that choice of ours is his choice of us. Rest secure in his choice, and let that shape your choice.*

JB

Day 150

Religion that breaks the command of God

MATTHEW 15:1–9 (MARK 7:1-13)

Then some Pharisees and teachers of the law came to Jesus from Jerusalem and asked, 'Why do your disciples break the tradition of the elders? They don't wash their hands before they eat!' Jesus replied, 'And why do you break the command of God for the sake of your tradition? For God said, "Honour your father and mother" and "Anyone who curses their father or mother is to be put to death." But you say that if anyone declares that what might have been used to help their father or mother is "devoted to God," they are not to "honour their father or mother" with it. Thus you nullify the word of God for the sake of your tradition. You hypocrites! Isaiah was right when he prophesied about you: "These people honour me with their lips, but their hearts are far from me. They worship me in vain; their teachings are merely human rules."'

What appears to be careful, faithful obedience to God might actually be far from that. Our public religious practices may look impeccable, but if they result in the neglect of our ordinary human responsibilities, God is not honoured.

These Pharisees had identified a way for people to divert money into the temple coffers that might have been used to provide for their parents. It made the giver look good, when actually they were neglecting their core duties, breaking the fifth commandment. Their worship was hollow, lacking in integrity. They had bought into outward religion, but lost their heart for God and his priorities.

The apostle James has a surprising, even shocking, definition of 'religion that is pure and undefiled' (James 1:27, NRSV). It has more to do with care of the vulnerable than public displays of either singing or giving. As our hearts are drawn close to God, they begin to pick up his heartbeat. Gradually our priorities become reshaped by his, and our worship finds a fresh expression. So, could worshipping God involve visiting an elderly parent, rather than attending a church service? Or being at home with a struggling teenager, rather than going to a prayer meeting? Or giving money to a needy neighbour, rather than to the church collection?

> *Lord, draw my heart to you. Help me to turn away from lip-service religion to hear your heart and take up your priorities. How are you calling me to worship you today?*

JB

Day 151

What makes a person unclean?

MATTHEW 15:10–20 (*MARK 7:14–23*)

Jesus called the crowd to him and said, 'Listen and understand. What goes into someone's mouth does not defile them, but what comes out of their mouth, that is what defiles them.' Then the disciples came to him and asked, 'Do you know that the Pharisees were offended when they heard this?' He replied, 'Every plant that my heavenly Father has not planted will be pulled up by the roots. Leave them; they are blind guides. If the blind lead the blind, both will fall into a pit.' Peter said, 'Explain the parable to us.' 'Are you still so dull?' Jesus asked them. 'Don't you see that whatever enters the mouth goes into the stomach and then out of the body? But the things that come out of a person's mouth come from the heart, and these defile them. For out of the heart come evil thoughts – murder, adultery, sexual immorality, theft, false testimony, slander. These are what defile a person; but eating with unwashed hands does not defile them.'

The Covid pandemic made hand-washing a topic of public interest because, done properly, it gives some protection against a serious viral threat. However, if we are already infected with the virus, no amount of hand-washing, mask-wearing or social distancing will help us.

For the Jews of Jesus' day, the purity and dietary laws were also about protection from an external threat. The infiltration of pagan practices and ideas, which led them away from the Lord, had been a persistent danger throughout their history. These laws emphasised and maintained Jewish identity, separate from the Gentile nations around them. However, they could do nothing about the condition of the human heart.

What defiles us is not external, but internal: our own hearts are the source of the problem. No amount of trying harder will change that. Only God can clean us on the inside. Thankfully, in Christ, he has promised just that: 'If we confess our sins, he is faithful and just and will forgive us our sins and purify us from all unrighteousness' (1 John 1:9).

> *Reflect on each of the following phrases and ask the Lord to help you take it in for yourself. He is faithful – he keeps this promise; and he is just – he will not demand a second payment after Christ's on the cross. He promises both forgiveness and cleansing, transformation of our hearts.*

JB

Day 152

The Canaanite woman

MATTHEW 15:21-28 (MARK 7:24-30)

Region of Tyre and Sidon
Leaving that place, Jesus withdrew to the region of Tyre and Sidon. A Canaanite woman from that vicinity came to him, crying out, 'Lord, Son of David, have mercy on me! My daughter is demon-possessed and suffering terribly.' Jesus did not answer a word. So his disciples came to him and urged him, 'Send her away, for she keeps crying out after us.' He answered, 'I was sent only to the lost sheep of Israel.' The woman came and knelt before him. 'Lord, help me!' she said. He replied, 'It is not right to take the children's bread and toss it to the dogs.' 'Yes it is, Lord,' she said. 'Even the dogs eat the crumbs that fall from their master's table.' Then Jesus said to her, 'Woman, you have great faith! Your request is granted.' And her daughter was healed at that moment.

At a time of family suffering, she cried out to the Lord for help. He did not answer. No response. Nothing. Her heartbreaking pleas met with nothing but silence. Have you experienced that? You've poured your heart out to God and... nothing.

This passage raises so many questions! Questions about Jesus, about faith, about prayer, about outsiders and insiders. Jesus had entered Gentile territory. This Canaanite woman with demonic issues in her family was not just an irritation to those Jewish disciples, she would have been regarded by them as an outsider, as unclean. Yet, she calls Jesus 'Lord' and asks for his mercy. Why, then, was he initially unresponsive to her?

Perhaps it is her response to him we are encouraged to look at. Far from putting her off, his silence seems to have stimulated her perseverance. Something about Jesus beckoned her. She drew near. She knelt before him. When he addressed her, with what seems a slight resistance, her faith came through all the stronger. Far from putting her down, he lifted her up. She is one of only two people (both Gentiles!) who we are told Jesus commended for their faith (see also Luke 7:9). I wonder what the disciples made of that?

> *What effect does God's apparent silence have on our faith? Do we withdraw and give up, or do we hold on, trusting that there is more? Might this actually be his invitation to us?*

JB

Day 153

Jesus heals many

MATTHEW 15:29–31 (MARK 7:31)

The Decapolis, eastern side of the Sea of Galilee
Jesus left there and went along the Sea of Galilee. Then he went up on a mountainside and sat down. Great crowds came to him, bringing the lame, the blind, the crippled, the mute and many others, and laid them at his feet; and he healed them. The people were amazed when they saw the mute speaking, the crippled made well, the lame walking and the blind seeing. And they praised the God of Israel.

There may be times when we feel the abundant life Jesus offers is for others, but not for us. We are convinced that there is something about us which excludes us. Maybe it's a sense of not being worthy enough, or spiritual enough, not having the right background, belonging to the right group or doing the right practices.

Those streaming up the hillside to see Jesus could have felt similar. Jesus was still in Gentile territory, on the eastern side of the Sea of Galilee (Mark 7:31), so this crowd was predominantly non-Jews, people of other nations and religious beliefs. No doubt they had heard about the Jews healed by Jesus on the other side of the lake (Matthew 14:34–36; Day 143). I wonder if they hesitated to set off for the climb. Would Jesus, a Jew, pay Gentiles any attention? Wouldn't he be reluctant to bless outsiders?

But up there on the mountain they were left in no doubt! Matthew paints a beautiful sketch of prophecy being fulfilled. The nations stream to God's anointed king on his mountain throne. The kingdom proclaimed and demonstrated as the blind, lame and mute are healed (see Isaiah 35:5–6; 52:7–10). Like the Canaanite woman in yesterday's passage, Gentiles were experiencing restoration and wholeness, too. (Not just crumbs, after all!)

Are there barriers you have erected in your mind that are holding you back from approaching Jesus? Know that he welcomes you warmly.

As you come to him, where do you sense your need for healing today? We all have attitudes and behaviours that limit us from receiving the full life we were created for. Bring that need, that brokenness to Jesus now, knowing that he delights to bring wholeness.

> *Praise the 'God of Israel' that you are included in his plans for restoration.*

Day 154

Healing the deaf man

MARK 7:32–37

The Decapolis, eastern side of the Sea of Galilee
There some people brought to him a man who was deaf and could hardly talk, and they begged Jesus to place his hand on him. After he took him aside, away from the crowd, Jesus put his fingers into the man's ears. Then he spat and touched the man's tongue. He looked up to heaven and with a deep sigh said to him, 'Ephphatha!' (which means 'Be opened!'). At this, the man's ears were opened, his tongue was loosed and he began to speak plainly. Jesus commanded them not to tell anyone. But the more he did so, the more they kept talking about it. People were overwhelmed with amazement. 'He has done everything well,' they said. 'He even makes the deaf hear and the mute speak.'

If yesterday you were concerned that the deaf of Isaiah 35:5–6 had somehow missed out on the fulfilment unfolding on the mountaintop, today you'll be pleased to see they are the focus of attention!

The melody of birdsong, the burble of a stream, the giggle of a child, conversation, banter, whispers, argument, laughter. Enforced silence drains the audible colour from life. It leaves a person cut off, less aware of what is going on, less able to join in. Inability to hear is a profound illustration of how deafness to the voice of God impacts our lives.

Jesus gave this man his full attention, communicating with him in very tangible ways. I wonder what the deaf man 'heard' as he felt Jesus' touch and his breath upon his face? Perhaps you're not aware of his voice, but could it be that Jesus is closer than you think, and speaking in unexpected ways?

With healing came hearing, and with hearing came speaking. No evangelism seminars needed! Even Jesus couldn't keep this man and his friends quiet! As we hear the voice of God – through the scriptures, through creation, through people and situations – how much do we relish it, enjoy it? And how often do we share it?

> Lord, open my ears, that I might hear you speak to me today; then, open my mouth, that others might hear me speak of you.

Day 155

Feeding the 4,000

MATTHEW 15:32–39

The Decapolis, eastern side of the Sea of Galilee
Jesus called his disciples to him and said, 'I have compassion for these people; they have already been with me three days and have nothing to eat. I do not want to send them away hungry, or they may collapse on the way.' His disciples answered, 'Where could we get enough bread in this remote place to feed such a crowd?' 'How many loaves do you have?' Jesus asked. 'Seven,' they replied, 'and a few small fish.' He told the crowd to sit down on the ground. Then he took the seven loaves and the fish, and when he had given thanks, he broke them and gave them to the disciples, and they in turn to the people. They all ate and were satisfied. Afterwards the disciples picked up seven basketfuls of broken pieces that were left over. The number of those who ate was four thousand men, besides women and children. After Jesus had sent the crowd away, he got into the boat and went to the vicinity of Magadan.

Rather like walking around an unfamiliar city, life sometimes seems to include a certain amount of going round in circles. 'This is familiar, haven't I been here before?' It can cause me to despair of ever learning the lesson God wants to teach me!

Perhaps the disciples had that sense of déjà vu when faced with thousands of hungry people miles from anywhere. Hadn't they been there before (Matthew 14:13–21; Day 141)? But, it seems they still didn't get it! Jesus, however, didn't rebuke them, but invited them again to participate with him. Patiently, step-by-step, he took them through a similar process, giving them another opportunity.

But this wasn't *exactly* the same situation. It was a different location and 'these people' who Jesus had compassion for were Gentiles. The invitation to the heavenly banquet, which this hillside picnic pointed to, is open to all. There is apparently plenty of the 'children's bread' (Matthew 15:26) for those who come to Jesus from outside Israel. The disciples may be back in a similar place, but there is a deeper lesson for them to learn this time.

> *Lord, I have so much yet to learn! Thank you for your patience with me. When it feels as though you've brought me back yet again to an old lesson, help me to be attentive to the new depth you want to take me to.*

JB

Day 156

Request for a sign

MATTHEW 16:1–4 (*MARK 8:11–13*)

> *The Pharisees and Sadducees came to Jesus and tested him by asking him to show them a sign from heaven. He replied, 'When evening comes, you say, "It will be fair weather, for the sky is red," and in the morning, "Today it will be stormy, for the sky is red and overcast." You know how to interpret the appearance of the sky, but you cannot interpret the signs of the times. A wicked and adulterous generation looks for a sign, but none will be given it except the sign of Jonah.' Jesus then left them and went away.*

If someone knocks at my door claiming to be the gas engineer to repair my boiler, it's important that I check their ID before letting them in. How much more important it is to have evidence of who Jesus is before I entrust my life to him. So, wasn't it entirely reasonable for these religious leaders to request concrete proof of identity from this travelling preacher, who was amassing a considerable following of people under their spiritual care?

Yes – but just how many more pieces of evidence did they need? Since the beginning of Jesus' ministry, he had demonstrated repeatedly who he was. Controlling the forces of nature, healing the sick, releasing the possessed, even raising the dead – each pointed to his messianic identity and the coming of the kingdom of God. Most recently, there in Galilee, the fulfilment of scriptural prophecy was clear (Isaiah 9:1–3; 35:1–6). The Pharisees and Sadducees, who studied the scriptures so thoroughly, should have been the first to grasp it. However, like the Israelites in the wilderness who repeatedly tested God (Psalm 78:18–20, 32), rejected his prophet Moses and refused to believe despite miraculous signs (Numbers 14:1–4, 11), they seemed blind to what was happening around them. Even the most conclusive sign of the coming kingdom – Jesus' resurrection (see Matthew 12:39–40) – would be missed because their minds were already made up.

For those who don't want to believe, miracles are rarely convincing. With some creativity, they can be explained away.

> *Lord, thank you for making yourself known. Help me to be open to the signs of your presence and your kingdom today, even if they challenge my preconceived ideas. (You may wish to pray for any known to you who seem to have closed their minds to the possibility of faith in Jesus.)*

JB

Day 157

Leaven

MATTHEW 16:5-12 (*MARK 8:14-21*)

Galilee
When they went across the lake, the disciples forgot to take bread. 'Be careful,' Jesus said to them. 'Be on your guard against the yeast of the Pharisees and Sadducees.' They discussed this among themselves and said, 'It is because we didn't bring any bread.' Aware of their discussion, Jesus asked, 'You of little faith, why are you talking among yourselves about having no bread? Do you still not understand? Don't you remember the five loaves for the five thousand, and how many basketfuls you gathered? Or the seven loaves for the four thousand, and how many basketfuls you gathered? How is it you don't understand that I was not talking to you about bread? But be on your guard against the yeast of the Pharisees and Sadducees.' Then they understood that he was not telling them to guard against the yeast used in bread, but against the teaching of the Pharisees and Sadducees.

From a multitude of sources – the media, the internet, colleagues, friends – many different voices, perspectives and opinions come to us every day. How discerning are we about their influence on us? Do we sift what we hear?

In warning the disciples about the influence of the Pharisees and Sadducees, Jesus' use of the metaphor of 'yeast' (or 'leaven') was powerful. Yeast is small, hardly noticeable, yet it pervades a whole batch of dough and has a very significant impact on it. The use of yeast was prohibited during Passover celebrations to remind the Israelites of their need to be ready when the moment of rescue from Egypt came (Exodus 12). The Pharisees and Sadducees' false understanding of the kingdom of God and their refusal to believe in Jesus would have a detrimental effect on any who were starting out in faith.

Like the disciples, we, too, should choose carefully who we listen to if we want to be ready for God's kingdom to grow in our lives. How alert are we to who is shaping our thinking, our values and our desires? Which voices are you vulnerable to? What is it about those ideas or values that are attractive? What, then, does it mean for you to be 'on your guard' against such potentially influential voices?

> *Hear again the voice of Jesus: 'The words I have spoken to you – they are full of the Spirit and life' (John 6:63).*

JB

Day 158

Healing a blind man

MARK 8:22–26

Bethsaida, north-east shore of Sea of Galilee
They came to Bethsaida, and some people brought a blind man and begged Jesus to touch him. He took the blind man by the hand and led him outside the village. When he had spat on the man's eyes and put his hands on him, Jesus asked, 'Do you see anything?' He looked up and said, 'I see people; they look like trees walking around.' Once more Jesus put his hands on the man's eyes. Then his eyes were opened, his sight was restored, and he saw everything clearly. Jesus sent him home, saying, 'Don't even go into the village.'

This healing is unique in the gospels in that it was done in two stages. That says nothing about Jesus' ability to heal, nor, apparently, about the faith of either the blind man or those who brought him to Jesus. Rather, it seems to be an illustration of the spiritual state of those around them: some still could not see the kingdom of God breaking in, others were beginning to see but lacked clarity. Only those whose spiritual eyes were opened could clearly see what was happening.

Today you might like to use your imagination to help you pray (see page 12). Read the passage three times, and with each reading imagine one of those three states of 'seeing': blindness; partial sight; clear sight. What was the experience like? How did it affect the man's life? How is that similar to 'spiritual sight' – yours and others? After each reading allow your thoughts to develop into prayer.

> *You may like to close by using the prayer of St Richard of Chichester (1197–1253): Thanks be to you, my Lord Jesus, for all the benefits you have given me, for all the pains and insults you have borne for me. O most merciful redeemer, friend and brother, of you three things I pray: to see you more clearly, love you more dearly and follow you more nearly, day by day.*

JB

Day 159

Peter's confession of Christ

MATTHEW 16:13–20 (MARK 8:27–30; LUKE 9:18–21)

Caesarea Philippi
When Jesus came to the region of Caesarea Philippi, he asked his disciples, 'Who do people say the Son of Man is?' They replied, 'Some say John the Baptist; others say Elijah; and still others, Jeremiah or one of the prophets.' 'But what about you?' he asked. 'Who do you say I am?' Simon Peter answered, 'You are the Messiah, the Son of the living God.' Jesus replied, 'Blessed are you, Simon son of Jonah, for this was not revealed to you by flesh and blood, but by my Father in heaven. And I tell you that you are Peter, and on this rock I will build my church, and the gates of Hades will not overcome it. I will give you the keys of the kingdom of heaven; whatever you bind on earth will be bound in heaven, and whatever you loose on earth will be loosed in heaven.' Then he ordered his disciples not to tell anyone that he was the Messiah.

Have you ever been asked a question that changed your life? After nearly three years together, the time had come for Jesus to ask his disciples such a question. First, however, he walked them 30 miles to a city which boasted a new temple dedicated to the worship of the Roman emperor. There was a clue in the context.

Just like the healing of the blind man yesterday, Jesus asked his 'Who am I?' question in two stages. While some people had made promising connections with Old Testament prophecy (Malachi 4:5; Deuteronomy 18:18), they remained 'partially sighted'. Jesus' second question was personal and, like the second touch to the eyes of the blind man, prompted from Peter a response of clear sight, a God-given revelation.

This was the crucial turning point in Jesus' ministry and in the lives of the disciples. Peter had come to the realisation that Jesus was not just announcing the kingdom of God, he had come as God's anointed king. This man, who they had seen repeatedly demonstrate his power through acts of compassion, was the only one who could rightly claim divine sonship. With this confession as its foundation, and under the loving authority of this king, the church would be established and protected.

> Hear Jesus' question as addressed to you, and allow your heart to worship him in response: 'What about you? Who do you say I am?'

JB

Day 160

Jesus predicts his death

MATTHEW 16:21–28 (MARK 8:31–9:1; LUKE 9:22–37)

From that time on Jesus began to explain to his disciples that he must go to Jerusalem and suffer many things at the hands of the elders, the chief priests and the teachers of the law, and that he must be killed and on the third day be raised to life. Peter took him aside and began to rebuke him. 'Never, Lord!' he said. 'This shall never happen to you!' Jesus turned and said to Peter, 'Get behind me, Satan! You are a stumbling-block to me; you do not have in mind the concerns of God, but merely human concerns.' Then Jesus said to his disciples, 'Whoever wants to be my disciple must deny themselves and take up their cross and follow me. For whoever wants to save their life will lose it, but whoever loses their life for me will find it. What good will it be for someone to gain the whole world, yet forfeit their soul? Or what can anyone give in exchange for their soul? For the Son of Man is going to come in his Father's glory with his angels, and then he will reward each person according to what they have done. Truly I tell you, some who are standing here will not taste death before they see the Son of Man coming in his kingdom.'

There is now a significant shift in the direction and tone of the story, as Jesus' death becomes the focus. While Peter saw his identity more clearly, he still had more to understand about Jesus' mission and how it would be achieved, and what his own part in it would involve.

Like Peter, none of us know what lies ahead and what following Christ might entail. However, denying ourselves and 'taking up our cross' is, at heart, about releasing into Christ's loving hands the control of our lives. What causes us to hesitate? Perhaps an under-estimation of both the love of Christ for us and the richness of life with him. We only begin to grasp that as we move beyond merely believing in him to surrendering to him and his love.

> 'He is no fool who gives up what he cannot keep to gain what he cannot lose' (Jim Elliot, 1927–56). Surrender to Christ is never a once-only event. Hear his invitation to you today to entrust your life to his love and to follow wherever he leads.

JB

the last few months

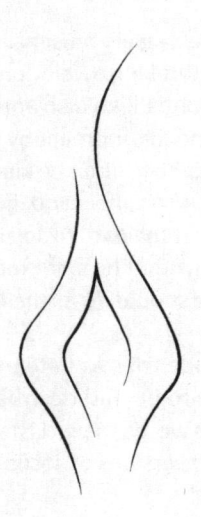

MELINDA HENDRY

Day 161

The transfiguration

MATTHEW 17:1–8 (MARK 9:2–13; LUKE 9:28–36)

A high mountain in the region of Caesarea Philippi
After six days Jesus took with him Peter, James and John the brother of James, and led them up a high mountain by themselves. There he was transfigured before them. His face shone like the sun, and his clothes became as white as the light. Just then there appeared before them Moses and Elijah, talking with Jesus. Peter said to Jesus, 'Lord, it is good for us to be here. If you wish, I will put up three shelters – one for you, one for Moses and one for Elijah.' While he was still speaking, a bright cloud covered them, and a voice from the cloud said, 'This is my Son, whom I love; with him I am well pleased. Listen to him!' When the disciples heard this, they fell face down to the ground, terrified. But Jesus came and touched them. 'Get up,' he said. 'Don't be afraid.' When they looked up, they saw no one except Jesus.

Jesus' transformation into his heavenly glory must have been bewildering for the disciples. It's a moment of unexpected, breathtaking revelation as the divine splendour of Jesus is unveiled before their eyes. Moses and Elijah also appear, testifying to Jesus' identity as the Messiah. Peter wants to enshrine this moment by setting up three tents, because this is the kind of Messiah that makes sense to him, the kind he can get behind. A Messiah who comes in glory and power, not one who suffers and dies as Jesus has predicted (Matthew 16:21). Peter does not yet realise that the path to Jesus' glory and victory will be through his death. But his actions also show that he's not ready to let go of his expectations of what Jesus should be and what he should do as the Messiah.

We sometimes have the same tendencies as Peter. We want Jesus to fit into our own agenda; to be what we want him to be and do what we want him to do. And so the Father's words to Peter are also his words to us, 'Listen to Jesus!' This is a word of grace to us, calling us back from the false versions of Jesus we can create because it's the real Jesus we need.

> How has your view of Jesus been challenged or enlarged as you've journeyed with him; and does that change how you live and respond to Jesus?

MH

Day 162

Elijah, Jesus and John

MATTHEW 17:9–13

Region of Caesarea Philippi
As they were coming down the mountain, Jesus instructed them, 'Don't tell anyone what you have seen, until the Son of Man has been raised from the dead.' The disciples asked him, 'Why then do the teachers of the law say that Elijah must come first?' Jesus replied, 'To be sure, Elijah comes and will restore all things. But I tell you, Elijah has already come, and they did not recognise him, but have done to him everything they wished. In the same way the Son of Man is going to suffer at their hands.' Then the disciples understood that he was talking to them about John the Baptist.

For centuries, God's people had been longing for the Messiah; eagerly looking for his coming and for his forerunner, Elijah, who would herald his arrival (Malachi 4:5–6). In this conversation, prompted by Elijah's appearance on the mountain, Jesus opens their eyes to what they had missed. Elijah had come as promised, not as they might have expected, but in the ministry of John the Baptist. However, it's not just the disciples who failed to recognise John's role as the new Elijah. The teachers of the law missed him too. Unlike the disciples, though, their lack of recognition became entrenched, leading them to reject both the messenger and the Messiah they had been waiting for. Was this their pride? Were they unable to move beyond their own conceptions of how God was going to fulfil his promises?

The disciples here stand in contrast to the teachers of the law. They still have some wrong expectations of Jesus as the Messiah, but they are humble, open and teachable. They are willing to ask questions and to have their understanding of God reshaped and corrected by Jesus.

Are you open to God showing up and working in unexpected ways? Are you humble, teachable and open to having your ideas about who God is and how he acts challenged and reshaped? The disciples here are a model for us, and show us the posture of a growing disciple.

> Lord God, may my heart be open and yielded to you. Guard me from pride and a belief in my own rightness; keep me humble and teachable, ready to hear your response to my questions. May I not miss your work when you show up or act in surprising ways.

MH

Day 163

Demon-possessed boy

MATTHEW 17:14–20 (MARK 9:14–29; LUKE 9:37–45)

Region of Caesarea Philippi
When they came to the crowd, a man approached Jesus and knelt before him. 'Lord, have mercy on my son,' he said. 'He has seizures and is suffering greatly. He often falls into the fire or into the water. I brought him to your disciples, but they could not heal him.' 'You unbelieving and perverse generation,' Jesus replied, 'how long shall I stay with you? How long shall I put up with you? Bring the boy here to me.' Jesus rebuked the demon, and it came out of the boy, and he was healed at that moment. Then the disciples came to Jesus in private and asked, 'Why couldn't we drive it out?' He replied, 'Because you have so little faith. Truly I tell you, if you have faith as small as a mustard seed, you can say to this mountain, "Move from here to there," and it will move. Nothing will be impossible for you.'

When Jesus descends from the mountain, he discovers his disciple's inability to heal a little boy. Jesus had given them authority to drive out demons (Matthew 10:1) and they've done it before. So why can't they now? Jesus says it's because they have 'little faith'. Mark helps us to understand what Jesus means here by adding that 'this kind can come out only by prayer' (Mark 9:29). It appears that rather than turning to God in prayer, the disciples' trust is oriented elsewhere in their attempts to heal. Perhaps they were trusting in the authority Jesus had given them, in their past success or in the words they spoke. Whatever the case, it's clear they are relying on something other than God's power to heal this boy. 'Little faith' then is not defined by its quantity but its direction.

The disciples were continually learning that they could do nothing in their power. This is a lesson we are also continually learning, with our own propensity to rely on our own strength, wisdom and experience rather than on God.

Jesus invites us to let go of our 'little faith' and to see just what he can do – in our lives, relationships and circumstances – if we will let go of our own efforts and entrust these things to his power and work.

> *Where are you living with little faith? What situations is Jesus inviting you to entrust to him in prayer?*

MH

Day 164

Death and resurrection foretold

MATTHEW 17:22–23 (MARK 9:30–32)

Galilee
When they came together in Galilee, he said to them, 'The Son of Man is going to be delivered into the hands of men. They will kill him, and on the third day he will be raised to life.' And the disciples were filled with grief.

This is the second time Jesus tells his disciples that he will be arrested, killed and then raised to life (see also Matthew 16:21). It's clear that Jesus wants them to be prepared for what's coming.

On this occasion, the words fill the disciples with grief, that deep sadness we all feel when we lose something or someone that is precious. I wonder, however, if these same words later filled them with awe and joy as they began to understand the full significance of Jesus' death and resurrection.

From the first announcement of the gospel in Genesis 3:15, God had been declaring again and again his intention to crush the curse of sin and death. He will not abandon his world or his people. Although the disciples don't understand it now, Jesus' words are more than just prediction or preparation. They stand in the long line of God's declarations of salvation. Here Jesus is proclaiming yet again God's settled intention and action to save.

The events that are about to happen are not by chance, but are the culmination of God's plan. Jesus will be arrested, he will be killed, he will be raised to life – and through those events God is bringing about his promised salvation.

> *Stop for a moment and think about God's settled intention and action to save you from the curse of sin and death. Think about Jesus' settled intention to go to the cross for you. What does this tell you about the heart of the Father and the Son? What do you discover about their desires and longings? Turn your reflections back to God in praise and prayer.*

MH

Day 165

Coin in the fish's mouth

MATTHEW 17:24–27

Capernaum
After Jesus and his disciples arrived in Capernaum, the collectors of the two-drachma temple tax came to Peter and asked, 'Doesn't your teacher pay the temple tax?' 'Yes, he does,' he replied. When Peter came into the house, Jesus was the first to speak. 'What do you think, Simon?' he asked. 'From whom do the kings of the earth collect duty and taxes – from their own children or from others?' 'From others,' Peter answered. 'Then the children are exempt,' Jesus said to him. 'But so that we may not cause offence, go to the lake and throw out your line. Take the first fish you catch; open its mouth and you will find a four-drachma coin. Take it and give it to them for my tax and yours.'

Matthew is the only gospel writer who records this story. Perhaps it's no surprise given his former life as a tax collector. The taxes in this narrative were for the upkeep of the temple, God's house. Paying them was culturally and religiously important. Yet, if Jesus is indeed the Son of the house, then surely he should be tax-exempt. However, Jesus does not stand on this right but pays what is due.

Jesus also pays Peter's debt through a miraculous provision. Placed soon after the account of the transfiguration, this story also points to the cross and to Jesus' payment of a far greater debt none of us could pay ourselves.

More than a lesson about paying taxes or tithes, or God's miraculous provision, this story speaks to us of a Jesus who does not cling on to his rights, but willingly gives them up to serve. Philippians 2 captures this same truth about Jesus: 'being in very nature God, did not consider equality with God something to be used to his own advantage… he humbled himself by becoming obedient to death – even death on a cross!' (vv. 6, 8).

> *Jesus' words and actions in this story reveal his character and leave us an example to follow. What rights might the Lord be calling you to lay down, so you can love and serve others?*

MH

Day 166

Who is the greatest?

MATTHEW 18:1-5 (MARK 9:33-37; LUKE 9:46-48)

Galilee
At that time the disciples came to Jesus and asked, 'Who, then, is the greatest in the kingdom of heaven?' He called a little child to him, and placed the child among them. And he said: 'Truly I tell you, unless you change and become like little children, you will never enter the kingdom of heaven. Therefore, whoever takes the lowly position of this child is the greatest in the kingdom of heaven. And whoever welcomes one such child in my name welcomes me.'

'Who, then, is greatest in the kingdom of heaven?' In Mark and Luke's telling, this is the question that occupied the disciples conversation after Jesus predicted his death for a second time. Jesus knows this and makes them give voice to it. It's almost hard to believe the sheer self-concern of the disciples, until I am forced to admit just how much this question occupies my own heart as well. Just like the disciples, we all have a natural absorption with our own position and status. And we all want to know how we stack up against others.

Jesus says that if we're concerned for our own greatness then not only will we miss out on greatness, but we are in danger of missing out on the kingdom altogether. Preoccupation with our status and position will always take us away from the life of Christ. Instead, life and greatness in the kingdom is found in becoming like a child. In Jesus' day, children had no status in society. They were needy and dependent. To become like a child is to let go of our egos, to acknowledge our helplessness, to recognise our lowliness; all of which cultivate humility in us. This is the kind of life that is considered great in the kingdom because it reflects the life of our Lord Jesus.

In his book *The Radical Disciple*, John Stott recounts advice that former Archbishop Michael Ramsey once gave to new ordinands: 'Do not worry about status. There is only one status that our Lord bids us to be concerned with, and that is the status of our proximity to himself.'[24]

> How might the preoccupation with status or position be evident in your own heart and life? What is Jesus wanting to say to you and do in you as you reflect on his words?

MH

Day 167

For or against

MARK 9:38–41 (*LUKE 9:49–50*)

> Capernaum
> *'Teacher,' said John, 'we saw someone driving out demons in your name and we told him to stop, because he was not one of us.' 'Do not stop him,' Jesus said. 'For no one who does a miracle in my name can in the next moment say anything bad about me, for whoever is not against us is for us. Truly I tell you, anyone who gives you a cup of water in my name because you belong to the Messiah will certainly not lose their reward.'*

At the start of his public ministry, Jesus specially appointed twelve disciples. He invested them with his authority and sent them out to heal the sick and to drive out evil spirits (Mark 6:7; Matthew 10:1). Just a short time ago, the disciples were unable to free a boy from an evil spirit because of their little faith. Now, they've encountered a man who's outside their group, doing the works they've been commissioned to do.

John no doubt expects Jesus to affirm the actions of the disciples. However, this turns out to be another teachable moment for them. Perhaps surprisingly, Jesus does not share the concern of the disciples. He sees a man demonstrating faith in the power and authority of his name. Jesus, however, is concerned with the attitude of his disciples. They seem to believe that the mission and the ministry of the kingdom is only for the select few who've been formally appointed or commissioned. Jesus here challenges their narrow thinking.

For those who've been specially appointed to a ministry, whether ordained or lay, Jesus' words remind us that our ministry is only a part of the wider ministry of the people of God. It also reminds us that ministry is not a 'right' that we have because of our education, experience or formal commissioning. For those uncertain about stepping into an area of ministry because of a lack of formal appointment or equipping, Jesus' words remind us that it's his power and authority, and not our own, that fuels kingdom work.

> *What ministry has the Lord called you to and gifted you for? How does this passage shape your thinking about that ministry?*

MH

Day 168

Lost sheep

MATTHEW 18:6-14 (*LUKE 15:3-7*)

Capernaum
'If anyone causes one of these little ones – those who believe in me – to stumble, it would be better for them to have a large millstone hung around their neck and to be drowned in the depths of the sea. Woe to the world because of the things that cause people to stumble! Such things must come, but woe to the person through whom they come! If your hand or your foot causes you to stumble, cut it off and throw it away. It is better for you to enter life maimed or crippled than to have two hands or two feet and be thrown into eternal fire. And if your eye causes you to stumble, gouge it out and throw it away. It is better for you to enter life with one eye than to have two eyes and be thrown into the fire of hell. See that you do not despise one of these little ones. For I tell you that their angels in heaven always see the face of my Father in heaven. What do you think? If a man owns a hundred sheep, and one of them wanders away, will he not leave the ninety-nine on the hills and go to look for the one that wandered off? And if he finds it, truly I tell you, he is happier about that one sheep than about the ninety-nine that did not wander off. In the same way your Father in heaven is not willing that any of these little ones should perish.'

Most of us are familiar with the picture of Jesus as a shepherd who searches after his wandering sheep. Perhaps we are less familiar, though, with the picture at the start of the passage. Here he is more akin to a mama bear who is fiercely protective of her cubs and goes against anyone who would bring them harm. Each of these images reveals an aspect God's love for us. It is passionate and protective, persistent and pursuing.

When we fear that we've sinned too much, been too unfaithful or wandered too far, these pictures remind us that we cannot out-sin or out-wander his love. He will always run after us and welcome us home.

> *Spend time meditating on the love of Jesus for you. How have you experienced these dimensions of love in your life? Turn your meditations back to him in praise.*

MH

Day 169

Accountability

MATTHEW 18:15-20

Galilee
If your brother or sister sins, go and point out their fault, just between the two of you. If they listen to you, you have won them over. But if they will not listen, take one or two others along, so that "every matter may be established by the testimony of two or three witnesses." If they still refuse to listen, tell it to the church; and if they refuse to listen even to the church, treat them as you would a pagan or a tax collector. Truly I tell you, whatever you bind on earth will be bound in heaven, and whatever you loose on earth will be loosed in heaven. Again, truly I tell you that if two of you on earth agree about anything they ask for, it will be done for them by my Father in heaven. For where two or three gather in my name, there am I with them.'

As any parent knows, love involves discipline, and seeking the best for a loved one can mean challenging harmful behaviour. The same principle applies in the family of believers, and Jesus' love for us motivates his teaching here as he describes how we are to apply discipline within the church community.

None of us finds accountability easy. It can be tempting to ignore someone's sinful behaviour or harmful conduct because we fear being seen as self-righteous. When we are the ones challenged, we can be defensive, justifying our own actions.

To love and follow Jesus is to share his concern for our own holiness and that of our spiritual brothers and sisters. Leaving sin unchallenged does not help us grow in Christlikeness, and we need each other to help us see the sin to which we are often blind. Growing in Jesus is never a solo endeavour. We need trusted friendships that seek the best for us just as we seek the best for them, even when that means speaking difficult truths.

> *How can you grow relationships of accountability in your life?*

MH

Day 170

Forgiveness

MATTHEW 18:21-35

Galilee
Then Peter came to Jesus and asked, 'Lord, how many times shall I forgive my brother or sister who sins against me? Up to seven times?' Jesus answered, 'I tell you, not seven times, but seventy-seven times. Therefore, the kingdom of heaven is like a king who wanted to settle accounts with his servants. As he began the settlement, a man who owed him ten thousand bags of gold was brought to him. Since he was not able to pay, the master ordered that he and his wife and his children and all that he had be sold to repay the debt. At this the servant fell on his knees before him. "Be patient with me," he begged, "and I will pay back everything." The servant's master took pity on him, cancelled the debt and let him go. But when that servant went out, he found one of his fellow servants who owed him a hundred silver coins. He grabbed him and began to choke him. "Pay back what you owe me!" he demanded. His fellow servant fell to his knees and begged him, "Be patient with me, and I will pay it back." But he refused. Instead, he went off and had the man thrown into prison until he could pay the debt. When the other servants saw what had happened, they were outraged and went and told their master everything that had happened. Then the master called the servant in. "You wicked servant," he said, "I cancelled all that debt of yours because you begged me to. Shouldn't you have had mercy on your fellow servant just as I had on you?" In anger his master handed him over to the jailers to be tortured, until he should pay back all he owed. This is how my heavenly Father will treat each of you unless you forgive your brother or sister from your heart.'

Forgiveness is to be one of the hallmarks of the Christian community, yet it does not come easy. When our brother or sister wrongs us, it can leave deep wounds, and we can empathise with Peter's question here.

> *Spend some time listening to the story Jesus tells. How does it speak into your own questions and struggles with forgiveness?*

MH

Day 171

Divorce

MATTHEW 19:1-12

Judea, across the Jordan

When Jesus had finished saying these things, he left Galilee and went into the region of Judea to the other side of the Jordan. Large crowds followed him, and he healed them there. Some Pharisees came to him to test him. They asked, 'Is it lawful for a man to divorce his wife for any and every reason?' 'Haven't you read,' he replied, 'that at the beginning the Creator "made them male and female," and said, "For this reason a man will leave his father and mother and be united to his wife, and the two will become one flesh"? So they are no longer two, but one flesh. Therefore what God has joined together, let no one separate.' 'Why then,' they asked, 'did Moses command that a man give his wife a certificate of divorce and send her away?' Jesus replied, 'Moses permitted you to divorce your wives because your hearts were hard. But it was not this way from the beginning. I tell you that anyone who divorces his wife, except for sexual immorality, and marries another woman commits adultery.' The disciples said to him, 'If this is the situation between a husband and wife, it is better not to marry.' Jesus replied, 'Not everyone can accept this word, but only those to whom it has been given. For there are eunuchs who were born that way, and there are eunuchs who have been made eunuchs by others – and there are those who choose to live like eunuchs for the sake of the kingdom of heaven. The one who can accept this should accept it.'

Jesus' teaching about marriage, singleness and divorce is as radical today as it was in the first century, and still as positive. He affirms that both marriage and singleness are sacred callings, and through both we have the opportunity to bear witness to the gospel. Married people testify to the faithfulness and security of God's love through the permanence of marriage. Single people testify to the sufficiency of God's love through sexual purity.

Jesus knows, though, that life is complex. Some Christian marriages sadly end in divorce. In these situations, God's grace is available and gives the possibility of beginning again. Many who've experienced divorce can bear witness to the gracious and redemptive nature of God's love.

> Whether married, single or divorced, how can you live faithfully for Jesus?

MH

Day 172

Jesus and his brothers

JOHN 7:1-13

Galilee and Jerusalem
After this, Jesus went around in Galilee. He did not want to go about in Judea because the Jewish leaders there were looking for a way to kill him. But when the Jewish Festival of Tabernacles was near, Jesus' brothers said to him, 'Leave Galilee and go to Judea, so that your disciples there may see the works you do. No one who wants to become a public figure acts in secret. Since you are doing these things, show yourself to the world.' For even his own brothers did not believe in him. Therefore Jesus told them, 'My time is not yet here; for you any time will do. The world cannot hate you, but it hates me because I testify that its works are evil. You go to the festival. I am not going up to this festival, because my time has not yet fully come.' After he had said this, he stayed in Galilee. However, after his brothers had left for the festival, he went also, not publicly, but in secret. Now at the festival the Jewish leaders were watching for Jesus and asking, 'Where is he?' Among the crowds there was widespread whispering about him. Some said, 'He is a good man.' Others replied, 'No, he deceives the people.' But no one would say anything publicly about him for fear of the leaders.

Most, if not all of us, have felt the weight of the expectation of others. We know the pressure that comes when others tell us what path we should follow or what decision to make. In this passage, we see that Jesus is no stranger to this experience. Jesus, however, knows that the most important voice is the voice of his Father. And the most important agenda is the agenda of his Father. Jesus will go to Jerusalem but the timing and manner will be determined by his Father, not by others. Jesus' response challenges us to think about our situations where the expectations of others might stop us from following God's agenda for us.

Whose voices tend to sway your actions and decisions? How might you grow in your attentiveness to God's voice and will?

MH

Day 173

Jesus teaches during the Feast of Tabernacles

JOHN 7:14–24

Jerusalem
Not until halfway through the festival did Jesus go up to the temple courts and begin to teach. The Jews there were amazed and asked, 'How did this man get such learning without having been taught?' Jesus answered, 'My teaching is not my own. It comes from the one who sent me. Anyone who chooses to do the will of God will find out whether my teaching comes from God or whether I speak on my own. Whoever speaks on their own does so to gain personal glory, but he who seeks the glory of the one who sent him is a man of truth; there is nothing false about him. Has not Moses given you the law? Yet not one of you keeps the law. Why are you trying to kill me?' 'You are demon-possessed,' the crowd answered. 'Who is trying to kill you?' Jesus said to them, 'I did one miracle, and you are all amazed. Yet, because Moses gave you circumcision (though actually it did not come from Moses, but from the patriarchs), you circumcise a boy on the Sabbath. Now if a boy can be circumcised on the Sabbath so that the law of Moses may not be broken, why are you angry with me for healing a man's whole body on the Sabbath? Stop judging by mere appearances, but instead judge correctly.'

Having entered Jerusalem quietly, Jesus now begins to teach publicly. As the listening crowds wonder where Jesus has gained such wisdom, he declares that his words are not his own but are his Father's. Jesus says the truth of his claims, however, will only be discerned by those want to do God's will. As David Ford comments: 'Some sorts of knowing can only happen through trusting and being in a committed relationship.'[25]

In our own lives, we might not question the divine origins of Jesus' teaching, but we may doubt whether obedience to his teaching will be for our good. But the principle and invitation are the same. It's only as we enter into Jesus' teaching through trusting obedience that we can know that Jesus' word is not only true, but also wise, beautiful, good and life-giving.

> Is there a teaching of Jesus that you resist because you doubt its goodness or because the cost of obedience feels too great? Jesus invites you to trust him in that area.

MH

Day 174

Jesus divides the opposition

JOHN 7:25–31

Jerusalem
At that point some of the people of Jerusalem began to ask, 'Isn't this the man they are trying to kill? Here he is, speaking publicly, and they are not saying a word to him. Have the authorities really concluded that he is the Messiah? But we know where this man is from; when the Messiah comes, no one will know where he is from.' Then Jesus, still teaching in the temple courts, cried out, 'Yes, you know me, and you know where I am from. I am not here on my own authority, but he who sent me is true. You do not know him, but I know him because I am from him and he sent me.' At this they tried to seize him, but no one laid a hand on him, because his hour had not yet come. Still, many in the crowd believed in him. They said, 'When the Messiah comes, will he perform more signs than this man?'

As we've seen, even before he arrives in Jerusalem, Jesus has been the talk of the town. Around the streets, questions about Jesus dominate the conversation. In giving voice to these questions in his narrative, John invites us to enter into them and to explore them for ourselves. He also invites us to ask our own questions of Jesus. If we ask them honestly and open-handedly, questions are so often catalysts to faith, maturity and a deeper understanding.

> As you've watched Jesus and listened to him, what questions have risen in your mind and heart? Take a moment now to capture them. How will you pursue those questions? God does not ask us to silence or suppress our questions or doubts, but invites us to bring them prayerfully to him and to his word. You may also want to talk about them with others. Let the questions of the crowds and your own questions take you closer to Jesus.

MH

Day 175

Pharisees seek to arrest Jesus

JOHN 7:32-36

Jerusalem
The Pharisees heard the crowd whispering such things about him. Then the chief priests and the Pharisees sent temple guards to arrest him. Jesus said, 'I am with you for only a short time, and then I am going to the one who sent me. You will look for me, but you will not find me; and where I am, you cannot come.' The Jews said to one another, 'Where does this man intend to go that we cannot find him? Will he go where our people live scattered among the Greeks, and teach the Greeks? What did he mean when he said, "You will look for me, but you will not find me," and "Where I am, you cannot come"?'

Jesus is becoming a growing threat to the Pharisees, and so they seek to arrest him. However, they have no real control over his destiny. Jesus knows that he has come from the Father and will return to him.

All throughout his dialogue with the crowds and Pharisees, Jesus has shown his deep sense of security. Even in the face of opposition and the threat of arrest, Jesus knows that the whole sweep of his life and ministry is in the hands of his Father. Nothing he encounters is out of his loving control. He also knows that he is the beloved Son, who is fulfilling his Father's mission. It's this confidence that strengthens Jesus and enables him to persist in his mission with courage.

The same loving Father who was in control of Jesus' story is also in control of our story. Nothing we encounter is a surprise to him, and nothing can thwart his loving plans and purposes for our life. Just as the Father was present with Jesus on his journey, so he is present with us on ours.

Jesus' confidence was often nurtured in the quiet places of prayer and communion with his Father. In those spaces of solitude and silence, Jesus was affirmed in his identity as the Son. He was given courage to face the journey ahead and confidence in his Father's sovereign control. Those quiet places of communion are essential for us too in our own journeys.

> How are you making space in your own life so you can be affirmed and strengthened by your loving Father?

MH

Day 176

Rivers of living water

JOHN 7:37–39

Jerusalem
On the last and greatest day of the festival, Jesus stood and said in a loud voice, 'Let anyone who is thirsty come to me and drink. Whoever believes in me, as scripture has said, rivers of living water will flow from within them.' By this he meant the Spirit, whom those who believed in him were later to receive. Up to that time the Spirit had not been given, since Jesus had not yet been glorified.

Each year crowds thronged to Jerusalem for the Festival of Tabernacles, remembering God's deliverance from Egypt and his sustaining provision in the desert (Leviticus 23:33–43). Each day of the festival a special water ceremony recalled how God miraculously supplied life-giving water to quench their thirst.

In extending his invitation against the backdrop of this ceremony, Jesus is using the metaphor of physical thirst to speak to our deeper spiritual thirsts and invites us to pay attention to the longings of our soul. The longings we have to be fully known and fully loved, for belonging, purpose, home, healing. In paying attention to our thirsts, we also become aware of all the ways we've sought to quench them without ever being fully satisfied.

Jesus alone is the true water for our souls, the one who can quench our soul's thirst and satisfy our deepest desires. All of our longings are ultimately longings for God, who has made us for relationship with himself. As we come to Jesus, he pours out his life, presence and transforming power in our life through the Holy Spirit.

Today Jesus invites you to come to him with the thirsts of your soul. As you hear this invitation from Jesus, will you come to him and drink? Will you look to him as the one who satisfies your needs and longings?

> Lord Jesus, I come to you as the only one who can quench my deepest thirsts. Would you pour out your Spirit in me today, so that streams of living water would flow within me.

MH

Day 177

Divided because of Jesus

JOHN 7:40-52

Jerusalem
On hearing his words, some of the people said, 'Surely this man is the Prophet.' Others said, 'He is the Messiah.' Still others asked, 'How can the Messiah come from Galilee? Does not scripture say that the Messiah will come from David's descendants and from Bethlehem, the town where David lived?' Thus the people were divided because of Jesus. Some wanted to seize him, but no one laid a hand on him. Finally the temple guards went back to the chief priests and the Pharisees, who asked them, 'Why didn't you bring him in?' 'No one ever spoke the way this man does,' the guards replied. 'You mean he has deceived you also?' the Pharisees retorted. 'Have any of the rulers or of the Pharisees believed in him? No! But this mob that knows nothing of the law – there is a curse on them.' Nicodemus, who had gone to Jesus earlier and who was one of their own number, asked, 'Does our law condemn a man without first hearing him to find out what he has been doing?' They replied, 'Are you from Galilee, too? Look into it, and you will find that a prophet does not come out of Galilee.'

Throughout the festival, Jesus has divided opinion. Some say he's a good man, others a deceiver and still others that he's demon-possessed. There are also many who believe that he's the promised Messiah. Jesus continues to divide opinion today.

C.S. Lewis famously said that Jesus is either a liar, a lunatic or Lord. He writes: 'You can shut him up for a fool, you can spit at him and kill him as a demon or you can fall at his feet and call him Lord and God, but let us not come with any patronizing nonsense about his being a great human teacher. He has not left that open to us. He did not intend to.'[26]

Jesus consistently insisted that he is Lord. If Jesus is deceived or a deceiver, then we can reject his claims and give him nothing. But if he is Lord, then our only response can be to give the whole of our lives to him in worship.

> *Imagine yourself in the crowd, what is your own response to Jesus? If Jesus is your Lord what difference does that make to your life and present circumstances?*

MH

Day 178

Adulterous woman

JOHN 8:1–11

Jerusalem
But Jesus went to the Mount of Olives. At dawn he appeared again in the temple courts, where all the people gathered round him, and he sat down to teach them. The teachers of the law and the Pharisees brought in a woman caught in adultery. They made her stand before the group and said to Jesus, 'Teacher, this woman was caught in the act of adultery. In the Law Moses commanded us to stone such women. Now what do you say?' They were using this question as a trap, in order to have a basis for accusing him. But Jesus bent down and started to write on the ground with his finger. When they kept on questioning him, he straightened up and said to them, 'Let any one of you who is without sin be the first to throw a stone at her.' Again he stooped down and wrote on the ground. At this, those who heard began to go away one at a time, the older ones first, until only Jesus was left, with the woman still standing there. Jesus straightened up and asked her, 'Woman, where are they? Has no one condemned you?' 'No one, sir,' she said. 'Then neither do I condemn you,' Jesus declared. 'Go now and leave your life of sin.'

Although this story is absent from the earliest manuscripts of John's gospel, there is little doubt as to its authenticity. Why not use the prayer of Richard of Chichester (see the Preface, page 5) to guide you in meditating on this woman's encounter with Jesus.

- What do you see of Jesus as you enter into this story?
- What captures your heart and moves you to greater love of Jesus?
- What way of life is Jesus inviting you into as you follow him?

MH

Day 179

The light of the world

JOHN 8:12

Jerusalem
When Jesus spoke again to the people, he said, 'I am the light of the world. Whoever follows me will never walk in darkness, but will have the light of life.'

During the Festival of Tabernacles, where Jesus continues to teach, Jerusalem was a spectacular sight. At night, four enormous golden lamps were lit on the temple mount, which illuminated the whole city. As the lamps' light pierced the darkness, they recalled the pillar of fire that guided Israel through the wilderness by night as they journeyed from Egypt to the promised land (Exodus 13:20–22). The pillar of fire was a visible sign of Yahweh's saving presence with them, illuminating the way, rescuing them from slavery and leading them to life and freedom.

It's against this backdrop that Jesus makes this declaration about himself. As Israel celebrates God's saving light, Jesus is proclaiming that he is the greater saving light, sent not just to the people of Israel but to the whole world. He is the presence of God with us and for us. He is the truth who illuminates and dispels the darkness. He is the rescuer who has come to free us from our slavery to sin and death. He is God come to give us life and bring us home.

As we hear Jesus' declaration that he is the light of the world, we must also hear his invitation. 'Will you follow me? Will you trust me to rescue you from your slavery to sin and death? Will you trust my truth to lead and guide? Will you open yourself to my light, so that I can heal the darkness that's in you? Will you abide in my word and trust that obedience to me will lead you into places of new life and freedom?' Jesus longs for us to walk in his light and experience his life.

> *Lord Jesus, be the light of my world. Shine your light into the darkest corners of my life. Lead me into your freedom and help me to follow you there.*

MH

Day 180

The Pharisees challenge Jesus

JOHN 8:13-20

Jerusalem
The Pharisees challenged him, 'Here you are, appearing as your own witness; your testimony is not valid.' Jesus answered, 'Even if I testify on my own behalf, my testimony is valid, for I know where I came from and where I am going. But you have no idea where I come from or where I am going. You judge by human standards; I pass judgment on no one. But if I do judge, my decisions are true, because I am not alone. I stand with the Father, who sent me. In your own Law it is written that the testimony of two witnesses is true. I am one who testifies for myself; my other witness is the Father, who sent me.' Then they asked him, 'Where is your father?' 'You do not know me or my Father,' Jesus replied. 'If you knew me, you would know my Father also.' He spoke these words while teaching in the temple courts near the place where the offerings were put. Yet no one seized him, because his hour had not yet come.

Jesus has just announced that he is the true light-giver, the one who gives the light and life of God to the world, but not everyone is willing to come into his light. The Pharisees response is to ask who can corroborate his claim. At face value, they are simply applying the Old Testament law to Jesus' testimony (Deuteronomy 19:15). But Jesus sees beyond the surface to their hearts. Their failure to recognise Jesus shows that, although they might be experts in the law, they do not know the God who is the giver of the law. If the Pharisees truly knew the Father, they would have recognised the Son. There is a sobering truth here. The Pharisees show us that it's possible to mistake knowledge about God for genuine knowledge of God. They reveal the capacity to know the word of God, without drawing near to the heart of God.

> *The example of the Pharisees causes us to reflect on the posture of our own hearts. As you've journeyed with Jesus, do you know him more or do you just know more about him? Have you drawn near to his heart in love and fellowship as you've encountered his word?*

MH

Day 181

Who are you?

JOHN 8:21-30

Jerusalem
Once more Jesus said to them, 'I am going away, and you will look for me, and you will die in your sin. Where I go, you cannot come.' This made the Jews ask, 'Will he kill himself? Is that why he says, "Where I go, you cannot come"?' But he continued, 'You are from below; I am from above. You are of this world; I am not of this world. I told you that you would die in your sins; if you do not believe that I am he, you will indeed die in your sins.' 'Who are you?' they asked. 'Just what I have been telling you from the beginning,' Jesus replied. 'I have much to say in judgment of you. But he who sent me is trustworthy, and what I have heard from him I tell the world.' They did not understand that he was telling them about his Father. So Jesus said, 'When you have lifted up the Son of Man, then you will know that I am he and that I do nothing on my own but speak just what the Father has taught me. The one who sent me is with me; he has not left me alone, for I always do what pleases him.' Even as he spoke, many believed in him.

Jesus speaks of his return to the Father for a second time, but again many of his listeners do not grasp what he's saying. The meaning of Jesus' words is obscured to them, not because he's being cryptic, but because of their unbelief. He warns them that if they persist in this choice, they will die in their sin.

Although Jesus' miraculous works have already supported his claims, he says that the ultimate confirmation of his divine nature and identity will come through his death, resurrection and ascension. Through these events, the Father will fully vindicate the Son, and the Son will return to the Father having accomplished everything he sent him to do.

As we encounter Jesus today, we meet the one who has already been vindicated by the Father. There is no more confirmation we need to be given about his identity. And the question now comes to us, 'Who do we believe Jesus is?' How we respond is a matter of life or death.

MH

Day 182

The truth will set you free

JOHN 8:31–41

Jerusalem
To the Jews who had believed him, Jesus said, 'If you hold to my teaching, you are really my disciples. Then you will know the truth, and the truth will set you free.' They answered him, 'We are Abraham's descendants and have never been slaves of anyone. How can you say that we shall be set free?' Jesus replied, 'Very truly I tell you, everyone who sins is a slave to sin. Now a slave has no permanent place in the family, but a son belongs to it for ever. So if the Son sets you free, you will be free indeed. I know you are Abraham's descendants. Yet you are looking for a way to kill me, because you have no room for my word. I am telling you what I have seen in the Father's presence, and you are doing what you have heard from your father.' 'Abraham is our father,' they answered. 'If you were Abraham's children,' said Jesus, 'then you would do what Abraham did. As it is, you are looking for a way to kill me, a man who has told you the truth that I heard from God. Abraham did not do such things. You are doing the works of your own father.' 'We are not illegitimate children,' they protested. 'The only Father we have is God himself.'

Freedom is one of the deep longings of the human heart. However, normal definitions of freedom, the ability to do whatever we want, don't leave us free but more enslaved to our destructive desires. Here Jesus shows us the path to true freedom.

Jesus says that apart from him we are slaves to sin; captive to ruinous ways of living which lead to death. But he is our liberator. However, it's not simply in knowing Jesus that we find freedom; it's also in following him. There's a strange irony here. True freedom is found not in doing what we want, but in being able to do what he wants, to live the kind of life he did. Transformed, we are freed to do and to want better things for ourselves.

> *Jesus invites you to step fully into the freedom he wants to offer you; to trust that obedience to his word leads to life. In what areas of your life do you need to trust that obedience to Jesus will lead to freedom rather than restriction?*

MH

Day 183

The father of lies

JOHN 8:42-47

Jerusalem
Jesus said to them, 'If God were your Father, you would love me, for I have come here from God. I have not come on my own; God sent me. Why is my language not clear to you? Because you are unable to hear what I say. You belong to your father, the devil, and you want to carry out your father's desires. He was a murderer from the beginning, not holding to the truth, for there is no truth in him. When he lies, he speaks his native language, for he is a liar and the father of lies. Yet because I tell the truth, you do not believe me! Can any of you prove me guilty of sin? If I am telling the truth, why don't you believe me? Whoever belongs to God hears what God says. The reason you do not hear is that you do not belong to God.'

Jesus' listeners have been protesting that they stand in the lineage of Abraham and have God as their Father. But children look like their parents, and Jesus says that they bear no family resemblance. If God was their Father, they would love his Son. If they were Abraham's true seed, they would welcome Jesus. They do, however, resemble their true father – the devil. In their desire to kill Jesus, they reflect his murderous nature. In their refusal to acknowledge the truth about Jesus, they reflect his lying nature. Just as Satan wilfully rejects and opposes Jesus, so do they. These are strong words and would have no doubt given his listeners pause. When Jesus exposes the truth about us, it's always painful, but it's always edged with grace, because it forces us to see the truth about ourselves so we can repent and seek change.

We must also pay attention to the way Jesus outlines Satan's nature and activity. Just as he stands against Jesus, he stands against his followers. We cannot be naïve to his schemes, the ways he wants to take us away from Christ or prevent us from experiencing the full life of Jesus. We need to be growing in discernment, so we can recognise and reject the voice of Satan when he speaks his lies to us.

Lord Jesus, when Satan comes at me with his lies, help me to discern his voice and hear your truth.

MH

Day 184

Jesus and Abraham

JOHN 8:48–59

Jerusalem
The Jews answered him, 'Aren't we right in saying that you are a Samaritan and demon-possessed?' 'I am not possessed by a demon,' said Jesus, 'but I honour my Father and you dishonour me. I am not seeking glory for myself; but there is one who seeks it, and he is the judge. Very truly I tell you, whoever obeys my word will never see death.' At this they exclaimed, 'Now we know that you are demon-possessed! Abraham died and so did the prophets, yet you say that whoever obeys your word will never taste death. Are you greater than our father Abraham? He died, and so did the prophets. Who do you think you are?' Jesus replied, 'If I glorify myself, my glory means nothing. My Father, whom you claim as your God, is the one who glorifies me. Though you do not know him, I know him. If I said I did not, I would be a liar like you, but I do know him and obey his word. Your father Abraham rejoiced at the thought of seeing my day; he saw it and was glad.' 'You are not yet fifty years old,' they said to him, 'and you have seen Abraham!' 'Very truly I tell you,' Jesus answered, 'before Abraham was born, I am!' At this, they picked up stones to stone him, but Jesus hid himself, slipping away from the temple grounds.

'I am!' These are two short words, yet they are cosmic in their significance. Throughout the festival, Jesus has used these two words to identify himself, but his meaning is only fully understood here at the climax of his dialogue. The penny finally drops on the enormity of what he is claiming for himself. In these two words, Jesus identifies himself as the God of Israel, the 'I am' who revealed himself and his name to Moses in the burning bush (Exodus 3:14). In Jesus, the divine Son, God has come to his world and among his people.

Therefore, in Jesus we see 'the radiance of God's glory and the exact representation of his being' (Hebrews 1:3). Everything we see about Jesus is who God is. In his words and actions, we see the whole unchanging heart, character, intentions and desires of the eternal God.

▌ *Let the wonderous reality of this lead you to worship.*

MH

Day 185

Man born blind

JOHN 9:1-7

Jerusalem
As he went along, he saw a man blind from birth. His disciples asked him, 'Rabbi, who sinned, this man or his parents, that he was born blind?' 'Neither this man nor his parents sinned,' said Jesus, 'but this happened so that the works of God might be displayed in him. As long as it is day, we must do the works of him who sent me. Night is coming, when no one can work. While I am in the world, I am the light of the world.' After saying this, he spat on the ground, made some mud with the saliva, and put it on the man's eyes. 'Go,' he told him, 'wash in the Pool of Siloam' (this word means 'Sent'). So the man went and washed, and came home seeing.

When the disciples notice this man, blind from birth, all they can see is a theological question. Whose sin caused this man's blindness? Jesus, however, sees this man's need and the opportunity to display the work his Father has sent him to do.

The backdrop of this healing is Jesus' announcement in John 8:12 that he is the light of the world. Here Jesus puts flesh on that statement and shows what that means. He gives sight to those in darkness.

As the narrative of John 9 unfolds, physical blindness becomes a metaphor for spiritual blindness, and we discover that the blind man's story is our story too. Estranged from God, we are all searching around, lost in the darkness.

Like the blind man, Jesus sees our need and desires to make us whole. Part of the work Jesus does in restoring our sight is to heal us from the false beliefs about God and ourselves that we've developed in our blindness. Perhaps we've carried the belief that we're not worthy of God's love, or that his love is something we must earn. These false beliefs are powerful forces in our lives. Jesus longs to free us from them and to bring us into the light of his truth. Will you trust in Jesus for the healing of your sight like the blind man did?

> Lord Jesus, I come to you for the healing of my own blindness. Open my eyes and give me sight, so that I can see you clearly and live in the light of your truth.

MH

Day 186

The man's testimony

JOHN 9:8–12

Jerusalem
His neighbours and those who had formerly seen him begging asked, 'Isn't this the same man who used to sit and beg?' Some claimed that he was. Others said, 'No, he only looks like him.' But he himself insisted, 'I am the man.' 'How then were your eyes opened?' they asked. He replied, 'The man they call Jesus made some mud and put it on my eyes. He told me to go to Siloam and wash. So I went and washed, and then I could see.' 'Where is this man?' they asked him. 'I don't know,' he said.

What must it have been like for this formerly blind man to see his surroundings for the first time? If he was expecting his neighbours to rejoice with him, it must have been surprising when they failed to recognise him! He must in some way look physically different; but I also wonder whether he's been so altered by the joy of what's happened to him that he appears to be a different man. Perhaps he walks taller, with a dance in his step and a smile that wasn't there before.

Whenever we encounter Jesus and respond in faith, we are changed. Some of us may have stories similar to this man, where the change has been so radical and instantaneous that our friends and family wonder how we could be the same person they knew previously. However, for most of us the process of becoming new, whole people in Christ is slow. It often takes time to see the transformative work Jesus has been doing in our lives. But there are moments where we can look back and discover we are not the person we were.

The process of becoming our true selves in Christ is never a straight line, but as we journey with Jesus scripture promises us that we are being transformed into his likeness (Romans 8:28–29). When the work is slow or imperceptible that's the promise we can hold on to as we keep going in the practices of faith that form us.

> *Spend some time reflecting on your own life. Where are the places in your heart and life where you've experienced the transforming work of Christ? What work does he want to do in you in this present season?*

MH

Day 187

The Pharisees investigate

JOHN 9:13-23

Jerusalem
They brought to the Pharisees the man who had been blind. Now the day on which Jesus had made the mud and opened the man's eyes was a Sabbath. Therefore the Pharisees also asked him how he had received his sight. 'He put mud on my eyes,' the man replied, 'and I washed, and now I see.' Some of the Pharisees said, 'This man is not from God, for he does not keep the Sabbath.' But others asked, 'How can a sinner perform such signs?' So they were divided. Then they turned again to the blind man, 'What have you to say about him? It was your eyes he opened.' The man replied, 'He is a prophet.' They still did not believe that he had been blind and had received his sight until they sent for the man's parents. 'Is this your son?' they asked. 'Is this the one you say was born blind? How is it that now he can see?' 'We know he is our son,' the parents answered, 'and we know he was born blind. But how he can see now, or who opened his eyes, we don't know. Ask him. He is of age; he will speak for himself.' His parents said this because they were afraid of the Jewish leaders, who already had decided that anyone who acknowledged that Jesus was the Messiah would be put out of the synagogue. That was why his parents said, 'He is of age; ask him.'

When this man is brought before the Pharisees, he is a living, seeing testimony to the transforming power and grace of Jesus. Although he's not able to fully explain, or even understand, who Jesus is yet, he knows what has happened to him and that his encounter with Jesus has not left him the same.

Our own stories of grace and transformation also bear witness to Jesus. We may feel ill-equipped to answer every question that might be asked of us, but we still have a story to share of our own experience of Christ which can be used powerfully by God.

> As you look back at your life, what testimony do you have of Jesus? Who is God calling you to share your story with?

MH

Day 188

The man thrown out

JOHN 9:24–34

Jerusalem
A second time they summoned the man who had been blind. 'Give glory to God by telling the truth,' they said. 'We know this man is a sinner.' He replied, 'Whether he is a sinner or not, I don't know. One thing I do know. I was blind but now I see!' Then they asked him, 'What did he do to you? How did he open your eyes?' He answered, 'I have told you already and you did not listen. Why do you want to hear it again? Do you want to become his disciples too?' Then they hurled insults at him and said, 'You are this fellow's disciple! We are disciples of Moses! We know that God spoke to Moses, but as for this fellow, we don't even know where he comes from.' The man answered, 'Now that is remarkable! You don't know where he comes from, yet he opened my eyes. We know that God does not listen to sinners. He listens to the godly person who does his will. Nobody has ever heard of opening the eyes of a man born blind. If this man were not from God, he could do nothing.' To this they replied, 'You were steeped in sin at birth; how dare you lecture us!' And they threw him out.

As the story unfolds, we see that there are two parallel journeys taking place. One is the journey of the Pharisees, who are becoming more entrenched in their spiritual blindness. The other is the journey of the man born blind, who is growing in spiritual sight.

> *Spend some time tracing these two journeys through John 9, paying attention to their response to Jesus. What moves the man born blind towards Jesus? What moves the Pharisees away from him? As you meditate on these journeys, what prayer is unfolding in your heart? Take time now to bring your prayer to the Lord.*

MH

Day 189

Lord, I believe

JOHN 9:35–41

Jerusalem
Jesus heard that they had thrown him out, and when he found him, he said, 'Do you believe in the Son of Man?' 'Who is he, sir?' the man asked. 'Tell me so that I may believe in him.' Jesus said, 'You have now seen him; in fact, he is the one speaking with you.' Then the man said, 'Lord, I believe,' and he worshipped him. Jesus said, 'For judgment I have come into this world, so that the blind will see and those who see will become blind.' Some Pharisees who were with him heard him say this and asked, 'What? Are we blind too?' Jesus said, 'If you were blind, you would not be guilty of sin; but now that you claim you can see, your guilt remains.'

The story of the man born blind culminates with the man restored to full physical and spiritual sight, while the Pharisees become more entrenched in their spiritual blindness.

Although given physical sight instantaneously, the man's spiritual sight develops over time. He first understands Jesus to be a prophet, then a man sent by God. But in his final encounter with Jesus the eyes of his heart are fully open and he recognises and confesses that Jesus is the Messiah. Physical sight has now led to spiritual sight and complete healing. It's worth noting that throughout his journey the man has remained receptive to Jesus, no doubt serving as a model for us in our own journey. The healing of our own spiritual sight comes as we too remain open to Jesus.

By contrast, the Pharisees become more entrenched in their blindness. They demonstrate a continued wilful resistance to Jesus. The Pharisees' refusal to see who Jesus is raises the question: what are they protecting by resisting Jesus? What are they so attached to that makes them unwilling to see?

In our own lives, we may resonate with both the man and the Pharisees. We may be open to the light of Jesus in some areas of our life, yet resistant to him in others. As you reflect on your own heart, are there places where you resist the light of Christ? If so, what are you holding on to? What would it look like to open those places up to Jesus?

> *Lord Jesus, help me to trust that your light brings healing and freedom. Help me to be open to you.*

MH

Day 190

Shepherd of the sheep

JOHN 10:1-6

Jerusalem
'Very truly I tell you Pharisees, anyone who does not enter the sheepfold by the gate, but climbs in by some other way, is a thief and a robber. The one who enters by the gate is the shepherd of the sheep. The gatekeeper opens the gate for him, and the sheep listen to his voice. He calls his own sheep by name and leads them out. When he has brought out all his own, he goes on ahead of them, and his sheep follow him because they know his voice. But they will never follow a stranger; in fact, they will run away from him because they do not recognise a stranger's voice.' Jesus used this figure of speech, but the Pharisees did not understand what he was telling them.

Following the Pharisees' investigation into the healing of the blind man, Jesus' teaching now focuses on the contrast between himself and the Pharisees. Shepherding imagery would have been familiar to his listeners and, importantly, an analogy used by the prophets. The Pharisees, however, miss the point. They do not recognise that Jesus is contrasting his leadership with theirs.

Jesus' teaching is a challenge to all his followers. Sheep need a shepherd. They cannot protect themselves. Sheep can survive, but without protection they become vulnerable to predators. They need a shepherd who will care for them and who knows them by name. One who desires their safety and flourishing. Jesus' encouragement is that the sheep will run away from those who mean them harm but run to the one who loves and protects them.

> We are often surrounded by different voices promising to care for us, but the voice we need to learn to attend to is the voice of Jesus. As we grow in Jesus, we become more attuned to his voice. As you have come to know the good shepherd, Jesus, how has that helped you recognise his voice above and before others? How will you allow that voice to grow louder in your life and keep following it?

MH

Day 191

Life in full

JOHN 10:7-13

Jerusalem
Therefore Jesus said again, 'Very truly I tell you, I am the gate for the sheep. All who have come before me are thieves and robbers, but the sheep have not listened to them. I am the gate; whoever enters through me will be saved. They will come in and go out, and find pasture. The thief comes only to steal and kill and destroy; I have come that they may have life, and have it to the full. I am the good shepherd. The good shepherd lays down his life for the sheep. The hired hand is not the shepherd and does not own the sheep. So when he sees the wolf coming, he abandons the sheep and runs away. Then the wolf attacks the flock and scatters it. The man runs away because he is a hired hand and cares nothing for the sheep.'

Having introduced his pastoral image, Jesus begins to develop it further, first, by describing himself as the gate to the sheepfold, and second, as the good shepherd caring for his flock.

The gate represents the truth that Jesus is the only way of God's salvation. But it also speaks to the protection he offers us as our shepherd. The sheepfolds of Jesus' day were walled enclosures, topped with thorny branches which kept predators and thieves out. The only way in or out was through the gate. When day breaks the sheep leave through the gate, led to good pastures by their good shepherd, returning to safety each night. With Jesus as our gate, we are secure and protected. He will not allow us to be snatched away. This is an image of flourishing, not just existing, under the love of the shepherd.

As the good shepherd, everything he does is for the sheep, including laying down his very life. Jesus has come to give his sheep life to the full. Rich, full, abundant life under his loving care and provision. How valuable the sheep must be to the shepherd for him to love and care for them to this extent.

> How have you experienced the protection and loving care of the good shepherd in your life? How might you grow more in the abundant life he has to offer?

MH

Day 192

I lay down my life

JOHN 10:14-21

Jerusalem
'I am the good shepherd; I know my sheep and my sheep know me – just as the Father knows me and I know the Father – and I lay down my life for the sheep. I have other sheep that are not of this sheepfold. I must bring them also. They too will listen to my voice, and there shall be one flock and one shepherd. The reason my Father loves me is that I lay down my life – only to take it up again. No one takes it from me, but I lay it down of my own accord. I have authority to lay it down and authority to take it up again. This command I received from my Father.' The Jews who heard these words were again divided. Many of them said, 'He is demon-possessed and raving mad. Why listen to him?' But others said, 'These are not the sayings of a man possessed by a demon. Can a demon open the eyes of the blind?'

Some of Israel's greatest leaders spent time working as shepherds, and Jesus' description of himself as a good shepherd would have been attractive to those listening. That is, until he began to describe his relationship with the Father. Jesus claims a profoundly intimate, personal relationship and union with the Father in these verses, a claim that declares his status, authority, mission and victory. He is not a hired hand or an under-shepherd. He is the sheep's worthy owner.

The good shepherd's willingness to give his life for his sheep is integral to his mission. It is a voluntary act born out of his Sonship, not a command a hired hand must follow. His voice will be recognised beyond Israel and attract Gentiles who will be welcomed into the fold, saved, protected and nurtured. What audacious claims. No wonder his audience were again divided. Is he mad, bad or actually someone unique and remarkable? There is no neutrality. He compels us to choose.

> *We are either moving towards Jesus, allowing him to dwell more fully in us, or going away from him, recoiling from the light. Which way are you moving? Remind yourself how much Jesus loves you, and consider how a love so complete changes you.*

MH

Day 193

I and the Father

JOHN 10:22-30

Jerusalem
Then came the Festival of Dedication at Jerusalem. It was winter, and Jesus was in the temple courts walking in Solomon's Colonnade. The Jews who were there gathered round him, saying, 'How long will you keep us in suspense? If you are the Messiah, tell us plainly.' Jesus answered, 'I did tell you, but you do not believe. The works I do in my Father's name testify about me, but you do not believe because you are not my sheep. My sheep listen to my voice; I know them, and they follow me. I give them eternal life, and they shall never perish; no one will snatch them out of my hand. My Father, who has given them to me, is greater than all; no one can snatch them out of my Father's hand. I and the Father are one.'

We have now moved on two months, and Jerusalem is celebrating Hanukkah. As Jesus is walking through one of the temple courtyards, he is surrounded by a crowd demanding he speaks plainly and gives them straight answers about who he claims to be. It is no surprise that there are sheep who do not recognise the good shepherd's voice. Jesus predicted this. As he becomes bolder and plainer in revealing his identity and purpose, there are those who deepen their resolve to oppose him and refuse to acknowledge the signs and teaching before them. Jesus repeats many elements of what he has already taught, including the affirmation that his works are from the Father.

Jesus tells those who have trusted in him that they will receive eternal life and that no one can snatch them away from him. As the good shepherd, Jesus has an unshakable and unbreakable grip on his sheep. This is a remarkable assurance for us as followers of Jesus. Our salvation does not depend on our ability to hold on to Jesus, but on his unfailing ability to hold on to us. When we experience seasons of doubt or when our love of and trust in Jesus feel small and weak, he keeps a grip on us and holds us firmly in his love and promises.

> What will help you to hold on to this truth in the different seasons and circumstances of life?

MH

Day 194

Blasphemy?

JOHN 10:31-39

Jerusalem
Again his Jewish opponents picked up stones to stone him, but Jesus said to them, 'I have shown you many good works from the Father. For which of these do you stone me?' 'We are not stoning you for any good work,' they replied, 'but for blasphemy, because you, a mere man, claim to be God.' Jesus answered them, 'Is it not written in your Law, "I have said you are 'gods'"? If he called them "gods", to whom the word of God came – and Scripture cannot be set aside – what about the one whom the Father set apart as his very own and sent into the world? Why then do you accuse me of blasphemy because I said, "I am God's Son"? Do not believe me unless I do the works of my Father. But if I do them, even though you do not believe me, believe the works, that you may know and understand that the Father is in me, and I in the Father.' Again they tried to seize him, but he escaped their grasp.

Jesus has just announced that he and the Father are one. This is one of the most direct claims to divinity that Jesus has made. There is no room for misunderstanding or misinterpretation. Those who have been pressing Jesus for an answer about his identity understand fully the claim he is making and seek to stone him immediately for blasphemy.

> We may not treat Jesus' claim as blasphemy, but there are times when our vision of Jesus is too small. We can reduce the full divinity of Jesus, and all its implications, in our minds and hearts. Take time to consider the implications and impact of what it means for Jesus to be God.

MH

Day 195

Ministry beyond the Jordan

JOHN 10:40-42

Transjordan
Then Jesus went back across the Jordan to the place where John had been baptising in the early days. There he stayed, and many people came to him. They said, 'Though John never performed a sign, all that John said about this man was true.' And in that place many believed in Jesus.

These verses mark the end of Jesus' public ministry. Here we see Jesus leaving Jerusalem and heading across the River Jordan. The next time he sets foot in Jerusalem, he will be arrested, tried and crucified. For now, he returns to where his public ministry began. It was where he was baptised and where the Father sent the Spirit to confirm Jesus' Sonship.

There will be several months before Jesus returns to Jerusalem. During that time, he will prepare for his return, not as the military liberator many hoped for but as the suffering, servant king whose death will accomplish a far greater victory than the people could comprehend. The location gives Jesus some respite from the opposition and threat he's faced in Jerusalem. But even more, this is a location of deep encouragement and assurance for him. This is where Jesus was baptised and where he heard the voice of his Father speaking to him, affirming his identity and assuring him of his Father's love and pleasure in him (Matthew 3:16–17). Jesus no doubt spends time remembering that moment and it would surely be a source of strength and assurance for Jesus as he looks ahead to the cross. But there is another encouragement in this place and time. Many are coming to Jesus and believing that he's the Messiah. This too would have been a source of encouragement to Jesus as he prepares for what's ahead.

> *Jesus shows us here that there are times and places when we need to retreat in order to prepare for what might be ahead. Times of retreat provide us with a refuge and can give us strength for future challenges, but they also give us space to rest and remember God's love and faithfulness to us. What challenges lie ahead for you? How can you prepare yourself now to meet those challenges with love, strength and trust in the faithfulness of God?*

MH

the journey to Jerusalem

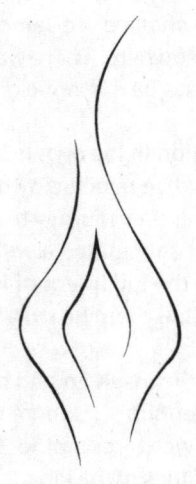

MAGS DUGGAN

Day 196

The journey to Jerusalem begins

LUKE 9:51–56

Leaving Galilee
As the time approached for him to be taken up to heaven, Jesus resolutely set out for Jerusalem. And he sent messengers on ahead, who went into a Samaritan village to get things ready for him; but the people there did not welcome him, because he was heading for Jerusalem. When the disciples James and John saw this, they asked, 'Lord, do you want us to call fire down from heaven to destroy them?' But Jesus turned and rebuked them. Then he and his disciples went to another village.

Rejection hurts: the sting of shame, the agony of betrayal, the pain of shattered expectations. Our instinct is to push back against the rejection – to hurt back, to lash out in retaliative anger – which is exactly what we see James and John, the aptly named 'sons of thunder' (Mark 3:17), wanting to do here. There was historical precedent – Elijah had done it (2 Kings 1:10–12)! But Jesus is having none of it.

He had already experienced rejection in his own hometown of Nazareth (Luke 4), and he knew that in Jerusalem he would be rejected by the elders, chief priests and scribes (Luke 9:22), but here at the start of his final journey to Jerusalem, he encounters an unexpected rejection. He had obviously anticipated a welcome – but it wasn't there. In this accumulation of rejections we see the fulfilment of Isaiah's prophecy that the Messiah would be despised and rejected (53:3) – and he truly was.

But unlike his disciples, Jesus lets the insult go and moves on. He had set face towards Jerusalem and nothing would deter him – so there would be no retaliation, no threat of getting even, not a single harsh word – except for his disciples for even suggesting a response that was so alien to the values of the kingdom that he was bringing into being. The character of the kingdom was embodied in Jesus; from start to finish, Jesus' ministry was shaped by a grace and a forgiveness which was so very evident that day as he began his journey to Jerusalem and all that awaited him there.

> *Lord Jesus, in those moments when the hurt of rejection pushes me inwards towards withdrawal and self-recriminations, or outwards towards harsh words and actions, draw me into your grace and forgiveness. Protect my heart from bitterness, free me from the desire to retaliate and help me to pursue your peace.*

MD

Day 197

The cost of discipleship

LUKE 9:57–62 (MATTHEW 8:19–22)

On the way to Samaria
As they were walking along the road, a man said to him, 'I will follow you wherever you go.' Jesus replied, 'Foxes have dens and birds have nests, but the Son of Man has nowhere to lay his head.' He said to another man, 'Follow me.' But he replied, 'Lord, first let me go and bury my father.' Jesus said to him, 'Let the dead bury their own dead, but you go and proclaim the kingdom of God.' Still another said, 'I will follow you, Lord; but first let me go back and say goodbye to my family.' Jesus replied, 'No one who puts a hand to the plough and looks back is fit for service in the kingdom of God.'

'*But first let me go…*' Their excuses seem so reasonable – until we understand what they were really saying. In the first century, it would be understood that the request to 'bury my father' (who is obviously not dead or this man, in accordance with the custom of the day, would not be on the road with Jesus!) meant, 'Let me wait until my dad has died – whenever that might be – then I'll follow you.' Even the request to first say goodbye was not about a quick hug and a kiss before leaving – it would involve lengthy dinner parties, lunches, long chats, etc.

These would-be disciples have obviously not grasped the nature or the urgency of Jesus' mission of proclaiming the kingdom – or its requirement for wholehearted, single-minded commitment. Their 'But first' was actually a demand that they be allowed to determine their own criteria for following Jesus – their own timing, their own way, not his.

In his invitation to follow him, Jesus is offering us his friendship and the chance to participate in his purpose of bringing the kingdom of God into our world, but I wonder if we have our own 'But first' as we consider this invitation? 'But first… let me experience more of life… settle into my job… raise a family… finish paying off the mortgage… figure out my retirement needs…'

> *Are you aware of any 'But firsts' in your life? Be honest with Jesus about them and ask him for the grace to surrender them to him even today.*

MD

Day 198

The 72 sent out

LUKE 10:1–12

Location unknown (not Galilee)
After this the Lord appointed seventy-two others and sent them two by two ahead of him to every town and place where he was about to go. He told them, 'The harvest is plentiful, but the workers are few. Ask the Lord of the harvest, therefore, to send out workers into his harvest field. Go! I am sending you out like lambs among wolves. Do not take a purse or bag or sandals; and do not greet anyone on the road. When you enter a house, first say, "Peace to this house." If someone who promotes peace is there, your peace will rest on them; if not, it will return to you. Stay there, eating and drinking whatever they give you, for the worker deserves his wages. Do not move around from house to house. When you enter a town and are welcomed, eat what is offered to you. Heal those there who are ill and tell them, "The kingdom of God has come near to you." But when you enter a town and are not welcomed, go into its streets and say, "Even the dust of your town we wipe from our feet as a warning to you. Yet be sure of this: the kingdom of God has come near." I tell you, it will be more bearable on that day for Sodom than for that town.'

I couldn't eat the food! I was in my first week as a new missionary in Hong Kong, housed with a local family who every mealtime generously covered the table with steaming plates of food – which literally turned my stomach. I thought I would never survive into the second week, my missionary career torpedoed over bowls of boiled pig's intestines and fish-head soup.

As the 72 set out on their first missionary journey, Jesus didn't seem too bothered about *where* these disciples went, but he was very particular about *how* they went. They were to be peace-bringers – not argumentative or contentious. They were to be uncomplaining, undemanding recipients of hospitality. They were to eat what they were given!

> As you seek to bring the good news of Jesus into your own contexts, where do the challenges of Jesus' instructions touch your life? What might need to change in your attitude or behaviour? What might you need to surrender?

MD

Day 199

The 72 return with joy

LUKE 10:13–20 (MATTHEW 11:20–24)

Location unknown
'Woe to you, Chorazin! Woe to you, Bethsaida! For if the miracles that were performed in you had been performed in Tyre and Sidon, they would have repented long ago, sitting in sackcloth and ashes. But it will be more bearable for Tyre and Sidon at the judgment than for you. And you, Capernaum, will you be lifted to the heavens? No, you will go down to Hades. Whoever listens to you listens to me; whoever rejects you rejects me; but whoever rejects me rejects him who sent me.' The seventy-two returned with joy and said, 'Lord, even the demons submit to us in your name.' He replied, 'I saw Satan fall like lightning from heaven. I have given you authority to trample on snakes and scorpions and to overcome all the power of the enemy; nothing will harm you. However, do not rejoice that the spirits submit to you, but rejoice that your names are written in heaven.'

I'd never heard of a 'Grandma's Boasting Book' until a friend pulled out a small photo album filled with photos of her grandchildren and their achievements. With great pride she showed me each child's photo and boasted about what that child had achieved.

The disciples could have compiled a 'Disciples' Boasting Book' that day when they excitedly returned to tell Jesus what they had accomplished in his name. But Jesus brings them down to earth with a reminder that what matters most is not their great success but that they were 'registered as citizens of heaven' (v. 20, TLB), which gave them a security and a status which would never change.[27] They could never have achieved this for themselves, no matter how accomplished or successful they were; it was all his doing.

It's no less for us.

The disciples rejoiced because they saw the effect their ministry was having, but we don't always have that privilege. We may not always see what our prayers, our service and our hard work have accomplished, and the truth is that we may not feel our lives are much to boast about either. But if we recognise what Jesus has done for us, then we have serious cause to celebrate!

> *How will you celebrate the gift of your salvation today?*

MD

Day 200

Jesus praises the Father and blesses the disciples

LUKE 10:21-24 (*MATTHEW 11:25-27*)

Location unknown
At that time Jesus, full of joy through the Holy Spirit, said, 'I praise you, Father, Lord of heaven and earth, because you have hidden these things from the wise and learned, and revealed them to little children. Yes, Father, for this is what you were pleased to do. All things have been committed to me by my Father. No one knows who the Son is except the Father, and no one knows who the Father is except the Son and those to whom the Son chooses to reveal him.' Then he turned to his disciples and said privately, 'Blessed are the eyes that see what you see. For I tell you that many prophets and kings wanted to see what you see but did not see it, and to hear what you hear but did not hear it.'

Praise, declaration, awe – all cradled in joyous, confident familiarity.

Jesus is praying. The words 'joy' and 'rejoice' throb their way like a heartbeat through the gospel of Luke. From the opening verses of his account of Jesus' life to its end, Luke shines a spotlight on joy. Here, in these verses, Luke skilfully plaits the theme of joy with another of his themes – prayer.

Jesus had just corrected his disciples' understanding of the source of their joy, and now his prayer reveals the source of his own exuberant joy: he is the Son of the sovereign Lord of all creation! Everything Jesus is, everything he has, everything he has already done or will ever do is grounded in this glorious truth: he is his Father's Son, with all the rights and privileges and responsibilities that come with this role and identity.

The moment we breathe the word 'Father' in prayer, we can be confident that, when we do so, it's because Jesus has revealed *his* Father to us *as our own*.

> *Whatever else is going on in our lives right now, this is our truest source of joy – and it will not change. Ever.*

MD

Day 201

The good Samaritan

LUKE 10:25-37

Location unknown
On one occasion an expert in the law stood up to test Jesus. 'Teacher,' he asked, 'what must I do to inherit eternal life?' 'What is written in the Law?' he replied. 'How do you read it?' He answered, '"Love the Lord your God with all your heart and with all your soul and with all your strength and with all your mind"; and, "Love your neighbour as yourself."' 'You have answered correctly,' Jesus replied. 'Do this and you will live.' But he wanted to justify himself, so he asked Jesus, 'And who is my neighbour?' In reply Jesus said: 'A man was going down from Jerusalem to Jericho, when he was attacked by robbers. They stripped him of his clothes, beat him and went away, leaving him half-dead. A priest happened to be going down the same road, and when he saw the man, he passed by on the other side. So too, a Levite, when he came to the place and saw him, passed by on the other side. But a Samaritan, as he travelled, came where the man was; and when he saw him, he took pity on him. He went to him and bandaged his wounds, pouring on oil and wine. Then he put the man on his own donkey, brought him to an inn and took care of him. The next day he took out two denarii and gave them to the innkeeper. "Look after him," he said, "and when I return, I will reimburse you for any extra expense you may have." Which of these three do you think was a neighbour to the man who fell into the hands of robbers?' The expert in the law replied, 'The one who had mercy on him.' Jesus told him, 'Go and do likewise.'

We know it as an exemplary story of extravagant compassion – but this is the parable that breathes life into Jesus' command to 'love your enemy… do something wonderful for the one who hates you…' (Matthew 5:44, TPT).

Despite the hatred which existed between Samaritans and Jews, this Samaritan crossed racial, religious and cultural barriers to respond to an enemy in need.

> As you consider Jesus' challenge to 'go and do likewise', what might 'likewise' look like in your context? What barriers might Jesus be inviting you to cross? Bring your reflection to God in prayer.

MD

Day 202

With Martha and Mary

LUKE 10:38–42

Bethany near Jerusalem
As Jesus and his disciples were on their way, he came to a village where a woman named Martha opened her home to him. She had a sister called Mary, who sat at the Lord's feet listening to what he said. But Martha was distracted by all the preparations that had to be made. She came to him and asked, 'Lord, don't you care that my sister has left me to do the work by myself? Tell her to help me!' 'Martha, Martha,' the Lord answered, 'you are worried and upset about many things, but few things are needed – or indeed only one. Mary has chosen what is better, and it will not be taken away from her.'

Pastor and author John Ortberg wrote, 'We live in the unceasing care of a relentlessly attentive and gracious God.'[28] In this little cameo, Martha reacts as though she believes that Jesus is not only inattentive but uncaring of the stress she is under, there in the kitchen as she prepares a meal for her dear friend and his disciples.

I imagine her as a confident, experienced hostess whose kitchen is probably her area of expertise – and it's in this very place of established competence that Martha seems to be overwhelmed. It's all more than she can handle and she erupts with a surprising question: 'Lord, don't you care?'

Have you ever whispered those words to Jesus, or thought them in those moments when you are feeling overwhelmed, even in those areas where you are usually competent and capable, and perhaps especially in those moments when you are trying so hard to serve and please God?

Martha didn't hide her frustration or disappointment, but brought them to Jesus himself, who, before leading her into a different place in her thinking, graciously reassured her that he did see her, that he did understand her anxiety and distress and the cause of it.

> *Is there any place in your own life today where you are feeling overwhelmed, frustrated, disappointed – even though you are trying so hard to get it all right? Perhaps like Martha, you may need to honestly say, 'Lord, don't you care?' What is the response you sense in your heart as you ask the Lord that question?*

MD

Day 203

Jesus and Beelzebul

LUKE 11:14–22 (*MATTHEW 12:22–25*)

In the area around Jerusalem
Jesus was driving out a demon that was mute. When the demon left, the man who had been mute spoke, and the crowd was amazed. But some of them said, 'By Beelzebul, the prince of demons, he is driving out demons.' Others tested him by asking for a sign from heaven. Jesus knew their thoughts and said to them: 'Any kingdom divided against itself will be ruined, and a house divided against itself will fall. If Satan is divided against himself, how can his kingdom stand? I say this because you claim that I drive out demons by Beelzebul. Now if I drive out demons by Beelzebul, by whom do your followers drive them out? So then, they will be your judges. But if I drive out demons by the finger of God, then the kingdom of God has come upon you. When a strong man, fully armed, guards his own house, his possessions are safe. But when someone stronger attacks and overpowers him, he takes away the armour in which the man trusted and divides up his plunder.'

'Gentle Jesus, meek and mild…' This is the wonderfully approachable Jesus, the one to whom we can safely come for comfort and care, to whom we can bring our burdens, our needs and our weariness (Matthew 11:28–30).

This is all good and true, but it is also flat and two-dimensional if we forget that this same Jesus is the one Zephaniah describes as 'the Mighty Warrior who saves' (3:17). In this passage, Jesus is aligning himself with the power of the 'the finger of God', which Pharoah encountered in Exodus 8:19, proving that the God of the exodus is both present and at work through him. He is that 'someone stronger' whose initial victory over Satan in the wilderness was fully completed on the cross.

Jesus is *our* 'someone stronger', who knows our every battle and understands our every struggle and temptation because he has been through it all – and come out the other side unscathed, except for the scars which bear testimony to his love for us.

> Lord Jesus, my mighty Saviour, you already know the struggles and the battles I face. Help me to trust your power and willingness to help me. Give me grace to recognise you at work in my life – and to respond to you with confident and willing obedience.

MD

Day 204

Trust and obey

LUKE 11:23-28 (MATTHEW 12:43-45)

On the road to Jerusalem
'Whoever is not with me is against me, and whoever does not gather with me scatters. When an impure spirit comes out of a person, it goes through arid places seeking rest and does not find it. Then it says, "I will return to the house I left." When it arrives, it finds the house swept clean and put in order. Then it goes and takes seven other spirits more wicked than itself, and they go in and live there. And the final condition of that person is worse than the first.' As Jesus was saying these things, a woman in the crowd called out, 'Blessed is the mother who gave you birth and nursed you.' He replied, 'Blessed rather are those who hear the word of God and obey it.'

Trust and obey, for there's no other way
to be happy in Jesus, but to trust and obey.

I sang those old words with gusto as a new believer in Jesus. Over the past 50 years I've come to deeply appreciate the wisdom of those simple words and the assurance of Jesus' blessing on those who hear, trust and obey his word.

But there is a warning here too. Having already dealt with those who claim he is in league with Satan (11:14-22), Jesus turns his attention to address those who want more evidence. They have seen the miracles, heard the teaching and are still sitting on the fence – an uncomfortable place which leaves them dangerously vulnerable to spiritual attack. They may be *open* to Jesus, but without a *commitment* to Jesus, that openness actually exposes them to other influences which may eventually harm their souls.

There can be no 'neutral' option, a 'take it or leave it' response when it comes to Jesus. Everything about him invites us into an unreserved surrender to his lordship and a wholehearted obedience to his word. Anything less could deprive us of the blessing he longs to pour into our lives.

Jesus is worthy of our trust; worthy of our obedience.

> Is there an invitation here for you? An area of your life perhaps in which you sense that the Lord might be inviting you to trust and obey? Bring whatever comes to mind to God in prayer.

MD

Day 205

Darkness and light

LUKE 11:29–36 (*MATTHEW 6:22–23*)

On the road to Jerusalem
As the crowds increased, Jesus said, 'This is a wicked generation. It asks for a sign, but none will be given it except the sign of Jonah. For as Jonah was a sign to the Ninevites, so also will the Son of Man be to this generation. The Queen of the South will rise at the judgment with the people of this generation and condemn them, for she came from the ends of the earth to listen to Solomon's wisdom; and now something greater than Solomon is here. The men of Nineveh will stand up at the judgment with this generation and condemn it, for they repented at the preaching of Jonah; and now something greater than Jonah is here. No one lights a lamp and puts it in a place where it will be hidden, or under a bowl. Instead they put it on its stand, so that those who come in may see the light. Your eye is the lamp of your body. When your eyes are healthy, your whole body also is full of light. But when they are unhealthy, your body also is full of darkness. See to it, then, that the light within you is not darkness. Therefore, if your whole body is full of light, and no part of it dark, it will be just as full of light as when a lamp shines its light on you.'

Age-related macular degeneration (AMD) is a degenerative eye condition which can lead to almost total blindness. It can be a life-limiting, loss-laden disease. Not necessarily genetic, AMD can be caused by lifestyle choices, which include being overweight and smoking. I know all this because my mother suffers from it.

I wonder if we can suffer from a form of spiritual AMD, caused by choosing not to seek out God's wisdom for our lives, choosing not to repent when God's word holds up a mirror to the sin in our lives?

> *Paul prayed for the Ephesian church that their hearts would be 'flooded with light' (Ephesians 1:18, NLT). It's a great prayer and one we can pray for ourselves today, asking the Lord to reveal to us anything within our hearts which clouds our ability to clearly see and respond to Jesus – to reveal anything which would keep us in the darkness of our ignorance or sin.*

MD

Day 206

Jesus criticises the Pharisees

LUKE 11:37–44

On the road to Jerusalem
When Jesus had finished speaking, a Pharisee invited him to eat with him; so he went in and reclined at the table. But the Pharisee was surprised when he noticed that Jesus did not first wash before the meal. Then the Lord said to him, 'Now then, you Pharisees clean the outside of the cup and dish, but inside you are full of greed and wickedness. You foolish people! Did not the one who made the outside make the inside also? But now as for what is inside you – be generous to the poor, and everything will be clean for you. Woe to you Pharisees, because you give God a tenth of your mint, rue and all other kinds of garden herbs, but you neglect justice and the love of God. You should have practised the latter without leaving the former undone. Woe to you Pharisees, because you love the most important seats in the synagogues and respectful greetings in the market-places. Woe to you, because you are like unmarked graves, which people walk over without knowing it.'

He said it before (Matthew 15:11), and he's saying it again here in these scathing denouncements: what matters most is what's on the inside.

The stinging insult of comparing the Pharisees to an unmarked grave would have been shocking. Jesus is referring to Numbers 19:16 and to the law which states that touching a grave or a dead body made a person unclean for seven days. To avoid this, graves were marked and whitewashed so that no one would inadvertently come into contact with them and be defiled. But Jesus is implying that when people came into contact with the Pharisees, they would be just as defiled – by their hypocrisy and pretentious holiness, by the lack of love and by the crippling legalism which flowed from the deadness of their hearts.

What is in our hearts matters, because whatever is on the inside *will*, eventually, come out – in our relationship with God and our relationship with others.

> Lord Jesus, let the overflow of your life in me – your kindness, your love, your grace – touch all whose lives I touch today. For your glory's sake.

MD

Day 207

Criticism of the legal experts

LUKE 11:45–54

On the road to Jerusalem
One of the experts in the law answered him, 'Teacher, when you say these things, you insult us also.' Jesus replied, 'And you experts in the law, woe to you, because you load people down with burdens they can hardly carry, and you yourselves will not lift one finger to help them. Woe to you, because you build tombs for the prophets, and it was your ancestors who killed them. So you testify that you approve of what your ancestors did; they killed the prophets, and you build their tombs. Because of this, God in his wisdom said, "I will send them prophets and apostles, some of whom they will kill and others they will persecute." Therefore this generation will be held responsible for the blood of all the prophets that has been shed since the beginning of the world, from the blood of Abel to the blood of Zechariah, who was killed between the altar and the sanctuary. Yes, I tell you, this generation will be held responsible for it all. Woe to you experts in the law, because you have taken away the key to knowledge. You yourselves have not entered, and you have hindered those who were entering.' When Jesus went outside, the Pharisees and the teachers of the law began to oppose him fiercely and to besiege him with questions, waiting to catch him in something he might say.

Jesus understood the lives of the men and women who crowded around him every day, thirsting for his words of grace. He saw how their struggle to be faithful to God was a never-ending, futile attempt to get everything right, every moment of every day.

The law was given to hold God's children within the circle of his love and blessing, but in the hands of the lawyers, that gracious intent had become distorted by rituals and rules which were impossible to keep and which made their lives a misery.

Jesus confronted this legalism head-on. But his withering condemnation of their hypocritical and soul-destroying practices didn't provoke repentance or remorse in them – only angry opposition. He was offering these leaders the chance to change, but they fiercely resisted.

> As you reflect on this reading, do you sense any areas in your own life which are ruled more by legalism than by God's loving grace? Bring your reflection to God in prayer.

MD

Day 208

Warnings and encouragements.

LUKE 12:1-12 (*MATTHEW 10:16-33*)

Perea (the region of Judea beyond the Jordan)
Meanwhile, when a crowd of many thousands had gathered, so that they were trampling on one another, Jesus began to speak first to his disciples, saying: 'Be on your guard against the yeast of the Pharisees, which is hypocrisy. There is nothing concealed that will not be disclosed, or hidden that will not be made known. What you have said in the dark will be heard in the daylight, and what you have whispered in the ear in the inner rooms will be proclaimed from the roofs. I tell you, my friends, do not be afraid of those who kill the body and after that can do no more. But I will show you whom you should fear: fear him who, after your body has been killed, has authority to throw you into hell. Yes, I tell you, fear him. Are not five sparrows sold for two pennies? Yet not one of them is forgotten by God. Indeed, the very hairs of your head are all numbered. Don't be afraid; you are worth more than many sparrows. I tell you, whoever publicly acknowledges me before others, the Son of Man will also acknowledge before the angels of God. But whoever disowns me before others will be disowned before the angels of God. And everyone who speaks a word against the Son of Man will be forgiven, but anyone who blasphemes against the Holy Spirit will not be forgiven. When you are brought before synagogues, rulers and authorities, do not worry about how you will defend yourselves or what you will say, for the Holy Spirit will teach you at that time what you should say.'

In responding to Jesus' words of warning and encouragement to his disciples, you might like to use the prayer prompts below as a springboard for your own prayers.

- 'Lord Jesus, help me to live my life with integrity, especially when...'
- 'Forgive me for being more scared of other people's opinions of me than I am of yours...'
- 'You know me intimately. You care about my life; so I bring you...'
- 'Help me to be bold and unashamed in my witness of you, especially with...'
- 'Thank you that you know all my fears and anxieties; I especially bring to you...'

MD

Day 209

Parable of the rich fool

LUKE 12:13–21

Perea
Someone in the crowd said to him, 'Teacher, tell my brother to divide the inheritance with me.' Jesus replied, 'Man, who appointed me a judge or an arbiter between you?' Then he said to them, 'Watch out! Be on your guard against all kinds of greed; life does not consist in an abundance of possessions.' And he told them this parable: 'The ground of a certain rich man yielded an abundant harvest. He thought to himself, "What shall I do? I have no place to store my crops." Then he said, "This is what I'll do. I will tear down my barns and build bigger ones, and there I will store my surplus grain. And I'll say to myself, 'You have plenty of grain laid up for many years. Take life easy; eat, drink and be merry.'" But God said to him, "You fool! This very night your life will be demanded from you. Then who will get what you have prepared for yourself?" This is how it will be with whoever stores up things for themselves but is not rich towards God.'

It's so easy to judge this rich man for his selfishness, his seeming disregard for the needs of the poor and hungry to whom he could have given away his surplus grain. But I wonder how many of us have caught ourselves thinking, 'I need a bigger wardrobe/shoe rack/pantry/garage/toolbox…'? It's so easy to appreciate the wise stewarding of his resources, his forward thinking, his retirement planning – and to be unsettled, perhaps, by how much his thinking mirrors our own.

He is not portrayed as wicked or stupid – yet God calls him a fool! Why?

This parable isn't primarily about wealth; it's about priorities and perspectives, about what we truly value. The issue is not that his field prospered – an abundant harvest is a good thing – it's about how he handled that abundant prosperity. It's about recognising that what matters most is not what's in our bank account, but that we are rich towards God: that our 'account' with God is healthy in the knowledge and love of God, in rich experiences of fellowship and partnering with him in his purposes for our world, in kindness and generosity towards others.

What does 'rich towards God' look like for you in practice? Could you be even richer?

MD

The journey to Jerusalem

Day 210

Be ready and waiting

LUKE 12:35–38 (MATTHEW 24:42–44)

Perea
'Be dressed ready for service and keep your lamps burning, like servants waiting for their master to return from a wedding banquet, so that when he comes and knocks they can immediately open the door for him. It will be good for those servants whose master finds them watching when he comes. Truly I tell you, he will dress himself to serve, will make them recline at the table and will come and wait on them. It will be good for those servants whose master finds them ready, even if he comes in the middle of the night or towards daybreak.'

The bag had been packed for days – ready for the first sign of labour which would prompt the journey to the hospital. Grandma and Grandpa were on hand to babysit at a moment's notice. There was a plentiful supply of food in the freezer and petrol in the car. This little family was as ready as they ever could be. All that was left to do now was to wait for the arrival of this new life. They knew the baby was coming; they just didn't know when exactly – which is just where these servants are in this gem of a parable.

Jesus is teaching his disciples – and us – what it means to be ready and waiting for his arrival, whether it's in anticipation of his final return or as he comes to us in the routine of our lives.

Being ready and waiting means:

- remaining faithful to who God has called us to be and to what he has called us to do
- being increasingly alert, attentive and responsive to the many different ways in which Jesus 'knocks' on the door of our lives
- waiting patiently for God to act, and letting go of our demands that God work according to our timetable and expectations
- being open to being surprised by new revelations of who God is, what God does and how God works. (A master who serves? Think of Lord Grantham serving Mrs Patmore in *Downton Abbey*.)

Which of the above struck a chord with you? Stirred up a desire in you? Revealed a need in your relationship with Jesus? Bring your reflections to the Lord in prayer.

MD

Day 211

The man and the mission

LUKE 12:49–53 (NLT) (*MATTHEW 10:34–38*)

Perea

'I have come to set the world on fire, and I wish it were already burning! I have a terrible baptism of suffering ahead of me, and I am under a heavy burden until it is accomplished. Do you think I have come to bring peace to the earth? No, I have come to divide people against each other! From now on families will be split apart, three in favour of me, and two against – or two in favour and three against. "Father will be divided against son and son against father; mother against daughter and daughter against mother; and mother-in-law against daughter-in-law and daughter-in-law against mother-in-law."'

Pause for a moment. Before reading on, go back and read Jesus' words again – out loud if possible.

How did you read? What was the tone of your voice? Sad? Forceful? Angry? Passionate? Resigned?

We don't know the tone in which Jesus spoke these words, but we do know that even as he spoke them, he was facing the reality of the suffering to come, a reality which weighed heavily on him. He knew what was coming in Jerusalem; he knew that every day, every step, brought him closer to the brutal events that lay ahead for him. He carried, too, the knowledge of what was coming for all who would follow him: not peace, but conflict; not harmony, but division. Their commitment to him had the potential to devastate their families, bringing discord and disruption. This was his daily burden. And it was heavy.

> Read the passage aloud again, and notice what captures your attention as you hear these words again. Bring that response to the Lord in prayer.

MD

Day 212

Interpreting the times

LUKE 12:54–59

Perea
He said to the crowd: 'When you see a cloud rising in the west, immediately you say, "It's going to rain," and it does. And when the south wind blows, you say, "It's going to be hot," and it is. Hypocrites! You know how to interpret the appearance of the earth and the sky. How is it that you don't know how to interpret this present time? Why don't you judge for yourselves what is right? As you are going with your adversary to the magistrate, try hard to be reconciled on the way, or your adversary may drag you off to the judge, and the judge turn you over to the officer, and the officer throw you into prison. I tell you, you will not get out until you have paid the last penny.'

Have you ever sat with a child and played 'Join the dots'? The pencil begins at 1, moves to 2, then 3… and before long a shape begins to form and the child starts guessing: 'It's a hippo!'; then, 'No! It's an elephant!' And on it goes until all is revealed.

After centuries of waiting, the Messiah had come and was ushering in the kingdom of God. The evidence was there in front of them in all of Jesus' words and actions. The crowd saw it all but didn't join the dots. Somehow, they didn't interpret what it meant, couldn't see that this moment in time was what all of Israel's history had been leading up to. It was the moment foretold by prophets down the centuries. The truth about Jesus was plain before their eyes, and yet so many refused to acknowledge it. Jesus is clearly frustrated with those who listened to him that day. A hypocrite is someone who knows what is right but lives in denial of it – and that's what they were doing. But Jesus doesn't give up on them. His little parable holds out the hope that there is still time to put that right, still time to recognise and acknowledge the truth of who he is, still time to turn their lives around.

As you refect on different events in your own life in these past days, can you trace any possible connection between them? What do you sense God may be wanting to say to you through them? Bring your reflections to God in prayer.

MD

Day 213

Of tyrants and towers and fruitless trees

LUKE 13:1–9

Perea
Now there were some present at that time who told Jesus about the Galileans whose blood Pilate had mixed with their sacrifices. Jesus answered, 'Do you think that these Galileans were worse sinners than all the other Galileans because they suffered this way? I tell you, no! But unless you repent, you too will all perish. Or those eighteen who died when the tower in Siloam fell on them – do you think they were more guilty than all the others living in Jerusalem? I tell you, no! But unless you repent, you too will all perish.' Then he told this parable: 'A man had a fig-tree growing in his vineyard, and he went to look for fruit on it but did not find any. So he said to the man who took care of the vineyard, "For three years now I've been coming to look for fruit on this fig-tree and haven't found any. Cut it down! Why should it use up the soil?" "Sir," the man replied, "leave it alone for one more year, and I'll dig round it and fertilise it. If it bears fruit next year, fine! If not, then cut it down."'

When tyrants rise and towers fall in all sorts of ways and under all sorts of circumstances, we are understandably shocked, and a question is shaken out of our bewildered hearts: 'Why?' It's not a question Jesus answers. He apportions no blame, offers no cause-and-effect rationale. Rather, he moves the focus away from the question *why* and places it on *how*: how do we live in a world where these kinds of things happen? His surprising answer is through repentance.

Repentance is not so much about sorrow over sin as much as it is about deliberately turning away from destructive and diminishing ways of thinking and living. It's about aligning ourselves with God's purposes for our lives and for our world. Repentance is shown in a life marked by love, compassion, forgiveness and other expressions of the life of Jesus within us.

Jesus is reminding us here that every single day is a 'grace day', providing us with fresh opportunities to repent – to start again, to live fully and fruitfully in whatever 'soil' we're planted.

> So today, what do you need to turn from, to turn to, in order to experience and express the grace of God for you?

MD

Day 214

Healing in the synagogue

LUKE 13:10–17

> Perea
> On a Sabbath Jesus was teaching in one of the synagogues, and a woman was there who had been crippled by a spirit for eighteen years. She was bent over and could not straighten up at all. When Jesus saw her, he called her forward and said to her, 'Woman, you are set free from your infirmity.' Then he put his hands on her, and immediately she straightened up and praised God. Indignant because Jesus had healed on the Sabbath, the synagogue leader said to the people, 'There are six days for work. So come and be healed on those days, not on the Sabbath.' The Lord answered him, 'You hypocrites! Doesn't each of you on the Sabbath untie your ox or donkey from the stall and lead it out to give it water? Then should not this woman, a daughter of Abraham, whom Satan has kept bound for eighteen long years, be set free on the Sabbath day from what bound her?' When he said this, all his opponents were humiliated, but the people were delighted with all the wonderful things he was doing.

'Eighteen long years'… until Jesus saw her, and set her free.

Jesus sees us. He sees us in all our brokenness and neediness, in all our crippling insecurities and fears. He sees all the things which bind us and which bow our heads low in guilt and shame and weariness. And when he looks at us, it's through eyes filled not with judgement, but with endless compassion for all that we are – and for all that we're not.

On that day, this dear woman praised God because she realised she'd come face to face with the God David described as 'the lifter of my head' (Psalm 3:3, ESV); the God who declared to his people, 'I have set you free; now walk with your heads held high' (Leviticus 26:13, CEV). From that moment on, she would literally walk with her head lifted high, a woman freed and free.

Hold tight today the truth that you are known; that you are seen by an infinitely compassionate Saviour who longs to release you from all that is bowing you down, all that is keeping you bound.

> Lord Jesus, you see me, you know me, you call me into your presence to love me into freedom and healing. I come to you now.

MD

Day 215

The organic growth of the kingdom

LUKE 13:18–21 (MATTHEW 13:31–33; MARK 4:30–32)

Perea
Then Jesus asked, 'What is the kingdom of God like? What shall I compare it to? It is like a mustard seed, which a man took and planted in his garden. It grew and became a tree, and the birds perched in its branches.' Again he asked, 'What shall I compare the kingdom of God to? It is like yeast that a woman took and mixed into about thirty kilograms of flour until it worked all through the dough.'

They had just witnessed a miracle. They had watched as Satan's hold on a needy woman's life was broken, her dignity, wholeness and freedom restored, providing clear evidence of the arrival of the kingdom of God among them. And now, springboarding from the healing of that one woman, Jesus teaches them about the nature and growth of the kingdom of God.

He talked to them about familiar things – seeds and yeast – small, ordinary, seemingly insignificant things which, when placed where they can have maximum effect, produce results that are out of all proportion to their size.

There may be times when we wonder how our own small, ordinary lives can make any impact on the growth of the kingdom of God around us, and yet if these parables teach us anything, it's that when we faithfully live out our redeemed lives where God has placed us, anything is possible! What matters is our presence and engagement in those places; the size of the seed, the quantity of the yeast is not what matters – but the seed must be *in* the ground, the yeast *in* the flour to make any difference.

If you have been touched by the miracle of God's grace, however small or insignificant you may feel, your life is already a witness to the reality of the presence of God in this world. So, where has God placed you? In what roles and relationships, locations and contexts are you already 'planted'?

> *Bring those places, those people and yourself to God in prayer now, with a confident expectation that God is able to do with our lives 'far more than we ever dare to ask or imagine' (Ephesians 3:20, JBP).*

MD

Day 216

The open door

LUKE 13:22-30 (MATTHEW 7:13-14)

Towns and villages on the way to Jerusalem
Then Jesus went through the towns and villages, teaching as he made his way to Jerusalem. Someone asked him, 'Lord, are only a few people going to be saved?' He said to them, 'Make every effort to enter through the narrow door, because many, I tell you, will try to enter and will not be able to. Once the owner of the house gets up and closes the door, you will stand outside knocking and pleading, "Sir, open the door for us." But he will answer, "I don't know you or where you come from." Then you will say, "We ate and drank with you, and you taught in our streets." But he will reply, "I don't know you or where you come from. Away from me, all you evildoers!" There will be weeping there, and gnashing of teeth, when you see Abraham, Isaac and Jacob and all the prophets in the kingdom of God, but you yourselves thrown out. People will come from east and west and north and south, and will take their places at the feast in the kingdom of God. Indeed there are those who are last who will be first, and first who will be last.'

However speculative the question may have been, Jesus' response was pointedly personal; he said in effect, 'This isn't about the few, it's about *you* – and this particular door will not stay open forever.'

There are times in our lives when God seems to present us with an open door. It may lead into a new relationship, a new role, a new experience of life or perhaps a new place in our faith journey. Unless we respond in trusting obedience at that moment, we may find the door closes, the moment passes, the opportunity is lost.

Many who listened to Jesus' teaching presumed that as Jews, they automatically had a guaranteed place at God's table, and so felt no urgency to understand or respond to Jesus' message about a new kind of kingdom, where entry was through repentance and faith *in him alone*. Tearfully, Jesus would later attribute Jerusalem's impending destruction to the fact that 'you have rejected the opportunity God offered you' (Luke 19:44, TLB).

> As you consider Jesus' words, do you have any sense that God is perhaps opening a new door somewhere in your life? How will you respond?

MD

Day 217

Healing on the sabbath

LUKE 14:1-6

On the way to Jerusalem
One Sabbath, when Jesus went to eat in the house of a prominent Pharisee, he was being carefully watched. There in front of him was a man suffering from abnormal swelling of his body. Jesus asked the Pharisees and experts in the law, 'Is it lawful to heal on the Sabbath or not?' But they remained silent. So taking hold of the man, he healed him and sent him on his way. Then he asked them, 'If one of you has a child or an ox that falls into a well on the Sabbath day, will you not immediately pull it out?' And they had nothing to say.

When Jesus said, 'Love your enemies, do good to those who hate you' (Luke 6:27), he wasn't telling us to do something he himself didn't do. His words were hewn from the rock of his own practice, his own commitment to embodying the love of God – for all.

The staggering truth is that Jesus loved these Pharisees every bit as much as he loved the man he healed. They were his enemies, they hated him, they were plotting to kill him – but he didn't give up on pursuing their law-hardened hearts.

He loved them enough to accept their invitation to dinner – probably knowing he was entering a trap. They had tried to trap him before (Luke 11:54), and here we are again: a repeat performance featuring The Sabbath, Pharisees, Experts in the Law, A Needy Person – and Jesus, trying again to help them understand the heart of the law, modelling for them the heart of God.

Jesus entered the trap that had been set for him, but on his own terms. He didn't allow them to manipulate him into compromising his convictions – or his character. He didn't lose his temper, his questions were direct but not rude, serving only to highlight their flawed understanding of the law.

In the same breath that he tells us to love our enemies, in a parallel passage Jesus tells us to 'pray for those who hurt you' (Matthew 5:44, ICB). We may not consider those who have hurt us as enemies – it doesn't really matter – we are to love them enough to pray for them.

▍ *As you reflect on this encounter, is there someone you need to pray for today?*

MD

Day 218

Teaching on honour, humility and hospitality

LUKE 14:7–14

On the way to Jerusalem
When he noticed how the guests picked the places of honour at the table, he told them this parable: 'When someone invites you to a wedding feast, do not take the place of honour, for a person more distinguished than you may have been invited. If so, the host who invited both of you will come and say to you, "Give this person your seat." Then, humiliated, you will have to take the least important place. But when you are invited, take the lowest place, so that when your host comes, he will say to you, "Friend, move up to a better place." Then you will be honoured in the presence of all the other guests. For all those who exalt themselves will be humbled, and those who humble themselves will be exalted.' Then Jesus said to his host, 'When you give a luncheon or dinner, do not invite your friends, your brothers or sisters, your relatives, or your rich neighbours; if you do, they may invite you back and so you will be repaid. But when you give a banquet, invite the poor, the crippled, the lame, the blind, and you will be blessed. Although they cannot repay you, you will be repaid at the resurrection of the righteous.'

I'd come home to find a stranger and her baby sitting on the sofa. She was being treated so warmly that I thought she was long-lost family. There was a pile of baby clothes next to her, which I recognised as my sister's, and one of mum's jackets folded underneath them. After a hearty lunch, she left, and it was only then that I discovered who she was: my dad had seen her sobbing and in distress at the side of the road, and he'd brought her home.

That was over 50 years ago, but I've never forgotten my dad's kindness that day. She wasn't expected, but she was welcomed like family into our home, treated with warmth and care and tender respect.

Honour, humility, respect, generous hospitality which cannot be repaid: these are challenging, but potentially life-changing, world-changing, attitudes when lived out in our individual contexts. Jesus didn't just teach about these qualities; he modelled them and calls us, his disciples, to live out these kingdom-stamped qualities wherever we are, whoever we're with.

> *Father, draw my attention today to the opportunities around me to live out these kingdom qualities.*

MD

Day 219

The great feast

LUKE 14:15-24

On the way to Jerusalem
When one of those at the table with him heard this, he said to Jesus, 'Blessed is the one who will eat at the feast in the kingdom of God.' Jesus replied: 'A certain man was preparing a great banquet and invited many guests. At the time of the banquet he sent his servant to tell those who had been invited, "Come, for everything is now ready." But they all alike began to make excuses. The first said, "I have just bought a field, and I must go and see it. Please excuse me." Another said, "I have just bought five yoke of oxen, and I'm on my way to try them out. Please excuse me." Still another said, "I have just got married, so I can't come." The servant came back and reported this to his master. Then the owner of the house became angry and ordered his servant, "Go out quickly into the streets and alleys of the town and bring in the poor, the crippled, the blind and the lame." "Sir," the servant said, "what you ordered has been done, but there is still room." Then the master told his servant, "Go out to the roads and country lanes and compel them to come in, so that my house will be full. I tell you, not one of those who were invited will get a taste of my banquet."'

Although rejected by those who'd been invited first, the host in this parable turns great insult into generous grace as he offers lavish hospitality to all who would accept it. Whoever they were, wherever they'd come from, however socially or religiously unacceptable they might have been, they were welcomed.

Every day, God offers me lavish grace, the honour of his company, unconditional acceptance. However undeserving I may feel, I belong at this feast because *God invited me* and *wants me* there.

So many of us find it hard to accept this gift of grace, but this parable invites us to trust the God who flings open the door of his home and says, 'Come on in! You are so welcomed here.'

> Father, help me to honour you by believing in your grace towards me – not only for when I first came to know you, but for every day of my life.

MD

Day 220

The cost of living

LUKE 14:25–35 (MATTHEW 5:13; MARK 9:50)

On the road to Jerusalem
Large crowds were travelling with Jesus, and turning to them he said: 'If anyone comes to me and does not hate father and mother, wife and children, brothers and sisters – yes, even their own life – such a person cannot be my disciple. And whoever does not carry their cross and follow me cannot be my disciple. Suppose one of you wants to build a tower. Won't you first sit down and estimate the cost to see if you have enough money to complete it? For if you lay the foundation and are not able to finish it, everyone who sees it will ridicule you, saying, "This person began to build and wasn't able to finish." Or suppose a king is about to go to war against another king. Won't he first sit down and consider whether he is able with ten thousand men to oppose the one coming against him with twenty thousand? If he is not able, he will send a delegation while the other is still a long way off and will ask for terms of peace. In the same way, those of you who do not give up everything you have cannot be my disciples. Salt is good, but if it loses its saltiness, how can it be made salty again? It is fit neither for the soil nor for the manure heap; it is thrown out. Whoever has ears to hear, let them hear.'

After weeks of agonised prayer, my friends finally left Ukraine with little more than the clothes on their backs. They left behind their home, possessions, beloved family members, lives they had established. They left everything for one reason only – they wanted to live. They had counted the cost, and chose life.

Jesus came to give us life in all its rich and satisfying fullness (John 10:10), but the only way to experience this life is as his disciple, learning from him as teacher, following him as Lord. Jesus doesn't hide the cost: 'If you're not willing to take what is dearest to you, whether plans or people, and kiss it good-bye, you can't be my disciple' (v. 33, MSG). Jesus' words might seem unduly harsh and demanding – until we recognise that *he is saving our lives.*

> Lord Jesus, I want to live. Help me kiss goodbye to whatever holds me back from following you with all my heart.

MD

Day 221

Lost sheep and lost coins: found

LUKE 15:1-10 (*MATTHEW 18:12-14*)

On the road to Jerusalem
Now the tax collectors and sinners were all gathering round to hear Jesus. But the Pharisees and the teachers of the law muttered, 'This man welcomes sinners, and eats with them.' Then Jesus told them this parable: 'Suppose one of you has a hundred sheep and loses one of them. Doesn't he leave the ninety-nine in the open country and go after the lost sheep until he finds it? And when he finds it, he joyfully puts it on his shoulders and goes home. Then he calls his friends and neighbours together and says, "Rejoice with me; I have found my lost sheep." I tell you that in the same way there will be more rejoicing in heaven over one sinner who repents than over ninety-nine righteous people who do not need to repent. Or suppose a woman has ten silver coins and loses one. Doesn't she light a lamp, sweep the house and search carefully until she finds it? And when she finds it, she calls her friends and neighbours together and says, "Rejoice with me; I have found my lost coin." In the same way, I tell you, there is rejoicing in the presence of the angels of God over one sinner who repents.'

Psalm 119:176 may be one of the most poignant verses in the Bible: 'I have wandered away like a lost sheep; come and find me' (TLB). After 175 verses extolling the wonder of God's word and his obedience to it, this is where the psalmist ends – with an acknowledgment of his lostness and a plea that God come and find him.

Perhaps it's this response that Jesus was coveting for the law-encrusted hearts of the Pharisees who listened to his parables that day. That they would not only recognise God's relentless pursuit of the lost – but also *their own* lostness.

We can get lost in so many places, can't we? In sin, in legalism, in hurts and disappointment. We can lose ourselves in our work, our hobbies, our relationships, our sincere but wearying efforts to be pleasing to God and others.

Wherever you may feel lost today, and however you came to be there, know that your God knows where you are and how you got there, and he will come and find you.

> *Today, you can make the psalmist's prayer your own: 'I have wandered away like a lost sheep; come and find me.'*

MD

Day 222

The wayward son

LUKE 15:11–24

On the road to Jerusalem

Jesus continued: 'There was a man who had two sons. The younger one said to his father, "Father, give me my share of the estate." So he divided his property between them. Not long after that, the younger son got together all he had, set off for a distant country and there squandered his wealth in wild living. After he had spent everything, there was a severe famine in that whole country, and he began to be in need. So he went and hired himself out to a citizen of that country, who sent him to his fields to feed pigs. He longed to fill his stomach with the pods that the pigs were eating, but no one gave him anything. When he came to his senses, he said, "How many of my father's hired servants have food to spare, and here I am starving to death! I will set out and go back to my father and say to him: Father, I have sinned against heaven and against you. I am no longer worthy to be called your son; make me like one of your hired servants." So he got up and went to his father. But while he was still a long way off, his father saw him and was filled with compassion for him; he ran to his son, threw his arms round him and kissed him. The son said to him, "Father, I have sinned against heaven and against you. I am no longer worthy to be called your son." But the father said to his servants, "Quick! Bring the best robe and put it on him. Put a ring on his finger and sandals on his feet. Bring the fattened calf and kill it. Let's have a feast and celebrate. For this son of mine was dead and is alive again; he was lost and is found." So they began to celebrate.'

Such a tragic story – a wayward, disrespectful son, and a father who never gave up on him, who, when he returns, welcomes him home with joy and forgiveness.

> *Now, read it again, with the following prompts in mind: What word or phrase draws your attention? What comes to you as you reflect on it? In what ways does this passage touch your life today? (Turn to page 13 for a fuller explanation of lectio divina.)*

MD

Day 223

The elder brother

LUKE 15:25–32

On the road to Jerusalem
'Meanwhile, the elder son was in the field. When he came near the house, he heard music and dancing. So he called one of the servants and asked him what was going on. "Your brother has come," he replied, "and your father has killed the fattened calf because he has him back safe and sound." The elder brother became angry and refused to go in. So his father went out and pleaded with him. But he answered his father, "Look! All these years I've been slaving for you and never disobeyed your orders. Yet you never gave me even a young goat so I could celebrate with my friends. But when this son of yours who has squandered your property with prostitutes comes home, you kill the fattened calf for him!" "My son," the father said, "you are always with me, and everything I have is yours. But we had to celebrate and be glad, because this brother of yours was dead and is alive again; he was lost and is found."'

In this parable, Jesus holds up a mirror to the hearts of the Pharisees – and perhaps to our own heart, too, as we witness the elder son's outraged responses to the generous, gracious actions of the father towards his profligate younger son.

In this elder son we see a picture of a dutiful, obedient, hard-working, self-sacrificing child, who is also joyless, self-righteous, angry, resentful and bitter. Lost in the wasteland of his grievances against his father, he seems unwilling to forgive his brother's sins or the ways in which those sins have impacted his own life.

The only path out of this lostness seems to be through believing and trusting his father's words to him: 'My son, you are always with me and everything I have is yours' (v. 31).

Do we see anything of ourselves in this picture of the elder son? Are there places where we too may be lost, hurting ourselves on rocks of resentment, of disappointment, of needs which were never met, of past hurts and unfair treatment? In leaving the ending of the parable open, Jesus leaves open the possibility of change – for the Pharisees, and for us too.

> Hear again the Father's words and bring your responses to those words to God in prayer: 'My child, you are always with me, and everything I have is yours.'

MD

Day 224

A day of reckoning

LUKE 16:1-9

On the road to Jerusalem
Jesus told his disciples: 'There was a rich man whose manager was accused of wasting his possessions. So he called him in and asked him, "What is this I hear about you? Give an account of your management, because you cannot be manager any longer." The manager said to himself, "What shall I do now? My master is taking away my job. I'm not strong enough to dig, and I'm ashamed to beg – I know what I'll do so that, when I lose my job here, people will welcome me into their houses." So he called in each one of his master's debtors. He asked the first, "How much do you owe my master?" "Three thousand litres of olive oil," he replied. The manager told him, "Take your bill, sit down quickly, and make it fifteen hundred." Then he asked the second, "And how much do you owe?" "Thirty tons of wheat," he replied. He told him, "Take your bill and make it twenty-four." The master commended the dishonest manager because he had acted shrewdly. For the people of this world are more shrewd in dealing with their own kind than are the people of the light. I tell you, use worldly wealth to gain friends for yourselves, so that when it is gone, you will be welcomed into eternal dwellings.'

Like the prodigal in the preceding parable (15:13), this dishonest manager has also squandered what was entrusted to him and is now facing the consequences. One day, like this steward, we too will give account – to God – of how we have stewarded the multi-faceted resources we've been entrusted with (Romans 14:12), not only our finances or possessions, but also our gifts, skills, temperaments, time. How we've allowed our life experiences to shape us more profoundly into the likeness of Jesus. How we've used the influence we've been given. How we've raised our voices in those places and spaces where they've needed to be heard. How we've stewarded and nurtured our relationships, and our relationship with God.

The prodigal 'came to his senses' (15:17) and this dishonest manager also had his 'light bulb moment' when he faced his master. As a result, they made changes that shaped their futures.

> As you consider all that God has so generously entrusted to you, are there changes you want to make in the days ahead? Bring those possible changes to the Lord in prayer.

MD

Day 225

The heart of the matter

LUKE 16:10–15

On the road to Jerusalem
'Whoever can be trusted with very little can also be trusted with much, and whoever is dishonest with very little will also be dishonest with much. So if you have not been trustworthy in handling worldly wealth, who will trust you with true riches? And if you have not been trustworthy with someone else's property, who will give you property of your own? No one can serve two masters. Either you will hate the one and love the other, or you will be devoted to the one and despise the other. You cannot serve both God and Money.' The Pharisees, who loved money, heard all this and were sneering at Jesus. He said to them, 'You are the ones who justify yourselves in the eyes of others, but God knows your hearts. What people value highly is detestable in God's sight.'

It's a catchy tune – so easy to sing – but so challenging to live these words: 'Riches I heed not nor man's empty praise… Thou and thou only first in my heart, high king of heaven my treasure thou art.' 'Be Thou My Vision' is one of our most beloved hymns – but it's a prayer too, in which we declare that we choose God as our treasure, our first and greatest love.

We know from experience that the choices we make shape our lives; they shape our priorities, our loyalties, our relationships, the use of our time and other resources. In this passage Jesus presented his hearers – and us – with a stark choice: Money or God – which one will we serve?

It's not that having money and having a relationship with God are mutually exclusive; it's rather that whichever is *first* in our hearts will control everything else about our lives. It has little to do with how much or how little money we have; rich and poor are faced with the same choice: to what will we give our hearts, our strength, our energies? To the pursuit of money, which 'cannot be trusted', or God, who 'takes care of us richly' (1 Timothy 6:17, ERV)?

> Father, I choose you this day. I choose to trust you with all and for all my life. Be my treasure, my only treasure.

MD

Day 226

The rich man and Lazarus

LUKE 16:19–31

On the road to Jerusalem
'There was a rich man who was dressed in purple and fine linen and lived in luxury every day. At his gate was laid a beggar named Lazarus, covered with sores and longing to eat what fell from the rich man's table. Even the dogs came and licked his sores. The time came when the beggar died and the angels carried him to Abraham's side. The rich man also died and was buried. In Hades, where he was in torment, he looked up and saw Abraham far away, with Lazarus by his side. So he called to him, "Father Abraham, have pity on me and send Lazarus to dip the tip of his finger in water and cool my tongue, because I am in agony in this fire." But Abraham replied, "Son, remember that in your lifetime you received your good things, while Lazarus received bad things, but now he is comforted here and you are in agony. And besides all this, between us and you a great chasm has been set in place, so that those who want to go from here to you cannot, nor can anyone cross over from there to us." He answered, "Then I beg you, father, send Lazarus to my family, for I have five brothers. Let him warn them, so that they will not also come to this place of torment." Abraham replied, "They have Moses and the Prophets; let them listen to them." "No, father Abraham," he said, "but if someone from the dead goes to them, they will repent." He said to him, "If they do not listen to Moses and the Prophets, they will not be convinced even if someone rises from the dead."'

'Amy!' 'Hey Joe!' Across the traffic, they waved to each other like old friends. He was begging in her neighbourhood when my friend first met him. She'd asked his name, heard his story – and opened her purse. After that, whenever she saw him, she stopped to chat – and to give.

Amy's kindness stands in stunning contrast to this rich man's disregard of the scriptures, which commanded the rich to care for the poor (Deuteronomy 15:7, 11). The parable was Jesus' clearest warning to the Pharisees that their callous lack of compassion for the needy had eternal consequences.

> We have the same scriptures, the same neediness around us, the same opportunities to care. How will we respond?

MD

Day 227

Rebuke, repentance and forgiveness

LUKE 17:1-10 (*MATTHEW 18:6-7; MARK 9:42*)

On the road to Jerusalem
Jesus said to his disciples: 'Things that cause people to stumble are bound to come, but woe to anyone through whom they come. It would be better for them to be thrown into the sea with a millstone tied around their neck than to cause one of these little ones to stumble. So watch yourselves. If your brother or sister sins against you, rebuke them; and if they repent, forgive them. Even if they sin against you seven times in a day and seven times come back to you saying "I repent," you must forgive them.' The apostles said to the Lord, 'Increase our faith!' He replied, 'If you have faith as small as a mustard seed, you can say to this mulberry tree, "Be uprooted and planted in the sea," and it will obey you. Suppose one of you has a servant ploughing or looking after the sheep. Will he say to the servant when he comes in from the field, "Come along now and sit down to eat"? Won't he rather say, "Prepare my supper, get yourself ready and wait on me while I eat and drink; after that you may eat and drink"? Will he thank the servant because he did what he was told to do? So you also, when you have done everything you were told to do, should say, "We are unworthy servants; we have only done our duty."'

I know how long she'd waited, how hard she'd prayed, how much she'd thought about it before speaking with me, because she told me later. Her rebuke was uncompromisingly clear. It was also gentle, wise, loving – and for my good. She rebuked me because she cared. And she forgave me, unconditionally, when I repented and asked for forgiveness.

It takes great courage to rebuke sin, and generous grace to forgive – especially when it's needed over and over again. Perhaps that's why the disciples asked for an increase in faith. Perhaps they recognised that it takes a profound trust and reliance on God to do what seems so impossible – to care enough to confront and to forgive sin in a way that reflects the heart of God. Humility too, perhaps, to recognise that we've done nothing outstandingly worthy when we do that!

> Father, thank you that you love me enough to rebuke me, to forgive me, time and time again.

MD

Day 228

A thankful leper

LUKE 17:11–19

On the road to Jerusalem
Now on his way to Jerusalem, Jesus travelled along the border between Samaria and Galilee. As he was going into a village, ten men who had leprosy met him. They stood at a distance and called out in a loud voice, 'Jesus, Master, have pity on us!' When he saw them, he said, 'Go, show yourselves to the priests.' And as they went, they were cleansed. One of them, when he saw he was healed, came back, praising God in a loud voice. He threw himself at Jesus' feet and thanked him – and he was a Samaritan. Jesus asked, 'Were not all ten cleansed? Where are the other nine? Has no one returned to give praise to God except this foreigner?' Then he said to him, 'Rise and go; your faith has made you well.'

I so appreciate – and enjoy – Anne Lamott's words, 'Here are the two best prayers I know: "Help me, help me, help me" and "Thank you, thank you, thank you."'[29] Yet in our reading, only one of ten healed men who called out to Jesus in their needy desperation that day returned to say thank you. And Jesus seems surprised by that.

I wonder if he is as surprised by our lack of gratitude?

It's so easy for us to fall into bed at the end of the day without any conscious acknowledgment of God's goodness to us in that day. Perhaps, like the other nine lepers, we take God's loving response to our neediness for granted.

An ancient prayer form, the Prayer of Examen, or Attentiveness, can help us become more aware of God's presence in our day, and more consciously thankful, especially as we notice how the Lord has answered our prayers. It's a simple process: at the end of the day, we take a few quiet moments to look back over the day, watching where God has been present with us, consciously recognising those moments when we have experienced the ways in which his love has been demonstrated to us – in kindness, in generosity, in moments of joy and laughter, in moments of encouragement and comfort. As we bring these moments to mind, thanksgiving and praise are the natural response.

> If you've never experienced this prayer form before, take a few moments now to be quiet, to acknowledge God's presence and to begin looking back over your day.

MD

Day 229

The coming of the kingdom of God

LUKE 17:20-25

On the road to Jerusalem
Once, on being asked by the Pharisees when the kingdom of God would come, Jesus replied, 'The coming of the kingdom of God is not something that can be observed, nor will people say, "Here it is," or "There it is," because the kingdom of God is in your midst.' Then he said to his disciples, 'The time is coming when you will long to see one of the days of the Son of Man, but you will not see it. People will tell you, "There he is!" or "Here he is!" Do not go running off after them. For the Son of Man in his day will be like the lightning, which flashes and lights up the sky from one end to the other. But first he must suffer many things and be rejected by this generation.'

'When, O Lord?' Who of us haven't asked that question as we've watched the news, and thought, 'When, O Lord? When will you return to set things right and deal with all that's wrong in our world?'

The Pharisees were asking the same question – 'When will the kingdom of God come?' For most Jews in the first century, 'kingdom' meant independence from foreign rule, a restoration of political power, economic prosperity, freedom. And there was no sign of that happening any time soon.

Their question presumed that the coming of the kingdom was a future event. In his response, Jesus doesn't focus on a future date when the kingdom truly would be seen in all its fullness; rather, he draws their attention to the present.

The kingdom was already present because the king was present in the presence and person of Jesus. The reign of God had already broken into their world and was clearly evident in Jesus' ministry – if only they had eyes to see it.

When we are tempted to despair over the state of our world, when we long for Jesus' return, Jesus' response to the Pharisees can encourage us to be more attentive to signs of God's kingdom already present in our lives. The risen Christ is present now, moving among us, seen in every word or deed or decision which expresses the Father's love, care, wisdom and grace.

> *Lord Jesus, give me eyes to recognise even the smallest signs of your kingdom in my day today.*

MD

The journey to Jerusalem

Day 230

Remember Lot's wife

LUKE 17:26-37

On the road to Jerusalem
'Just as it was in the days of Noah, so also will it be in the days of the Son of Man. People were eating, drinking, marrying and being given in marriage up to the day Noah entered the ark. Then the flood came and destroyed them all. It was the same in the days of Lot. People were eating and drinking, buying and selling, planting and building. But the day Lot left Sodom, fire and sulphur rained down from heaven and destroyed them all. It will be just like this on the day the Son of Man is revealed. On that day no one who is on the housetop, with possessions inside, should go down to get them. Likewise, no one in the field should go back for anything. Remember Lot's wife! Whoever tries to keep their life will lose it, and whoever loses their life will preserve it. I tell you, on that night two people will be in one bed; one will be taken and the other left. Two women will be grinding corn together; one will be taken and the other left.' 'Where, Lord?' they asked. He replied, 'Where there is a dead body, there the vultures will gather.'

In a cryptic conversation, heavy with images and warnings of impending disaster and future judgement, Jesus drew his disciples' attention to Lot's wife. Why?

In Judaism, Lot's wife was a symbol of wilful disobedience. Contrary to the clear word of God's messengers to flee and to not look back, she looked back (Genesis 19:17, 26). Such a simple action – but one which cost her life. She'd been given no reason for the command, but it was a word to be obeyed. She could have had no idea what her disobedience would cost, just as we have no idea what our own lack of trust and obedience may cost us.

Although it may not cost our lives, there will be a cost if we too look back and hold on to the past when God is urging us forward into the future and into his good and loving purposes for us. There will be a price to pay when we consciously disregard and disobey God's word to us.

> *Father, as I remember Lot's wife, help me to recognise where I'm slipping into her shoes and walking in her ways. Help me walk in your footsteps.*

MD

Day 231

The persistent widow

LUKE 18:1–8

On the road to Jerusalem
Then Jesus told his disciples a parable to show them that they should always pray and not give up. He said: 'In a certain town there was a judge who neither feared God nor cared what people thought. And there was a widow in that town who kept coming to him with the plea, "Grant me justice against my adversary." For some time he refused. But finally he said to himself, "Even though I don't fear God or care what people think, yet because this widow keeps bothering me, I will see that she gets justice, so that she won't eventually come and attack me!"' And the Lord said, 'Listen to what the unjust judge says. And will not God bring about justice for his chosen ones, who cry out to him day and night? Will he keep putting them off? I tell you, he will see that they get justice, and quickly. However, when the Son of Man comes, will he find faith on the earth?'

It's a study in contrasts. She is not your stereotypical image of a widow – helpless, vulnerable, dependent! Jesus portrays her as feisty, demanding, engaged. She is not afraid to confront authority in her pursuit of vengeance. No cowering wallflower, she batters the judge with her pleas until he eventually gives in and supports her cause.

Jesus tells us to 'learn a lesson' from this judge (v. 6, NLT), because in contrast to him, God is no unconcerned judge, impatient with our needs, frustrated by our persistence, bothered by our prayers. We don't need to beg, plead, threaten or cajole God to answer our prayers. We may pray often and long, but he heard us the first time!

We are his chosen ones (Ephesians 1:4). Because of Christ, the judge of all the earth is our Abba, our Father (Genesis 18:25; Romans 8:15), so we can be confident that when we bring our requests to him, he will respond in loving kindness and wisdom.

But will we keep trusting him? It's the question Jesus asked. How will we answer?

> *Father, thank you that I can pour out my heart to you in fearless confidence, even now, as I bring my concerns to you, especially my concern for those places in the world at large, and in my own world, where justice, fairness, is in short supply.*

MD

Day 232

The Pharisee and the tax collector: a parable

LUKE 18:9–14

On the road to Jerusalem

To some who were confident of their own righteousness and looked down on everyone else, Jesus told this parable: 'Two men went up to the temple to pray, one a Pharisee and the other a tax collector. The Pharisee stood by himself and prayed: "God, I thank you that I am not like other people – robbers, evildoers, adulterers – or even like this tax collector. I fast twice a week and give a tenth of all I get." But the tax collector stood at a distance. He would not even look up to heaven, but beat his breast and said, "God, have mercy on me, a sinner." I tell you that this man, rather than the other, went home justified before God. For all those who exalt themselves will be humbled, and those who humble themselves will be exalted.'

'Confidently self-righteous' and 'contemptuous of others' are not ways we would ever want to be described. Yet the moment we look askance at other Christians, other churches, other Christian practices, the moment we look down on those whose lives and lifestyles are not what or how *we* would live, in that moment when we feel the surging strength of our own righteousness, we are in danger of standing in the shoes of this Pharisee.

The Pharisee was so right to be thankful to God for the blessings of a godly life – but the moment he started measuring himself against others, he lost the plot, literally, of God's story of redemption. 'God… didn't choose you because you were big and important – the fact is, there was almost nothing to you. He did it out of sheer love' (Deuteronomy 7:7, MSG). It was all grace. Every blessing, every advantage – all grace – and great love.

In contrast, when he stood in God's presence that day, the tax collector seemed confident of only two things: God was merciful; he was sinful. His prayer was shaped by both of those truths.

Jesus shocked his audience that day by declaring this tax collector justified – the recipient of a righteousness he didn't, couldn't, ever earn, but which was freely and generously given to a humbled man who seemed to understand who he was praying to.

> As you reflect on this reading, what do you want to say to God? To confess? To acknowledge? To ask?

MD

Day 233

Come as a child

LUKE 18:15–17 (MATTHEW 19:13–15; MARK 10:13–16)

Towns and villages, journeying towards Jerusalem
People were also bringing babies to Jesus for him to place his hands on them. When the disciples saw this, they rebuked them. But Jesus called the children to him and said, 'Let the little children come to me, and do not hinder them, for the kingdom of God belongs to such as these. Truly I tell you, anyone who will not receive the kingdom of God like a little child will never enter it.'

He reaches up and tucks his hand into mine. He has no idea where we're going or what we're doing, but he's happy. When he stumbles, I haul him up just before he hits the ground. He thinks it's a game and, giggling, does it again. Before long, he wordlessly lifts his arms in that universal gesture that says, 'Carry me, I'm tired.' And I do. He has no shame in asking, and I have no hesitation in responding. Later, he falls asleep on my shoulder. His trust of me is complete. His dependence natural. He knows from experience that when he calls, I'll be there. He knows that wherever we are, I won't leave him; he's safe. He knows I love him.

My two-year-old godson is dependent, defenceless, needy – and carefree in my care. He is typical for his age – not unlike those little ones who were brought to Jesus for his blessing that day. In Jesus' day, children were largely ignored as unimportant, unworthy of much attention, and yet Jesus draws attention to these children to further his disciples' understanding of the kingdom of God.

Jesus teaches that the kingdom of God is a gift which can only be received by those who understand that they can bring nothing to God but their neediness. Who finally understand that all their goodness, their achievements, their worthiness cannot earn them a place in the kingdom – they can only depend on what Jesus has done for them.

God invites us to live in his kingdom without pretence or pretentiousness; in unashamed dependence on his kindness, trusting in his love for us, humbly acknowledging our neediness, fearlessly abandoning ourselves into the arms of his mercy and grace and goodness.

> Can we live like this? Dare we take Jesus' words seriously and come to him as a child – in all our neediness? To rest, carefree in his care? May it be so.

MD

Day 234

The rich young ruler

LUKE 18:18–27 (MATTHEW 19:16–26; MARK 10:17–27)

Towns and villages, journeying towards Jerusalem
A certain ruler asked him, 'Good teacher, what must I do to inherit eternal life?' 'Why do you call me good?' Jesus answered. 'No one is good – except God alone. You know the commandments: "You shall not commit adultery, you shall not murder, you shall not steal, you shall not give false testimony, honour your father and mother."' 'All these I have kept since I was a boy,' he said. When Jesus heard this, he said to him, 'You still lack one thing. Sell everything you have and give to the poor, and you will have treasure in heaven. Then come, follow me.' When he heard this, he became very sad, because he was very wealthy. Jesus looked at him and said, 'How hard it is for the rich to enter the kingdom of God! Indeed, it is easier for a camel to go through the eye of a needle than for someone who is rich to enter the kingdom of God.' Those who heard this asked, 'Who then can be saved?' Jesus replied, 'What is impossible with man is possible with God.'

By now the disciples would have learned that salvation couldn't be earned; it could only be received as a gift by those who acknowledged their need for mercy (like the tax collector) and who were willing to come to God with nothing but the trust of a little child. This young ruler came to Jesus with his question, sensing perhaps that there was something lacking in his relationship with God and wanting to know what he needed to do. Surprisingly, Jesus seems to be in agreement that there was something he could do! But Jesus is not laying down the terms for salvation here, rather he's exposing the reality of this man's claims. Despite his faithful observance of the commandments, he was actually breaking the first and most important – 'You shall have no other gods before me' (Exodus 20:3). His response demonstrated that wealth was his true god, the one he couldn't give up even for all the 'treasure in heaven'.

Wealth may not be your god, but is there something in your life which you sense may be holding you back from a wholehearted commitment to following Jesus? From fully experiencing the life God wants for you?

▌ *Father, reveal my heart to me; lead me into truth and into your richest, fullest life for me.*

MD

Day 235

It will be worth it all

LUKE 18:28–30 (MATTHEW 19:27–30; MARK 10:28–31)

On the road to Jerusalem
Peter said to him, 'We have left all we had to follow you!' 'Truly I tell you,' Jesus said to them, 'no one who has left home or wife or brothers or sisters or parents or children for the sake of the kingdom of God will fail to receive many times as much in this age, and in the age to come eternal life.'

Looking back over 20 years as a missionary in Asia, one song stands out. I sang and sobbed and whispered it so many times over those years, especially in those early days when it all felt too hard, the cost too great.

You may know the song – 'It Will Be Worth It All' (Esther Kerr Rusthoi, 1909–62). The words of the song held out the promise that on the day we stand face-to-face with Jesus, we will recognise that every sacrifice we've ever made, every loss we've ever suffered because of our choice to follow Jesus will be worth it – because *he* is worth it.

It seems that the closer he gets to Jerusalem, the more explicit Jesus is about the cost of following him. Through witnessing Jesus' interaction with the rich young ruler, the disciples are faced again with the reality that being Jesus' disciple demands total commitment. Peter, perhaps speaking for the others, seems to be reminding Jesus that they have given just that; they'd left everything to follow him – their homes, their jobs, their families, their security for the future, everything. And Jesus is assuring these disciples that it really would be worth it all; one day they would know that.

Do you ever have moments when you wonder if it really is worth it all? If being a follower of Jesus is worth the hassle, the cost, the hard decisions, the losses? If you do, take those thoughts to Jesus in prayer and ask him for a renewed vision of who he is and why he is worth it all.

> If this isn't your question, praise God! But pray now for someone you know who may be struggling with following Jesus.

MD

Day 236

The generosity of God

MATTHEW 20:1–16

On the road to Jerusalem
'For the kingdom of heaven is like a landowner who went out early in the morning to hire workers for his vineyard. He agreed to pay them a denarius for the day and sent them into his vineyard. About nine in the morning he went out and saw others standing in the market-place doing nothing. He told them, "You also go and work in my vineyard, and I will pay you whatever is right." So they went. He went out again about noon and about three in the afternoon and did the same thing. About five in the afternoon he went out and found still others standing around. He asked them, "Why have you been standing here all day long doing nothing?" "Because no one has hired us," they answered. He said to them, "You also go and work in my vineyard." When evening came, the owner of the vineyard said to his foreman, "Call the workers and pay them their wages, beginning with the last ones hired and going on to the first." The workers who were hired about five in the afternoon came and each received a denarius. So when those came who were hired first, they expected to receive more. But each one of them also received a denarius. When they received it, they began to grumble against the landowner. "These who were hired last worked only one hour," they said, "and you have made them equal to us who have borne the burden of the work and the heat of the day." But he answered one of them, "I am not being unfair to you, friend. Didn't you agree to work for a denarius? Take your pay and go. I want to give the one who was hired last the same as I gave you. Don't I have the right to do what I want with my own money? Or are you envious because I am generous?" So the last will be first, and the first will be last.'

Jesus is again teaching about the nature of the kingdom of God and draws it all to a close with a question: 'Are you envious because I am generous?'

> Let Jesus' question linger in your heart. What does it stir in you? Bring those stirrings to the Lord in prayer, perhaps beginning with the words, 'Generous God…' and go on from there.

MD

Day 237

Jesus predicts his death a third time

LUKE 18:31–34 (MATTHEW 20:17–19; MARK 10:32–34)

> On the road to Jerusalem
> *Jesus took the Twelve aside and told them, 'We are going up to Jerusalem, and everything that is written by the prophets about the Son of Man will be fulfilled. He will be handed over to the Gentiles. They will mock him, insult him and spit on him; they will flog him and kill him. On the third day he will rise again.' The disciples did not understand any of this. Its meaning was hidden from them, and they did not know what he was talking about.*

He was not a victim. However it might appear in the days ahead, especially to the uncomprehending disciples (who are being told for the third time what lay ahead in Jerusalem), Jesus was not the hapless victim of tragic circumstances. He knew that everything that would happen to him had already been woven into God's redeeming purposes.

All through his life, Jesus had lived with the knowledge of what lay ahead of him in Jerusalem, because he knew the prophecies surrounding his death. Every detail of his suffering by crucifixion had been spelled out by Isaiah (Isaiah 50:6; 53:3–7) and by David (Psalm 22:6–8) long before the Romans ever existed as a fearsome world power. Nothing in the days ahead would be unexpected. It had been prophesied. It would happen.

Jesus knew the suffering he would face – but he also knew that everything was under his Father's control. From the outside it might look like others had taken control, that he would be delivered over to his enemies without any say in the matter, but Jesus knew that ultimately it was *God* who was delivering him into those hands (Isaiah 53:10; Romans 8:32). And it was God who would raise him to life again. Jesus could surely testify with David, who proclaimed: 'But I trust in you, Lord; I say, "You are my God." My destiny is in *your hands*' (Psalm 31:15–16, NAB; emphasis mine).

This truth cradled his peace, his resolute purpose, his willing, sacrificial obedience, his steadfast walk towards Jerusalem.

> *Father, as I look at the circumstances of my life today, give me grace to trust that every detail of those circumstances is under your wise and kind control. Help me to trust that even when things look so hopeless, so dead, you are able to bring new life, even in the circumstances which come to mind now…*

MD

Day 238

An audacious request

MATTHEW 20:20-28 (MARK 10:35-40)

On the road to Jerusalem
Then the mother of Zebedee's sons came to Jesus with her sons and, kneeling down, asked a favour of him. 'What is it you want?' he asked. She said, 'Grant that one of these two sons of mine may sit at your right and the other at your left in your kingdom.' 'You don't know what you are asking,' Jesus said to them. 'Can you drink the cup I am going to drink?' 'We can,' they answered. Jesus said to them, 'You will indeed drink from my cup, but to sit at my right or left is not for me to grant. These places belong to those for whom they have been prepared by my Father.' When the ten heard about this, they were indignant with the two brothers. Jesus called them together and said, 'You know that the rulers of the Gentiles lord it over them, and their high officials exercise authority over them. Not so with you. Instead, whoever wants to become great among you must be your servant, and whoever wants to be first must be your slave – just as the Son of Man did not come to be served, but to serve, and to give his life as a ransom for many.'

It's easy to shake our heads in disbelief at this mother's misguided request and her sons' collusion with it just moments after Jesus has shared the brutal details of what he will face when they reach Jerusalem. The level of indifference to his suffering and seeming disregard of all that he has taught them about the distinctive nature of his kingdom may be painfully uncomfortable for us to witness – and yet their audacious request, the reaction of the other disciples and Jesus' response may hold up a mirror to our own lives – and raise uncomfortable questions.

For example, do you always need to be the one in charge or in control of events to be happy? How do you feel when others are promoted, recognised, applauded – and you are not? How do you feel when your voice is ignored, your input casually dismissed when decisions are being made? When you are overlooked, taken advantage of, treated like a servant?

> What do we see when we look into this mirror – and how will we respond to what we see? Bring your reflections to the Lord in prayer.

MD

Day 239

The faith of a blind beggar

LUKE 18:35-43 (MATTHEW 20:29-34; MARK 10:46-52)

Outside Jericho
As Jesus approached Jericho, a blind man was sitting by the roadside begging. When he heard the crowd going by, he asked what was happening. They told him, 'Jesus of Nazareth is passing by.' He called out, 'Jesus, Son of David, have mercy on me!' Those who led the way rebuked him and told him to be quiet, but he shouted all the more, 'Son of David, have mercy on me!' Jesus stopped and ordered the man to be brought to him. When he came near, Jesus asked him, 'What do you want me to do for you?' 'Lord, I want to see,' he replied. Jesus said to him, 'Receive your sight; your faith has healed you.' Immediately he received his sight and followed Jesus, praising God. When all the people saw it, they also praised God.

'He honoured me by the magnitude of his request.' These words were allegedly spoken by Napoleon about a young officer who boldly interrupted the celebrations enjoyed by Napoleon and his generals after a significant military victory. On being asked what he wanted, the young officer responded, 'Give me this island.' The generals were astonished when Napoleon there and then signed the hard-won island over to the young man. His reason – 'He honoured me with the magnitude of his request.'

And this is exactly what this blind beggar did here. When asked what he wanted, he didn't hesitate. He went for broke – and asked for a miracle.

Despite his blindness this beggar had seen what so many in the crowd seem to have missed – that Jesus was not just 'of Nazareth', but the Son of David, the Anointed One of God – the Messiah. He recognised the power and majesty of Jesus through the eyes of faith, and in light of what he saw, he yelled, unashamedly, for mercy. And received so much more.

The faith that Jesus heard in that yell stopped him in his tracks. I like to think it comforted him as he faced what lay ahead for him in Jerusalem – that his kingdom continued to grow in the unlikeliest of lives.

> 'What do you want me to do for you?' In the quietness of your heart, hear those words of Jesus addressing you as his heart is touched by your faith, your need. How will your answer honour him?

MD

The journey to Jerusalem 261

Day 240

Jesus encounters Zacchaeus

LUKE 19:1–10

Jericho

Jesus entered Jericho and was passing through. A man was there by the name of Zacchaeus; he was a chief tax collector and was wealthy. He wanted to see who Jesus was, but because he was short he could not see over the crowd. So he ran ahead and climbed a sycamore-fig tree to see him, since Jesus was coming that way. When Jesus reached the spot, he looked up and said to him, 'Zacchaeus, come down immediately. I must stay at your house today.' So he came down at once and welcomed him gladly. All the people saw this and began to mutter, 'He has gone to be the guest of a sinner.' But Zacchaeus stood up and said to the Lord, 'Look, Lord! Here and now I give half of my possessions to the poor, and if I have cheated anybody out of anything, I will pay back four times the amount.' Jesus said to him, 'Today salvation has come to this house, because this man, too, is a son of Abraham. For the Son of Man came to seek and to save the lost.'

Through this account of Jesus' last encounter with an individual before he reaches Jerusalem, Luke draws together many of the threads of Jesus' teaching and actions these many months. There's the thread of stewardship and the use of wealth. There's the thread of sight – of seeing, or not. We see the thread of Jesus' blatant involvement with those who, for all sorts of reasons, are despised, marginalised, treated with contempt. There's the mounting resistance to his ministry of seeking and saving the lost. All of these threads – and more – are drawn together in the person of Zacchaeus.

But he's more than just a thread holder! Zacchaeus is every one of us who longs for a transformative encounter with God. He is the reminder that my past does not define me and that my present circumstances don't limit me, because when Jesus is present my future becomes filled with endless possibilities. He is the embodied hope of a different, more generous, expansive way of living. He is the living, breathing evidence of Jesus' passionate pursuit of my heart; of his desire to be involved in my life.

> Lord Jesus, Zacchaeus welcomed you gladly into his home that day. And I gladly welcome you to step into my home today with all your transforming power. Amen.

MD

the last few weeks

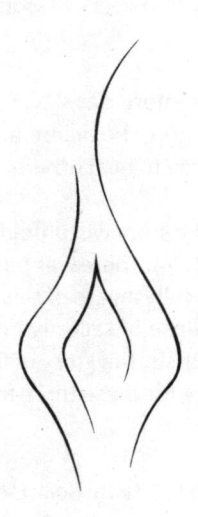

JENNY BROWN

Day 241

Lazarus falls ill

JOHN 11:1-7

A day's journey from Bethany
Now a man named Lazarus was ill. He was from Bethany, the village of Mary and her sister Martha. (This Mary, whose brother Lazarus now lay ill, was the same one who poured perfume on the Lord and wiped his feet with her hair.) So the sisters sent word to Jesus, 'Lord, the one you love is ill.' When he heard this, Jesus said, 'This illness will not end in death. No, it is for God's glory so that God's Son may be glorified through it.' Now Jesus loved Martha and her sister and Lazarus. So when he heard that Lazarus was ill, he stayed where he was two more days, and then he said to his disciples, 'Let us go back to Judea.'

In a crisis, we sense the need to act, and act fast. When crisis hit their family, it was obvious to Mary and Martha what they needed to do: send for Jesus. He had power to heal and he was their dear friend. They had every reason to be confident in both his ability and his willingness to help.

'So… he stayed where he was two more days' (v. 6). That little word 'so' bothers me. Jesus loved those three siblings and yet he deliberately delayed. It seems so unlike the compassionate Jesus who was ready to heal others.

Although we don't yet know how the story will unfold, there is another 'so' which makes all the difference: 'it is… so that…' (v. 4). There was purpose in his delay, although it could not be seen at the time. Jesus was fully aware of this situation. His words of confidence about Lazarus' future brought a sense of security into the confusion. This was not yet the end of the story. Through this crisis, the glory of God would somehow be displayed. His delay did not contradict his love for these three friends. On the contrary, his love for them is the basis of his actions.

> *It can be painfully hard to understand why God doesn't respond to our cries for help in the way we think we need. Are there situations in your own life, or the lives of others you care about, where it seems as though the Lord is delaying? What is the Lord saying to you for that situation through these verses? What do you want to say to him in response?*

JB

Day 242

Jesus goes to Lazarus

JOHN 11:8-16

A day's journey from Bethany
'But Rabbi,' they said, 'a short while ago the Jews there tried to stone you, and yet you are going back?' Jesus answered, 'Are there not twelve hours of daylight? Anyone who walks in the day-time will not stumble, for they see by this world's light. It is when a person walks at night that they stumble, for they have no light.' After he had said this, he went on to tell them, 'Our friend Lazarus has fallen asleep; but I am going there to wake him up.' His disciples replied, 'Lord, if he sleeps, he will get better.' Jesus had been speaking of his death, but his disciples thought he meant natural sleep. So then he told them plainly, 'Lazarus is dead, and for your sake I am glad I was not there, so that you may believe. But let us go to him.' Then Thomas (also known as Didymus) said to the rest of the disciples, 'Let us also go, that we may die with him.'

To stay or to go? Yesterday it was Jesus' delay that was hard to understand. Today, it is his decision to go that is questioned! How you view the situation is affected by who you are and where you stand in the story.

We are finite and have a limited perspective on what happens around us. The only way to walk through life without stumbling is in the light of Christ, to follow him. We may not understand the route or the timing, but we will be led through securely. What does it mean for you today to walk with Jesus in his light?

Dead or asleep? From the perspective of Jesus, the giver of life, Lazarus was merely asleep. 'Death is not a full stop to life… Physical death happens, but it is relativized by Jesus.'[30] How gracious of God that every day, as we fall asleep, he gives us practice for the moment of our death, so that we need not fear.

> *You might like to use these words from the Psalms tonight: 'Into your hand I commit my spirit; you have redeemed me, O Lord God of truth' (Psalm 31:5, NKJV); 'In peace I will lie down and sleep, for you alone, Lord, make me dwell in safety' (Psalm 4:8).*

JB

Day 243

Jesus and Martha

JOHN 11:17-27

> Bethany
> *On his arrival, Jesus found that Lazarus had already been in the tomb for four days. Now Bethany was less than two miles from Jerusalem, and many Jews had come to Martha and Mary to comfort them in the loss of their brother. When Martha heard that Jesus was coming, she went out to meet him, but Mary stayed at home. 'Lord,' Martha said to Jesus, 'if you had been here, my brother would not have died. But I know that even now God will give you whatever you ask.' Jesus said to her, 'Your brother will rise again.' Martha answered, 'I know he will rise again in the resurrection at the last day.' Jesus said to her, 'I am the resurrection and the life. The one who believes in me will live, even though they die; and whoever lives by believing in me will never die. Do you believe this?' 'Yes, Lord,' she replied, 'I believe that you are the Messiah, the Son of God, who is to come into the world.'*

There are events in life which we do not understand and which cause us to feel disappointed, even angry, with God. For Martha and Mary, the death of their brother must have tested their confidence in Jesus' love for them.

'If only...' Through this touching conversation, Jesus leads Martha on a journey. He starts with the faith she *could* articulate, even if she was clinging on to it by her fingertips. From the present situation, he points her eyes to the future. Then he takes her seed of future hope back to the present, showing that he is the place where that hope is rooted and will flourish. Step by step, Martha was invited to raise her gaze from the crisis to Jesus himself. As a result, her faith grew, embracing Jesus' true identity and mission, and becoming a model for all John's readers (John 20:31).

As Tom Wright says, Jesus urged Martha to 'exchange her "if only..." for an "if Jesus..."'[31] If Jesus is Messiah, Son of God, resurrection-in-person and life itself, that changes everything. Not only for Martha, but for all who believe in him.

> *Hear Jesus' invitation to bring your 'If only...' to him, to voice your disappointment. Be attentive to where he leads you in prayer. Focus on his trustworthiness rather than on your ability to trust.*

JB

Day 244

Jesus and Mary

JOHN 11:28-37

Bethany
After she had said this, she went back and called her sister Mary aside. 'The Teacher is here,' she said, 'and is asking for you.' When Mary heard this, she got up quickly and went to him. Now Jesus had not yet entered the village, but was still at the place where Martha had met him. When the Jews who had been with Mary in the house, comforting her, noticed how quickly she got up and went out, they followed her, supposing she was going to the tomb to mourn there. When Mary reached the place where Jesus was and saw him, she fell at his feet and said, 'Lord, if you had been here, my brother would not have died.' When Jesus saw her weeping, and the Jews who had come along with her also weeping, he was deeply moved in spirit and troubled. 'Where have you laid him?' he asked. 'Come and see, Lord,' they replied. Jesus wept. Then the Jews said, 'See how he loved him!' But some of them said, 'Could not he who opened the eyes of the blind man have kept this man from dying?'

Grief can feel so isolating. We have no energy to interact with others; we have no words to express how we feel.

With Martha, Jesus had shared theological truth to reassure her. With Mary, however, he responds differently, though equally tenderly. He is simply present, drawing alongside her. He doesn't minimise her pain or try to stop her tears. Rather, he meets her in her grief and weeps with her.

This is not merely a response of empathy from his mind. It wells up from the centre of his being, from his Spirit, the point of his deepest connection with the Father. Jesus is moved, troubled, even angered, in the face of death, an intrusion in God's good creation. Foreshadowing the grief of Gethsemane, when he will face his own experience of death, he feels more than anyone what separation from the life of the Father would mean. Far from being detached from the pain of grief, Jesus has entered most fully into it.

> *Is there something that is causing you sadness, pain, grief? Perhaps it is a bereavement – recent or in the past. Will you allow Jesus to join you in it? What difference does it make to know that he has fully experienced grief himself?*

JB

Day 245

Lazarus is raised

JOHN 11:38–44

Bethany

Jesus, once more deeply moved, came to the tomb. It was a cave with a stone laid across the entrance. 'Take away the stone,' he said. 'But, Lord,' said Martha, the sister of the dead man, 'by this time there is a bad odour, for he has been there four days.' Then Jesus said, 'Did I not tell you that if you believe, you will see the glory of God?' So they took away the stone. Then Jesus looked up and said, 'Father, I thank you that you have heard me. I knew that you always hear me, but I said this for the benefit of the people standing here, that they may believe that you sent me.' When he had said this, Jesus called in a loud voice, 'Lazarus, come out!' The dead man came out, his hands and feet wrapped with strips of linen, and a cloth round his face. Jesus said to them, 'Take off the grave clothes and let him go.'

'Dead man walking' is a term that refers to a condemned prisoner walking to his death. But here is a liberated man walking away from his death! Or was it more of a shuffle?

Lazarus was pulled back into life without apparent struggle. It was a clear, authoritative call from the one who is the resurrection and the life (John 11:25), the shepherd who 'calls his own sheep by name and leads them out' (John 10:3). But those restrictive grave clothes needed to be removed before Lazarus could live his renewed life fully.

Mags Duggan writes:

> Each one of us came into our new life a bit like Lazarus... with life-limiting attitudes, beliefs and behaviours... Even after years of knowing Jesus, there can be areas of our lives where we are as bound as Lazarus was... hardly aware of the way they are restricting us from living the life that Jesus promised us.[32]

As well as negative patterns, our 'grave clothes' might include good practices, which have served us well but now need to change.

> *Knowing you are safe in the love of God, why not ask him to show you a 'grave cloth' that is keeping you from living fully with Jesus? Surrender it to Father God, and ask to be released, trusting him to lead you into the greater freedom he desires for you. Be attentive to how he does that.*

Day 246

Conspiracy to kill Jesus

JOHN 11:45-53

Jerusalem
Therefore many of the Jews who had come to visit Mary, and had seen what Jesus did, believed in him. But some of them went to the Pharisees and told them what Jesus had done. Then the chief priests and the Pharisees called a meeting of the Sanhedrin. 'What are we accomplishing?' they asked. 'Here is this man performing many signs. If we let him go on like this, everyone will believe in him, and then the Romans will come and take away both our temple and our nation.' Then one of them, named Caiaphas, who was high priest that year, spoke up, 'You know nothing at all! You do not realise that it is better for you that one man die for the people than that the whole nation perish.' He did not say this on his own, but as high priest that year he prophesied that Jesus would die for the Jewish nation, and not only for that nation but also for the scattered children of God, to bring them together and make them one. So from that day on they plotted to take his life.

In judo (Japanese for 'the gentle way'), one fundamental principle is to turn the force coming against you and direct it back, using it as the means to defeat your opponent.

The force coming against Jesus was building. The religious authorities responded to his gift of new life to a dead man by plotting Jesus' own death. However, John recognises this outburst from the high priest as an unwitting prophecy.

Jesus would indeed be killed. At the time it must have seemed a terrible end, a cruel tragedy. But John is clear that Jesus' death would open the door to eternal life for multitudes (John 1:29; 3:16). God was at work, not just despite, but *through* their anxious plotting. God, the 'supreme judo champion', using the actions of his opponents to bring about the fulfilment of his purposes (Acts 2:23, 36).

As Joseph said of his brothers: 'You intended to harm me, but God intended it all for good. He brought me to this position so I could save the lives of many people' (Genesis 50:20, NLT).

> *Reflect back on your life. Can you see traces of this redemptive pattern of God at work to bring blessing out of what seemed at the time so bad? How does that strengthen you as you look ahead?*

JB

Day 247

The end of public ministry

JOHN 11:54-57

Ephraim and Jerusalem
Therefore Jesus no longer moved about publicly among the people of Judea. Instead he withdrew to a region near the wilderness, to a village called Ephraim, where he stayed with his disciples. When it was almost time for the Jewish Passover, many went up from the country to Jerusalem for their ceremonial cleansing before the Passover. They kept looking for Jesus, and as they stood in the temple courts they asked one another, 'What do you think? Isn't he coming to the festival at all?' But the chief priests and the Pharisees had given orders that anyone who found out where Jesus was should report it so that they might arrest him.

Imagine what it might have been like for those newest of believers. They had originally gone to comfort Mary and Martha for the loss of their brother Lazarus, to sit with them, to weep with them. The last thing they had expected to see was Lazarus walking out of his tomb four days later!

Such a powerful experience had moved them to believe in the man who had raised Lazarus back to life. Now they wanted to be with Jesus, to hear his teaching, to watch what he would do next. And it was Passover – a time of great expectation. They went to the temple courts as usual, but Jesus didn't come. They looked for him, but could not find him. As the hostility towards Jesus built, he had withdrawn to Ephraim (about 12–15 miles from Jerusalem) to bide his time and prepare those who had been with him over the last three years for what would come next.

What do you think might have gone through their minds? What questions, hopes and fears?

With your knowledge of what followed, what would you want to say to these new believers?

> *Whether a new believer or a seasoned disciple, where are you looking for Jesus? What questions, hopes and fears are on your mind? What would you like to say to him?*

JB

the last week

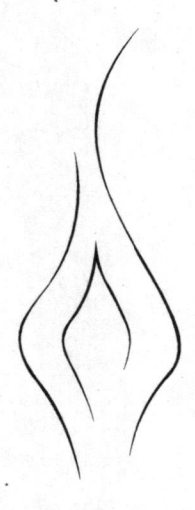

TONY HORSFALL

Saturday

Day 248

Jesus anointed at Bethany

JOHN 12:1-11

Bethany[33]

Six days before the Passover, Jesus came to Bethany, where Lazarus lived, whom Jesus had raised from the dead. Here a dinner was given in Jesus' honour. Martha served, while Lazarus was among those reclining at the table with him. Then Mary took about half a litre of pure nard, an expensive perfume; she poured it on Jesus' feet and wiped his feet with her hair. And the house was filled with the fragrance of the perfume. But one of his disciples, Judas Iscariot, who was later to betray him, objected, 'Why wasn't this perfume sold and the money given to the poor? It was worth a year's wages.' He did not say this because he cared about the poor but because he was a thief; as keeper of the money bag, he used to help himself to what was put into it. 'Leave her alone,' Jesus replied. 'It was intended that she should save this perfume for the day of my burial. You will always have the poor among you, but you will not always have me.' Meanwhile a large crowd of Jews found out that Jesus was there and came, not only because of him but also to see Lazarus, whom he had raised from the dead. So the chief priests made plans to kill Lazarus as well, for on account of him many of the Jews were going over to Jesus and believing in him.

The focus is now on the coming Passover and the death of Jesus. Bruce Milne comments:

> As the pilgrims prepare to sacrifice the Passover lamb in commemoration of God's gracious liberation from slavery, so God's own true Lamb is prepared and ready at the Father's summons to offer himself in bloody sacrifice for the sins of the world.[34]

Jesus may have headed to Jerusalem with a steely determination, but he was not without feelings and emotional need. The meal in his honour provided him with much-needed affirmation, consolation and comfort. No disciple needs to make themselves emotionally impregnable as they face the challenges of their calling. Even Jesus appreciated the warmth of touch and the encouragement of recognition and feeling special. Dark forces are already at work, operating through Judas and the religious leaders, but the Father provides solace and strength for the Son.

▌ *How are your own emotional needs being acknowledged and met?*

TH

Sunday

Day 249

Triumphal entry

MARK 11:1-11 (*MATTHEW 21:1-11; LUKE 19:29-44; JOHN 12:12-19*)

Bethphage and Bethany

As they approached Jerusalem and came to Bethphage and Bethany at the Mount of Olives, Jesus sent two of his disciples, saying to them, 'Go to the village ahead of you, and just as you enter it, you will find a colt tied there, which no one has ever ridden. Untie it and bring it here. If anyone asks you, "Why are you doing this?" say, "The Lord needs it and will send it back here shortly."' They went and found a colt outside in the street, tied at a doorway. As they untied it, some people standing there asked, 'What are you doing, untying that colt?' They answered as Jesus had told them to, and the people let them go. When they brought the colt to Jesus and threw their cloaks over it, he sat on it. Many people spread their cloaks on the road, while others spread branches they had cut in the fields. Those who went ahead and those who followed shouted, 'Hosanna!' 'Blessed is he who comes in the name of the Lord!' 'Blessed is the coming kingdom of our father David!' 'Hosanna in the highest heaven!' Jesus entered Jerusalem and went into the temple courts. He looked around at everything, but since it was already late, he went out to Bethany with the Twelve.

Messianic expectations are high as Jesus reaches Jerusalem and enters the city, but his surprising mode of transport sends out a clear message that he is no political messiah intent on rebellion. Yes, he comes in fulfilment of the prophecy of Zechariah 9:9, a king with a kingdom, but he comes in lowliness, riding on a donkey not a white stallion. Humility, not self-display, is his mark; strength of character, not force of personality, is his style. Neither is he seduced by popular acclaim. We must not, however, mistake his gentleness for weakness or his meekness for softness. Jesus is strong, brave and courageous beyond his enemies.

There are tears. As he looks over the city he weeps (Luke 19:41–42), but not for himself. His sorrow stems from the knowledge that many will reject the kingdom he represents. Strong people do cry, especially in the face of spiritual folly.

> *In what ways is your idea of strength influenced by that of society? Do you see humility as weakness? When were you last moved to tears?*

TH

Monday

Day 250

Cleansing the temple

MARK 11:15–19 (MATTHEW 21:12-13; LUKE 19:45-46)

Jerusalem, the temple
On reaching Jerusalem, Jesus entered the temple courts and began driving out those who were buying and selling there. He overturned the tables of the money-changers and the benches of those selling doves, and would not allow anyone to carry merchandise through the temple courts. And as he taught them, he said, 'Is it not written: "My house will be called a house of prayer for all nations"? But you have made it "a den of robbers".' The chief priests and the teachers of the law heard this and began looking for a way to kill him, for they feared him, because the whole crowd was amazed at his teaching. When evening came, Jesus and his disciples went out of the city.

Here is an example of the fact that Jesus, although meek and lowly in heart, is not a weak man. Sadly, the temple courts had become commercialised and exploitation of the worshippers was rife. The purpose of the house of God had been completely lost and prayer neglected for monetary gain. The hurly-burly of the marketplace had replaced the stillness of the sanctuary. It was time for reformation. Radical change was needed, and Jesus did not shrink back from holy confrontation.

It is all too easy to be critical of the contemporary western church, which in the drive to become relevant may be tempted to adopt questionable means to achieve popularity. Yet we must be brave enough to consider how we ourselves are faring and whether or not prayer is still central to the life of our church. It is the acid test of spirituality, and regular personal and corporate prayer must be the foundation of any Christ-centred congregation.

> *The brave action of Jesus intensified the opposition against him, an accelerant to the flames of hatred. Do I have the courage to speak out against something I know to be wrong and risk a backlash of hostility? How brave am I? How brave are you?*

TH

Day 251

Praise of the children

MATTHEW 21:14–17 (*LUKE 19:47–48; MARK 11:19*)

Jerusalem, the temple
The blind and the lame came to him at the temple, and he healed them. But when the chief priests and the teachers of the law saw the wonderful things he did and the children shouting in the temple courts, 'Hosanna to the Son of David,' they were indignant. 'Do you hear what these children are saying?' they asked him. 'Yes,' replied Jesus, 'have you never read, "From the lips of children and infants you, Lord, have called forth your praise"?' And he left them and went out of the city to Bethany, where he spent the night.

The humility and approachability of Jesus drew to him many who were otherwise considered unworthy of much attention, in particular the sick and the young. Even though time is now running out, and opposition to him is reaching boiling point, Jesus finds space to heal the blind and the lame and encourage the children.

It is worth noticing from this passage that children have an in-built capacity to recognise the presence and activity of God, their very childlikeness making them more amenable to spiritual encounter and their innocence opening them to the unseen realm. Their praise registers a stark contrast to the cynical indignation of the adults around them, and I feel sure that their exclamations strengthened Jesus in much the same way as the anointing had done earlier.

> *Why not use this passage as a basis for lectio divina? Listen to what God may be saying to you through the words of this passage following the guidelines given earlier.*

TH

Tuesday

Day 252

Fig tree withered

MATTHEW 21:18-22 (MARK 11:12-14)

Jerusalem
Early in the morning, as Jesus was on his way back to the city, he was hungry. Seeing a fig-tree by the road, he went up to it but found nothing on it except leaves. Then he said to it, 'May you never bear fruit again!' Immediately the tree withered. When the disciples saw this, they were amazed. 'How did the fig-tree wither so quickly?' they asked. Jesus replied, 'Truly I tell you, if you have faith and do not doubt, not only can you do what was done to the fig-tree, but also you can say to this mountain, "Go, throw yourself into the sea," and it will be done. If you believe, you will receive whatever you ask for in prayer.'

Matthew gives us here an insight into the true humanity of Jesus when he writes, 'He was hungry.' Even the Son of God experienced hunger pains and woke feeling ready for his breakfast. Indeed, a good appetite is a sign of health. There is something reassuring in this note of normality with its reminder that Jesus knows and understands what it is to be human.

The cursing of the fig tree, however, is not an act of human petulance. Jesus has not lost his temper and he does not speak out of angry frustration. Rather, this is an acted parable. In the Old Testament, the fig tree (like the vine) stands for Israel, which in spiritual terms is unfruitful. The coming of the Messiah should have awakened faith, yet the entry into the city, the events in the temple and the growing hostility against him all bear witness to unbelief, especially among the religious leaders.

By contrast, those who have faith are the ones who will bear fruit. This will be expressed particularly through prayer, something sadly absent from the temple. Those who are true believers will grow in their understanding of God and his ways, and it will become natural for them to pray his will into being. Here is a challenge for us all. How potent is our prayer life? Do we have the faith to ask God to intervene in situations and show his glory?

> Just as it is normal to feel hunger, so it is normal to turn to God in prayer and see him answer those requests. What request will you make? Where do you place your faith?

TH

Day 253

His authority questioned

MATTHEW 21:23–27 (*MARK 11:27–33; LUKE 20:1–8*)

Jerusalem, the temple courts
Jesus entered the temple courts, and, while he was teaching, the chief priests and the elders of the people came to him. 'By what authority are you doing these things?' they asked. 'And who gave you this authority?' Jesus replied, 'I will also ask you one question. If you answer me, I will tell you by what authority I am doing these things. John's baptism – where did it come from? Was it from heaven, or of human origin?' They discussed it among themselves and said, 'If we say, "From heaven", he will ask, "Then why didn't you believe him?" But if we say, "Of human origin" – we are afraid of the people, for they all hold that John was a prophet.' So they answered Jesus, 'We don't know.' Then he said, 'Neither will I tell you by what authority I am doing these things.'

In following the ministry of Jesus in the temple courts we will see the fierce controversy between himself and various groups of religious leaders in the city gain momentum, starting here with the chief priests and elders, those who ruled by position and the respect of age.

The question they raise is one of authority. Who has authorised Jesus to teach and act in the way he does? What are his qualifications? What training has he had, and who has validated his ministry? As Michael Green says: 'What right did an unordained carpenter have to make such a nuisance of himself?'[35]

The response of Jesus is not a clever ploy to divert attention from his own lack of training, but to draw out a similarity between himself and John – both were sent by God, and that is the basis of their authority. If his detractors accept that John had divine authorisation (from heaven), they should have repented as he said; if they say he had no such qualification (of human origin), they will lose respect among the people who know John was sent by God. They are silenced but left with the implication that the authority of Jesus is also from heaven.

Training for ministry is vitally important, but we must not replace educational qualification for divine anointing or organisational authorisation for the calling of God. Hopefully the two go together; but being sent by God is the more important.

▌ *Ponder what it means to be sent by God.*

TH

Day 254

Parable of two sons

MATTHEW 21:28-32

Jerusalem, the temple courts
'What do you think? There was a man who had two sons. He went to the first and said, "Son, go and work today in the vineyard." "I will not," he answered, but later he changed his mind and went. Then the father went to the other son and said the same thing. He answered, "I will, sir," but he did not go. Which of the two did what his father wanted?' 'The first,' they answered. Jesus said to them, 'Truly I tell you, the tax collectors and the prostitutes are entering the kingdom of God ahead of you. For John came to you to show you the way of righteousness, and you did not believe him, but the tax collectors and the prostitutes did. And even after you saw this, you did not repent and believe him.'

There now follows three parables, all directed at the religious leaders, each warning of the danger of rejecting the message of the kingdom.

Most parents know the struggle to get their children to do what they are told, and to do so at once. Reluctant obedience is an issue in family life, and Jesus uses this familiar scenario to teach about obedience to God. Of the two sons, the first refuses to obey but later does; the other promises to obey, but actually does not.

Like the first boy, many tax collectors and prostitutes initially lived sinful lives but on hearing the message of the kingdom turned in repentance. The religious leaders, although hearing the message through John the Baptist, were like the second boy, listening to his preaching but failing to repent.

Disciples are called to live in the way of righteousness, choosing day by day to respond obediently to the will of God. This is kingdom living. We may sometimes obey hesitantly, but even hesitant obedience is better than disobedience. Lip service is not a good enough response, and good intentions are insufficient. The Father looks for swift and joyful obedience, and the delight that comes from doing his will.

> *How do you rate your own obedience to your heavenly Father? When have you been conscious of choosing to obey even when it seemed hard or costly? Have there been moments of hesitancy, even refusal? Why not talk things over with him in this moment and yield your will to him once again?*

TH

Day 255

Parable of the tenants

MATTHEW 21:33-41 (*MARK 12:1-9; LUKE 20:9-16*)

Jerusalem, the temple courts
'Listen to another parable: there was a landowner who planted a vineyard. He put a wall round it, dug a winepress in it and built a watchtower. Then he rented the vineyard to some farmers and moved to another place. When the harvest time approached, he sent his servants to the tenants to collect his fruit. The tenants seized his servants; they beat one, killed another, and stoned a third. Then he sent other servants to them, more than the first time, and the tenants treated them in the same way. Last of all, he sent his son to them. "They will respect my son," he said. But when the tenants saw the son, they said to each other, "This is the heir. Come, let's kill him and take his inheritance." So they took him and threw him out of the vineyard and killed him. Therefore, when the owner of the vineyard comes, what will he do to those tenants?' 'He will bring those wretches to a wretched end,' they replied, 'and he will rent the vineyard to other tenants, who will give him his share of the crop at harvest time.'

Here is a second parable, where the details are important. The landowner is God, the vineyard is the nation of Israel, the farmers are the religious leaders, the servants are various prophets and the son is Jesus. It provides in brief an accurate summary of the spiritual history of Israel and shows that Jesus knew exactly what was happening and how events would unfold.

The religious leaders hear the story and are drawn to its obvious conclusion but fail to recognise that it is speaking about their own rejection of God's messengers, including his Son. They are in fact condemning themselves. How easy it is to hear God's word and apply it to others, rather than to realise the message is directed towards us personally. We deflect the sharp sword of conviction by thinking of the shortcomings of others, and thereby prevent it from piercing our own hearts.

> *How well do you listen to the word of God? Do you listen to it primarily on your own behalf, applying it to your own life first and foremost, whether promise or rebuke? A heart attuned to God in this way is vital for spiritual growth.*

TH

Day 256

The stone the builders rejected

MATTHEW 21:42-46 (*MARK 12:10-12; LUKE 20:17-19*)

Jerusalem, the temple courts
Jesus said to them, 'Have you never read in the Scriptures: "The stone the builders rejected has become the cornerstone; the Lord has done this, and it is marvellous in our eyes"? Therefore I tell you that the kingdom of God will be taken away from you and given to a people who will produce its fruit. Anyone who falls on this stone will be broken to pieces; anyone on whom it falls will be crushed.' When the chief priests and the Pharisees heard Jesus' parables, they knew he was talking about them. They looked for a way to arrest him, but they were afraid of the crowd because the people held that he was a prophet.

Thoughts about his forthcoming death are never far away from the mind of Jesus during this last week. He sees everything through the lens of scripture and the fulfilment of the purpose of God. Although it was not easy, this clear perspective must have strengthened his resolve. Like an obedient son, he sets out to obey his Father's will, swiftly and with joy.

The scripture foremost in his thinking at this moment is Psalm 118:22-23, a well-known messianic psalm often sung at major festivals. The focus is on his rejection by people, but also the transformation of his fortunes under God. He knows he will die, but also is convinced that this will not be the end of the story. He will be raised to life and exalted to God's right hand. The stone the builders have rejected will become the chief cornerstone. How marvellous is that!

In Hebrew there is a close connection between son (*ben*) and stone (*eben*). Jesus is both son and stone. In their foolish rejection of this particular stone, the builders (the spiritual leaders of Israel) have thrown out God's chosen and precious stone (Isaiah 28:16; 1 Peter 2:6). What a big mistake. The very stone they have rejected will in the plan of God become the cornerstone, the main building block in the spiritual temple that God is constructing. Such radical teaching further enflames the religious leaders, who are now set on his destruction.

> *Have you experienced rejection? Let this truth strengthen your own resolve. God can turn defeat into victory, and failure into success. We may be rejected by others yet accepted by God; cast aside by human judgement but embraced and used by God.*

TH

Day 257

Parable of the wedding banquet

MATTHEW 22:1-14 (*LUKE 14:16-24*)

Jerusalem, the temple courts
Jesus spoke to them again in parables, saying: 'The kingdom of heaven is like a king who prepared a wedding banquet for his son. He sent his servants to those who had been invited to the banquet to tell them to come, but they refused to come. Then he sent some more servants and said, "Tell those who have been invited that I have prepared my dinner: my oxen and fattened cattle have been slaughtered, and everything is ready. Come to the wedding banquet." But they paid no attention and went off – one to his field, another to his business. The rest seized his servants, ill-treated them and killed them. The king was enraged. He sent his army and destroyed those murderers and burned their city. Then he said to his servants, "The wedding banquet is ready, but those I invited did not deserve to come. So go to the street corners and invite to the banquet anyone you find." So the servants went out into the streets and gathered all the people they could find, the bad as well as the good, and the wedding hall was filled with guests. But when the king came in to see the guests, he noticed a man there who was not wearing wedding clothes. He asked, "How did you get in here without wedding clothes, friend?" The man was speechless. Then the king told the attendants, "Tie him hand and foot, and throw him outside, into the darkness, where there will be weeping and gnashing of teeth." For many are invited, but few are chosen.'

Life in the kingdom is meant to be a joyful celebration, and those invited are privileged indeed. In this third parable, surprisingly, many of those so honoured refuse to attend. They miss out on the festivities, to their detriment. Others, from more humble and broken backgrounds, come gladly and are welcomed.

The man without a wedding garment reminds us that we cannot enter God's kingdom if we are trusting in our own goodness. Everyone needs to be clothed in the garments of righteousness, which God freely supplies in Christ (Isaiah 61:10; 64:6; Philippians 3:9).

The saying 'Many are invited, but few are chosen' (v. 14) suggests that only those who respond to the invitation will be able to sit and enjoy the banquet. They become the chosen. Divine invitation requires human response.

▎ *Ponder what it means to be chosen.*

TH

Day 258

Tribute to Caesar

MATTHEW 22:15-22 (MARK 12:13-17; LUKE 20:19-26)

Then the Pharisees went out and laid plans to trap him in his words. They sent their disciples to him along with the Herodians. 'Teacher,' they said, 'we know that you are a man of integrity and that you teach the way of God in accordance with the truth. You aren't swayed by others, because you pay no attention to who they are. Tell us then, what is your opinion? Is it right to pay the poll-tax to Caesar or not?' But Jesus, knowing their evil intent, said, 'You hypocrites, why are you trying to trap me? Show me the coin used for paying the tax.' They brought him a denarius, and he asked them, 'Whose image is this? And whose inscription?' 'Caesar's,' they replied. Then he said to them, 'So give back to Caesar what is Caesar's, and to God what is God's.' When they heard this, they were amazed. So they left him and went away.

It is amazing how natural enemies can come together to destroy a perceived common threat. Normally Pharisees, a strict religious group, and Herodians, a more politically based party, did not get on, but here they scheme together for the downfall of Jesus. They seek to outsmart Jesus with a trick question but find themselves outsmarted!

The wise answer of Jesus avoids both dangers of total capitulation to Rome and outright rebellion against the system. It has also become the basis of the Christian approach to the church's relationship with the state. It is right to pay taxes and be supportive of secular rulers, but the greatest allegiance is always to God. We are to be good citizens, but our true citizenship is in heaven (Philippians 3:20; Romans 13:6-7; 1 Peter 2:13-14; Acts 5:29).

Michael Green makes a very helpful point: 'One delightful touch comes through in the Greek word translated give (*apodote*), which means "give back". The coin bears Caesar's image: give it back to him. You bear God's image: so give yourself back to him!'[36]

That is the rub of the matter, isn't it? Groups like the Pharisees and Herodians were not surrendered to God, which meant they could not discern the kingdom of God.

> What does it mean for you to be a true disciple and a good citizen in the society where you live? When is there a clash between the two?

TH

Day 259

Question of the resurrection

MATTHEW 22:23-33 (MARK 12:18-27; LUKE 20:27-40)

Jerusalem, the temple courts
That same day the Sadducees, who say there is no resurrection, came to him with a question. 'Teacher,' they said, 'Moses told us that if a man dies without having children, his brother must marry the widow and raise up offspring for him. Now there were seven brothers among us. The first one married and died, and since he had no children, he left his wife to his brother. The same thing happened to the second and third brother, right on down to the seventh. Finally, the woman died. Now then, at the resurrection, whose wife will she be of the seven, since all of them were married to her?' Jesus replied, 'You are in error because you do not know the Scriptures or the power of God. At the resurrection people will neither marry nor be given in marriage; they will be like the angels in heaven. But about the resurrection of the dead – have you not read what God said to you, "I am the God of Abraham, the God of Isaac, and the God of Jacob"? He is not the God of the dead but of the living.' When the crowds heard this, they were astonished at his teaching.

Now a third religious group, the Sadducees, come to question Jesus. Made up of wealthy aristocrats and powerful priestly families, they were very influential in Jerusalem, but denied any idea of an afterlife. The conundrum they pose is designed to show how ridiculous such an idea is, and they expect Jesus to agree with them. Jesus, however, shows they are wrong because they do not know the scriptures well enough and they underestimate God's power.

Resurrection is possible because God is all-powerful. He *is* the God of Abraham, Isaac and Jacob and, though they have died, their relationship with God remains intact; death cannot sever that connection. Further, in the life to come it is our relationship with God that will be central, not our married status. Their question is irrelevant and reveals their ignorance.

> *Error often occurs because of unfamiliarity with the scriptures and not fully believing in God's power. How might you increase your knowledge and understanding of the Bible? Does your unbelief limit what you perceive God can do? Whatever our churchmanship, there is always room to increase our grasp of God's word and to develop our faith.*

TH

Day 260

The greatest commandment

MATTHEW 22:34–40 (*MARK 12:28–34; LUKE 10:25–28*)

Jerusalem, the temple courts
Hearing that Jesus had silenced the Sadducees, the Pharisees got together. One of them, an expert in the law, tested him with this question: 'Teacher, which is the greatest commandment in the Law?' Jesus replied: '"Love the Lord your God with all your heart and with all your soul and with all your mind." This is the first and greatest commandment. And the second is like it: "Love your neighbour as yourself." All the Law and the Prophets hang on these two commandments.'

I am not a great fan of red-letter Bibles, where the words of Jesus are highlighted in red. But if any passage of scripture deserves to be given such treatment, it is surely the response of Jesus to this question. Here we have the heart of true religion in a minimum of words, yet with unmistakeable clarity. Loving God (the first four commandments) and loving our neighbour (the last six commandments) are what it is all about. These two statements encapsulate the entire message of the Old Testament and summarise kingdom living in a nutshell.

First and foremost, we are called to love God with our whole being. Since our love for God is a response to his extravagant love for us (1 John 4:19), we are to love him wholeheartedly, with every fibre of our being. There is no room for lukewarmness or a carefully measured approach to faith. It is all or nothing. We must give ourselves totally to the God who is our maker and redeemer.

Secondly, and flowing from the first, we are called to love our neighbour (our fellow human beings with whom we come into contact) in a way that reflects the love of God for them. We receive love, and then we give love back – to God, and to the people around us. Such love is to be practical and down-to-earth rather than mere sentiment. It is to be expressed in tangible expressions of service that meets the needs of others.

Clearly, none of us is capable of this in our own strength. The starting point must always be the grace of God and his unconditional and unchanging love for us. Love flows into us, and then outwards in worship and service.

> *How are you receiving the love of God? And what does the overflow look like in terms of your heartfelt worship and willing involvement?*

TH

Day 261

Concerning the Lord

MATTHEW 22:41-46 (MARK 12:35-37; LUKE 20:41-44)

Jerusalem, the temple courts
While the Pharisees were gathered together, Jesus asked them, 'What do you think about the Messiah? Whose son is he?' 'The son of David,' they replied. He said to them, 'How is it then that David, speaking by the Spirit, calls him "Lord"? For he says, "The Lord said to my Lord: 'Sit at my right hand until I put your enemies under your feet.'" If then David calls him "Lord", how can he be his son?' No one could say a word in reply, and from that day on no one dared to ask him any more questions.

Until this point Jesus has been the one being questioned, but now he takes the initiative and begins to ask the questions. He is not afraid of lively debate and controversy. He uses the interest that his presence on the temple courts has aroused to lay down some teaching of his own, so that both opponents and followers can see that the scriptures actually point to him.

The common expectation in Israel was that the Messiah would be descended from King David, one who would deliver them from their enemies. This belief was based on Psalm 110:1 but was not totally accurate. Jesus asks them to look more carefully and to notice that David addresses the Messiah as 'my Lord', recognising that the coming Saviour would be more than just a man – he would in fact be divine as well. Not just the Son of David, then, but the Son of God as well. Scripture therefore confirms what he has been claiming through his words and demonstrating by his powerful works all along. He is the Lord of whom David is speaking.

The attestation of the title 'Lord' to Jesus is a weighty one, and one which came to distinguish true believers as the gospel spread. 'Jesus is Lord' became their watchword, and 'Jesus is *my* Lord' their basic confession, for which they were willing to die (1 Corinthians 12:3; Romans 10:9; John 13:13; Acts 10:36; Philippians 2:11; Colossians 2:6). To give him this title means we recognise both his divinity and his right to reign in our lives, which is why it cannot be said lightly.

> *Have you come to this place of recognition yet? And what does it mean for you to bow the knee before him in surrender to his lordship? Can you say sincerely, 'Jesus is Lord'?*

TH

Day 262

Warning against the religious leaders

MATTHEW 23:1-12 (MARK 12:38-40; LUKE 20:45-47)

Jerusalem, the temple courts
Then Jesus said to the crowds and to his disciples: 'The teachers of the law and the Pharisees sit in Moses' seat. So you must be careful to do everything they tell you. But do not do what they do, for they do not practise what they preach. They tie up heavy, cumbersome loads and put them on other people's shoulders, but they themselves are not willing to lift a finger to move them. Everything they do is done for people to see: they make their phylacteries wide and the tassels on their garments long; they love the place of honour at banquets and the most important seats in the synagogues; they love to be greeted with respect in the market-places and to be called "Rabbi" by others. But you are not to be called "Rabbi", for you have one Teacher, and you are all brothers. And do not call anyone on earth "father", for you have one Father, and he is in heaven. Nor are you to be called instructors, for you have one Instructor, the Messiah. The greatest among you will be your servant. For those who exalt themselves will be humbled, and those who humble themselves will be exalted.'

The content of the next few days will repay careful study. Jesus exposes the leadership failings of many of the Jerusalem-based scribes and Pharisees. These hard-hitting words apply to anyone in leadership, especially church leadership, and at whatever level. We must pay close attention to his words.

We live in a time of celebrity culture, where leadership is based on personality before integrity, and where abuse of position and power is sadly too common. Leaders have an important role to play, which we must respect, but they have a duty to set a good example, to live out what they teach. Hypocrisy is therefore highlighted as a major danger, along with overloading people and being addicted to position, fame and recognition. We must beware of making too much of ourselves, thereby usurping the place of Jesus.

The antidote is to adopt a posture of humble servant-leadership after the pattern of Jesus. To do so is to let go of pride, self-seeking and ungodly ambition and to be as happy in the background as in the limelight.

> *How do these words speak to you? How can you guard yourself against the temptations of leadership?*

TH

Day 263

Warnings (1)

MATTHEW 23:13–22 (MARK 12:40; LUKE 11:45–46)

Jerusalem, the temple courts
'Woe to you, teachers of the law and Pharisees, you hypocrites! You shut the door of the kingdom of heaven in people's faces. You yourselves do not enter, nor will you let those enter who are trying to. Woe to you, teachers of the law and Pharisees, you hypocrites! You travel over land and sea to win a single convert, and when you have succeeded, you make them twice as much a child of hell as you are. Woe to you, blind guides! You say, "If anyone swears by the temple, it means nothing; but anyone who swears by the gold of the temple is bound by that oath." You blind fools! Which is greater: the gold, or the temple that makes the gold sacred? You also say, "If anyone swears by the altar, it means nothing; but anyone who swears by the gift on the altar is bound by that oath." You blind men! Which is greater: the gift, or the altar that makes the gift sacred? Therefore, anyone who swears by the altar swears by it and by everything on it. And anyone who swears by the temple swears by it and by the one who dwells in it. And anyone who swears by heaven swears by God's throne and by the one who sits on it.'

There is no doubt that the Pharisees appear in the gospels like the baddies in a pantomime, and every time they appear we want to boo them. Some, however, were motivated by a genuine desire to live out the stipulations of the law in obedience and faith, but with such a rules-based approach legalism was never far away. It was really among the religious elite in Jerusalem that we see the greatest failure, and their jealousy of the popularity of Jesus was the principal factor in their hatred of him.

Needless to say, they made disciples in their own image, and burdened converts with a multitude of unachievable rules and regulations. Their own unwillingness to accept the teachings of Jesus inevitably held others back. Their hair-splitting mentality meant that every religious custom (like the making of oaths) became an occasion for the minutest disagreement over interpretation. We must not judge too harshly. There is a little Pharisee inside each of us.

> *Has legalism infected your spirit? How can you find freedom? (See Galatians 5:1.)*

TH

Day 264

Warnings (2)

MATTHEW 23:23-28 (*LUKE 11:39-44*)

Jerusalem, the temple courts
'Woe to you, teachers of the law and Pharisees, you hypocrites! You give a tenth of your spices – mint, dill and cumin. But you have neglected the more important matters of the law – justice, mercy and faithfulness. You should have practised the latter, without neglecting the former. You blind guides! You strain out a gnat but swallow a camel. Woe to you, teachers of the law and Pharisees, you hypocrites! You clean the outside of the cup and dish, but inside they are full of greed and self-indulgence. Blind Pharisee! First clean the inside of the cup and dish, and then the outside also will be clean. Woe to you, teachers of the law and Pharisees, you hypocrites! You are like whitewashed tombs, which look beautiful on the outside but on the inside are full of the bones of the dead and everything unclean. In the same way, on the outside you appear to people as righteous but on the inside you are full of hypocrisy and wickedness.'

When we say that someone has a blind spot, we mean that they cannot see a fault in themselves that is perfectly obvious to everyone else. Here Jesus describes the Pharisees as blind guides for this very reason – they are pitifully unaware of their true spiritual condition and do not see their own shortcomings. How can they lead others?

It is pride that makes us blind, and sadly many in Christian leadership are also blind to character flaws and unhelpful personality traits that hinder their ministry. It is vital that we get to know ourselves, both strengths and weaknesses, if we are to mature in our faith and be more greatly used by God.

Jesus highlights two common shortcomings. The first is to focus on non-essentials at the expense of more major concerns – for example, being obsessed with a tiny detail of behaviour but forgetting the importance of being just, showing mercy and being faithful.

Then, the temptation to focus on external appearances without giving attention to the state of our heart; to look good before people yet be messed up on the inside. This is a common trap for those in the public eye, who keep up appearances 'on stage' but in private are falling apart.

> *What are you doing to get to know yourself better? What steps can you take to grow in self-awareness?*

TH

Day 265

Warnings (3)

MATTHEW 23:29–36 (*LUKE 11:47–54*)

Jerusalem, the temple courts
'Woe to you, teachers of the law and Pharisees, you hypocrites! You build tombs for the prophets and decorate the graves of the righteous. And you say, "If we had lived in the days of our ancestors, we would not have taken part with them in shedding the blood of the prophets." So you testify against yourselves that you are the descendants of those who murdered the prophets. Go ahead, then, and complete what your ancestors started! You snakes! You brood of vipers! How will you escape being condemned to hell? Therefore I am sending you prophets and sages and teachers. Some of them you will kill and crucify; others you will flog in your synagogues and pursue from town to town. And so upon you will come all the righteous blood that has been shed on earth, from the blood of righteous Abel to the blood of Zechariah son of Berekiah, whom you murdered between the temple and the altar. Truly I tell you, all this will come upon this generation.'

It is alarmingly easy to degrade the present by idealising the past, saying, 'That would never have happened in our day.' Likewise, we can stand in judgement on those who went before us, belittling their contribution and criticising their behaviour and values, saying, 'How could they have done such a thing?' Either approach can make us oblivious to the faults in our own behaviour.

A sad fact of the history of Israel was how many times the people of God rejected, often violently, those whom God had sent to them. The contemporary religious hierarchy were claiming they would never do such a thing, yet Jesus dismisses their claims, declaring that they will do exactly the same. No doubt he has in mind the way they will treat him, and also his followers. The gospel accounts and the story of Acts show sadly that history repeats itself.

> *How do we look back on our predecessors, whether in our church, denomination or organisation? We may revere them uncritically or we may cast aspersions on their work. Neither attitude is helpful. It is far better to examine ourselves honestly and to ensure that we are responding to God as wholeheartedly as we can, obeying what he is saying to us in our day, rather than comparing ourselves with those who have gone before.*

TH

Day 266

Lament for Jerusalem

MATTHEW 23:37–39 (LUKE 13:31–35)

Jerusalem, the temple courts
'Jerusalem, Jerusalem, you who kill the prophets and stone those sent to you, how often I have longed to gather your children together, as a hen gathers her chicks under her wings, and you were not willing. Look, your house is left to you desolate. For I tell you, you will not see me again until you say, "Blessed is he who comes in the name of the Lord."'

Jerusalem had a special place in the heart of Jesus. Since his first exciting visit as a child (Luke 2:41–50), he had been there many times, becoming familiar with streets and alleyways and knowing the landmark buildings intimately. He knew in detail the history of this great city, on which God had set his name and where his presence could be felt.

Here we see his sorrow over Jerusalem as the pattern of rejecting God's servant is being repeated once again. His sadness is real and deep. He had previously wept over the city (Luke 19:41); now he feels only pain at the prospect of the desolation that will come upon the city in days to come. There is no bitterness in his voice, nor any vindictive sense of 'I told you so' in his words. Simply deep regret that the city had once again ignored the time of its visitation.

This passage reveals the compassionate and merciful heart of Jesus. Like a mother hen, he is always ready to gather to himself those who are willing to be saved. He gives repeated opportunities; it is never too late. How sad then to read the words 'You were not willing' (v. 37).

Each of us must be careful not to take advantage of the patience of God or to harden our hearts before his gracious invitations. Is there any matter between you and God where you have been unwilling to respond? Who do you know who, despite many opportunities to receive the gift of salvation, is still unwilling? Can you feel the pain in the heart of God? Do you pray for them with tears?

> Ask that God will form something of his own compassionate heart within you for the people and places still unreached by his love.

TH

Day 267

The widow's gift

MARK 12:41-44 (*LUKE 21:1-4*)

The temple treasury
Jesus sat down opposite the place where the offerings were put and watched the crowd putting their money into the temple treasury. Many rich people threw in large amounts. But a poor widow came and put in two very small copper coins, worth only a few pence. Calling his disciples to him, Jesus said, 'Truly I tell you, this poor widow has put more into the treasury than all the others. They all gave out of their wealth; but she, out of her poverty, put in everything – all she had to live on.'

As my mother grew older and became housebound, she could no longer attend church, but every week she would still set aside a little brown envelope containing her offering, saving them up until someone from church came to collect them. A widow for many years, with not much income, she never lost the joy of giving to God.

I can't help but think of her as I read of the poor widow in the temple. Many rich people were giving ostentatiously, hoping their generosity was noted by others and by God. They quite literally trumpeted their good deeds, but since they were very rich, they hardly felt the pain of giving even large amounts to the treasury.

Jesus noticed the widow despite the crowds and the hurly-burly and saw the great generosity of her heart. No doubt she crept in quietly, made her offering secretly and left as quickly as possible, feeling ashamed that she could give so little and not wanting to be seen. Yet Jesus saw her and uses the moment to teach his disciples about true giving – not to be seen by others or to gain favour with God, but to express sacrificially our gratitude to him. It is not the amount we give that matters but the spirit in which our offering is made.

> *Giving is a spiritual discipline that reveals what is in our hearts. Regularly practised, it breaks the grip of materialism on our lives and releases us to receive the blessing that accompanies generosity of heart. How is this being worked out in your life? What resistance do you feel to giving sacrificially? How do you ensure your giving continues to be free of impure motives?*

TH

Day 268

End times (1)

MATTHEW 24:1-8 (*MARK 13:1-8; LUKE 21:5-9*)

Mount of Olives
Jesus left the temple and was walking away when his disciples came up to him to call his attention to its buildings. 'Do you see all these things?' he asked. 'Truly I tell you, not one stone here will be left on another; every one will be thrown down.' As Jesus was sitting on the Mount of Olives, the disciples came to him privately. 'Tell us,' they said, 'when will this happen, and what will be the sign of your coming and of the end of the age?' Jesus answered: 'Watch out that no one deceives you. For many will come in my name, claiming, "I am the Messiah," and will deceive many. You will hear of wars and rumours of wars, but see to it that you are not alarmed. Such things must happen, but the end is still to come. Nation will rise against nation, and kingdom against kingdom. There will be famines and earthquakes in various places. All these are the beginning of birth-pains.'

Most of Matthew 24 is taken up with the themes of the destruction of Jerusalem and the temple, the return of Christ and the end of the world. All these topics have been hinted at already, but now they come to the forefront. They are interwoven, and not surprisingly there is much that is hard to understand!

Who in Jerusalem could imagine the temple not being there? It was such a massive and imposing building, a permanent reminder of the presence of God, yet Jesus says the day is coming when it will be destroyed. This actually happened in AD70 when the Romans, following a dreadful siege, stormed the city and the temple. These terrible events foreshadow the end of the world. Other cataclysmic events will take place throughout the earth – wars, political turmoil, natural disasters, false messiahs and so on. Yet these will not herald the actual end of the world, only the beginning of the end.

As believers, we are to be aware that history will climax with the return of Jesus, but as that day draws near and the world increases in turmoil, we are not to be alarmed. We are to be at peace because we know God is in control and history is moving under his direction.

> How can these truths steady your faith amid the chaos of our present times?

TH

Day 269

End times (2)

MATTHEW 24:9-14 (MARK 13:9-11; LUKE 21:10-18)

Mount of Olives
'Then you will be handed over to be persecuted and put to death, and you will be hated by all nations because of me. At that time many will turn away from the faith and will betray and hate each other, and many false prophets will appear and deceive many people. Because of the increase of wickedness, the love of most will grow cold, but the one who stands firm to the end will be saved. And this gospel of the kingdom will be preached in the whole world as a testimony to all nations, and then the end will come.'

Biblically speaking we are already living in the 'last days', since scripture uses this term to refer to the period from Christ's first coming to his glorious return. But as time passes and that day comes closer, we are getting nearer than ever to the end of the world.

The church has always been persecuted, but opposition on a global scale will be a reality as the time for Christ's return gets nearer. We should not be surprised if the church is marginalised and vilified, even hated and opposed. This will mean that many will abandon their faith because they do not want to suffer; their love will grow cold, and they will fail to stand firm in their faith. They will fall prey to false teachings and pseudo messiahs with a false gospel. True disciples will need great resilience and to learn how to live in a hostile world.

At the same time, this in-between period will give opportunity for the gospel to spread. Brave pioneers will cross cultural boundaries to proclaim the good news of Christ, and his kingdom will come even in hostile places. There will be contraction in some places but expansion in others; some will grow cold while others get hot!

How do we develop a resilient faith at such a difficult time? By understanding the times and not being taken by surprise, but also by digging our roots deep into Christ and the scriptures. We must build strong relationships with other believers, understand the faith, worship regularly and be willing to suffer. The key is to stand firm.

How are you preparing yourself to live in a hostile world? Is your faith shaky or are you well rooted in Christ?

TH

Day 270

End times (3)

MATTHEW 24:15-25 (MARK 13:14-19; LUKE 21:19-24)

Mount of Olives
'So when you see standing in the holy place "the abomination that causes desolation," spoken of through the prophet Daniel – let the reader understand – then let those who are in Judea flee to the mountains. Let no one on the housetop go down to take anything out of the house. Let no one in the field go back to get their cloak. How dreadful it will be in those days for pregnant women and nursing mothers! Pray that your flight will not take place in winter or on the Sabbath. For then there will be great distress, unequalled from the beginning of the world until now – and never to be equalled again. If those days had not been cut short, no one would survive, but for the sake of the elect those days will be shortened. At that time if anyone says to you, "Look, here is the Messiah!" or, "There he is!" do not believe it. For false messiahs and false prophets will appear and perform great signs and wonders to deceive, if possible, even the elect. See, I have told you in advance.'

Warning signs are everywhere – a red light on the dashboard, a flashing light on an emergency vehicle or a message on a motorway gantry. They signal danger and should be heeded. The prophet Daniel gave a graphic warning sign predicting the downfall of the temple. Here Jesus returns the focus to the fall of Jerusalem, reminding his hearers that what had been foretold will happen soon.

It is unclear exactly what Daniel meant by the 'abomination that causes desolation', but most scholars think it refers to an act of sacrilege in the temple. When this happens those in Judea should understand what is happening and act accordingly. They should flee to the mountains, for it will signal a period of unprecedented distress. All this came to pass when the Roman emperor Titus attacked the city in AD70.

The implication is clear. Scripture warns us in advance of the terrible events that will characterise the end times, and we also should prepare ourselves. We must read the signs, take precautions and pray for protection. We must beware of those who would try to deceive us with false claims and pseudo-miracles. We are to be on our guard and stay alert.

> *What warning signs do you see? Are you staying alert?*

TH

Day 271

End times (4)

MATTHEW 24:26–31 (MARK 13:20–27; LUKE 21:25–28)

Mount of Olives
'So if anyone tells you, "There he is, out in the desert," do not go out; or, "Here he is, in the inner rooms," do not believe it. For as lightning that comes from the east is visible even in the west, so will be the coming of the Son of Man. Wherever there is a carcass, there the vultures will gather. Immediately after the distress of those days "the sun will be darkened, and the moon will not give its light; the stars will fall from the sky, and the heavenly bodies will be shaken." Then will appear the sign of the Son of Man in heaven. And then all the peoples of the earth will mourn when they see the Son of Man coming on the clouds of heaven, with power and great glory. And he will send his angels with a loud trumpet call, and they will gather his elect from the four winds, from one end of the heavens to the other.'

In my youth it was common to see people in city centres with placards warning 'The end is nigh'. No one took them seriously, and they were scorned and mocked. Life was too good to think it may end soon. Gradually that form of outreach has been abandoned, and the church generally has become silent about the second coming, but things are changing. The urgent threat posed by climate change, worldwide pandemics and economic collapse along with frightening political instability and dramatic social breakdown all create within us a feeling of fragility and concern that the world cannot go on forever as it is.

The Christian gospel is clear that not only did Jesus come a first time, but he will come again a second time. If the first happened, so will the second. His return will be in person, highly visible and dramatic. No one will be able to ignore it. It will signal the end of 'business as usual' on planet earth, to the sadness of many. There will be a great separation as Jesus gathers his people together. It will set in motion a chain of events that show God is in control.

> *How does belief in the return of Jesus shape your thinking and inform your behaviour? What difference does it make to the way you live and how you act?*

TH

Day 272

End times (5)

MATTHEW 24:32–35 (MARK 13:28–31; LUKE 21:29–33)

Mount of Olives
'Now learn this lesson from the fig-tree: as soon as its twigs become tender and its leaves come out, you know that summer is near. Even so, when you see all these things, you know that it is near, right at the door. Truly I tell you, this generation will certainly not pass away until all these things have happened. Heaven and earth will pass away, but my words will never pass away.'

It is not surprising that the creator can be seen in his creation, or that his mind is expressed in the things he has made. This is true on the macro scale – creation as a whole in its grandeur displays the glory of God – but also in the micro scale – creation is impregnated with his word, and parables of nature can be seen everywhere, even in the tiniest details. God speaks to us through creation if we have eyes to see and ears to hear.

Jesus loved to draw people's attention to the world around them and spoke of birds and trees, of animals and flowers, of the weather and the wind. Here the humble fig tree carries a message about the end times if we are willing to notice. When we see buds forming and then leaves bursting forth, we know that summer is almost here. We can see the signs around us. Likewise, when we look around and see the kind of events he has been speaking about – persecution, false messiahs, natural disasters, wars, changes in the heavenlies and so on – we should justifiably deduce that the time of Christ's return is getting closer. He is standing at the door.

Each generation has felt his nearness, but none has been as close to his coming as this generation. We must not get carried away with speculation, but we must also be aware that his word is true and his promise is certain – he will return, and we should live in the expectation of that glorious day, for it is the only hope for our world.

> *Becoming more aware of God in creation is part of growing in our attentiveness to his voice. Spend some time this week prayerfully pondering the created world. Ask God to speak to you through majestic vistas as well as in tiny details. Take photos, draw or paint, write poetry. What do you hear God saying?*

TH

Day 273

End times (6)

MATTHEW 24:36-44 (MARK 13:32-34; LUKE 21:34-36)

Mount of Olives
'But about that day or hour no one knows, not even the angels in heaven, nor the Son, but only the Father. As it was in the days of Noah, so it will be at the coming of the Son of Man. For in the days before the flood, people were eating and drinking, marrying and giving in marriage, up to the day Noah entered the ark; and they knew nothing about what would happen until the flood came and took them all away. That is how it will be at the coming of the Son of Man. Two men will be in the field; one will be taken and the other left. Two women will be grinding with a hand mill; one will be taken and the other left. Therefore keep watch, because you do not know on what day your Lord will come. But understand this: if the owner of the house had known at what time of night the thief was coming, he would have kept watch and would not have let his house be broken into. So you also must be ready, because the Son of Man will come at an hour when you do not expect him.'

A key characteristic of the return of Jesus is that it will happen *unexpectedly*. Yes, there will be signs pointing to his arrival, but even so when it happens it will take everyone by surprise. Why is this?

First, because no one knows the precise time of his coming, except the Father. Even Jesus does not know the exact hour. Therefore, there is no value in speculating when it will happen or trying to fix dates. We must have a perpetual state of readiness.

Second, because life will be going on as normal. In the days of Noah no one expected the flood. They went about their daily lives and disregarded the warnings, then suddenly it happened – the earth was flooded! It will be like that when Jesus returns. It will happen on 'just another day'.

Third, because some will have left it too late. Those who put off deciding to follow Jesus will find time has run out, the chance has gone. One will be taken, and another left.

> We must become watchful people, living our lives yet consciously waiting for his return. How is your state of readiness?

TH

Day 274

Faithful and wise servants

MATTHEW 24:45–51 (MARK 13:35–37)

Mount of Olives
'Who then is the faithful and wise servant, whom the master has put in charge of the servants in his household to give them their food at the proper time? It will be good for that servant whose master finds him doing so when he returns. Truly I tell you, he will put him in charge of all his possessions. But suppose that servant is wicked and says to himself, "My master is staying away a long time," and he then begins to beat his fellow servants and to eat and drink with drunkards. The master of that servant will come on a day when he does not expect him and at an hour he is not aware of. He will cut him to pieces and assign him a place with the hypocrites, where there will be weeping and gnashing of teeth.'

There is a saying, 'When the cat's away, the mice will play.' It expresses the human tendency to behave badly when the boss is absent from work or the teacher out of the classroom.

Matthew now records a series of four parables all concerned with how disciples behave during the period when Jesus is no longer with them. Each emphasises the fact that his coming will not be immediate but may be delayed. How will we behave during this interval?

Clearly Jesus is expecting his followers to be faithful and wise servants, going diligently about their kingdom business and waiting patiently for his return, but he is aware of the danger of boredom and relapse. Delay can lead to a loss of focus and discipline, and with it a slide into bad behaviour – abuse of others (always a danger in leadership) and intemperate living. Delay, however, does not mean cancellation. He will return, suddenly and unexpectedly, so his servants need to maintain their state of readiness or risk losing the blessing that might have been theirs.

Remember that not every detail in a parable is to be taken literally. Jesus is not violent like the master in this story (or the others), but he does hold his servants to account.

Do the words 'faithful' and 'wise' describe your service? Are you staying diligent over the long haul of life and ministry? Are you still expectant of Christ's return?

TH

Day 275

Parable of the ten virgins

MATTHEW 25:1-13

Mount of Olives
'At that time the kingdom of heaven will be like ten virgins who took their lamps and went out to meet the bridegroom. Five of them were foolish and five were wise. The foolish ones took their lamps but did not take any oil with them. The wise ones, however, took oil in jars along with their lamps. The bridegroom was a long time in coming, and they all became drowsy and fell asleep. At midnight the cry rang out: "Here's the bridegroom! Come out to meet him!" Then all the virgins woke up and trimmed their lamps. The foolish ones said to the wise, "Give us some of your oil; our lamps are going out." "No," they replied, "there may not be enough for both us and you. Instead, go to those who sell oil and buy some for yourselves." But while they were on their way to buy the oil, the bridegroom arrived. The virgins who were ready went in with him to the wedding banquet. And the door was shut. Later the others also came. "Lord, Lord," they said, "open the door for us!" But he replied, "Truly I tell you, I don't know you." Therefore keep watch, because you do not know the day or the hour.'

Here is another parable highlighting the importance of staying alert, especially since the coming of Jesus may not be for some time. When it does happen, it will be sudden and unexpected, therefore we are to keep watch.

This parable expands on what it means to be wise and, through the story of the two groups of virgins waiting for the bridegroom to arrive, teaches the need to be prepared – to think beforehand about what is needed and to make preparations accordingly. It is folly to assume that we can leave things to the last minute. The oil and the lamps speak to me about the inner life of the believer and being filled with the Holy Spirit. It is essential to maintain our spiritual vitality in the last days, and to keep the flame burning brightly in our hearts.

> *A second danger is that of spiritual drowsiness, becoming sluggish spiritually and not quite awake. What are you doing to maintain your walk with God? How are you staying fresh and vital as you wait for Christ's return?*

TH

Day 276

Parable of the bags of gold (1)

MATTHEW 25:14-23 (LUKE 19:12-19)

Mount of Olives

'Again, it will be like a man going on a journey, who called his servants and entrusted his wealth to them. To one he gave five bags of gold, to another two bags, and to another one bag, each according to his ability. Then he went on his journey. The man who had received five bags of gold went at once and put his money to work and gained five bags more. So also, the one with two bags of gold gained two more. But the man who had received one bag went off, dug a hole in the ground and hid his master's money. After a long time the master of those servants returned and settled accounts with them. The man who had received five bags of gold brought the other five. "Master," he said, "you entrusted me with five bags of gold. See, I have gained five more." His master replied, "Well done, good and faithful servant! You have been faithful with a few things; I will put you in charge of many things. Come and share your master's happiness!" The man with two bags of gold also came. "Master," he said, "you entrusted me with two bags of gold: see, I have gained two more." His master replied, "Well done, good and faithful servant! You have been faithful with a few things; I will put you in charge of many things. Come and share your master's happiness!"'

Jesus is here compared to a wealthy businessman who goes on a long journey and is away for some considerable time. He allocates to his servants different amounts of money with the expectation that they will use it wisely while he is away, so that there is a return for his investment.

The implication is clear. We are to use the gifts and abilities God has given us as we wait for his return to be a blessing to others, rather than sit idly by and wait lazily for that day. Good and faithful servants will be rewarded for their diligence, sharing the master's joy and being entrusted with more responsibility.

> We are called to be faithful servants and, even though we have different capacities and capabilities, to use what we have well. How are you stewarding what has been given to you by God? How is your life impacting others, even in small ways?

TH

Day 277

Parable of the bags of gold (2)

MATTHEW 25:24–30 (*LUKE 19:20–27*)

Mount of Olives
'Then the man who had received one bag of gold came. "Master," he said, "I knew that you are a hard man, harvesting where you have not sown and gathering where you have not scattered seed. So I was afraid and went out and hid your gold in the ground. See, here is what belongs to you." His master replied, "You wicked, lazy servant! So you knew that I harvest where I have not sown and gather where I have not scattered seed? Well then, you should have put my money on deposit with the bankers, so that when I returned I would have received it back with interest. So take the bag of gold from him and give it to the one who has ten bags. For whoever has will be given more, and they will have an abundance. Whoever does not have, even what they have will be taken from them. And throw that worthless servant outside, into the darkness, where there will be weeping and gnashing of teeth."'

In the British TV programme *Dragons' Den*, different entrepreneurs share their ideas for making money with a panel of investors, hoping one will back them financially. Some have crazy ideas and are rejected out of hand, but others have their ideas accepted and given the chance to make them work. What I love about the participants is that they are willing to risk failure in order to succeed.

Serving God requires faith, and faith often means taking risks, which is why some choose to play it safe and do nothing. They are afraid of failure, thinking God will be displeased with them if that happens. They imagine God to be like the man in the story, harsh and demanding and hard to please, but he is not like that. I believe that God loves adventurous faith and rejoices when we step out boldly with a plan or idea to make the gospel known and to share his love. Even if we fail, he rejoices in our attempts. He loves to see us using what he has given us to bring glory to his name.

> *To be faithful is not to be staid and cautious, but to hear God's voice and step out in faith and obedience to fulfil his calling. How adventurous are you? What brave steps are you willing to take to please the master?*

TH

Day 278

Parable of the sheep and goats (1)

MATTHEW 25:31–40

Mount of Olives
'When the Son of Man comes in his glory, and all the angels with him, he will sit on his glorious throne. All the nations will be gathered before him, and he will separate the people one from another as a shepherd separates the sheep from the goats. He will put the sheep on his right and the goats on his left. Then the King will say to those on his right, "Come, you who are blessed by my Father; take your inheritance, the kingdom prepared for you since the creation of the world. For I was hungry and you gave me something to eat, I was thirsty and you gave me something to drink, I was a stranger and you invited me in, I needed clothes and you clothed me, I was ill and you looked after me, I was in prison and you came to visit me." Then the righteous will answer him, "Lord, when did we see you hungry and feed you, or thirsty and give you something to drink? When did we see you a stranger and invite you in, or needing clothes and clothe you? When did we see you ill or in prison and go to visit you?" The King will reply, "Truly I tell you, whatever you did for one of the least of these brothers and sisters of mine, you did for me."'

A feature of the return of Christ will be the separation of those who have truly believed (sheep) from those who have merely simulated faith (goats). The genuineness of faith is seen not just in words, but in deeds, especially in caring for those in need.

Mother Teresa became famous for her work among the poor and dying on the streets of Calcutta. When she cared for the most destitute, she felt she was caring for Jesus in disguise. This belief, arising out of this passage, was the motivation for her amazing work. What we learn here is the deep identification that Jesus has with the needy. He is one with them.

Notice that true goodness is largely unselfconscious. People motivated by love to serve the poor do so instinctively, without thinking of reward or recognition.

> How is your faith being expressed in terms of caring for others? Social justice is not simply a political issue; it is at the heart of Christian discipleship.

TH

Day 279

Parable of the sheep and goats (2)

MATTHEW 25:41–46

Mount of Olives
'Then he will say to those on his left, "Depart from me, you who are cursed, into the eternal fire prepared for the devil and his angels. For I was hungry and you gave me nothing to eat, I was thirsty and you gave me nothing to drink, I was a stranger and you did not invite me in, I needed clothes and you did not clothe me, I was ill and in prison and you did not look after me." They also will answer, "Lord, when did we see you hungry or thirsty or a stranger or needing clothes or ill or in prison, and did not help you?" He will reply, "Truly I tell you, whatever you did not do for one of the least of these, you did not do for me." Then they will go away to eternal punishment, but the righteous to eternal life.'

The theme of separation is surprisingly prominent in this parable. While we must beware of pressing the details too far or taking everything literally, we cannot escape the fact that human behaviour will be judged and not all will enjoy eternal life. This is a sobering fact. Genuine faith is not simply a matter of assent to doctrinal truth or church attendance. Its reality is seen in how we live and care for others.

As we read this parable, we can see that those described as 'goats' are the most selfish and self-centred of people. At best they are so full of themselves they become oblivious to the needs around them. At worst they wilfully close their hearts to the pain they see and stubbornly refuse to help or get involved in alleviating the needs of others. All the time they notionally say they follow Jesus, yet they are blind to his presence in the person of the hungry stranger they encounter on the street. They are without excuse. They are guilty of rejecting Christ.

Such people are left to their own heartless self-centredness and find themselves without compassion even as they had shown no compassion themselves. Whatever is meant by eternal fire, it must include the burning regret that will consume those who lived only for themselves. Just as they closed their hearts to the destitute, so heaven itself will be closed to them.

> *What are your thoughts and feelings as you read this parable?*

TH

Wednesday

Day 280

The plot against Jesus

MATTHEW 26:1-5 (*MARK 14:1-2; LUKE 22:1-2*)

Jerusalem
When Jesus had finished saying all these things, he said to his disciples, 'As you know, the Passover is two days away – and the Son of Man will be handed over to be crucified.' Then the chief priests and the elders of the people assembled in the palace of the high priest, whose name was Caiaphas, and they schemed to arrest Jesus secretly and kill him. 'But not during the festival,' they said, 'or there may be a riot among the people.'

Tuesday had been a long, tiring and stressful day for Jesus. I wonder how he slept that night? Did the one who slept in a boat through the storm rest peacefully, or was his sleep fitful and broken?

As the day breaks, his thoughts are focused on what he knows will be the ultimate outcome, death on a cross. We enter now the passion narratives. There will be no more public teaching, only the recounting of the events leading to his trial, crucifixion and resurrection. This is holy ground. We marvel at his courage and worship as the plan of salvation reaches a climax.

Two strands are converging, one divine, the other human.

From heaven's perspective, the time has come in the eternal purpose of God to save a lost world, for the Son of Man to be handed over to his enemies. This will coincide with the great Passover festival, and by divine design. That which commemorated the exodus of Israel from slavery in Egypt will be the pattern for another, greater deliverance from slavery to sin to be accomplished at Calvary.

From a human perspective the scheming to get rid of Jesus that began when he first appeared on the scene at the Jordan river is also coming to climax. Orchestrated by Caiaphas, and backed by a powerful religious elite, the cunning plan to kill him cannot now be reversed..

Powerful forces are at work here, including the authority of Rome and the malevolence of Satan. Human scheming and the purpose of God, but the divine will coming to pass.

> *Take time to worship. Behold the Lamb of God, ready to lay down his life.*

TH

Day 281

Greeks seeking Jesus

JOHN 12:20-26

Jerusalem
Now there were some Greeks among those who went up to worship at the festival. They came to Philip, who was from Bethsaida in Galilee, with a request. 'Sir,' they said, 'we would like to see Jesus.' Philip went to tell Andrew; Andrew and Philip in turn told Jesus. Jesus replied, 'The hour has come for the Son of Man to be glorified. Very truly I tell you, unless a grain of wheat falls to the ground and dies, it remains only a single seed. But if it dies, it produces many seeds. Anyone who loves their life will lose it, while anyone who hates their life in this world will keep it for eternal life. Whoever serves me must follow me; and where I am, my servant also will be. My Father will honour the one who serves me.'

As a young man I learned to preach in the Methodist chapels in the north of England where I grew up. On the pulpit of one chapel was a small brass plaque with the words 'Sir, we would see Jesus.' It became a permanent reminder to me of my job as a preacher.

Taken in context, the request from a group of Gentiles visiting Jerusalem for the Passover signalled to Jesus that his hour had indeed come, the moment when as the Son of Man he would be 'glorified' by laying down his life – a strange but positive way to speak about his death.

The picture of the seed falling into the ground is a powerful metaphor by which to understand the death of Jesus, and also the true nature of discipleship. The message is clear: life comes out of death, and without dying there is no harvest. Jesus had to fall into the ground in death, but by his death many would be saved. Likewise, when his followers die to their own will in order to follow Jesus, their lives will bear much fruit.

There is a cost to discipleship, for we must follow Jesus along the Calvary Road. Jim Elliot (1927–56), an American missionary, martyred as he sought to reach the Huaorani people in Ecuador, said, 'He is no fool who gives what he cannot keep in order to gain what he cannot lose.'

▌ *Where does the cross intersect with your life today? How might people see Jesus in you?*

TH

Day 282

Jesus speaks about his death

JOHN 12:27-36

Jerusalem

'Now my soul is troubled, and what shall I say? "Father, save me from this hour"? No, it was for this very reason I came to this hour. Father, glorify your name!' Then a voice came from heaven, 'I have glorified it, and will glorify it again.' The crowd that was there and heard it said it had thundered; others said an angel had spoken to him. Jesus said, 'This voice was for your benefit, not mine. Now is the time for judgment on this world; now the prince of this world will be driven out. And I, when I am lifted up from the earth, will draw all people to myself.' He said this to show the kind of death he was going to die. The crowd spoke up, 'We have heard from the Law that the Messiah will remain for ever, so how can you say, "The Son of Man must be lifted up"? Who is this "Son of Man"?' Then Jesus told them, 'You are going to have the light just a little while longer. Walk while you have the light, before darkness overtakes you. Whoever walks in the dark does not know where they are going. Believe in the light while you have the light, so that you may become children of light.' When he had finished speaking, Jesus left and hid himself from them.

The reality of his coming death now sweeps over Jesus in a shockwave of emotion, but he is steadied by his own commitment to his Father's purpose and the timely voice from heaven. He was aware of *how* he would die (lifted up on a cross) and *why* (to deal with sin, defeat the devil and draw people back to God). There is no doubt that this clear sense of mission strengthened his resolve at a moment when he may have hesitated, but that does not mean it was easy for him. It took remarkable courage to walk into the storm of hostility that would soon swirl so violently around him.

There is a moment of challenge too for the crowd who heard the heavenly voice to believe and receive the light he offers. It is a day of opportunity that will soon be past.

> *Where do you need courage as you follow Jesus? How can his example strengthen your resolve to keep following?*

TH

Day 283

Second anointing at Bethany

MATTHEW 26:6-13 (*MARK 14:3-9*)

Bethany
While Jesus was in Bethany in the home of Simon the Leper, a woman came to him with an alabaster jar of very expensive perfume, which she poured on his head as he was reclining at the table. When the disciples saw this, they were indignant. 'Why this waste?' they asked. 'This perfume could have been sold at a high price and the money given to the poor.' Aware of this, Jesus said to them, 'Why are you bothering this woman? She has done a beautiful thing to me. The poor you will always have with you, but you will not always have me. When she poured this perfume on my body, she did it to prepare me for burial. Truly I tell you, wherever this gospel is preached throughout the world, what she has done will also be told, in memory of her.'

There are similarities between this incident and that which we read earlier from John 12:1–11 (see Day 248). But there are also significant differences, which suggests this is a second anointing – this takes place at the home of Simon the Leper, centres on an unnamed woman and features an alabaster jar. We cannot be certain either way, but at such a moment of emotional need for Jesus, it would have provided another tangible expression of comfort and solace.

The main point of the story seems to be that this extravagant act of love was done *to* Jesus. It was for him alone. It was intensely personal, an intimate interaction between himself and a woman who was grateful for what he had done for her. Some considered it a waste, but not the master. He received the gift gladly and the love that it expressed with joy. It ministered to him, soothed his body and helped prepare him for what was to come. He delighted in the offering.

It reminds us that we must never allow our service for Jesus to replace our love for him. We must enjoy times of intimate worship and communion with Jesus that flow out of a grateful heart. And in all we do, our worship and service, we must not be afraid to be extravagant, to go far beyond the minimum requirements, even if others consider us extreme. We love because he first loved us.

What beautiful thing might you do for Jesus? How can you demonstrate your love to him?

TH

Thursday

Day 284

Preparations for Passover

MATTHEW 26:14-19 (MARK 14:12-16; LUKE 22:7-13)

Bethany
Then one of the Twelve – the one called Judas Iscariot – went to the chief priests and asked, 'What are you willing to give me if I deliver him over to you?' So they counted out for him thirty pieces of silver. From then on Judas watched for an opportunity to hand him over. On the first day of the Festival of Unleavened Bread, the disciples came to Jesus and asked, 'Where do you want us to make preparations for you to eat the Passover?' He replied, 'Go into the city to a certain man and tell him, "The Teacher says: my appointed time is near. I am going to celebrate the Passover with my disciples at your house."' So the disciples did as Jesus had directed them and prepared the Passover.

We are uncertain what motivated Judas to treacherously betray Jesus. We know he was greedy for money and dishonest (John 12:6), but if he believed Jesus to be a political messiah, perhaps he wanted to force a confrontation with the authorities. Even those living close to Jesus, known as disciples and within his inner circle, were capable of living parallel lives and not being what they seemed. It is a warning for us all.

The annual Passover meal was of great significance to the Jewish people, commemorating their escape from slavery in Egypt. Back then each household had been told to slaughter a lamb, sprinkle the blood on the doorposts and then eat the meat. When the angel of death passed through that place, he 'passed over' the homes protected by the blood, and they were spared.

There is no doubt that Jesus celebrated the meal with his disciples because he wanted to be with them and needed their companionship, but he also had things to say to them. He wanted to teach them more about the deliverance he would accomplish for the world through his own sacrificial death as the Lamb of God (John 1:29), the 'Passover that would eclipse all Passovers'.[37] The meal then provided a moment of much-needed comradeship and support. It also beautifully illustrated why his death was necessary and what it would achieve – freedom and deliverance from sin.

If you feel weak in your discipleship, remember what Christ has done for you. Forgiveness is always available, no matter how far we have strayed.

TH

Day 285

The last supper

MATTHEW 26:20–30 (MARK 14:17–25; LUKE 22:14–23)

Jerusalem, the upper room
When evening came, Jesus was reclining at the table with the Twelve. And while they were eating, he said, 'Truly I tell you, one of you will betray me.' They were very sad and began to say to him one after the other, 'Surely you don't mean me, Lord?' Jesus replied, 'The one who has dipped his hand into the bowl with me will betray me. The Son of Man will go just as it is written about him. But woe to that man who betrays the Son of Man! It would be better for him if he had not been born.' Then Judas, the one who would betray him, said, 'Surely you don't mean me, Rabbi?' Jesus answered, 'You have said so.' While they were eating, Jesus took bread, and when he had given thanks, he broke it and gave it to his disciples, saying, 'Take and eat; this is my body.' Then he took a cup, and when he had given thanks, he gave it to them, saying, 'Drink from it, all of you. This is my blood of the covenant, which is poured out for many for the forgiveness of sins. I tell you, I will not drink from this fruit of the vine from now on until that day when I drink it new with you in my Father's kingdom.' When they had sung a hymn, they went out to the Mount of Olives.

Betrayal is an act of disloyalty, the breaking of an assumed bond of trust which usually causes great pain to the one who is betrayed. We can think of unfaithfulness in marriage, the breaking of a confidence or the dishonouring of a promise. Jesus was deeply hurt by the betrayal of Judas, for it involved someone whom he had welcomed into his most intimate moments. The disciples rightly are provoked to examine their hearts, but even then, Judas feigns innocence.

The Passover meal becomes an opportunity for Jesus to model what will become known as the Lord's Supper, a way of remembering him and understanding his death that has been central to church life ever since. It is often accompanied by a time of self-reflection and, given the visible tokens of his broken body and shed blood, the assurance of forgiveness and cleansing.

▎ *What does Communion mean to you? How does it both challenge you and reassure you?*

TH

Day 286

Washing the disciples' feet

JOHN 13:1-11

Jerusalem, the upper room
It was just before the Passover Festival. Jesus knew that the hour had come for him to leave this world and go to the Father. Having loved his own who were in the world, he loved them to the end. The evening meal was in progress, and the devil had already prompted Judas, the son of Simon Iscariot, to betray Jesus. Jesus knew that the Father had put all things under his power, and that he had come from God and was returning to God; so he got up from the meal, took off his outer clothing, and wrapped a towel round his waist. After that, he poured water into a basin and began to wash his disciples' feet, drying them with the towel that was wrapped round him. He came to Simon Peter, who said to him, 'Lord, are you going to wash my feet?' Jesus replied, 'You do not realise now what I am doing, but later you will understand.' 'No,' said Peter, 'you shall never wash my feet.' Jesus answered, 'Unless I wash you, you have no part with me.' 'Then, Lord,' Simon Peter replied, 'not just my feet but my hands and my head as well!' Jesus answered, 'Those who have had a bath need only to wash their feet; their whole body is clean. And you are clean, though not every one of you.' For he knew who was going to betray him, and that was why he said not every one was clean.

John's intimate account of the time in the upper room begins after the Passover meal and starts with a reminder of the great love Jesus had for his disciples, even Judas. Why not try to visualise the event (see page 12), and place yourself into the story as if you were a disciple or a servant standing by?

- How do you imagine the evening has been going?
- How do you feel when Jesus disrobes and takes the towel and basin?
- What do you make of Peter's response, and how Jesus deals with him?
- Imagine Jesus comes to wash your feet. What does that feel like? What do you say to him? How does he respond to you?

> *Turn your thoughts into prayer; journal about anything that has surfaced for you.*

TH

Day 287

Wash one another's feet

JOHN 13:12-20

Jerusalem, the upper room
When he had finished washing their feet, he put on his clothes and returned to his place. 'Do you understand what I have done for you?' he asked them. 'You call me "Teacher" and "Lord", and rightly so, for that is what I am. Now that I, your Lord and Teacher, have washed your feet, you also should wash one another's feet. I have set you an example that you should do as I have done for you. Very truly I tell you, no servant is greater than his master, nor is a messenger greater than the one who sent him. Now that you know these things, you will be blessed if you do them. I am not referring to all of you; I know those I have chosen. But this is to fulfil this passage of Scripture: "He who shared my bread has turned against me." I am telling you now before it happens, so that when it does happen you will believe that I am who I am. Very truly I tell you, whoever accepts anyone I send accepts me; and whoever accepts me accepts the one who sent me.'

In any form of instruction, the example set by the teacher is as powerful as anything that is said or written. We all need to see truth demonstrated, which is why modelling is such a vital part in discipling or mentoring. If there is any disparity between a teacher's words and their actions, the impact of their teaching will be significantly lessened.

Jesus is a great example of servant leadership, where authority is exercised in humility, not for personal gain or prestige but for the benefit of those being led. We are to be servants first and leaders second. In washing the disciples' feet, Jesus took a lowly place and ministered to their need.

The question now is: are we willing to follow his example? To wash one another's feet means to be willing to put the needs of others before our own and to attend to their concerns. It means to use the gifts we have for the benefit of others. This requires humility and love, two key characteristics of the kingdom and the new community (church) that Jesus is bringing into being.

> *What has shaped your understanding of leadership? What do you think it means to be a servant leader?*

TH

Day 288

Jesus and Judas

JOHN 13:21–30 (MATTHEW 26:14–16; MARK 14:10–11; LUKE 22:1–6)

Jerusalem, the upper room
After he had said this, Jesus was troubled in spirit and testified, 'Very truly I tell you, one of you is going to betray me.' His disciples stared at one another, at a loss to know which of them he meant. One of them, the disciple whom Jesus loved, was reclining next to him. Simon Peter motioned to this disciple and said, 'Ask him which one he means.' Leaning back against Jesus, he asked him, 'Lord, who is it?' Jesus answered, 'It is the one to whom I will give this piece of bread when I have dipped it in the dish.' Then, dipping the piece of bread, he gave it to Judas, the son of Simon Iscariot. As soon as Judas took the bread, Satan entered into him. So Jesus told him, 'What you are about to do, do quickly.' But no one at the meal understood why Jesus said this to him. Since Judas had charge of the money, some thought Jesus was telling him to buy what was needed for the festival, or to give something to the poor. As soon as Judas had taken the bread, he went out. And it was night.

Here we have the first self-description of the writer of the fourth gospel. John calls himself 'the disciple whom Jesus loved' and will refer to himself in this way four more times (19:26; 20:2; 21:7, 20). This is neither a false modesty nor a boastful self-accolade but simply a statement of fact. John knew himself to be loved by Jesus and this became the basis for his identity, as it is for any child of God.

Brennan Manning writes, 'Define yourself radically as one beloved by God. This is the true self. Every other identity is an illusion.'[38] John reclined next to Jesus, a place of intimacy and friendship, but that same relationship of tenderness and affection is for all his followers. It is true to say that the spiritual life is a journey into our own discovery that we too are deeply loved by God.

Judas presents such a contrast, sharing the intimacy of the broken bread yet contemplating betrayal. Satan seems to have manipulated his wounded self and taken advantage of his brokenness, but the decision was still his own.

> *Which path will you tread – that of the beloved or the betrayer?*

TH

Day 289

Prediction of Peter's denial

JOHN 13:31–38 (MATTHEW 26:31–35; MARK 14:27–32; LUKE 22:31–38)

Jerusalem, the upper room
When he was gone, Jesus said, 'Now the Son of Man is glorified and God is glorified in him. If God is glorified in him, God will glorify the Son in himself, and will glorify him at once. My children, I will be with you only a little longer. You will look for me, and just as I told the Jews, so I tell you now: where I am going, you cannot come. A new command I give you: Love one another. As I have loved you, so you must love one another. By this everyone will know that you are my disciples, if you love one another.' Simon Peter asked him, 'Lord, where are you going?' Jesus replied, 'Where I am going, you cannot follow now, but you will follow later.' Peter asked, 'Lord, why can't I follow you now? I will lay down my life for you.' Then Jesus answered, 'Will you really lay down your life for me? Very truly I tell you, before the cock crows, you will disown me three times!'

Leisurely mealtimes can provide great opportunities for meaningful conversation, and here in the upper room Jesus begins what has been called his farewell discourse, sharing with his closest friends the things most on his heart.

Repeatedly he tells them that he is going away, implying that he is soon to die. He seeks to prepare them for life without him. His goal is to leave behind a new community (the church), a visible expression of the kingdom, which will be founded on love – love received from him, then shared with each other.

This is his one new commandment: his followers are to love one another. This will be their distinctive mark, that which even an unbelieving society will recognise. In all our strategising for church growth, this has to remain the most important principle: a loving church will be a growing church.

Peter allows his enthusiasm to run away with him, claiming for himself that which Jesus knows he will not be able to deliver. A gentle rebuke from the master brings him down to earth and reminds us to not overestimate our own potential. Denial is not betrayal, but it is still not good.

> *Lord, grant me a realistic assessment of myself, and a vision for your church as a community of love.*

TH

Day 290

Words of comfort

JOHN 14:1-7

Jerusalem, the upper room
'Do not let your hearts be troubled. You believe in God; believe also in me. My Father's house has many rooms; if that were not so, would I have told you that I am going there to prepare a place for you? And if I go and prepare a place for you, I will come back and take you to be with me that you also may be where I am. You know the way to the place where I am going.' Thomas said to him, 'Lord, we don't know where you are going, so how can we know the way?' Jesus answered, 'I am the way and the truth and the life. No one comes to the Father except through me. If you really know me, you will know my Father as well. From now on, you do know him and have seen him.'

My son and his family live in Australia, and although they visit here from time to time, their going back home is always a painful moment for me, and the separation does not get easier. We can probably all sympathise with the disciples at the thought of losing Jesus when he returns to the Father. He has been their rock for the past three years. How will they manage without him now?

All separation from those we love involves a bereavement, and Jesus speaks to ease their fears. Not surprisingly this passage is often read at funerals because it gives us assurance of a life beyond the grave. The antidote to a troubled heart is to trust. His promise is that he is going to prepare a place for them and will one day come back to take them there (either at death or at his return). They are invited to trust his promise and rest on his word.

The disciples have many questions in their minds and Thomas is the first to speak, since they are not clear where Jesus is going. Jesus is returning to the Father, and it is his desire to lead them there as well. He is opening *the way* to God, has made known *the truth* about God and offers *the life* from God to any who believe. That is the gospel.

> What loss or separation are you facing? How can faith in Jesus help you through troubled times, especially bereavement?

TH

Day 291

The Father and I

JOHN 14:8-14

Jerusalem, the upper room
Philip said, 'Lord, show us the Father and that will be enough for us.' Jesus answered: 'Don't you know me, Philip, even after I have been among you such a long time? Anyone who has seen me has seen the Father. How can you say, 'Show us the Father'? Don't you believe that I am in the Father, and that the Father is in me? The words I say to you I do not speak on my own authority. Rather, it is the Father, living in me, who is doing his work. Believe me when I say that I am in the Father and the Father is in me; or at least believe on the evidence of the works themselves. Very truly I tell you, whoever believes in me will do the works I have been doing, and they will do even greater things than these, because I am going to the Father. And I will do whatever you ask in my name, so that the Father may be glorified in the Son. You may ask me for anything in my name, and I will do it.'

Mentioning my son yesterday reminds me that people often say he is like me – like father, like son. This was certainly true of Jesus, who perfectly reflected the heavenly Father's likeness.

To Philip's request to see the Father, Jesus replies with certainty: 'If you have seen me, you have already seen the Father.' God is invisible to the human eye, but in Jesus he has become visible and is made known (John 1:14, 18). When we see Jesus, we see God; when we hear Jesus, we hear God.

We are given an insight here of how Jesus worked in partnership with the Father – 'It is the Father, living in me, who is doing his work' (v. 10). That is how Jesus operated, and as we will see later, when Jesus speaks about the vine and its branches (John 15:1-8), it is how we are to work as well.

With this relationship of dependency and intimacy in place, believers will do similar supernatural works to those of Jesus, God working in and through them. 'Greater works', though, may not mean greater in power, but either greater in number (the whole of church history) or greater in nature (the miracle of salvation).

Lord, let me be like you, as you are like the Father.

TH

Day 292

The comforter

JOHN 14:15–21

Jerusalem, the upper room
'If you love me, keep my commands. And I will ask the Father, and he will give you another advocate to help you and be with you for ever – the Spirit of truth. The world cannot accept him, because it neither sees him nor knows him. But you know him, for he lives with you and will be in you. I will not leave you as orphans; I will come to you. Before long, the world will not see me anymore, but you will see me. Because I live, you also will live. On that day you will realise that I am in my Father, and you are in me, and I am in you. Whoever has my commands and keeps them is the one who loves me. The one who loves me will be loved by my Father, and I too will love them and show myself to them.'

When my car broke down one day at the side of a busy motorway, I was relieved to know I had breakdown cover and could call for help, which arrived quickly. Thankfully, I was soon on my way again.

A major plus for the disciples in the future will be the presence of the Holy Spirit. The Spirit's ministry is described here with the Greek word *parakletos*, literally one who draws alongside us to help. Although translated in the passage above as 'advocate' (a legal helper), and often as 'comforter' or 'counsellor', the emphasis is on one who comes to our aid as and when we need it.

The helper will not only be with us, but also within us – he will take residence in our hearts and work powerfully through us. This means the disciples will not be left as abandoned orphans when Jesus leaves but will continue to know the divine presence constantly. Further, the Spirit living within them will enable them to live out the commandments of Jesus and do his will.

Notice that obedience is not merely compliance to rules but an expression of love. As David Benner writes, 'Christian obedience should always be based on surrender to a person, not simply acceptance of an obligation. It is surrender to love, not submission to a duty.'[39]

> *What difference does the Spirit make to your life? How is your love for God being expressed in obedience?*

TH

Day 293

Peace I leave with you

JOHN 14:22-27

Jerusalem, the upper room
Then Judas (not Judas Iscariot) said, 'But, Lord, why do you intend to show yourself to us and not to the world?' Jesus replied, 'Anyone who loves me will obey my teaching. My Father will love them, and we will come to them and make our home with them. Anyone who does not love me will not obey my teaching. These words you hear are not my own; they belong to the Father who sent me. All this I have spoken while still with you. But the Advocate, the Holy Spirit, whom the Father will send in my name, will teach you all things and will remind you of everything I have said to you. Peace I leave with you; my peace I give you. I do not give to you as the world gives. Do not let your hearts be troubled and do not be afraid.'

An orphanage is a home for orphans, those who have no parents to care for them and no home of their own. Jesus promised not to leave his disciples as orphans and, as well as a helper to guide them, he promises a home to shelter them.

Those who love Jesus, and who express that love in their obedience, will discover that their hearts have become the dwelling place of God. Father and Son will come, by the work of the Spirit, to abide within them, creating a relationship closer than any they had known before.

Further, the Spirit will continue to teach them spiritual truth and remind them of all that Jesus had previously taught them. Even more consoling is the promise that this new intimate relationship will be characterised by a deep inner peace unlike anything the world can offer. It will be the peace that Jesus himself experienced as he lived day by day under the protective gaze of the Father. That same promise is applicable to all who obediently follow Jesus.

Circumstances will always challenge our emotional equilibrium, but an inner stability is available to us as we are mindful of the divine life within us and the peace available to us. When we learn to dwell in the shelter of the Most High, we find God is our refuge and fortress (Psalm 91:1-2).

▍ *Lord, teach me to hide myself in you. Grant me your peace. Be the anchor for my soul today.*

TH

Day 294

The prince of this world

JOHN 14:28–31

Jerusalem, the upper room
'You heard me say, "I am going away and I am coming back to you." If you loved me, you would be glad that I am going to the Father, for the Father is greater than I. I have told you now before it happens, so that when it does happen you will believe. I will not say much more to you, for the prince of this world is coming. He has no hold over me, but he comes so that the world may learn that I love the Father and do exactly what my Father has commanded me. Come now; let us leave.'

The expression 'Forewarned is forearmed' means that you can deal more effectively with difficult circumstances if you have an idea beforehand of the challenges you will face. The strategy of Jesus has been to prepare the disciples for his departure, and the consequences of that for them. He has told them clearly that he will soon be returning to the Father and has hidden nothing from them; but he is also spelling out the resources that are available to them once he has left.

If the disciples truly love Jesus, they will rejoice at what is happening, for it marks the next stage in his mission and in his obedience to the Father's plan. They may not like it, but they will come to understand why it is necessary. The time has arrived for the confrontation between Jesus and the powers of darkness to come to a head. The prince of the world (Satan) is coming, with the aim of thwarting the purpose of God. Jesus will not shrink back, however, and will meet the enemy head-on.

'Let us leave' may mean more than leaving the meeting place. It carries the weight of 'Let us go to meet the advancing enemy.' The teaching will continue for a while, but the determination to face the challenge of the enemy's approach has been accepted. That very willingness reveals the love of Jesus for the Father, and his commitment to fulfilling his mission. When we understand this, we love Jesus even more for saving us. He is our champion, going to do battle on our behalf.

> *Take time to ponder what it meant for Jesus to go to the cross. What was he feeling in these moments? How do you respond?*

TH

Day 295

The vine and the branches

JOHN 15:1-8

Jerusalem, the upper room
'I am the true vine, and my Father is the gardener. He cuts off every branch in me that bears no fruit, while every branch that does bear fruit he prunes so that it will be even more fruitful. You are already clean because of the word I have spoken to you. Remain in me, as I also remain in you. No branch can bear fruit by itself; it must remain in the vine. Neither can you bear fruit unless you remain in me. I am the vine; you are the branches. If you remain in me and I in you, you will bear much fruit; apart from me you can do nothing. If you do not remain in me, you are like a branch that is thrown away and withers; such branches are picked up, thrown into the fire and burned. If you remain in me and my words remain in you, ask whatever you wish, and it will be done for you. This is to my Father's glory, that you bear much fruit, showing yourselves to be my disciples.'

If I were shipwrecked on a desert island and could salvage only one page from my Bible, this would be the one. Here is everything we need to live the Christian life effectively and enjoyably.

Perhaps there was a vine growing outside the upper room. Maybe Jesus had in mind the golden vine that adorned the temple. Either way, the vine provides the perfect illustration of how we are to live the Christian life – by abiding in Christ.

The main point is this: separated from the vine, a branch can bear no fruit, but connected to the vine (and given proper care and attention), it will bear much fruit. Likewise, when a believer maintains a living relationship of dependency and faith with Jesus, that person will produce much spiritual fruit. That will be in terms of Christlike character (the fruit of the Spirit, Galatians 5:22–23) and Christlike service (compassionate acts of service, Colossians 1:10).

It takes time to abide in Christ, and in a busy world, that is the greatest challenge for modern-day disciples. Through prayer and scripture, obedience and love, and with submission to the Father, we maintain our pace of abiding in Christ, and so bear much fruit.

> Do you know that 'apart from Jesus, you can do nothing'?

TH

Day 296

Chosen and appointed

JOHN 15:9-17

Jerusalem, the upper room

'As the Father has loved me, so have I loved you. Now remain in my love. If you keep my commands, you will remain in my love, just as I have kept my Father's commands and remain in his love. I have told you this so that my joy may be in you and that your joy may be complete. My command is this: love each other as I have loved you. Greater love has no one than this: to lay down one's life for one's friends. You are my friends if you do what I command. I no longer call you servants, because a servant does not know his master's business. Instead, I have called you friends, for everything that I learned from my Father I have made known to you. You did not choose me, but I chose you and appointed you so that you might go and bear fruit – fruit that will last – and so that whatever you ask in my name the Father will give you. This is my command: love each other.'

The disciples were a mixed bunch and each an unlikely person to be at the heart of the new kingdom that Jesus was inaugurating. Yet, he had chosen them personally and over three years trained and shaped them, so they were ready to take forward his mission when he returned to the Father.

They were not just servants to him but friends whose company he enjoyed and from whom he derived strength and support. He would soon demonstrate his love by laying down his life for them (and the whole world). As his friends, he was now sharing with them his most intimate thoughts about the future.

At the heart of his mission was the formation of a new community which would be built around their love for each other. This would not be easy because human beings are by nature selfish and self-centred. Only people who know themselves to be loved, and who are willing to live sacrificially, could bring such a community into being.

Obeying this commandment need not be a joyless task. As they abide in Jesus, and his life is in them, they will also know his joy bubbling up within them.

What is the difference between a servant and a friend? How do you see yourself?

TH

Day 297

Hated without a reason

JOHN 15:18–25

Jerusalem, the upper room
'If the world hates you, keep in mind that it hated me first. If you belonged to the world, it would love you as its own. As it is, you do not belong to the world, but I have chosen you out of the world. That is why the world hates you. Remember what I told you: "A servant is not greater than his master." If they persecuted me, they will persecute you also. If they obeyed my teaching, they will obey yours also. They will treat you this way because of my name, for they do not know the one who sent me. If I had not come and spoken to them, they would not be guilty of sin; but now they have no excuse for their sin. Whoever hates me hates my Father as well. If I had not done among them the works no one else did, they would not be guilty of sin. As it is, they have seen, and yet they have hated both me and my Father. But this is to fulfil what is written in their Law: "They hated me without reason."'

Jesus is a realist. He does not sugar-coat his picture of the future, pretending the task he is giving the disciples will be easy. He does not deceive them about what lies ahead, but warns them bluntly that their work will be opposed and they will be hated. They will need great courage to continue his work.

The principle is clear: 'A servant is not greater than his master' (v. 20). We have seen throughout the gospel story that Jesus was hated and rejected by those he came to save, by his own people and those who purported to know God. If he was rejected, then his followers will be also. He was hated without reason – he did nothing wrong and was not deserving of such treatment. The hatred was a hatred of God himself, a sinful rejection of his rule and purpose.

Most of us seek to be popular. We want to please and hope to be appreciated. We are kind and compassionate and seek to do good. Why do people not like us? It is irrational, yet realistically to be expected when we bear the name of Jesus.

> *Pray for grace to bear reproach for Christ's sake, and for all who feel the daily sting of persecution and ostracism.*

TH

Day 298

Put out of the synagogues

JOHN 15:26–16:4

Jerusalem, the upper room
'When the Advocate comes, whom I will send to you from the Father – the Spirit of truth who goes out from the Father – he will testify about me. And you also must testify, for you have been with me from the beginning. All this I have told you so that you will not fall away. They will put you out of the synagogue; in fact, the time is coming when anyone who kills you will think they are offering a service to God. They will do such things because they have not known the Father or me. I have told you this, so that when their time comes you will remember that I warned you about them.'

The disciples will face harsh and brutal opposition, and they must be well prepared or they may be overwhelmed. They will experience ostracism – be put out of the synagogue and socially isolated, a high price to pay for their beliefs. More than that, some will actually be put to death because of their allegiance to Christ. The book of Acts, and church history, confirm the reality of this.

Fortunately, they will not be alone. The Holy Spirit will be with them, empowering and emboldening them in their witness. He will continue to teach them about the work that Jesus has accomplished so that they can give public testimony to what they know to be true. They are eyewitnesses, and this will be an essential part of their ministry. Having been with Jesus from the beginning, they are well-placed to bear witness to all they had seen and heard, and to share their discovery that Jesus was indeed the long-awaited Messiah.

Every believer has a story to tell and a testimony to give. We too are called to be witnesses, to share sensitively and in appropriate ways what we know to be true. We are to point others to Jesus by our words and our lives, and we have to learn how to do that amid a hostile world that does not always want to hear our message. We will feel intimidated, but we have the Holy Spirit to make us bold and to go ahead of us to create openings for appropriate sharing. Our responsibility is to speak when the opportunity arises.

▍ *Lord, release me from fear and make me a bold and sensitive witness for you.*

TH

Day 299

The counsellor will come

JOHN 16:4–11

Jerusalem, the upper room
'I did not tell you this from the beginning because I was with you, but now I am going to him who sent me. None of you asks me, "Where are you going?" Rather, you are filled with grief because I have said these things. But very truly I tell you, it is for your good that I am going away. Unless I go away, the Advocate will not come to you; but if I go, I will send him to you. When he comes, he will prove the world to be in the wrong about sin and righteousness and judgment: about sin, because people do not believe in me; about righteousness, because I am going to the Father, where you can see me no longer; and about judgment, because the prince of this world now stands condemned.'

It is often said that grief is the price we pay for loving. Grief is that bundle of sad and painful emotions that rise up inside us when we lose something or someone that is precious to us. Certainly, the departure of Jesus signalled a huge loss to the disciples; they are already feeling bereft and destabilised.

Yet, surprisingly, it is to their advantage that he is going away. Why? Because when Jesus leaves the Holy Spirit will come and he will work on their behalf. The work they have to do is not exactly their work – it is God's work, and the Spirit will help them to accomplish the task in three significant ways. He will convict people of their sin; he will show them how to find the righteousness that is from God; and he will apply the victory that Jesus has won over Satan by setting his captives free.

Two things follow. First, we are to realise that we are not alone in the work of mission. The Spirit is secretly and invisibly at work in the world, and we are to work in partnership with him. We must not take all the responsibility on our own shoulders or feel we have to do it in our own strength – indeed we cannot.

Second, we can be assured of the accompanying supernatural work of the Spirit, 'the unleashing of the powers of the promised kingdom of God in the world'.[40]

▎ *You are not alone; but are you depending on the help of the Spirit?*

TH

Day 300

The Spirit of truth

JOHN 16:12-18

Jerusalem, the upper room

'I have much more to say to you, more than you can now bear. But when he, the Spirit of truth, comes, he will guide you into all the truth. He will not speak on his own; he will speak only what he hears, and he will tell you what is yet to come. He will glorify me because it is from me that he will receive what he will make known to you. All that belongs to the Father is mine. That is why I said the Spirit will receive from me what he will make known to you.' Jesus went on to say, 'In a little while you will see me no more, and then after a little while you will see me.' At this, some of his disciples said to one another, 'What does he mean by saying, "In a little while you will see me no more, and then after a little while you will see me," and "Because I am going to the Father"?' They kept asking, 'What does he mean by "a little while"? We don't understand what he is saying.'

I remember sitting in a class at school for A-level mathematics and thinking, 'I don't get this.' My brain could not take in the information being given. I seemed unable to think in the way that was required to grasp the theory involved. Not surprisingly, I failed that particular subject.

I guess the disciples often felt inadequate as they tried to grasp the teaching of Jesus. Sometimes it left them baffled, and they must have despaired of ever understanding properly. Yet help was at hand in the form of the Holy Spirit, who would become their resident, internalised teacher.

The promise is that, as the Spirit of truth, he will guide them into all truth; that is, give them understanding and insight of what they need to know regardless of their simple backgrounds and lack of learning. He will instruct them and reveal the truth to them, opening their eyes to grasp spiritual realities. This is the joyful work of the Spirit – to take what he is given by Jesus and make it live in the hearts and lives of the disciples.

This work of revelation continues today. He is the best teacher ever, and he will give you understanding.

> Holy Spirit, be my teacher. Open my eyes, give me understanding.

TH

Day 301

Grief and joy

JOHN 16:19-24

Jerusalem, the upper room
Jesus saw that they wanted to ask him about this, so he said to them, 'Are you asking one another what I meant when I said, "In a little while you will see me no more, and then after a little while you will see me"? Very truly I tell you, you will weep and mourn while the world rejoices. You will grieve, but your grief will turn to joy. A woman giving birth to a child has pain because her time has come; but when her baby is born she forgets the anguish because of her joy that a child is born into the world. So with you: now is your time of grief, but I will see you again and you will rejoice, and no one will take away your joy. In that day you will no longer ask me anything. Very truly I tell you, my Father will give you whatever you ask in my name. Until now you have not asked for anything in my name. Ask and you will receive, and your joy will be complete.'

Jesus does not hide the fact that a time of acute sadness lies ahead for his followers. They will know the sting of grief, the particular disabling anguish that follows the violent death of a loved one. They will weep, for sure, and feel miserable and lost. It will feel like the world has been plunged into darkness and that the sun will never shine again.

It is right and proper to grieve well, and Jesus does not circumvent the process of grieving. He acknowledges the validity of feeling the loss created by his departure, and not rushing through the normal stages of grief. Yet he also assures them that they need not be trapped in sadness forever. Their grief will eventually turn to joy as they understand all that his death has accomplished.

Giving birth is extremely painful and can last for a long time, but it does end. When a mother sees her newborn baby she is usually filled with joy and forgets her pain. Likewise, as the disciples receive the benefits that flow from the cross, they will rejoice at what has been gained and forget the pain of loss.

> *What grief is inside you? Remember, it is important to grieve well. Don't avoid or anaesthetise the pain.*

TH

Day 302

Returning to the Father

JOHN 16:25–33

Jerusalem, the upper room
'Though I have been speaking figuratively, a time is coming when I will no longer use this kind of language but will tell you plainly about my Father. In that day you will ask in my name. I am not saying that I will ask the Father on your behalf. No, the Father himself loves you because you have loved me and have believed that I came from God. I came from the Father and entered the world; now I am leaving the world and going back to the Father.' Then Jesus' disciples said, 'Now you are speaking clearly and without figures of speech. Now we can see that you know all things and that you do not even need to have anyone ask you questions. This makes us believe that you came from God.' 'Do you now believe?' Jesus replied. 'A time is coming and in fact has come when you will be scattered, each to your own home. You will leave me all alone. Yet I am not alone, for my Father is with me. I have told you these things, so that in me you may have peace. In this world you will have trouble. But take heart! I have overcome the world.'

The policy of radical honesty continues as Jesus shares his heart with the disciples, whom he loves. A clear statement of his intentions helps to secure them: 'I came from the Father and entered the world; now I am leaving the world and going back to the Father' (v. 28). His words are a masterful summary of two great themes in theology – incarnation and ascension. Now the disciples have a handle on what he is doing and where he is going, and their faith is strengthened.

Yet Jesus knows their faith is still weak and refuses to sugar-coat the pill. Placed under pressure, his disciples will desert him and he will be left alone, but they need not be despondent. They can experience peace because he will overcome the world. Trouble will come, but he will lead them victoriously through it.

How easily we feel strong when things are going well and misjudge our true spiritual condition. Peace comes, not through self-confidence, but by trusting in Jesus to bring us through even when we are weak.

> Lord, I am weak, but you are strong. Hold me in the storm.

TH

Day 303

Jesus prays: glorify your Son

JOHN 17:1–5

Jerusalem, the upper room
After Jesus said this, he looked towards heaven and prayed: 'Father, the hour has come. Glorify your Son, that your Son may glorify you. For you granted him authority over all people that he might give eternal life to all those you have given him. Now this is eternal life: that they know you, the only true God, and Jesus Christ, whom you have sent. I have brought you glory on earth by finishing the work you gave me to do. And now, Father, glorify me in your presence with the glory I had with you before the world began.'

If, during the teaching time in the upper room, we have been standing in the holy place, surely now, as we eavesdrop on Jesus at prayer, we have entered the holy of holies. To hear another pray is to see into their very soul; to listen to Jesus pray is to hear the very heartbeat of God. Ponder slowly and carefully over the next few days these Holy Spirit-crafted words.

Jesus shows us how to mix teaching with prayer, and how to water the seed of the word with spiritual longing. Jesus prays for himself and his disciples, but first for himself – another significant pointer. His overwhelming desire is to glorify the Father, and to do this by finishing the work entrusted to him. He longs to be in the presence of God again, to receive the glory he is due for finishing his course and bringing salvation to the world. His hopes and dreams are centred four-square upon doing the Father's will and pleasing him. Is this where my longing rests?

The whole reason for his coming is so that people may have eternal life, and here we have his own definition of this important concept: eternal life is to know, in an experiential way, both Father and Son; to be brought into a deeply personal relationship with both. Therefore, we must ask, 'Do I know God in this way? Am I growing in connection to Jesus as friend to friend? Is my great desire to show others how to know Father and Son? Do my prayers reflect these priorities?'

> *Eternal life continues beyond the grave, but it begins in this life. We can have eternal life now and enjoy the life of God pulsating through our veins. What a privilege.*

TH

Day 304

Jesus prays: protect them

JOHN 17:6–12

Jerusalem, the upper room
'I have revealed you to those whom you gave me out of the world. They were yours; you gave them to me and they have obeyed your word. Now they know that everything you have given me comes from you. For I gave them the words you gave me and they accepted them. They knew with certainty that I came from you, and they believed that you sent me. I pray for them. I am not praying for the world, but for those you have given me, for they are yours. All I have is yours, and all you have is mine. And glory has come to me through them. I will remain in the world no longer, but they are still in the world, and I am coming to you. Holy Father, protect them by the power of your name, the name you gave me, so that they may be one as we are one. While I was with them, I protected them and kept them safe by that name you gave me. None has been lost except the one doomed to destruction so that Scripture would be fulfilled.'

I wonder how you pray for your children, or the little ones within your circle of love? Almost certainly you will pray for their safety and protection. We are not surprised to hear Jesus praying for his 'children' (John 13:33) in much the same way.

The principle by which Jesus lived was one of receiving everything from the Father. All is gift. He does nothing apart from the Father and passes on only what has been given to him. The disciples have witnessed this way of living, and it will be a pattern for them (and us) to follow. Jesus does not claim ownership of his followers, only stewardship, for they belong to God. As he returns to the Father, he entrusts them confidently into the Father's care.

Having warned them of trials and opposition ahead, Jesus prays for their protection, from the devil and a hostile world. This does not imply a total immunity to suffering but a protection from the schemes and attacks that might damage the church in its infancy. They will be persecuted, and some may die, but the church will not be wiped out as her enemies would desire.

▍ *Are you learning to live like Jesus? Who do you pray for?*

TH

Day 305

Jesus prays: sanctify them

JOHN 17:13–19

Jerusalem, the upper room
'I am coming to you now, but I say these things while I am still in the world, so that they may have the full measure of my joy within them. I have given them your word and the world has hated them, for they are not of the world any more than I am of the world. My prayer is not that you take them out of the world but that you protect them from the evil one. They are not of the world, even as I am not of it. Sanctify them by the truth; your word is truth. As you sent me into the world, I have sent them into the world. For them I sanctify myself, that they too may be truly sanctified.'

It is a common caricature of Christians that they are joyless, sombre people. Perhaps some are, but not those who live in relationship with Jesus, for his prayer is that we may know the full measure of his joy within us. Ponder that for a moment.

Jesus was anointed with the oil of gladness beyond what was normal (Psalm 45:7), which means fun and laughter, good humour and joyfulness were part of his being and characterised his relationships. He promised his followers his joy would be in them so that their joy might be complete (John 15:11), and now he prays that promise into being. The challenges they face will be lightened by the joy that they will have whatever the circumstances. We share in that joy, regardless of our temperament. Why be miserable?

Notice that holiness and joy are not mutually exclusive. Those who sanctify themselves, that is, set themselves apart to do God's will, have not abandoned fun and laughter or taken a pledge of seriousness. It is sin that makes us miserable and the further we are from it, the happier we will be. Those who live surrendered lives live within the bounty of God and know deep, abiding joy.

We are to enter the world full of holy joy, not to burden people further (as the Pharisees did), but to lift their burdens from them and bring them into the eternal life that Jesus offers. That is our calling, and to that task we happily give ourselves.

> *How do you understand the connection between joy and holiness? What does it mean to be light in the darkness?*

TH

Day 306

Jesus prays: make them one

JOHN 17:20–26

Jerusalem, the upper room

'My prayer is not for them alone. I pray also for those who will believe in me through their message, that all of them may be one, Father, just as you are in me and I am in you. May they also be in us so that the world may believe that you have sent me. I have given them the glory that you gave me, that they may be one as we are one – I in them and you in me – so that they may be brought to complete unity. Then the world will know that you sent me and have loved them even as you have loved me. Father, I want those you have given me to be with me where I am, and to see my glory, the glory you have given me because you loved me before the creation of the world. Righteous Father, though the world does not know you, I know you, and they know that you have sent me. I have made you known to them, and will continue to make you known in order that the love you have for me may be in them and that I myself may be in them.'

As a young believer I was confused about the multiplicity of churches, and still am. Why, when Jesus so desires his church to be one, do we continue to fragment and divide over so many minor issues?

Not that unity is the same as uniformity. Different churches suit different people, and a variety of styles can be good. What Jesus seeks is a heart unity where churches love and respect each other and can easily work together for the common concern of sharing the gospel. If each individual church is submitted to his lordship and leadership, it follows that we will move in the same direction, being guided by the Spirit.

Unity comes about because God's love is within us, and Christ lives in us as we live in him (remember John 15?). If we are secure in our identity, then we dare cross boundaries and work together. In a hostile world we need each other, and the world will believe when they see our love for one another and how we live in the way that Jesus taught us.

> *How are you reaching out to other believers? Is the unity of the church important to you?*

TH

arrest and trial

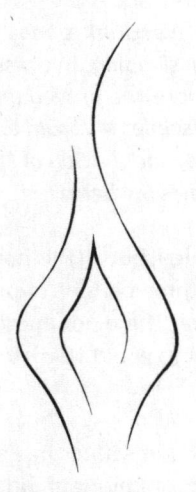

JENNY BROWN AND TONY HORSFALL

Day 307

Jesus in Gethsemane

MATTHEW 26:36–46 (MARK 14:32–34; LUKE 22:40; JOHN 18:1)

Garden of Gethsemane, Jerusalem

Then Jesus went with his disciples to a place called Gethsemane, and he said to them, 'Sit here while I go over there and pray.' He took Peter and the two sons of Zebedee along with him, and he began to be sorrowful and troubled. Then he said to them, 'My soul is overwhelmed with sorrow to the point of death. Stay here and keep watch with me.' Going a little farther, he fell with his face to the ground and prayed, 'My Father, if it is possible, may this cup be taken from me. Yet not as I will, but as you will.' Then he returned to his disciples and found them sleeping. 'Couldn't you men keep watch with me for one hour?' he asked Peter. 'Watch and pray so that you will not fall into temptation. The spirit is willing, but the flesh is weak.' He went away a second time and prayed, 'My Father, if it is not possible for this cup to be taken away unless I drink it, may your will be done.' When he came back, he again found them sleeping, because their eyes were heavy. So he left them and went away once more and prayed the third time, saying the same thing. Then he returned to the disciples and said to them, 'Are you still sleeping and resting? Look, the hour has come, and the Son of Man is delivered into the hands of sinners. Rise! Let us go! Here comes my betrayer!'

Jesus is usually so calm and controlled, but on this hardest of nights the disciples witness a Jesus who is overwhelmed. His three periods of prayer reflect the three temptations at the beginning of his ministry. Was there not another way? Wrestling with the reality of what lay ahead, the temptation to avoid God's will was broken through his honest prayer to his Father.

Then, three times, Jesus submitted himself to the Father's will: twice in prayer, then in action: 'Let us go!' As Jesus put his commitment into practice, he invited the struggling disciples to join him.

> *Where are you feeling tempted to avoid God's will? In the face of that, speak honestly to the Father. You may want to ask his help to pray Jesus' prayer: 'Yet not as I will, but as you will.' Is there a first step of action that God is inviting you to?*

JB

Day 308

Judas arrives with soldiers

JOHN 18:2-9

Garden of Gethsemane, Jerusalem
Now Judas, who betrayed him, knew the place, because Jesus had often met there with his disciples. So Judas came to the garden, guiding a detachment of soldiers and some officials from the chief priests and the Pharisees. They were carrying torches, lanterns and weapons. Jesus, knowing all that was going to happen to him, went out and asked them, 'Who is it you want?' 'Jesus of Nazareth,' they replied. 'I am he,' Jesus said. (And Judas the traitor was standing there with them.) When Jesus said, 'I am he,' they drew back and fell to the ground. Again he asked them, 'Who is it you want?' 'Jesus of Nazareth,' they said. Jesus answered, 'I told you that I am he. If you are looking for me, then let these men go.' This happened so that the words he had spoken would be fulfilled: 'I have not lost one of those you gave me.'

A garden of fellowship, intimacy and shared memories becomes a place of betrayal. In Gethsemane tonight there are echoes of Eden. Like Eve and Adam, Judas, who had been so close to Jesus, has been persuaded by the words of those who oppose him. Sometimes the reasoning of the world seems so plausible. We, like them, can doubt the purposes of God, the way of Jesus, and be drawn away.

Jesus' question, cutting through the darkness, finds them before they find him: 'Who is it you want?' They use his most 'human' title: 'Jesus of Nazareth'. But his response – 'I am he' – echoes from the great self-revelation of the living God to Moses at the burning bush: 'I am who I am' (Exodus 3:14). Jesus, carpenter from Nazareth, is the one who was 'with God and was God' (John 1:1). Whether they realise it or not, the Jesus they are looking for among the trees of Gethsemane is the God who sought out Adam and Eve among the trees of Eden. In finding Jesus, they have found the one who seeks out those who have been taken in by the enemy.

'For the Son of Man came to seek and to save the lost' (Luke 19:10).

> Does intimacy with Jesus feel like a thing of the past? Has the 'world's reasoning' persuaded you and numbed your fellowship with him? 'Who is it you want?' How do you respond?

JB

Day 309

Jesus arrested

MATTHEW 26:47–56 (MARK 14:43–49; LUKE 22:47–53)

Garden of Gethsemane, Jerusalem
While he was still speaking, Judas, one of the Twelve, arrived. With him was a large crowd armed with swords and clubs, sent from the chief priests and the elders of the people. Now the betrayer had arranged a signal with them: 'The one I kiss is the man; arrest him.' Going at once to Jesus, Judas said, 'Greetings, Rabbi!' and kissed him. Jesus replied, 'Do what you came for, friend.' Then the men stepped forward, seized Jesus and arrested him. With that, one of Jesus' companions reached for his sword, drew it out and struck the servant of the high priest, cutting off his ear. 'Put your sword back in its place,' Jesus said to him, 'for all who draw the sword will die by the sword. Do you think I cannot call on my Father, and he will at once put at my disposal more than twelve legions of angels? But how then would the scriptures be fulfilled that say it must happen in this way?' In that hour Jesus said to the crowd, 'Am I leading a rebellion, that you have come out with swords and clubs to capture me? Every day I sat in the temple courts teaching, and you did not arrest me. But this has all taken place that the writings of the prophets might be fulfilled.' Then all the disciples deserted him and fled.

Surely it is one of the worst kinds of pain to inflict on a friend: false loyalty, false affection and words of love that cover over a heart of indifference, or worse, of unfaithfulness.

Even though Jesus sees through Judas' facade, he still calls him 'friend'. He had called the other disciples 'friends' a few hours before (John 15:15), but Judas had already left. Despite his betrayal, Jesus doesn't exclude Judas from that relationship. Just as no one can take his life from him, so also no one can take his friends from him (John 10:18, 28). Even though Satan had 'entered into' Judas (John 13:27), the power of Jesus' commitment to Judas is stronger than that of the evil one. As Paul later wrote: nothing 'in all creation will be able to separate us from the love of God that is in Christ Jesus our Lord' (Romans 8:39).

> What does it mean for you today to hear Jesus call you 'friend'?

Day 310

Everyone deserts Jesus

MARK 14:50–52

Garden of Gethsemane, Jerusalem
Then everyone deserted him and fled. A young man, wearing nothing but a linen garment, was following Jesus. When they seized him, he fled naked, leaving his garment behind.

'What's your most embarrassing moment?' I dread being asked that question! For the very reason that it *was* so embarrassing, I have tried to forget it, and I certainly don't want to relive it in front of another audience!

As well as being embarrassing for obvious reasons, deserting Jesus would doubtless have been a cause of shame for this young disciple. He was probably John Mark. Later Barnabas and Paul took him along with them on their first missionary journey. But again he fled – perhaps in fear of the opposition they faced (Acts 13). Branding him a 'deserter', Paul refused to take him on his next mission (Acts 15:38). John Mark could have been crippled by shame and fear of failure, discounting himself from ever being useful to Jesus.

And yet, he is, almost certainly, the 'Mark' who wrote this gospel. Alone among the gospel writers, he recorded this, his most embarrassing and shameful moment, for generations to read. It seems that years after the event he is happy to own it, not airbrush it out. Why?

Although Paul rejected him, Barnabas gave John Mark another opportunity (Acts 15:37–40). Just as he had helped Paul in his early days (Acts 9:27; 11:25), so Barnabas, the encourager, took John Mark and, it seems, nurtured his faith and restored him to ministry (see Colossians 4:10; Philemon 24; 2 Timothy 4:11; 1 Peter 5:13).

No matter our past failures, the God of grace can restore us and is pleased to work through us to achieve his purposes. John Mark, in recording these verses, came to know what God also revealed to Paul. It is not just that he uses us *despite* our weaknesses, but he even works *through* those very weaknesses to display his glory and power (2 Corinthians 4:7).

> He said to me, 'My grace is sufficient for you, for my power is made perfect in weakness.'
> 2 CORINTHIANS 12:9

How does the story of this young man impact you? Can you identify with him? Or perhaps with Paul, or with Barnabas? Receive the all-sufficient grace of Christ.

Day 311

Peter's first denial

JOHN 18:12-18 (MATTHEW 26:69-70; MARK 14:66-68; LUKE 22:55-57)

Courtyard of the high priest, Jerusalem
Then the detachment of soldiers with its commander and the Jewish officials arrested Jesus. They bound him and brought him first to Annas, who was the father-in-law of Caiaphas, the high priest that year. Caiaphas was the one who had advised the Jewish leaders that it would be good if one man died for the people. Simon Peter and another disciple were following Jesus. Because this disciple was known to the high priest, he went with Jesus into the high priest's courtyard, but Peter had to wait outside at the door. The other disciple, who was known to the high priest, came back, spoke to the servant-girl on duty there and brought Peter in. 'You aren't one of this man's disciples too, are you?' she asked Peter. He replied, 'I am not.' It was cold, and the servants and officials stood around a fire they had made to keep warm. Peter also was standing with them, warming himself.

How I wished I could turn the clock back! In a moment of thoughtlessness some words had slipped out and now they could never be 'un-said'. Ah! We probably all have painful memories of such experiences.

Peter had tried so hard to keep this situation under control. He had protested against Jesus' talk of death, tried to deter him from going to Jerusalem, vowed to stay with him, professed undying loyalty, done his best in the garden – to pray, to resist arrest. Finally, he had followed along behind Jesus, with John (possibly). But now, tired, afraid, confused, it took only a question from a servant girl for him to say something he'd regret.

His motives and emotions were all mixed and muddled, and now he lost it. Peter couldn't hold it together any longer. The other disciple didn't seem to struggle in the same way as Peter. Maybe that made it worse.

It's hard to keep our life of discipleship together sometimes, isn't it? And our regrets can wear away at the very heart of us. We try so hard to do better, but instead we can surrender these struggles and regrets to Jesus by honestly acknowledging them and then placing them into his hands.

> *Peter's 'I am not' contrasts with Jesus' 'I am he' (John 18:5-6). So now shift your focus from yourself, your failures and frailties, on to Jesus and who he is. And receive his grace again.*

Day 312

Jesus before Annas

JOHN 18:19–24 (MATTHEW 26:57–58; MARK 14:53–54; LUKE 22:54)

The high priest's house, Jerusalem
Meanwhile, the high priest questioned Jesus about his disciples and his teaching. 'I have spoken openly to the world,' Jesus replied. 'I always taught in synagogues or at the temple, where all the Jews come together. I said nothing in secret. Why question me? Ask those who heard me. Surely they know what I said.' When Jesus said this, one of the officials near by slapped him in the face. 'Is this the way you answer the high priest?' he demanded. 'If I said something wrong,' Jesus replied, 'testify as to what is wrong. But if I spoke the truth, why did you strike me?' Then Annas sent him bound to Caiaphas the high priest.

Some elements of this part of the story are unclear and confusing. Which high priest is being referred to? Caiaphas, the current one, or Annas, his father-in-law and former high priest, who still wields a lot of influence?

The confusion of the night, along with Peter's false answers, contrast with Jesus' openness, clarity and truth-telling. He had made a point of teaching openly in places where teaching is expected. He hadn't gathered a group behind closed doors and whispered plans of revolution – religious or political. He had taught in the temple, the synagogues, in the open air where anyone could come and hear him. He had never acted violently or tried to run away, and yet those questioning Jesus feel the need to slap him and tie his hands.

Is my life marked by plain speech? Do I whisper in corners? Do I give a different story openly to the one I tell behind closed doors? Or am I a person of integrity, open and consistent no matter to whom or where I am speaking?

> 'Set a guard over my mouth, Lord; keep watch over the door of my lips' (Psalm 141:3).

JB

Day 313

Jesus before the Sanhedrin

MATTHEW 26:59–68 (MARK 14:53–65; LUKE 22:63–65)

> The high priest's house, Jerusalem
> The chief priests and the whole Sanhedrin were looking for false evidence against Jesus so that they could put him to death. But they did not find any, though many false witnesses came forward. Finally two came forward and declared, 'This fellow said, "I am able to destroy the temple of God and rebuild it in three days."' Then the high priest stood up and said to Jesus, 'Are you not going to answer? What is this testimony that these men are bringing against you?' But Jesus remained silent. The high priest said to him, 'I charge you under oath by the living God: Tell us if you are the Messiah, the Son of God.' 'You have said so,' Jesus replied. 'But I say to all of you: from now on you will see the Son of Man sitting at the right hand of the Mighty One and coming on the clouds of heaven.' Then the high priest tore his clothes and said, 'He has spoken blasphemy! Why do we need any more witnesses? Look, now you have heard the blasphemy. What do you think?' 'He is worthy of death,' they answered. Then they spat in his face and struck him with their fists. Others slapped him and said, 'Prophesy to us, Messiah. Who hit you?'

Chief priests looking for false witnesses. Really?! Those charged with upholding the law of God are seeking to partner with those who will break it (Exodus 20:16).

'This fellow' they call him. The false witnesses see Jesus as just an ordinary, dispensable bloke. The chief priests think the living God is on their side. Yet Jesus will sit at the right hand of that Mighty One. He is the true Messiah, the Son of God and the Son of Man who has all authority, glory and power (Daniel 7:13). They accuse him of blasphemy, but it is they, in declaring him 'worthy of death', who are blasphemous. They condemn him, yet he, through his death, will rescue them from the penalty they have effectively pronounced upon themselves.

Sometimes we are in danger of holding so strongly to an opinion, convinced of our rightness, that we go against God in order to fulfil our aim.

> *Refocus on Jesus himself. Reflect on his titles – and worship him. This is the one who died the death we are worthy of. Give thanks to him.*

Day 314

Peter's further denials

LUKE 22:58–62 (MATTHEW 26:71–75; MARK 14:69–72; JOHN 18:25–27)

Courtyard of the high priest, Jerusalem
A little later someone else saw him and said, 'You also are one of them.' 'Man, I am not!' Peter replied. About an hour later another asserted, 'Certainly this fellow was with him, for he is a Galilean.' Peter replied, 'Man, I don't know what you're talking about!' Just as he was speaking, the cock crowed. The Lord turned and looked straight at Peter. Then Peter remembered the word the Lord had spoken to him: 'Before the cock crows today, you will disown me three times.' And he went outside and wept bitterly.

We've all been there, haven't we? Downplayed our involvement with Jesus, kept silent when he is the subject of banter or joined in the condemnation of his body, the church.

As Jesus turned to look Peter in the eye, Luke refers to him as 'Lord'. Peter's inner heart was exposed under the gaze of the one who knows all things and will judge all peoples, the one who saw Peter's heart before he saw it himself.

Driven by shame, Peter took himself outside, removing himself from Jesus' presence, fleeing from his gaze. It broke him. He wept uncontrollably, tears of humiliation. He surely felt the pain of vulnerability we have all felt. That inner pain of being known and found wanting, of having to face the fact that our true self does not match our outer image. But Peter's tears also reveal his heart. Tears flow out of a heart that loves. Peter's moment of weakness did not deny his love for Jesus.

I wonder what Peter could see across the dark courtyard, through the smoke of the fire? Could he see the expression on the face of Jesus as he looked straight at him? If Peter's tears expressed his love for Jesus, how did Jesus' gaze express his greater love for Peter?

As Jesus looks at you today, what is the expression on his face? It is not only our guilt that Jesus took to the cross, but also our shame.

> Tears can be the start of healing, bringing us to a point where all we can do is look up for mercy and grace. 'A broken and contrite heart you, God, will not despise' (Psalm 51:17); 'No one who hopes in you will ever be put to shame' (Psalm 25:3).

JB

Day 315

From the council to Pilate

LUKE 22:63—23:1 (MATTHEW 26:62-67; MARK 15:1)

Sanhedrin, Jerusalem
The men who were guarding Jesus began mocking and beating him. They blindfolded him and demanded, 'Prophesy! Who hit you?' And they said many other insulting things to him. At daybreak the council of the elders of the people, both the chief priests and the teachers of the law, met together, and Jesus was led before them. 'If you are the Messiah,' they said, 'tell us.' Jesus answered, 'If I tell you, you will not believe me, and if I asked you, you would not answer. But from now on, the Son of Man will be seated at the right hand of the mighty God.' They all asked, 'Are you then the Son of God?' He replied, 'You say that I am.' Then they said, 'Why do we need any more testimony? We have heard it from his own lips.' Then the whole assembly rose and led him off to Pilate.

As we delve into the narrative about the various trials that Jesus faced, we can be overwhelmed by the details, or we can stand back and see the bigger picture that shows Jesus beginning to walk the path of suffering on our behalf. This is how I want us to approach the next few days, and I invite you to visualise what is happening and to empathise with Jesus in his pain. Feel compassion for him in his agony, even as he feels compassion for you in your suffering. Be there as a companion, not as a detached observer.

Alex Aronis says:

> The final days of the earthly life of Jesus provide us with a unique opportunity to understand more fully the courage, compassion, and grace with which Jesus bore the most grievous suffering. If we believe that he endured everything out of love for us and for our sins, we will be drawn to an ever more profound love of him.[41]

For the Jewish leaders, this is the decisive moment in their plot to get rid of Jesus (Matthew 26:1-5). The claim of Jesus to be the Son of God is what has disturbed them most, and he does not deny it. How could he? It is his true identity. At this moment they stand in judgement over him, but the day will come when he will stand in judgement of them.

▎ *What suffering do you see Jesus experiencing? How do you respond to it?*

TH

Day 316

Jesus before Pilate (1)

JOHN 18:28–32

Roman governor's palace
Then the Jewish leaders took Jesus from Caiaphas to the palace of the Roman governor. By now it was early morning, and to avoid ceremonial uncleanness they did not enter the palace, because they wanted to be able to eat the Passover. So Pilate came out to them and asked, 'What charges are you bringing against this man?' 'If he were not a criminal,' they replied, 'we would not have handed him over to you.' Pilate said, 'Take him yourselves and judge him by your own law.' 'But we have no right to execute anyone,' they objected. This took place to fulfil what Jesus had said about the kind of death he was going to die.

It is worth taking the time to note every aspect of the suffering that Jesus went through, even before he is crucified. It was all part of his being the Lamb of God:

> He was oppressed and afflicted, yet he did not open his mouth; he was led like a lamb to the slaughter, and as a sheep before its shearers is silent, so he did not open his mouth. By oppression and judgment he was taken away.
> ISAIAH 53:7–8

We have seen him betrayed, disowned and abandoned by his closest friends. During his trials he endures rejection, hatred, hostility, physical abuse, mistreatment, mockery, ridicule and scorn. His trials are unfair and unjust. He is the victim of religious hypocrisy, personal jealousy and political convenience.

Somewhere in this list it will be possible for you to identify with him, because he has suffered what you have suffered. This realisation, that he suffers not only for us, but with us, is what Paul calls 'participation in his sufferings' (Philippians 3:10). This deeper intimacy with Jesus is a privilege, but one seldom chosen or even realised.

The Jewish leaders have only one purpose in mind in taking him to Pilate – to ensure the death penalty. Unwittingly they are playing into the hands of God, for Jesus already knew that he would be not only rejected but also crucified. Even through adversity, injustice and hatred, the will of God is being worked out.

> In what ways can you empathise with Jesus? Where is his pain your pain, and your pain his? Gently allow yourself to feel that pain in his presence. He knows, he understands.

TH

Day 317

The remorse of Judas

MATTHEW 27:3-10 (*MATTHEW 27:10*)

Jerusalem, the temple
When Judas, who had betrayed him, saw that Jesus was condemned, he was seized with remorse and returned the thirty pieces of silver to the chief priests and the elders. 'I have sinned,' he said, 'for I have betrayed innocent blood.' 'What is that to us?' they replied. 'That's your responsibility.' So Judas threw the money into the temple and left. Then he went away and hanged himself. The chief priests picked up the coins and said, 'It is against the law to put this into the treasury, since it is blood money.' So they decided to use the money to buy the potter's field as a burial place for foreigners. That is why it has been called the Field of Blood to this day. Then what was spoken by Jeremiah the prophet was fulfilled: 'They took the thirty pieces of silver, the price set on him by the people of Israel, and they used them to buy the potter's field, as the Lord commanded me.'

It may well be that Judas, with his roots in the radical movement of the Zealots, had betrayed Jesus in order to force his hand and propel him into revolt, but his plans backfired. Realising his actions would lead to the death of Jesus, Judas is full of remorse and guilt. 'What hell he went through in the hours that followed we cannot know,' says Michael Green, 'but he certainly saw the horror of what he had done.'[42] A dark despair grips his soul and he can see no way out other than to take his own life.

Human despair can bring us to a dark and destructive place. Without hope, the cocktail of punishing emotions that accompany deep remorse distorts reality. The balance of the mind can be disturbed when self-hatred takes over and only pain is felt. Suicide is the tragic exit strategy for Judas, as for many others.

Later the disciples will try to make sense of how the life of one of their number could end like this (Acts 1:15-19). Matthew sees a fulfilment of prophecy, notably from Zechariah (11:12-13) and Jeremiah (32:6-9), but this seems a cold comfort, and the tragedy remains a mystery.

> Look out for anyone close to you whose mental health is unsteady. If you are troubled yourself, seek help and counsel as soon as possible.

TH

Day 318

Pilate sends Jesus to Herod

LUKE 23:2-7 (MATTHEW 27:11-14; MARK 15:2-5)

Jerusalem
And they began to accuse him, saying, 'We have found this man subverting our nation. He opposes payment of taxes to Caesar and claims to be Messiah, a king.' So Pilate asked Jesus, 'Are you the king of the Jews?' 'You have said so,' Jesus replied. Then Pilate announced to the chief priests and the crowd, 'I find no basis for a charge against this man.' But they insisted, 'He stirs up the people all over Judea by his teaching. He started in Galilee and has come all the way here.' On hearing this, Pilate asked if the man was a Galilean. When he learned that Jesus was under Herod's jurisdiction, he sent him to Herod, who was also in Jerusalem at that time.

Jesus has given us a wonderful example of how to face unjust suffering and the persecution that comes to those who seek to follow him amid a hostile world.

The apostle Peter emphasises this as he writes to encourage those believers scattered throughout the then known world for the sake of their faith, quoting from Isaiah 53:9 concerning the suffering servant:

> If you suffer for doing good and you endure it, this is commendable before God. To this you were called, because Christ suffered for you, leaving you an example, that you should follow in his steps. 'He committed no sin, and no deceit was found in his mouth.'
> 1 PETER 2:20-22

Throughout his ordeal, Jesus did not retaliate when insulted and made no threats in response to the attacks upon him. 'Instead, he entrusted himself to him who judges justly' (1 Peter 2:23). As we carefully watch Jesus during his trials, we see that this posture of trust is the reason for his calmness under pressure and his peace in the face of injustice.

Pilate knows that Jesus has done nothing wrong and makes a public declaration to that effect. Yet Pilate is a weak man and sees an opportunity to 'pass the buck'. Since Jesus is a Galilean, he should be tried by Herod, a convenient way of avoiding an unpopular decision.

> How does the example of Jesus speak to you today? What issues do you need to entrust to God?

TH

Day 319

Jesus before Herod

LUKE 23:8-12

> Jerusalem
> When Herod saw Jesus, he was greatly pleased, because for a long time he had been wanting to see him. From what he had heard about him, he hoped to see him perform a sign of some sort. He plied him with many questions, but Jesus gave him no answer. The chief priests and the teachers of the law were standing there, vehemently accusing him. Then Herod and his soldiers ridiculed and mocked him. Dressing him in an elegant robe, they sent him back to Pilate. That day Herod and Pilate became friends – before this they had been enemies.

Jesus is pushed from pillar to post, hands bound like a criminal. He is under fire night and day, with little respite, mistreated continually and held in an atmosphere of hostility and hatred. Eventually he stands before Herod, who was conveniently in Jerusalem at the time. This is the same Herod who had beheaded John and whom Jesus called 'that fox' (Mark 6:14–15; Luke 13:32) because of his duplicitous nature. Hardly a fit person to pass judgement on anyone, he was nonetheless a powerful ruler, even if only with Rome's approval.

Herod had apparently long wanted to meet Jesus, having heard of his reputation as a miracle-worker, and fearing that he was John the Baptist come back to life (such is the unease of a guilty conscience, Matthew 14:1–2). To satisfy his natural curiosity Herod hopes to see some supernatural display from Jesus, but he has no spiritual hunger, just as he has no interest in passing judgement on these religious accusations. Jesus, however, refuses to respond and remains silent throughout.

Leon Morris summarises the situation accurately:

> The interview must have disappointed Herod. He got no answer to his many questions. What could Jesus say to this trifler who wanted nothing more than a mild sensation? He never refused a sincere questioner, but Herod was not in that class. He is the only person to whom Jesus said nothing at all.[43]

Notice how Jesus is ridiculed and mocked, at Herod's instigation. Such is his arrogant depravity, he has no idea in whose presence he stands.

> What are your feelings for Jesus at this point? Have you known humiliation and ridicule, like him? How did you respond?

TH

Day 320

Jesus before Pilate (2)

JOHN 18:33–38 (MATTHEW 27:11–14; MARK 15:2–5)

Jerusalem
Pilate then went back inside the palace, summoned Jesus and asked him, 'Are you the king of the Jews?' 'Is that your own idea,' Jesus asked, 'or did others talk to you about me?' 'Am I a Jew?' Pilate replied. 'Your own people and chief priests handed you over to me. What is it you have done?' Jesus said, 'My kingdom is not of this world. If it were, my servants would fight to prevent my arrest by the Jewish leaders. But now my kingdom is from another place.' 'You are a king, then!' said Pilate. Jesus answered, 'You say that I am a king. In fact, the reason I was born and came into the world is to testify to the truth. Everyone on the side of truth listens to me.' 'What is truth?' retorted Pilate. With this he went out again to the Jews gathered there and said, 'I find no basis for a charge against him.'

The merry-go-round continues as Jesus is returned to Pilate for judgement. Realising that charges of blasphemy will carry no weight with the Romans, the accusers continue with the line of attack that Jesus is a threat to Rome because of his claims to be a king. Thus Pilate asks the pointed question, 'Are you the king of the Jews' (v. 33)?

In one sense it is an astute question, and the heart of the matter, since Jesus spoke so often about the kingdom of God. Yet it is unlikely that Pilate was aware of that. His concern is that Jesus may be a revolutionary, although there is no evidence of it and he seems an unlikely terrorist.

Without directly asserting his kingship Jesus acknowledges the spiritual nature of his kingdom, one not of this world, that is, not political. In fact, it is a kingdom based on truth and recognised by anyone who is willing to submit to the truth when they find it. This places Pilate in a moral dilemma, since he knows Jesus is innocent (v. 38) and yet fears to act according to what he knows to be true. That is his weakness, and the reason he can make no spiritual progress. He is not 'on the side of truth' (v. 37).

> *What does it mean for you to be on the side of truth? What do you learn about Jesus from his conversation with Pilate?*

TH

Day 321

Pilate declares Jesus innocent

LUKE 23:13-23

Jerusalem
Pilate called together the chief priests, the rulers and the people, and said to them, 'You brought me this man as one who was inciting the people to rebellion. I have examined him in your presence and have found no basis for your charges against him. Neither has Herod, for he sent him back to us; as you can see, he has done nothing to deserve death. Therefore, I will punish him and then release him.' But the whole crowd shouted, 'Away with this man! Release Barabbas to us!' (Barabbas had been thrown into prison for an insurrection in the city, and for murder.) Wanting to release Jesus, Pilate appealed to them again. But they kept shouting, 'Crucify him! Crucify him!' For the third time he spoke to them: 'Why? What crime has this man committed? I have found in him no grounds for the death penalty. Therefore I will have him punished and then release him.' But with loud shouts they insistently demanded that he be crucified, and their shouts prevailed.

Jesus said clearly before he went up to Jerusalem that he would be 'delivered into the hands of men' (Mark 9:31) and that this would mean both the Jewish religious leaders as well as Gentile rulers. Here we see that his fate (from a human perspective) is not in his own hands. Jesus is hardly involved in the conversation anymore from this point onwards. He is totally at the mercy of others.

The innocence of Jesus shines through in the accounts of his various trials. Pilate himself is convinced of this, and says so clearly (Luke 23:4, 15, 22). Herod agreed with his assessment that this man 'has done nothing to deserve death' (v. 15). It is only those whose minds are biased and whose hearts are closed who persist in their demand for Jesus to be punished.

That Jesus was innocent is important since only the 'just' could die for the 'unjust', and so bring us to God (1 Peter 3:18). However, his innocence shows the suggestion of Pilate to punish him and then release him to be an abuse of power – if he is innocent, he should be released immediately. No doubt Pilate was trying to appease the Jewish religious leaders, but his appeasement failed anyway. The crowd, demanding blood, cry out, 'Crucify him.'

> How would you feel if you were Jesus?

TH

Day 322

Jesus or Barabbas?

MATTHEW 27:15-19 (MARK 15:6-11)

Jerusalem
Now it was the governor's custom at the festival to release a prisoner chosen by the crowd. At that time they had a well-known prisoner whose name was Jesus Barabbas. So when the crowd had gathered, Pilate asked them, 'Which one do you want me to release to you: Jesus Barabbas, or Jesus who is called the Messiah?' For he knew it was out of self-interest that they had handed Jesus over to him. While Pilate was sitting on the judge's seat, his wife sent him this message: 'Don't have anything to do with that innocent man, for I have suffered a great deal today in a dream because of him.'

It must have seemed to Pilate like another way out of his dilemma. He knew Jesus was innocent of any charge and should be released, yet he feared upsetting the Jewish religious hierarchy. Why not, therefore, follow his usual custom of releasing a prisoner during the festival as a goodwill gesture? And why not give the people a choice between a notorious criminal (Barabbas) and a good man (Jesus) who had done nothing wrong? Surely, they would choose Jesus?

What a contrast between the two men. Barabbas, an insurrectionist; Jesus, the prince of peace. Barabbas, a murderer and taker of life; Jesus, the one who came to give life. Barabbas, a common criminal and guilty; Jesus, a good man, innocent and wrongly accused.

Before the choice can be made, there is a warning for Pilate from his wife, who has been disturbed by a dream she has had about Jesus. She too knows he is innocent. Has she been following proceedings from a distance? God has many ways to speak to us and to disturb our peace if we are heading in the wrong direction. Dreams are just one medium he uses. It is important to recognise when we are inwardly disturbed about a choice of action.

Here is another moment when Pilate's conscience is touched and there is the opportunity to stay on the side of truth and choose a different path. But Pilate is weak and easily swayed. The baying of the crowd is insistent, and his pride too great. He cannot climb down now.

> *What do you learn about Pilate from his handling of the trial? How do you make your decisions?*

TH

Day 323

Barabbas released

MATTHEW 27:20-26 (MARK 15: 12-15; LUKE 23:22-25; JOHN 18:40)

Jerusalem
But the chief priests and the elders persuaded the crowd to ask for Barabbas and to have Jesus executed. 'Which of the two do you want me to release to you?' asked the governor. 'Barabbas,' they answered. 'What shall I do, then, with Jesus who is called the Messiah?' Pilate asked. They all answered, 'Crucify him!' 'Why? What crime has he committed?' asked Pilate. But they shouted all the louder, 'Crucify him!' When Pilate saw that he was getting nowhere, but that instead an uproar was starting, he took water and washed his hands in front of the crowd. 'I am innocent of this man's blood,' he said. 'It is your responsibility!' All the people answered, 'His blood is on us and on our children!' Then he released Barabbas to them. But he had Jesus flogged, and handed him over to be crucified.

Faced with the choice between the innocent Jesus (the Messiah) and the guilty Barabbas (the rebel), the crowd without hesitation choose Barabbas. Why is this? Most likely because they were a mob of his supporters seeing an opportunity to engineer their leader's freedom. Stirred up by the Jewish religious leaders, they bay for his execution, for his crucifixion – the fate they thought would befall their hero, Barabbas. Now another will take his place. The cross prepared for the rascal will be made ready for the redeemer.

It is impossible not to see in this exchange a beautiful picture of the way in which the cross works. It involves a divine exchange, the innocent Son of God taking the place on the cross of sinful men and women. It is only one way of understanding the mystery of salvation, but it is in my opinion a very helpful one. It is what we have already seen in Peter's declaration that 'Christ also suffered once for sins, the righteous for the unrighteous, to bring you to God' (1 Peter 3:18).

Hymnwriter Philip Bliss (1838–76) captured this well when he wrote, 'Bearing shame and scoffing rude, in my place condemned he stood; sealed my pardon with his blood. Hallelujah! What a Saviour!'

Once we have understood the cross in this way, our love for Jesus is deepened beyond measure and we find a strong assurance for our confidence before God.

> *Take time to ponder this, and to respond with thankfulness. He died for you.*

TH

Day 324

Here is the man

JOHN 19:1-7

Jerusalem
Then Pilate took Jesus and had him flogged. The soldiers twisted together a crown of thorns and put it on his head. They clothed him in a purple robe and went up to him again and again, saying, 'Hail, king of the Jews!' And they slapped him in the face. Once more Pilate came out and said to the Jews gathered there, 'Look, I am bringing him out to you to let you know that I find no basis for a charge against him.' When Jesus came out wearing the crown of thorns and the purple robe, Pilate said to them, 'Here is the man!' As soon as the chief priests and their officials saw him, they shouted, 'Crucify! Crucify!' But Pilate answered, 'You take him and crucify him. As for me, I find no basis for a charge against him.' The Jewish leaders insisted, 'We have a law, and according to that law he must die, because he claimed to be the Son of God.'

Pilate's famous words, most often remembered as 'Behold the man' (*Ecce homo* in Latin), reach down to us through the centuries as a call to take in what is happening in this dreadful moment.

To 'behold' is to look at something intently, to gaze with wonder and awe. Our instinct may be to turn away from a sight we consider too gruesome, yet only by truly looking with the eyes of faith can we plunge the depths of the love Jesus showed for us in these moments, of the agony he endured on our behalf. If we sanitise it or airbrush from the picture the details we find uncomfortable, we may rob ourselves of an appreciation of the magnitude of heavenly love for lost sinners.

William Barclay comments:

> The Roman scourge was a terrible thing. The criminal was bent and bound in such a way that his back was exposed. The scourge was a long leathern thong, studded here and there with sharpened pieces of lead and bits of bone. It literally tore a man's back to ribbons.[44]

> *This physical abuse was followed by the public humiliation of being dressed up and paraded as a 'king'. And this was only the beginning of his sufferings for us. Why not meditate on this verse today: 'He was despised and rejected by mankind, a man of suffering, and familiar with pain' (Isaiah 53:3).*

TH

Day 325

Handed over

JOHN 19:8-16

Jerusalem
When Pilate heard this, he was even more afraid, and he went back inside the palace. 'Where do you come from?' he asked Jesus, but Jesus gave him no answer. 'Do you refuse to speak to me?' Pilate said. 'Don't you realise I have power either to free you or to crucify you?' Jesus answered, 'You would have no power over me if it were not given to you from above. Therefore the one who handed me over to you is guilty of a greater sin.' From then on, Pilate tried to set Jesus free, but the Jewish leaders kept shouting, 'If you let this man go, you are no friend of Caesar. Anyone who claims to be a king opposes Caesar.' When Pilate heard this, he brought Jesus out and sat down on the judge's seat at a place known as the Stone Pavement (which in Aramaic is Gabbatha). It was the day of Preparation of the Passover; it was about noon. 'Here is your king,' Pilate said to the Jews. But they shouted, 'Take him away! Take him away! Crucify him!' 'Shall I crucify your king?' Pilate asked. 'We have no king but Caesar,' the chief priests answered. Finally Pilate handed him over to them to be crucified.

The trials reach their conclusion, but not justly. The ending is far from satisfactory as Pilate remains convinced of the innocence of Jesus, but weakly gives in to external pressure and fear of losing favour with Caesar. It is emotional blackmail. The Jewish leaders by now have lost all integrity in their demands, happy to curry favour with Rome if it means being rid of Jesus.

Jesus is 'handed over', surrendered to the will of the people through the envy of the religious leaders, the treachery of Judas, the ignorance of Herod, the weakness of Pilate and the machinations of Satan. Yet, from God's perspective, it is better described as Jesus being 'offered up', for this is the way that sin will be dealt with and salvation achieved.

Significantly the next day will be the Passover, when lambs will be slain in remembrance of the great Exodus deliverance. And at Calvary, the Lamb of God will give himself to die to accomplish an even greater deliverance for the world.

> Lord, I yield before the beauty of your salvation plan, bringing good out of evil and triumphing over sin.

TH

the crucifixion

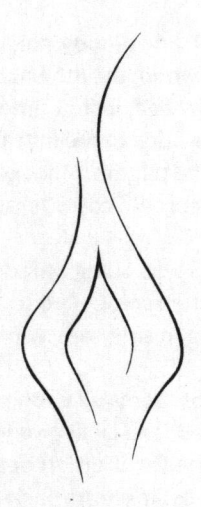

STEVE AISTHORPE

Day 326

On the way to Golgotha

LUKE 23:26–31 (MATTHEW 27:32–33; MARK 15:21–22; JOHN 19:17–19)

Jerusalem
As the soldiers led him away, they seized Simon from Cyrene, who was on his way in from the country, and put the cross on him and made him carry it behind Jesus. A large number of people followed him, including women who mourned and wailed for him. Jesus turned and said to them, 'Daughters of Jerusalem, do not weep for me; weep for yourselves and for your children. For the time will come when you will say, "Blessed are the childless women, the wombs that never bore and the breasts that never nursed!" Then "they will say to the mountains, 'Fall on us!' and to the hills, 'Cover us!'" For if people do these things when the tree is green, what will happen when it is dry?'

Two men meet: one of them, beaten and bloody, staggers and stumbles under the sheer weight and awkwardness of dense wood; the other is coming in 'from the country', nearing the climax of an 800-mile pilgrimage, just in time for Passover. The gospels are full of anonymous characters, but Luke adds to the intimacy of his narrative by giving both name and address for this exhausted pilgrim. Mark goes further still and names his two sons, perhaps eager that his readers could corroborate the events.

Both men appear powerless. Jesus was being paraded and humiliated as an example to others. Simon was 'seized' and then compelled to about-turn, shoulder the crippling load and take his position in that agonising convoy of cruelty.

At first this deeply poignant incident seems all wrong. The rabbi who said 'Come to me, all you who are weary and burdened, and I will give you rest' (Matthew 11:28) is utterly exhausted; the one who came to be the 'burden bearer' for humanity (Isaiah 53:5–6) needs help from a footsore passer-by. It seems back-to-front, topsy-turvy, but here we glimpse the mysterious truth of the incarnation, God made flesh-and-blood in Christ.

This withholding and refusing to call on divine power reminds us that in becoming one of us, Jesus 'did not consider equality with God something to be used to his own advantage; rather, he made himself nothing by taking the very nature of a servant' (Philippians 2:6–7).

> *Simon turned around, shouldered the cross and walked in the footsteps of Jesus. In what ways are you called to do likewise?*

SA

Day 327

Crucified with criminals

LUKE 23:32-35

Jerusalem
Two other men, both criminals, were also led out with him to be executed. When they came to the place called the Skull, they crucified him there, along with the criminals – one on his right, the other on his left. Jesus said, 'Father, forgive them, for they do not know what they are doing.' And they divided up his clothes by casting lots. The people stood watching, and the rulers even sneered at him. They said, 'He saved others; let him save himself if he is God's Messiah, the Chosen One.'

From the earliest days of the Christian faith the cross has been our principal symbol. At first its use would have been radically countercultural. Crucifixion was the most extreme punishment for the most serious crimes, reserved for slaves and foreigners. People associated it with wrongdoing, suffering and shame. Two millennia later, the cross is sometimes seen as little more than a badge of affiliation or even a fashion item, but any thoughtful reflection on the crucifixion of Jesus and its enduring significance must confront the awful reality behind the symbol.

Crucifixion was not just a means of execution. It was designed to inflict maximum suffering for as long as possible and to do so in public. Archaeological discoveries and accounts from the Roman era show how this instrument of torture and the techniques of attaching the condemned person were carefully designed to ensure a slow and excruciating death.

As so often in his life, we find Jesus in his last hours surrounded by men who were widely despised, seen as contemptible. With a convicted criminal on either side and his cruel executioners around, as prophesied centuries earlier, he willingly 'shared the fate of evil men' (Isaiah 53:12, GNT) and prayed that they might be forgiven. When we are under extreme pressure, what is inside comes out; as Jesus endured the most dreadful ordeal imaginable, he did not call down judgement, but pleaded with his Father for forgiveness for those who inflicted such cruelty on him and others.

> *As followers of this man whose love led him to willingly endure such horror, we receive both the forgiveness he cried out for and made possible and the highest calling: 'to live a life of love, just as Christ loved us and gave himself up for us as a fragrant offering and sacrifice to God' (Ephesians 5:2).*

SA

Day 328

A sign for all

JOHN 19:19-22 (MARK 15:25-26; LUKE 23:38)

Jerusalem
Pilate had a notice prepared and fastened to the cross. It read: JESUS OF NAZARETH, THE KING OF THE JEWS. Many of the Jews read this sign, for the place where Jesus was crucified was near the city, and the sign was written in Aramaic, Latin and Greek. The chief priests of the Jews protested to Pilate, 'Do not write "The King of the Jews", but that this man claimed to be king of the Jews.' Pilate answered, 'What I have written, I have written.'

On the surface, these events are normal and pragmatic. It was usual for a signboard to inform passers-by of the crime that led the mutilated person before them to such a place of suffering and death. At Passover, with many pilgrims coming into the city from far afield, it made sense for the sign to be multilingual.

Pilate could have chosen words that expressed the charge of sedition in a straightforward matter, but his intention was to mock. Philo of Alexandria, an important first-century Jewish philosopher, recorded Pilate's term as prefect of Judea as full of insults, cruelty and executions without trial. However, while his intention was to jeer and ridicule, Pilate inadvertently made a declaration of truth. When the priests pressured him to edit his proclamation, the previously dithering Pilate was decisive and unyielding. The bold announcement of the kingship of Jesus remained. Not for the first or last time, someone antagonistic to Christ and his purposes became an unintentional prophet.

The trilingual placard also has connotations far beyond its straightforward legal and scornful purposes. These three languages represented the spheres of life that together made up the totality of human life and culture. Greek was the language of philosophy and art. Latin was associated with politics and power, the language of the empire. Aramaic was the ancient vernacular, the mother tongue of many people local to that region. The implications are clear: the rule of Christ the King knows no borders.

> *Any boundaries or distinctions that we might be tempted to draw between public and private, politics and religion, science and faith, sacred and secular are meaningless. As the Dutch theologian Abraham Kuyper stated with simplicity and clarity, 'There is not a square inch in the whole domain of our human existence over which Christ, who is Sovereign over all, does not cry: "Mine!"'*

SA

Day 329

Gambling for his garment

JOHN 19:23-24 (MATTHEW 27:35-36; MARK 15:24)

Jerusalem
When the soldiers crucified Jesus, they took his clothes, dividing them into four shares, one for each of them, with the undergarment remaining. This garment was seamless, woven in one piece from top to bottom. 'Let's not tear it,' they said to one another. 'Let's decide by lot who will get it.' This happened that the scripture might be fulfilled that said, 'They divided my clothes among them and cast lots for my garment.' So this is what the soldiers did.

The gospel accounts of the crucifixion arouse a multitude of emotions, questions and realisations. Among the feelings evoked is a sense of the profound humiliation that Jesus endured. After the stripping, flogging, spitting and taunting at the hands of the 'whole company of soldiers' (Mark 15:16), there was the spiteful goading as they draped him in a mock royal robe and placed a crown of thorns on his head. All this was only the prelude to the horror of the main event. In a prophetic glimpse of these sickening experiences, the author of Psalm 22 wrote: 'Dogs surround me, a pack of villains encircles me; they pierce my hands and my feet. All my bones are on display; people stare and gloat over me' (vv. 16–17).

It was common practice for the convicted person to be stripped and their clothing divided among the execution squad as a perverse perk of the job. All of the gospels record the soldiers distributing Jesus' clothes between themselves, but only John explains how one item was treated differently. Here too Psalm 22 is astounding in its precise prophetic detail: 'They divide my clothes among them and cast lots for my garment' (v. 18).

In his gospel, John is always eager to highlight 'signs' that reveal who Jesus is, and the seamless undergarment he mentions is another example. Such a piece of clothing was unusual. The soldiers noticed the uncommon quality and value of it, but John was recognising prophecy fulfilled and realising the connection with the tradition of the high priest wearing such an item, as instructed in the Hebrew scriptures (Exodus 28). John wants us to know that this is the pivotal point in history foreseen many centuries earlier.

> On the cross we witness the perfect sacrifice and encounter the great high priest. 'Christ was sacrificed once to take away the sins of many' (Hebrews 9:28).

SA

Day 330

Jesus and his mother

JOHN 19:25–27

Jerusalem
Near the cross of Jesus stood his mother, his mother's sister, Mary the wife of Clopas, and Mary Magdalene. When Jesus saw his mother there, and the disciple whom he loved standing near by, he said to her, 'Woman, here is your son,' and to the disciple, 'Here is your mother.' From that time on, this disciple took her into his home.

Many gathered to witness the demise of the three men strung up on Calvary that day. Most were onlookers, attracted by the gruesome spectacle, drawn together into a baying pack. However, John draws our attention to a faithful huddle, mainly women, including Jesus' mother and an anonymous disciple we assume to be John. Amid the mob, surrounded by hatred and mockery, their courage and faithfulness comforted Jesus and inspire us.

For his mother, the words spoken by Simeon when presenting her young son at the temple would have been reverberating through her soul: 'This child is destined to cause the falling and rising of many in Israel… And a sword will pierce your own soul too' (Luke 2:34–35).

In first-century Palestine the concept of a household was quite different to our modern ideas of family. It was an economic unit of up to a hundred people, who were included because of their relationship to the head of the household, the *pater familias*. During the preceding months and years Jesus had been inaugurating a radical reconfiguration of the household. When he pointed to his disciples and said, 'Here are my mother and my brothers' (Matthew 12:49), he indicated that a new way of belonging together was emerging. Rather than being based on the leadership of a senior patriarch, it would be based on the relationship of people with God. Hence his words, 'For whoever does the will of my Father in heaven is my brother and sister and mother' (Matthew 12:50).

In his tender words from the cross to his beloved mother and disciple, he makes it clear that this is no theoretical concept. Those who follow Jesus are not called to a hypothetical love for everyone in general, but rather to a love that has practical implications in our daily relationships, responsibilities and priorities.

> *As you pray 'Our Father', sense the global and eternal family you are part of and ask who and how Jesus calls you to love today.*

SA

Day 331

Mockery and insults

MATTHEW 27:39–44

Jerusalem
Those who passed by hurled insults at him, shaking their heads and saying, 'You who are going to destroy the temple and build it in three days, save yourself! Come down from the cross, if you are the Son of God!' In the same way the chief priests, the teachers of the law and the elders mocked him. 'He saved others,' they said, 'but he can't save himself! He's the king of Israel! Let him come down now from the cross, and we will believe in him. He trusts in God. Let God rescue him now if he wants him, for he said, "I am the Son of God."' In the same way the rebels who were crucified with him also heaped insults on him.

Battered and bloody from his cruel beating, already mocked and humiliated, Jesus now became the focus of a barrage of merciless taunts. His critics and hecklers comprised a wide-ranging cast of characters, from religious officials to convicted insurgents and random passers-by.

During those hours of agony, and in the face of an unending tirade of ridicule and insult, Jesus' intimate knowledge of the Psalms provided a deep well of reassurance, and they reminded him of his unique role in the cosmic conflict that was unfolding. 'All who see me mock me; they hurl insults' (Psalm 22:7); 'I am an object of scorn to my accusers' (Psalm 109:25). The sneer 'Where is your God?' is a recurring echo in the Psalms. 'My tears have been my food day and night, while people say to me all day long, "Where is your God?"' (Psalm 42:3).

To onlookers, Jesus appeared weak and abandoned. His apparent inability to invoke divine intervention seemed to confirm their jibes. However, it was neither his own helplessness nor the power of those who nailed him there that kept Jesus on that cross. Rather it was his complete obedience to God and his fathomless love for you, me, those who hurled insults and everyone else. For Jesus, his absolute commitment to enduring this awful battle was confirmed the previous evening in Gethsemane, as he prayed, 'My Father, if it is not possible for this cup to be taken away unless I drink it, may your will be done' (Matthew 26:42).

> 'Amazing love! How can it be… that Thou, my God, should die for me?' (Charles Wesley, 1707–88).

SA

Day 332

Two robbers respond

LUKE 23:39–43

Jerusalem
One of the criminals who hung there hurled insults at him: 'Aren't you the Messiah? Save yourself and us!' But the other criminal rebuked him. 'Don't you fear God,' he said, 'since you are under the same sentence? We are punished justly, for we are getting what our deeds deserve. But this man has done nothing wrong.' Then he said, 'Jesus, remember me when you come into your kingdom.' Jesus answered him, 'Truly I tell you, today you will be with me in paradise.'

It was not unusual for criminals to be crucified together. Perhaps crucifying Jesus alongside two robbers was designed to add to his humiliation. Whatever the reason, it was no happenstance that these three men were there together. Centuries earlier, having caught a prophetic glimpse of these awful proceedings, Isaiah wrote: 'He poured out his life unto death, and was numbered with the transgressors' (Isaiah 53:12).

The crucifixion and resurrection of Jesus are the fulcrum, the turning point, of history. There is no bigger or more important story. Yet, while describing these events of cosmic and eternal significance, Luke zooms in on a personal, three-way conversation. Millenia later we get to eavesdrop on the exchange between three men in their last moments.

At first both criminals 'heaped insults on [Jesus]' (Matthew 27:44), but as the dialogue continues we witness a transformation in the attitude of one. It was not that he finally worked out a challenging mental puzzle, but rather that the blinkers that had blinded him to the identity of Jesus fell away. His appeal to the other criminal, 'Don't you fear God' points to a dawning of realisation. There is a self-humbling and recognition of his own wrongdoing: 'We are getting what our deeds deserve' (v. 41). There is an acknowledgement that, unlike them, Jesus is innocent and deserves nothing of this excruciating punishment. Finally, recognising implicitly that Jesus is indeed king, he makes the simple, heartfelt request, 'Jesus, remember me when you come into your kingdom' (v. 42).

Imagine the influx of hope as, in the midst of agony and surrounded by the contemptuous crowd, Jesus turned his loving eyes towards the man and assured him, 'Today you will be with me in paradise.'

> Be still and become aware of the grace-filled gaze of Jesus. Allow his waves of peace to wash over you.

SA

Day 333

Darkness descends

MATTHEW 27:45-50 (MARK 15:35-36; LUKE 23:36-37; JOHN 19:29)

Jerusalem
From noon until three in the afternoon darkness came over all the land. About three in the afternoon Jesus cried out in a loud voice, 'Eli, Eli, lema sabachthani?' (which means 'My God, my God, why have you forsaken me?'). When some of those standing there heard this, they said, 'He's calling Elijah.' Immediately one of them ran and got a sponge. He filled it with wine vinegar, put it on a staff, and offered it to Jesus to drink. The rest said, 'Now leave him alone. Let's see if Elijah comes to save him.' And when Jesus had cried out again in a loud voice, he gave up his spirit.

Throughout the Bible the state of being distanced or separated from God is often characterised by darkness. In contrast, being brought into a place of acceptance by and closeness with God is often symbolised by light. When the plagues inflicted on the Egyptians in order to free the Israelites from captivity approached their climax, God brought darkness upon them for three days. It was a 'darkness that [could] be felt' (Exodus 10:21), preceding and foreshadowing the death of the firstborn sons. When communicating the terrifying vision he received, the prophet Amos wrote, 'Will not the day of the Lord be darkness, not light – pitch-dark, without a ray of brightness?' (Amos 5:20). Now, as God's plan for redeeming broken creation and reconciling estranged people approaches its climax, darkness descends.

As we have seen, Psalm 22 had inevitably been on Jesus' mind over the preceding hours, full as it is with prophetic forebodings of this day. Now, with a strength of voice remarkable in view of all he had suffered, he cried out its chilling opening line: 'My God, my God, why have you forsaken me?' None of us can fully fathom the mysteries of all that occurred in that instant, of how the consequences of the Saviour's death ricocheted and flowed throughout space and eternity. In the moment of that awful cry, as he shouldered the full burden of humankind's rebellious nature, he plumbed the darkest depths of the human condition and tasted the awfulness of alienation from God. However, in doing so, Jesus made possible the reconciliation between creator and humankind forever.

> *'For you were once darkness, but now you are light in the Lord. Live as children of light'* (Ephesians 5:8).

SA

Day 334

It is finished

JOHN 19:30 (MATTHEW 27:50; MARK 15:37; LUKE 23:46)

Jerusalem
When he had received the drink, Jesus said, 'It is finished.' With that, he bowed his head and gave up his spirit.

If we had been following only John's gospel, we would be conscious of progressing along a countdown towards a long-anticipated climax, and with that word 'finished' we reach its culmination. Jesus was fully aware of the eternal plan that was unfolding. To his mother at the wedding in Cana he said, 'My hour has not yet come' (John 2:4). Seven times we are told, 'A time is coming.' His persecutors could not touch him because 'his hour had not yet come' (John 7:30). As the time of his death and resurrection approached, he prayed, 'Father, the hour has come' (John 17:1). Likewise, three times John describes Jesus talking or praying about his need to 'finish' the task his Father has given him to complete. Now, with his dying breath he declares, 'It is finished', a cry of victory that was and is true in several ways.

Jesus spoke about his work of bringing good news to the people he encountered in terms of finishing his Father's work (John 4:34). That was now finished. His miracles were also part of the work he needed to 'finish' (John 5:36). John, more than any other gospel writer, explains how Jesus' miracles were 'signs' that provided windows into the character of God and the identity of Jesus. Having fed thousands, Jesus revealed himself as the 'bread of life' (6:48), and while healing a blind man, Jesus explained that he was 'the light of the world' (9:5). All those signs were now completed or 'finished'.

With his triumphant pronouncement, Jesus also pointed to how everything that has been said of him in the scriptures had been fulfilled. In the previous verses, John explains, 'Knowing that everything had now been finished, and so that Scripture would be fulfilled, Jesus said, "I am thirsty"' (v. 28). So, even in that act he fulfilled a final prophetic word: 'They... gave me vinegar for my thirst' (Psalm 69:21).

The incomprehensible riches of all Jesus accomplished are summarised in his anguished but triumphant cry, 'It is finished.' The way of salvation for humankind is realised. The conquest of evil is accomplished.

> Because Jesus could say 'It is finished', we can say 'There is now no condemnation for those who are in Christ Jesus' (Romans 8:1).

SA

Day 335

Temple curtain torn

MATTHEW 27:51–56 (MARK 15:38–40; LUKE 23:45–49)

Jerusalem
At that moment the curtain of the temple was torn in two from top to bottom. The earth shook, the rocks split and the tombs broke open. The bodies of many holy people who had died were raised to life. They came out of the tombs after Jesus' resurrection and went into the holy city and appeared to many people. When the centurion and those with him who were guarding Jesus saw the earthquake and all that had happened, they were terrified, and exclaimed, 'Surely he was the Son of God!' Many women were there, watching from a distance. They had followed Jesus from Galilee to care for his needs. Among them were Mary Magdalene, Mary the mother of James and Joseph, and the mother of Zebedee's sons.

Each of the wonderful happenings that Matthew describes has its own potent symbolism. It is impossible to exaggerate the significance of the heavy curtain that separated the holy of holies from the holy place being ripped open. This was the barrier between people and the presence of God. Only God's appointed mediator, the high priest, could pass this ornate drape, and even he could only do so once a year and after following the prescribed rituals of the day of atonement. Suddenly, the barrier between the holy God and sinful people was opened and the fact that the curtain was torn 'from top to bottom' underscores that this was the work of God.

People 'raised to life' was a clear demonstration of victory over death. As well as the way to God being thrown wide open, death has lost its sting. The grave no longer holds any fear for those who follow Jesus. The handful of faithful women who continued to show their devotion while others deserted him could never have imagined how Jesus' promise, 'And I, when I am lifted up from the earth, will draw all people to myself' (John 12:32) would be fulfilled, how multitudes in every generation and from every 'nation, tribe, people and language' (Revelation 7:9) would find hope, purpose and salvation in Jesus. And yet here was a first sign in one of the Roman guards, there to oversee the grisly proceedings, but then heard to recognise in the now battered and twisted corpse the 'Son of God'.

> Let's rejoice with Paul: 'Where, O death, is your victory? Where, O death, is your sting?' (1 Corinthians 15:55).

SA

Day 336

Legs broken, pierced

JOHN 19:31-37

Jerusalem
Now it was the day of Preparation, and the next day was to be a special Sabbath. Because the Jewish leaders did not want the bodies left on the crosses during the Sabbath, they asked Pilate to have the legs broken and the bodies taken down. The soldiers therefore came and broke the legs of the first man who had been crucified with Jesus, and then those of the other. But when they came to Jesus and found that he was already dead, they did not break his legs. Instead, one of the soldiers pierced Jesus' side with a spear, bringing a sudden flow of blood and water. The man who saw it has given testimony, and his testimony is true. He knows that he tells the truth, and he testifies so that you also may believe. These things happened so that the scripture would be fulfilled: 'Not one of his bones will be broken,' and, as another scripture says, 'They will look on the one they have pierced.'

Death by crucifixion was a matter of slow suffocation, and breaking the victim's legs was an act of mercy. The fact that the body of Jesus remained unbroken is significant. As the 'Lamb of God' hung on a cross, religious people prepared to sacrifice and eat a lamb, as prescribed by the law. The decrees for the Passover lamb stated, 'Do not break any of the bones' (Exodus 12:46).

Oblivious to their cooperation with divine providence, the soldiers, seeing that Jesus was already dead, plunged a spear deep into his side. The blood and 'water' that poured out suggest they penetrated the heart and released the fluid that gathers in the membranes around the heart and lungs during extreme trauma. More words of prophecy echoed down through the ages, this time from Zechariah: 'They will look on me, the one they have pierced, and they will mourn for him as one mourns for an only child' (12:10).

John's eyewitness knew the crucial importance of what he witnessed. It testified to the fact that Jesus was dead. The ancient creeds could not be clearer: Jesus 'was crucified, died and was buried'.

> Lord Jesus, no words can convey my gratitude that you 'humbled yourself by becoming obedient to death – even death on a cross' (Philippians 2:8) – for me. Amen.

SA

Day 337

Joseph claims the body

MATTHEW 27:57-61 (MARK 15:42-47; LUKE 23:50-54; JOHN 19:38-42)

Jerusalem
As evening approached, there came a rich man from Arimathea, named Joseph, who had himself become a disciple of Jesus. Going to Pilate, he asked for Jesus' body, and Pilate ordered that it be given to him. Joseph took the body, wrapped it in a clean linen cloth, and placed it in his own new tomb that he had cut out of the rock. He rolled a big stone in front of the entrance to the tomb and went away. Mary Magdalene and the other Mary were sitting there opposite the tomb.

From our perspective, the death of Jesus may seem dreadfully protracted and his burial strangely rushed. However, by the norms of the day, the death of Jesus, while unimaginably awful, was unusually swift. Death by crucifixion could take days. So, when Joseph asked for the body of Jesus, Pilate 'was surprised to hear that he was already dead' (Mark 15:44).

The need for haste in burying Jesus becomes clear when we explore the circumstances. It was commonplace for corpses to be left to be picked over by birds as a gruesome example to passers-by, but this was not just any Roman province. The tension with the religious authorities was acute and the Jewish law was adamant in prohibiting the leaving of corpses overnight (Deuteronomy 21:22-23). In addition, the following day was the sabbath and part of the Passover celebrations.

The gospel writers together paint a multifaceted portrait of the man who requested the body of Jesus and donated his own tomb. Matthew tells us that Joseph was wealthy and a follower of Jesus. Mark tells us he was a prominent member of the Jewish legislative assembly and someone who had been 'waiting for the kingdom of God'. Luke describes Joseph as 'a good and upright man' and assures us that, despite being a member of the Sanhedrin, he had not consented to the execution of Jesus.

John enriches our understanding of Joseph by explaining that he had been keeping his trust in Jesus a secret 'because he feared the Jewish leaders'. This makes his courageous approach to Pilate all the more astounding. Here was a man in a position of public prominence who, forced to choose between his personal safety and reputation and his devotion to Christ, exercised his faith and 'went boldly to Pilate' (Mark 15:43).

▍ *'Perfect love drives out fear' (1 John 4:18).*

SA

Day 338

Joseph and Nicodemus

JOHN 19:38-42

Jerusalem
Later, Joseph of Arimathea asked Pilate for the body of Jesus. Now Joseph was a disciple of Jesus, but secretly because he feared the Jewish leaders. With Pilate's permission, he came and took the body away. He was accompanied by Nicodemus, the man who earlier had visited Jesus at night. Nicodemus brought a mixture of myrrh and aloes, about thirty-five kilograms. Taking Jesus' body, the two of them wrapped it, with the spices, in strips of linen. This was in accordance with Jewish burial customs. At the place where Jesus was crucified, there was a garden, and in the garden a new tomb, in which no one had ever been laid. Because it was the Jewish day of Preparation and since the tomb was near by, they laid Jesus there.

Here we discover that Joseph had an accomplice. Nicodemus too was a member of the legislative assembly, the Sanhedrin, and a Pharisee. Like Joseph, there was a time when he feared the consequences of aligning himself with Jesus and kept his identity as a disciple secret, visiting Jesus 'at night' (John 3:2). However, each time we meet him in the pages of John's gospel Nicodemus grows bolder. When opposition to Jesus was gathering pace and the religious leaders pressured the temple guards to arrest Jesus, it was Nicodemus who found the courage to challenge them to give Jesus a fair hearing (John 7:50-51).

Now, with the corpse of Jesus hanging on a cross, at a time when many believed the Jesus movement was finished and his promises worthless, Joseph and Nicodemus joined forces in fearless collaboration. Willing to make themselves ritually unclean according to the law and at significant risk to their safety and reputations, they treated Jesus' crucified body with reverence and dignity. Together, they joined forces in generous devotion: Joseph donating his family tomb, carved into a rocky outcrop in the garden; Nicodemus contributing a quantity of spices fitting for the burial of a king.

As they took the body of Jesus, crucified between two criminals, and laid it in wealthy Joseph's family sepulchre, I wonder if they remembered the prophecy of Isaiah, in which the one who was 'led like a lamb to the slaughter' is 'assigned a grave with the wicked, and with the rich in his death' (53:7, 9).

> Lord, please help me to grow in faith and courage day by day. Amen.

SA

Day 339

The women

LUKE 23:55–56

Jerusalem
The women who had come with Jesus from Galilee followed Joseph and saw the tomb and how his body was laid in it. Then they went home and prepared spices and perfumes. But they rested on the Sabbath in obedience to the commandment.

Within these three short sentences some vital characteristics of being a faithful disciple of Jesus are demonstrated. When we talk about 'the disciples of Jesus', we tend to think about 'the Twelve', his inner circle of particularly close companions, those he called into the ultimate adventure with the words 'Follow me', the men he 'appointed… that they might be with him and that he might send them out' (Mark 3:14).

However, when we search the gospel accounts of Jesus' agonising journey towards Golgotha, his death, burial and resurrection, again and again we find that there is a group of women who remain close by, attentive to his situation, words and needs. Some of them are named, as we saw in John's account: 'His mother, his mother's sister, Mary the wife of Clopas, and Mary Magdalene' (19:25). At other times they are anonymous, like the 'many women' who 'were there, watching from a distance' in Matthew's account, but never far away. In scenes when more prominent disciples are noticeably absent, these women model consistency and commitment. They are with Jesus through thick and thin, keeping close, dependably diligent.

Responding to all they had witnessed, they 'prepared spices and perfumes' (v. 56). Their devotion was not just a sentiment; it was conveyed in their practical actions. Even now that Jesus was dead and buried, their faithfulness overflowed into loving service.

No doubt there were countless things they were then tempted to do, numerous places they could have gone. Surely, they longed to gather with others, to discuss all that had happened and to pray. However, their absolute loyalty now showed itself in obedience to what they already knew of God's way. Despite the heart-rending and eternally momentous nature of the events unfolding around them, 'they rested on the Sabbath' (v. 56). The basic principles of walking in God's way were not open to negotiation or compromise. Throughout the accounts of the crucifixion and burial of Jesus, this group of devout woman model faithfulness by their presence, actions and obedience.

> Lord, help me to be consistent in my attentiveness to you, courageous in my actions and unswerving in my obedience. Amen.

SA

Day 340

The tomb secured

MATTHEW 27:62-66

Jerusalem
The next day, the one after Preparation Day, the chief priests and the Pharisees went to Pilate. 'Sir,' they said, 'we remember that while he was still alive that deceiver said, "After three days I will rise again." So give the order for the tomb to be made secure until the third day. Otherwise, his disciples may come and steal the body and tell the people that he has been raised from the dead. This last deception will be worse than the first.' 'Take a guard,' Pilate answered. 'Go, make the tomb as secure as you know how.' So they went and made the tomb secure by putting a seal on the stone and posting the guard.

To grasp the gravity of these events, we need to understand the significance of those words, 'the next day'. This was a sabbath. Not only that, it was one of a handful of days considered 'high days' and, therefore, deemed especially holy. A recurrent theme in the gospels is the conflict between the religious authorities and Jesus over what was allowable on the sabbath, and yet here 'the chief priests and the Pharisees', renowned for their meticulous attention to every detail of the law, went to plead with Pilate and get involved in sealing a tomb. By their own standards, it was outrageous behaviour.

What could drive these men, so fervent in their fastidious observance of the sabbath, to violate their own codes so blatantly? The answer is simple and, considering the astonishing events that took place around the death of Jesus, it is unsurprising. These men, usually so confident in their virtue, were in a state of extreme anxiety. This was just hours after an inexplicable and chilling darkness descended, a terrifying earthquake had shaken the land and the profoundly symbolic temple curtain suddenly ripped from top to bottom. The shocking behaviour of these religious leaders was provoked by panic. They were afraid and desperate. While their words convey concern that the disciples might orchestrate a hoax, the recent events must have stirred a deeper fear of the claims of Jesus being true.

Scholars tell us that the language used by Pilate was a blunt rebuff: the Jewish authorities must employ their own guards. They are on their own.

> *Consider the ludicrous futility of trying to contain or constrain what Paul called the 'incomparably great power' (Ephesians 1:19).*

SA

the resurrection and aftermath

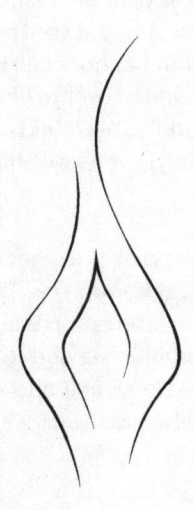

TONY HORSFALL

Day 341

The two women meet Jesus

MATTHEW 28:1-7 (MARK 16:1-8; LUKE 24:1-8)

Jerusalem, the tomb
After the Sabbath, at dawn on the first day of the week, Mary Magdalene and the other Mary went to look at the tomb. There was a violent earthquake, for an angel of the Lord came down from heaven and, going to the tomb, rolled back the stone and sat on it. His appearance was like lightning, and his clothes were white as snow. The guards were so afraid of him that they shook and became like dead men. The angel said to the women, 'Do not be afraid, for I know that you are looking for Jesus, who was crucified. He is not here; he has risen, just as he said. Come and see the place where he lay. Then go quickly and tell his disciples: "He has risen from the dead and is going ahead of you into Galilee. There you will see him." Now I have told you.'

The climax of the gospel story arrives with the realisation that Jesus, having definitely been crucified and buried, has risen and is alive. These are the most exciting chapters in the whole Bible and mean his death has not been in vain. It is exactly what Jesus said would happen – that he would be handed over to his enemies, be crucified and then on the third day come back to life (Mark 8:31–32; 9:31–32; 10:32–34). He had emphasised it continually, spoken about it plainly, yet as we shall see, the disciples were far from expecting it to happen!

The events of the first Easter morning are somewhat confused, and it is difficult to piece them together in a tidy chronological framework. This is to be expected, and actually confirms the veracity of the story. A fabrication would be much neater. In reality, the eyewitness accounts of such a mind-blowing and fear-inducing moment are authentically jumbled and inconsistent. The shock of it all would have made remembering the finer details (like what happened when and who was where when it happened) much harder to recall.

The two Marys are entrusted with passing on the news of the resurrection, a reminder of the significant part that women have played ever since in spreading the gospel.

> *How do you greet the news that Jesus is risen? Does the joy and wonder of the greatest event in history continue to inspire and uplift you?*

TH

Day 342

The women meet Jesus

MATTHEW 28:8–10

Jerusalem, the tomb
So the women hurried away from the tomb, afraid yet filled with joy, and ran to tell his disciples. Suddenly Jesus met them. 'Greetings,' he said. They came to him, clasped his feet and worshipped him. Then Jesus said to them, 'Do not be afraid. Go and tell my brothers to go to Galilee; there they will see me.'

It is popular in our fast-paced society to seek to eliminate hurry from our lives, but some matters are urgent and do require haste – like passing on the news that Jesus is alive! So, when the women leave the tomb, they are running, eager to tell the other disciples the most exciting news ever and do so as quickly as possible.

Their emotional state at this time is one of understandable turmoil, a mixture of fear (from the earthquake and encountering an angel) and indescribable joy (that Jesus has been raised). It is about to be disturbed even more, for unexpectedly, they are actually encountered by Jesus. He comes to them with a greeting that means 'Be full of joy!', which seems in the context to be something of an understatement.

Their instinctive response is to worship him, and to do so by grasping his feet and holding on to him as if they never want to let him go. This is a natural grief reaction, a response of love that has known separation and does not want to feel pain again. But this is not a time for clinging. Jesus calms their fears and sends them to prepare the disciples to head north to Galilee where they will meet him again.

It is striking that the task of announcing the resurrection is entrusted to the women, who had little standing in society and would have no credibility as witnesses. Michael Green calls this 'simply astounding' and describes the fact that God attests the resurrection, his greatest act since the creation of the world, through the lips of those so widely undervalued as 'the supreme irony' and 'Magnificent!'[45]

> *Why not take a moment to re-create this scene in your mind? Imagine in your busyness you are interrupted by meeting Jesus. How does he greet you? How do you respond to his presence? What else does he say to you?*

TH

Day 343

The women inform the disciples

LUKE 24:9-12

Jerusalem
When they came back from the tomb, they told all these things to the Eleven and to all the others. It was Mary Magdalene, Joanna, Mary the mother of James, and the others with them who told this to the apostles. But they did not believe the women, because their words seemed to them like nonsense. Peter, however, got up and ran to the tomb. Bending over, he saw the strips of linen lying by themselves, and he went away, wondering to himself what had happened.

It may be apocryphal, but apparently Oliver Cromwell told the artist Peter Lely to paint his portrait 'warts and all' – that is, as he truly was, without concealing his blemishes. The gospel writers never conceal the weaknesses of the apostles, and Luke here does nothing to hide the shame they must have felt later when their rough refusal to believe the women's announcement of the resurrection is disclosed. It is perhaps their lowest moment.

Such authenticity is, however, to be admired. If we project only an image of perfection and attainment, we are not true to our own reality which can make following Jesus seem daunting to others more conscious of failure. It is far better to be appropriately open about our struggles and mistakes. This keeps us humble and shows others that God can use weak and fallible people.

But why did the apostles refuse to believe the women? Was it because they unconsciously looked down on them, doubting their credibility? Sadly, men have often held prejudice towards women and refused to learn from them. But this was a staggering truth to grasp, even though Jesus had told them he would rise again. People who have died do not normally come back to life. Rationally that doesn't happen. To the men it seemed like nonsense.

Only Peter breaks through the prejudice and scepticism in the room. Luke's account does not sit easily with the other gospel records on this point, but it is perfectly possible he went to the tomb alone. His belief in the resurrection came slowly and in stages, as faith so often does.

> *What prejudices stop you from receiving new truth? Do you find yourself cynical when it comes to the supernatural? If you are a man, is your attitude towards women wholesome, like that of Jesus?*

TH

Day 344

The guards' report

MATTHEW 28:11-15

Jerusalem
While the women were on their way, some of the guards went into the city and reported to the chief priests everything that had happened. When the chief priests had met with the elders and devised a plan, they gave the soldiers a large sum of money, telling them, 'You are to say, "His disciples came during the night and stole him away while we were asleep." If this report gets to the governor, we will satisfy him and keep you out of trouble.' So the soldiers took the money and did as they were instructed. And this story has been widely circulated among the Jews to this very day.

Ever since Donald Trump became president of the United States, the expression 'fake news' has passed into everyday conversation. 'Fake news' refers to the falsification of what is true, and the broadcasting or publication of that which is not true but promoted as being true. It is the creation of a false narrative to sway public opinion. 'Fake news' has become a fact of life in societies influenced by social media, but it is far from a new phenomenon, as today's passage illustrates.

Interestingly, the women were not the only witnesses to the resurrection – the men sent to guard the tomb also knew what had happened and reported it to the religious leaders. The reason they had placed guards there was because they knew the claims that Jesus had made to rise again, and they feared his body would be stolen to make it look as if he had (Matthew 27:62–66). They did not expect it to actually happen, so now they had to create a false narrative to stop people believing the truth. With a little bribery and a lot of intimidation, they managed to construct another version of events, that the disciples had stolen the body. It was, however, fake news.

Each of us will have our own way of dealing with inconvenient truth. Jesus Christ demands our allegiance, and that is not always welcomed. We may be tempted to deflect his claims upon us by interpreting his words in a way that fits better with our own desires. Only if we are committed to obeying the truth will we be able to live truly as his disciples.

❚ *How are you responding to the claims of Jesus, especially his lordship?*

TH

Day 345

Peter and John at the tomb

JOHN 20:1-10 (*MARK 16:9-11*)

Jerusalem, the tomb
Early on the first day of the week, while it was still dark, Mary Magdalene went to the tomb and saw that the stone had been removed from the entrance. So she came running to Simon Peter and the other disciple, the one Jesus loved, and said, 'They have taken the Lord out of the tomb, and we don't know where they have put him!' So Peter and the other disciple started for the tomb. Both were running, but the other disciple outran Peter and reached the tomb first. He bent over and looked in at the strips of linen lying there but did not go in. Then Simon Peter came along behind him and went straight into the tomb. He saw the strips of linen lying there, as well as the cloth that had been wrapped round Jesus' head. The cloth was still lying in its place, separate from the linen. Finally the other disciple, who had reached the tomb first, also went inside. He saw and believed. (They still did not understand from Scripture that Jesus had to rise from the dead.) Then the disciples went back to where they were staying.

I cannot read this story without thinking of my school sports days. I was a fast runner, but another boy could always run slightly faster than me. I never did beat him, so I know how Peter felt. On this occasion, though, coming second didn't matter.

Running and the Easter story go together. If Mary's report is true, then it really matters. Peter and John lose no time in racing to the tomb to see for themselves. John may be faster, but Peter is bolder, and he enters the tomb first. The evidence is there for them to see. There is no body, but the grave clothes are lying there in such a way as to suggest something supernatural has happened. It is as if the body has passed through them. The clothes are as they would have been, minus the body. This is not the work of grave robbers. It is the work of God. This is resurrection. They saw and believed.

Seeing and believing are connected. Understanding through scripture will come later, validating their experience, but personal encounter is equally convincing.

▎ *Lord, thank you for the truth of the resurrection, and the assurance that you are alive.*

TH

Day 346

Mary meets Jesus

JOHN 20:11-18

Jerusalem, the tomb

Now Mary stood outside the tomb crying. As she wept, she bent over to look into the tomb and saw two angels in white, seated where Jesus' body had been, one at the head and the other at the foot. They asked her, 'Woman, why are you crying?' 'They have taken my Lord away,' she said, 'and I don't know where they have put him.' At this, she turned round and saw Jesus standing there, but she did not realise that it was Jesus. He asked her, 'Woman, why are you crying? Who is it you are looking for?' Thinking he was the gardener, she said, 'Sir, if you have carried him away, tell me where you have put him, and I will get him.' Jesus said to her, 'Mary.' She turned towards him and cried out in Aramaic, 'Rabboni!' (which means 'Teacher'). Jesus said, 'Do not hold on to me, for I have not yet ascended to the Father. Go instead to my brothers and tell them, "I am ascending to my Father and your Father, to my God and your God."' Mary Magdalene went to the disciples with the news: 'I have seen the Lord!' And she told them that he had said these things to her.

The resurrection stories make fascinating reading as we see how individual disciples come to terms with the incredible fact that Jesus is alive. At the heart of the narrative is Mary Magdalene, who, given her background, appears surprisingly as the gatekeeper to the resurrection.

Mary had a troubled past. We read that Jesus delivered her from demonic oppression, and that she became one of a group of women who travelled with him, supporting him in his ministry (Luke 8:1-3). Tradition describes her as a former prostitute, but this is not certain. Her grief at the death of Jesus is authentic and understandable. Her tears flow freely, and her anger bubbles beneath the surface.

How tenderly Jesus comes to meet her, giving her individual attention and calling her gently by name. He is indeed the good shepherd caring mercifully for his sheep. Now she has a testimony of her own, a witness not just of an empty tomb but to a risen Saviour.

> *Thank you, Lord, for times when you have come to me in my sadness, loss and confusion, and called me by name.*

TH

Day 347

On the road to Emmaus (1)

LUKE 24:13–16 (*MARK 16:12–13*)

Towards Emmaus
Now that same day two of them were going to a village called Emmaus, about seven miles from Jerusalem. They were talking with each other about everything that had happened. As they talked and discussed these things with each other, Jesus himself came up and walked along with them; but they were kept from recognising him.

Do you like walking? I rediscovered the joy of walking during the Covid pandemic and spent many hours walking the countryside in the company of a close friend. Walking helped me cope with my grief after my wife's passing, and to ease my loneliness.

It is easy to picture these companions, Cleopas and most probably his wife, walking and talking as they head back to their home in Emmaus. But this is no happy jaunt. As part of the inner circle of the disciples of Jesus, they are devastated and disappointed at what has happened. Their hopes have died with Jesus. Their steps are heavy with grief and loss, the weight of shattered dreams sagging their shoulders, their faces downcast with the pain of defeat.

At some point a stranger draws alongside them, but they hardly notice him, such is their absorption in sorrow. They are kept from recognising Jesus, perhaps because his risen appearance is slightly different, but more likely because they are preoccupied. Yet still Jesus comes to search them out and bring comfort to them.

Only Luke, with a doctor's compassion and awareness of the human condition, records this story of the walk to Emmaus. It highlights two important lessons for us. The first is the importance of developing close friendships and of talking openly about how we are thinking and feeling. Such spiritual companionship is a gift from God and a way of bringing healing to us in our sorrow.

The second is the reminder that Jesus, the man of sorrows, is always with us in our sadness. He does not stand aloof from human weakness and need but comes to us in our brokenness to bring healing and restoration. He is always there, if we open our eyes.

> *With whom do you share your deepest needs? How does this picture of Jesus drawing alongside encourage your faith? Who might you help in their sadness?*

TH

Day 348

On the road to Emmaus (2)

LUKE 24:17-21

Towards Emmaus
He asked them, 'What are you discussing together as you walk along?' They stood still, their faces downcast. One of them, named Cleopas, asked him, 'Are you the only one visiting Jerusalem who does not know the things that have happened there in these days?' 'What things?' he asked. 'About Jesus of Nazareth,' they replied. 'He was a prophet, powerful in word and deed before God and all the people. The chief priests and our rulers handed him over to be sentenced to death, and they crucified him; but we had hoped that he was the one who was going to redeem Israel. And what is more, it is the third day since all this took place.'

We love Jesus because, as we have seen, he is the man of sorrows who identifies with us in our grief and loss. He is also the Wonderful Counsellor (Isaiah 9:6), whose wisdom leads and guides us through our difficult days. Somewhere on the journey to Emmaus the two friends acknowledge his presence, and with some carefully chosen questions and good listening, Jesus begins to open up the conversation and set them on the path to healing.

For a moment they come to a standstill (v. 17). Stopping can be vitally important, for it reflects the recognition that something significant is happening to us that requires our full attention. A failure to be still can rob us of such moments and the possibility of transformation and healing. Stillness is essential to the deeper work of God.

Provoked by the questions of Jesus, Cleopas opens his heart to disclose not only the facts of what has happened in Jerusalem, but also their impact upon them. His words 'we had hoped' give the game away – their dreams have been shattered, their hearts are broken and they do not know what to do next. They invested so much in following Jesus, but to no avail.

An essential part in healing is to name our pain, to acknowledge what has happened to us, to identify our wounds and to verbalise our feelings. This requires great courage, and sometimes the help of a skilled counsellor or wise spiritual director. It is painful, but yields rich rewards, especially when we offer our pain to God.

> *What pain do you find in your heart? Can you name it? With whom can you share your need of healing?*

TH

Day 349

On the road to Emmaus (3)

LUKE 24:22-27

Towards Emmaus
'In addition, some of our women amazed us. They went to the tomb early this morning but didn't find his body. They came and told us that they had seen a vision of angels, who said he was alive. Then some of our companions went to the tomb and found it just as the women had said, but they did not see Jesus.' He said to them, 'How foolish you are, and how slow to believe all that the prophets have spoken! Did not the Messiah have to suffer these things and then enter his glory?' And beginning with Moses and all the Prophets, he explained to them what was said in all the Scriptures concerning himself.

While it is important to sympathise with those who are hurting, sometimes at the right moment, and always with tenderness and love, it is right to challenge any ways of thinking that may be hindering recovery and replace them with the truth. Jesus understands the couple's hurt, but it is partly their own making. They are not thinking clearly.

Their interpretation of the weekend's events is based upon their refusal to receive the testimony of the women and their mistaken expectation that Jesus was a political Messiah. Jesus does not mince his words, describing them as 'thick-headed' and 'slow-hearted' (v. 25, MSG). If they had been less sceptical, been better informed from the scriptures and listened more carefully to the teaching of Jesus, they would have believed.

This rebuke would have shaken them badly, but it is followed by perhaps the most amazing Bible study ever given, as Jesus explains how the scriptures speak about him. The heart of the matter is that suffering leads to glory, and death to resurrection. That is the key to making sense of all that has happened.

How much of our mental pain is in fact due to faulty thinking? We hold preconceived ideas and fixed ways of thinking that are inaccurate yet have gone unchallenged. To heal we must remain open-minded, submitting our inherited thoughts to the truth of scripture and exposing ourselves to the wisdom of God. In this way our minds will be renewed (Romans 12:2; 2 Corinthians 10:5).

> *Are you aware how your thinking influences your emotions and behaviours? Can you see how wrong thinking can be damaging? How can you align your thinking more firmly with God's word?*

TH

Day 350

On the road to Emmaus (4)

LUKE 24:28–35

Towards Emmaus
As they approached the village to which they were going, Jesus continued on as if he were going further. But they urged him strongly, 'Stay with us, for it is nearly evening; the day is almost over.' So he went in to stay with them. When he was at the table with them, he took bread, gave thanks, broke it and began to give it to them. Then their eyes were opened and they recognised him, and he disappeared from their sight. They asked each other, 'Were not our hearts burning within us while he talked with us on the road and opened the Scriptures to us?' They got up and returned at once to Jerusalem. There they found the Eleven and those with them, assembled together and saying, 'It is true! The Lord has risen and has appeared to Simon.' Then the two told what had happened on the way, and how Jesus was recognised by them when he broke the bread.

A simple act of hospitality proves to be a major turning point for the disheartened couple. Jesus, perhaps deliberately seeking to test their hearts, appears to be going further, but acquiesces to their invitation to stay. Jesus never imposes himself on us; he waits to be invited.

Over an ordinary meal the two disciples finally realise they are entertaining the Lord. The revelation comes in two ways. First, in the manner in which he broke the bread and gave thanks. Perhaps a memory stirred of the feeding of the 5,000 (Luke 9:16) or even of the meal in the upper room (Luke 22:19). Perhaps it was a familiar mannerism or the sound of his voice that awakened them. Either way, around the table their eyes were opened.

Then second, as they reflected on their conversation with him, they noticed how their hearts had been 'burning' within them as he taught them. Had they experienced that before – the warmth of God's love, the kindling of affection for him as they listed to his teaching?

Suddenly certainty burst into their consciousness; they knew they had seen Jesus and that he was alive. Newly restored and re-energised, they immediately hurry back to Jerusalem to tell the others, adding their testimony to that of Simon.

> *How has God brought assurance to your heart? In what ways has he shown himself alive (Acts 1:3)?*

TH

Day 351

Jesus appears to the disciples

LUKE 24:36-43 (MARK 16:14)

Jerusalem
While they were still talking about this, Jesus himself stood among them and said to them, 'Peace be with you.' They were startled and frightened, thinking they saw a ghost. He said to them, 'Why are you troubled, and why do doubts rise in your minds? Look at my hands and my feet. It is I myself! Touch me and see; a ghost does not have flesh and bones, as you see I have.' When he had said this, he showed them his hands and feet. And while they still did not believe it because of joy and amazement, he asked them, 'Do you have anything here to eat?' They gave him a piece of broiled fish, and he took it and ate it in their presence.

With such evidence before them we might expect the disciples to be immediately convinced of the resurrection. But no, they are still hesitant. Hiding behind locked doors for fear of arrest (John 20:19), they cower in nervous apprehension.

When Jesus appears with his message of peace, their heightened senses are triggered and they assume it is a ghost, since they did not let him in. What tricks the mind can play when we are afraid! He has come to bring peace, but instead they are more alarmed.

With great compassion, Jesus seeks to allay their fears and establish for them his identity. First, he shows them the wounds in his hands and feet and invites them to touch him. He is a real human being, with flesh and blood. They need not fear; it truly is Jesus.

The disciples are still hovering between joy that he is risen and doubt that such a thing could actually happen, so to further convince them and underline his humanity he next asks for something to eat. His resurrection self may look slightly different, but it is the same Jesus, and he still needs food. This is such a touching detail in the story, and to see Jesus eating the broiled fish must have left the disciples gobsmacked.

Doubt is not the same as unbelief. To have questions does not mean that we do not believe. Sometimes to grow in faith we must work through our reservations so that doubt can become certainty. Jesus seems at ease with such a process.

▍ *Meditate on this: 'Peace be with you' (v. 36).*

TH

Day 352

Called to be witnesses

LUKE 24:44–49

Jerusalem
He said to them, 'This is what I told you while I was still with you: everything must be fulfilled that is written about me in the Law of Moses, the Prophets and the Psalms.' Then he opened their minds so they could understand the Scriptures. He told them, 'This is what is written: the Messiah will suffer and rise from the dead on the third day, and repentance for the forgiveness of sins will be preached in his name to all nations, beginning at Jerusalem. You are witnesses of these things. I am going to send you what my Father has promised; but stay in the city until you have been clothed with power from on high.'

Into the confusion and uncertainty of the disciples, Jesus speaks a word of clarity and direction. It is just what they need to get back on track and prepare for what is to come.

First, he grounds them in the objective truth of scripture, reminding them that from beginning to end they speak about him and his mission, and that these same scriptures are now being fulfilled. The events of the past few days are not random happenings, but part of God's eternal plan and purpose.

Second, he opens their minds to understand and grasp for themselves that the promised Messiah was destined to suffer, that his death and resurrection were essential to the divine plan. They must be convinced in their own minds that a suffering Messiah is not a contradiction in terms. His sacrificial death makes salvation possible.

Third, he outlines for them the task ahead which he is giving them – to preach a message of repentance and forgiveness in Jerusalem and the rest of the world. What a big vision that is! How daunting it must have seemed.

Finally, he assures them that they will receive the power of the Holy Spirit so they can accomplish their God-given task. It is not possible in human strength alone; they will need divine assistance, and this will be granted.

We share this same call to be witnesses, but there is no need to be confused about our mission or inadequate for the job. The task is daunting, but the resources still adequate and available.

> How does your life align with the purpose of God for his church?

TH

Day 353

They are commissioned

JOHN 20:19–23

Jerusalem
On the evening of that first day of the week, when the disciples were together, with the doors locked for fear of the Jewish leaders, Jesus came and stood among them and said, 'Peace be with you!' After he said this, he showed them his hands and side. The disciples were overjoyed when they saw the Lord. Again Jesus said, 'Peace be with you! As the Father has sent me, I am sending you.' And with that he breathed on them and said, 'Receive the Holy Spirit. If you forgive anyone's sins, their sins are forgiven; if you do not forgive them, they are not forgiven.'

John's account of the appearance of Jesus to the gathered group of disciples differs slightly from that of Luke, containing an expansion of his promise of the Holy Spirit. We notice the same fear in their hearts, but greater emphasis on the peace that Jesus brings them and a little more detail about their commission.

Their sending into the world is a continuation of the ministry of Jesus. He does not delegate the work to them and then absent himself. Rather he invites them to partner with him in the work the Father has given him to do. He will continue to operate through the Holy Spirit, who will make it possible for them to fulfil their calling.

His breathing on them appears to be a symbolic act, preparing them for Pentecost, when the Spirit will come like a mighty rushing wind. Perhaps it also provides a foretaste of what is to come, an empowering for the present moment that will be intensified when the Spirit is given in full measure. This prophetic action clearly reminds us that the work of God requires the power of God. Christian ministry will not be effective without the Spirit's help.

His words about forgiveness underline the fact that providing an antidote for sin is at the heart of the gospel. Sometimes confessing one's sin to a trusted person may be helpful in knowing that we are forgiven. A personal, subjective approach may not adequately deal with guilt and shame; objective confirmation from another will bring greater release. Likewise, forgiveness should not be offered cheaply if repentance is not evident. Pastoral wisdom always encourages genuine, not superficial, response.

▋ *How do the words of Jesus shape your understanding of the task he has given us?*

TH

Day 354

Thomas meets Jesus

JOHN 20:24-29

Jerusalem
Now Thomas (also known as Didymus), one of the Twelve, was not with the disciples when Jesus came. So the other disciples told him, 'We have seen the Lord!' But he said to them, 'Unless I see the nail marks in his hands and put my finger where the nails were, and put my hand into his side, I will not believe.' A week later his disciples were in the house again, and Thomas was with them. Though the doors were locked, Jesus came and stood among them and said, 'Peace be with you!' Then he said to Thomas, 'Put your finger here; see my hands. Reach out your hand and put it into my side. Stop doubting and believe.' Thomas said to him, 'My Lord and my God!' Then Jesus told him, 'Because you have seen me, you have believed; blessed are those who have not seen and yet have believed.'

For some reason Thomas has isolated himself from the other disciples. It is never wise to be cut adrift from supportive friends, especially in times of crisis. His pessimistic outlook had emerged earlier with his sardonic response to the desire of Jesus to return to Jerusalem, 'Let us also go, that we may die with him' (John 11:16). The thing he most feared had happened. Perhaps he thought it safer to be alone than identified with the others.

His absence meant he missed the appearance of Jesus, but he is far from convinced by the testimony he hears. Thomas requires tangible proof. A week later there is a softening in his attitude. He is present when Jesus appears again and speaks directly to him and his doubts. Here is the good shepherd, in mercy and love looking for the sheep that had gone astray. There is no angry rebuke at his faithlessness, only the vulnerability of an invitation to see and touch the wounds of Calvary.

Such tenderness is Thomas' undoing. His doubt evaporates, and faith bursts forth in a responsive surrender to the love he has received: 'My Lord and my God', he cries.

Jesus reminds them that faith will not always be built on sight. The way of discipleship more often requires trust, and not seeing.

> 'My Lord and my God.' Are you able to make such a response? What do these words mean to you?

TH

Day 355

That you may believe

JOHN 20:30-31 (*JOHN 21:24-25*)

Jesus performed many other signs in the presence of his disciples, which are not recorded in this book. But these are written that you may believe that Jesus is the Messiah, the Son of God, and that by believing you may have life in his name.

Modern TV dramas often have very unsatisfactory endings, where nothing is resolved and the viewer is left hanging with no proper conclusion. John makes no such mistake with his readers. He leaves them in no doubt about his purpose in writing, or the response he desires to see in them. He doesn't even wait for the story to finish!

John has been selective in his writing. He could have included many other examples of the miraculous signs he records. Not everything about the life of Jesus has been written down; that would have been too great a task. What he has recorded, though, should be enough to bring people to faith.

For John, the miracles that Jesus performed are signs, pointing the way to his true identity as the promised Messiah and Son of God. That is his first objective in writing, to help us to see who Jesus really is – not just a rabbi or prophet, more than a wonderworker or great teacher, but the one promised long ago who would come to save his people. And not just an ordinary man, however special. Human, yes, but equally divine – in fact the Son of God, God in human form, revealing the nature of God to us by becoming one with us.

Intellectual conviction of the identity of Jesus is not enough, however. John's second objective is that by reading his book we might come to believe for ourselves, to place our trust in Jesus and commit our lives to him, and in doing so receive the gift of his very life within us. In other words, to love him more dearly and follow him more nearly, beginning a journey of personal transformation.

> *At this point, may I ask a very personal question on behalf of all the gospel writers? As you have been reading, have you come to any conclusion as to who Jesus is? And if you have, have you placed your trust in him to save you, and offered your life to him to guide you? If so, why not tell someone your good news?*

TH

Day 356

The disciples go fishing

JOHN 21:1–6

Galilee
Afterwards Jesus appeared again to his disciples, by the Sea of Galilee. It happened this way: Simon Peter, Thomas (also known as Didymus), Nathanael from Cana in Galilee, the sons of Zebedee, and two other disciples were together. 'I'm going out to fish,' Simon Peter told them, and they said, 'We'll go with you.' So they went out and got into the boat, but that night they caught nothing. Early in the morning, Jesus stood on the shore, but the disciples did not realise that it was Jesus. He called out to them, 'Friends, haven't you any fish?' 'No,' they answered. He said, 'Throw your net on the right side of the boat and you will find some.' When they did, they were unable to haul the net in because of the large number of fish.

There is something special about going 'home', back to one's roots and familiar places. Peter and some of the others were drawn back to Galilee, partly by the homing instinct that can be so strong, but more importantly by the command of Jesus that he would meet them there (Mark 16:7).

Jerusalem was not a safe place, and to be further prepared for what lay before them they needed to step back from the hurly-burly of the city into the quiet of the countryside. They needed time and space to process all that had happened, and to reconnect with their original calling and vision.

Peter returns to what is most familiar to him, a fishing trip on the lake. There on the sea his mind could clear and he could relax. The others come too, valuing the camaraderie at a time of high uncertainty. Their all-night fishing yields nothing but sets the scene for a reminder of a lesson learned much earlier, a lesson which had resulted in Peter and others leaving everything to follow Jesus (Luke 5:1–11).

When Jesus appears and shows them what to do, and the result is another miraculous catch, the implication must have been obvious: this is a time for a new surrender and willingness to leave all to follow him. Such moments are always scary, but when Jesus is leading us into something larger and different, he invites rather than commands. His ability requires only our availability. What we cannot achieve ourselves, he can do through us.

> *Where might you go to reconnect with God?*

TH

Day 357

Breakfast on the beach

JOHN 21:7–14 (LUKE 24:36–43)

Galilee
Then the disciple whom Jesus loved said to Peter, 'It is the Lord!' As soon as Simon Peter heard him say, 'It is the Lord,' he wrapped his outer garment round him (for he had taken it off) and jumped into the water. The other disciples followed in the boat, towing the net full of fish, for they were not far from shore, about a hundred metres. When they landed, they saw a fire of burning coals there with fish on it, and some bread. Jesus said to them, 'Bring some of the fish you have just caught.' So Simon Peter climbed back into the boat and dragged the net ashore. It was full of large fish, 153, but even with so many the net was not torn. Jesus said to them, 'Come and have breakfast.' None of the disciples dared ask him, 'Who are you?' They knew it was the Lord. Jesus came, took the bread and gave it to them, and did the same with the fish. This was now the third time Jesus appeared to his disciples after he was raised from the dead.

It is well-known that those involved in Christian ministry are good at caring for others, but poor at looking after themselves. This lack of self-care is a major cause of attrition among missionaries and a reason for the high drop-out rate among clergy and full-time workers.

Today's story can be approached from many different angles, but it speaks to me about the care Jesus has for his servants and the delight he takes in attending to their well-being. Jesus had helped the disciples with the task of fishing, perhaps a parable for the work of mission that they were called to in the future. But now he welcomes them ashore and invites them to a meal. A warm fire and a hearty breakfast were just what they needed. Times of rest and relaxation, of being cared for and looked after, of receiving rather than giving, are crucial in sustaining ministry over the long haul. Here Jesus legitimises the validity of self-care.

Peter's characteristic enthusiasm to dive in and get involved is commendable, but dangerous too. Zeal without wisdom can lead to burnout. It is highly significant that, even before their work begins, the disciples should be invited to sit and eat.

> How do you practise self-care? Who cares for you?

TH

Day 358

Jesus and Peter

JOHN 21:15-19

Galilee
When they had finished eating, Jesus said to Simon Peter, 'Simon son of John, do you love me more than these?' 'Yes, Lord,' he said, 'you know that I love you.' Jesus said, 'Feed my lambs.' Again Jesus said, 'Simon son of John, do you love me?' He answered, 'Yes, Lord, you know that I love you.' Jesus said, 'Take care of my sheep.' The third time he said to him, 'Simon son of John, do you love me?' Peter was hurt because Jesus asked him the third time, 'Do you love me?' He said, 'Lord, you know all things; you know that I love you.' Jesus said, 'Feed my sheep. Very truly I tell you, when you were younger you dressed yourself and went where you wanted; but when you are old you will stretch out your hands, and someone else will dress you and lead you where you do not want to go.' Jesus said this to indicate the kind of death by which Peter would glorify God. Then he said to him, 'Follow me!'

Difficult conversations are, for some of us, best avoided. So far Peter has avoided talking about his triple denial of Jesus, but now comes the moment of facing up to his failure and doing the necessary soul work that will not only bring healing, but also prepare him to lead the disciples after Jesus has ascended.

The key question for Peter – and for all who take discipleship seriously – is simply this: 'Do you love me? And do you love me more than anything else?'

Church leader Mark Brickman writes, 'Peter needs to do two things: give up his idealized self-image as Jesus' perfect follower and forfeit his self-love for love of Jesus' sheep.'[46] The invitation is to become authentic and real, receive forgiveness and grace, and then take up the call to follow Jesus into a new phase of leadership. That is the doorway to maturity, but it is a small door and requires humility to pass through.

A chastened Peter responds with a resounding 'Yes' to Jesus and offers himself afresh to the master. It is a huge turning point, where he finds freedom from the past and confidence for the future.

> Are there any issues in your life that you withhold from God? Why not have that honest conversation right now?

TH

Day 359

John's testimony

JOHN 21:20-25

Galilee
Peter turned and saw that the disciple whom Jesus loved was following them. (This was the one who had leaned back against Jesus at the supper and had said, 'Lord, who is going to betray you?') When Peter saw him, he asked, 'Lord, what about him?' Jesus answered, 'If I want him to remain alive until I return, what is that to you? You must follow me.' Because of this, the rumour spread among the believers that this disciple would not die. But Jesus did not say that he would not die; he only said, 'If I want him to remain alive until I return, what is that to you?' This is the disciple who testifies to these things and who wrote them down. We know that his testimony is true. Jesus did many other things as well. If every one of them were written down, I suppose that even the whole world would not have room for the books that would be written.

Peter and John were friends, but also rivals. Isn't that often the way? Men in particular seem to view each other as rivals and cannot help comparing themselves. Competitiveness throbs beneath the surface of many relationships, even within Christian ministry. For the sake of the future church, this particular boil needs to be lanced so that these two men can lead well, not as rivals but as collaborators.

Peter's question, 'What about this man?' reveals his tendency towards comparing, and his own ambition. The answer is to refuse to be concerned about what others are doing, and instead concentrate on what Jesus is asking us to do. Selfish ambition, envy and rivalry have no place in the heart of the Christian leader and must be ruthlessly rooted out.

John, for his part, must be content with the calling given to him. Peter will be the one to stand before the crowds and gather in multitudes. John will be the more reflective one, focused on loving God and carefully writing down the gospel story for others to read. Extroverted preacher and introverted teacher will both have a part to play, and the church will need both activist and contemplative strands.

> *Think for a moment. Who do you envy or see as a rival? How can you avoid unhelpful comparisons? Can you build up the other person and appreciate them for who they are?*

TH

Day 360

The great commission

MATTHEW 28:16-20 (MARK 16:15-18)

Galilee
Then the eleven disciples went to Galilee, to the mountain where Jesus had told them to go. When they saw him, they worshipped him; but some doubted. Then Jesus came to them and said, 'All authority in heaven and on earth has been given to me. Therefore go and make disciples of all nations, baptising them in the name of the Father and of the Son and of the Holy Spirit, and teaching them to obey everything I have commanded you. And surely I am with you always, to the very end of the age.'

Long before business leaders thought about mission statements to sharpen the focus of their efforts, Jesus was giving clear instructions to the disciples – and all subsequent generations of leaders – about the purpose and mission of the church.

Here is the vision of Jesus for his church. To ignore it is to ignore him. We are called to make disciples; that is, bring others to know Jesus and then give their lives to following him. This directive happens when it is accompanied by three specific activities.

1. *Going* – there must be an outward movement that will take us away from our own small worlds, into all the world and every group of people, with the intention of calling them to Christ.

2. *Baptising* – marking them out as disciples and bringing them into a trinitarian relationship with God as Father, the Son as Saviour and the Spirit as Helper.

3. *Teaching* – instructing them in the fundamentals of the faith by word and example so they become strong and mature and able in turn to disciple others.

This may be a formidable task, but Jesus gives two reassurances. First, he authorises us to do so, sharing his heavenly authority with us (v. 18). Second, as we go his presence will be with us, protecting us, leading and guiding us, making all this possible. He will be with us wherever he sends us (v. 20). In the light of this, God's people are either 'senders' or 'goers' – either supporting the work of mission through prayer and giving or becoming actively involved in the specific tasks of outreach, evangelism and mission.

> *How does the great commission inform what your church does? How does it impact how you live your life?*

TH

Day 361

Promise and blessing

LUKE 24:48–49 (ACTS 1:4–5)

Galilee
'You are witnesses of these things. I am going to send you what my Father has promised; but stay in the city until you have been clothed with power from on high.'

We covered these verses on Day 352, but it seems important to follow up yesterday's reading on the great commission with this reminder that, before engaging with the task of mission, the disciples must wait for the promised Holy Spirit.

It is easy for disciples with an activist mindset to throw themselves into a whirl of activity in order to get the job done. That is a very natural, human response. We see the challenge, and in response we roll up our sleeves and set about the task. However, this enormous vision cannot be realised by human energy alone.

I was part of a mission agency whose strapline was 'The speediest evangelisation of East Asia's millions'. This approach is typical of many similar agencies who take the great commission seriously, see its urgency and set themselves big targets to be accomplished as soon as possible. This often results in a culture of drivenness, placing a huge sense of burden on the workers.

Nowadays people understand 'mission' in a much broader sense than making disciples. It also includes involvement in social justice, a concern for the environment and climate change, and matters of inclusion and racial equality. All are justifiable concerns but add enormously to the size of the task, especially if we see it as something *we* have to accomplish.

The Father does not want to wear his children out or see them become so preoccupied with the task that they forget the joy of knowing him. It remains his work, in which he invites us to share, and he also promises the help we need by giving us his Spirit. Our priority is to ensure that we are 'clothed' with divine power before we set about our task.

This 'clothing' happens as we wait on him in our weakness and dependency. This may be daily, weekly as we join others for worship or intermittently as we take time aside for retreat and spiritual refreshment. But wait we must.

> *Do you feel driven? How can you incorporate more 'waiting' into your life?*

TH

Day 362

The ascension

LUKE 24:50–53 (MARK 16:19–20)

Bethany, Jerusalem
When he had led them out to the vicinity of Bethany, he lifted up his hands and blessed them. While he was blessing them, he left them and was taken up into heaven. Then they worshipped him and returned to Jerusalem with great joy. And they stayed continually at the temple, praising God.

How do you find saying goodbye? It is never easy, especially if it is a final goodbye, the kind of separation that is going to be permanent and involves parting from a loved one. Jesus had spoken so much about his coming departure, and now the time has arrived for him to return to the Father. Luke, who also wrote the book of Acts, describes this moment of ascension more fully there (Acts 1:9–11).

As he leaves, Jesus blesses the disciples, presumably asking that God will be with them and enable them as they learn to live without his physical presence. The idea of blessing others is thoroughly biblical, whether from the perspective of a priest (Numbers 6:22–27), a leader (Deuteronomy 33:1) or a parent (Genesis 48:15–16). It is far more than wishing someone well. Blessing another person like this imparts spiritual life and releases them positively into the next phase of life.

Having received his blessing, the disciples are now ready to return to Jerusalem, the scene for them of such trauma and fear, but they do so now with joy, released from those shackles and renewed in their confidence and sense of purpose.

Notice how worship of Jesus becomes a feature of their life from now on. They could only do this because they were absolutely convinced that he is God. Their understanding has matured, and they are absolutely certain of his identity as the Son of God. Worship is therefore an appropriate response.

We also notice that they give themselves to praising God and doing so in the temple. How far they have come since the time they were huddled together behind locked doors for fear of the Jewish leaders. This is the point where they enter into a time of waiting to be clothed with power from on high, spending time together in prayer in the upper room (Acts 1:12–14).

▌ *When have you given or received a blessing? Why is it important and helpful?*

TH

Day 363

In retrospect (1) – the Word

JOHN 1:1-5

In the beginning was the Word, and the Word was with God, and the Word was God. He was with God in the beginning. Through him all things were made; without him nothing was made that has been made. In him was life, and that life was the light of all mankind. The light shines in the darkness, and the darkness has not overcome it.

We have now completed our journey through the gospels, following as chronologically as we can the story of Jesus and the disciples. This brings us to a place where we can step back and see the bigger picture behind the story, and we do so through John's prologue to the fourth gospel, which for us becomes our epilogue.

John describes Jesus as the Word. This expression suggests that through Jesus God is speaking to the world, but there is more to it than that. Here is an echo of the beginning of creation when God spoke the world into being. The Son of God was there, sharing the Father's eternal nature and being actively involved in creation. The Jesus we have met in the gospels actually pre-existed the world and was involved in its making. Heaven was his home, and there he enjoyed intimacy with the Father.

When the Son came into the world, he left behind him the glory of heaven but brought heaven with him. As the creator of life, he came to give eternal life to the whole of creation, and his coming brought the light of revelation into a darkened world. Previously God was distant and remote, and not easy to know. In the coming of the Son, he became visible, accessible and touchable. This is why he was given the name Immanuel, meaning God with us (Matthew 1:22-23). Through his life and teaching, his words and actions, the light of God can now be seen.

Such a coming was bound to meet resistance from Satan, the 'ruler' of the darkness in the world. From his birth, Satanic powers sought his destruction but failed. Throughout his life there was continuous opposition and hatred, but nothing Satan could do was able to stop the dawning of the new era ushered in by the Son.

> *Step back and behold in worship the glory of Jesus, the Son of God, now ascended and glorified again.*

TH

Day 364

In retrospect (2) – children of God

JOHN 1:6–13

There was a man sent from God whose name was John. He came as a witness to testify concerning that light, so that through him all might believe. He himself was not the light; he came only as a witness to the light. The true light that gives light to everyone was coming into the world. He was in the world, and though the world was made through him, the world did not recognise him. He came to that which was his own, but his own did not receive him. Yet to all who did receive him, to those who believed in his name, he gave the right to become children of God – children born not of natural descent, nor of human decision or a husband's will, but born of God.

John the Baptist came as a forerunner, sent ahead of Jesus to prepare the way. He became extremely popular but was only a signpost pointing people to Jesus, the Son of God and true light of the world.

We may have thought that his coming would be universally welcomed, but as we have seen through the gospel story his arrival was a challenge to some. Amazingly, although he had been involved in the creation of the world, people did not recognise him. His personal example, miraculous works and powerful teaching were lost on them. They chose not to believe. That was true even of the religious leaders who were blinded by their pride and envy of him.

Many, however, did believe. They saw the character of God in his life, witnessed the power of God through his miracles and heard the voice of God in his teaching. They welcomed him, and as a result became children of God. That was always the intention behind his coming – to seek and to save the lost, to bring people back into a relationship with God the Father.

A big theme for John is that of the new birth, as in the story of Nicodemus (John 3:1–8). We do not become children of God by right; it is nothing to do with natural birth. We become God's children when we believe in Jesus and welcome him into our lives. Then a miracle of God takes place, and we are born again.

> Are you a child of God? If so, rejoice. If not, now is your opportunity.

TH

Day 365

In retrospect (3) – God made flesh

JOHN 1:14–18

The Word became flesh and made his dwelling among us. We have seen his glory, the glory of the one and only Son, who came from the Father, full of grace and truth. (John testified concerning him. He cried out, saying, 'This is the one I spoke about when I said, "He who comes after me has surpassed me because he was before me."') Out of his fullness we have all received grace in place of grace already given. For the law was given through Moses; grace and truth came through Jesus Christ. No one has ever seen God, but the one and only Son, who is himself God and is in closest relationship with the Father, has made him known.

John gives no account of the birth of Jesus, so much enjoyed and celebrated at Christmas, but more than any other gospel writer majors on the significance of his coming.

For John, the focus is on the incarnation, the truth that in Jesus God appeared in human form – or, as *The Message* puts it, 'The Word became flesh and blood, and moved into the neighbourhood' (v. 14). This assumes all that Matthew and Luke tell us about his miraculous conception and birth, but emphasises his true identity as God become man, fully God and completely human.

Those with the eyes of faith saw his glory, the life and light of God radiating through his words and actions. They became aware of the truth he spoke and the grace (unconditional love) that he displayed in his interactions with people. John says that Jesus made God known, helped us to see what God was really like, gave us a living demonstration of his nature and character. Perhaps you have seen this too as you have been reading day by day?

The new way of relating to God that Jesus introduced built on the old covenant brought by Moses, but instigated a different approach, based not on rules and regulations but on grace and truth. This new approach is intensely experiential, because we are all in need of God's mercy, grace and forgiveness. In Jesus there is an endless supply of grace from which we keep on receiving moment by moment, and day by day. It is the only way to live.

> Can you see the difference between law and grace? Which is the basis of your way of living?

TH

Day 366

Final reflection

Thanks be to you, my Lord Jesus, for all the benefits you have given me, for all the pains and insults you have borne for me. O most merciful redeemer, friend and brother, of you three things I pray: to see you more clearly, love you more dearly, follow you more nearly, day by day.
RICHARD OF CHICHESTER (1197–1253)

The famous prayer that has been the inspiration behind this book forms the basis of our final reflection, one which might only be read when it is a leap year! But taking an extra day to think over the past year will pay rich dividends, and using the following questions may stimulate your thinking. They could make an outline for a quiet day or personal retreat.

To see you more clearly

In what ways have you got to know Jesus better? What have you learnt about his life and work that was new to you? What have you understood about him that you didn't know before? How has your perception of Jesus changed?

To love you more dearly

How has your love for Jesus been kindled? What have you come to appreciate about him and admire in him? How has he spoken to you during the past year? In what ways has his grace flowed towards you? What has made you thankful and grateful as you have interacted with the gospel stories?

To follow you more nearly

How have you heard the call to follow Jesus? Has your discipleship been deepened as a result of these readings? What challenges have you faced? Have you made any changes to the way you live and behave? Do you feel closer to Jesus now than before? Have you made any significant life choices based on your reading? Do you feel more surrendered to him now?

TH

list of Bible translations

Unless otherwise stated, scripture quotations are taken from The Holy Bible, New International Version® (Anglicised edition) NIV® Copyright © 1973, 1978, 1984, 2011 by Biblica, Inc. Reproduced with permission of Hodder & Stoughton Limited through PLSclear. All rights reserved worldwide.

Scripture quotations marked with the following abbreviations are taken from the version shown.

CEV   The Contemporary English Version. New Testament © American Bible Society 1991, 1992, 1995. Old Testament © American Bible Society 1995. Anglicisations © British & Foreign Bible Society 1996. Used by permission.

EHV   The Holy Bible, Evangelical Heritage Version® (EHV®) © 2019 Wartburg Project, Inc. All rights reserved. Used by permission.

ERV   The Easy-to-Read Version, copyright © 2006 by Bible League International.

ESV   The Holy Bible, English Standard Version, published by HarperCollins Publishers, © 2001 Crossway Bibles, a division of Good News Publishers. Used by permission. All rights reserved.

GNT   The Good News Bible published by The Bible Societies/HarperCollins Publishers Ltd, UK © American Bible Society 1966, 1971, 1976, 1992, used with permission.

ICB   The Holy Bible, International Children's Bible® Copyright© 1986, 1988, 1999, 2015 by Tommy Nelson™, a division of Thomas Nelson. Used by permission.

JBP   The New Testament in Modern English by J.B Phillips copyright © 1960, 1972 J.B. Phillips. Administered by The Archbishops' Council of the Church of England. Used by permission.

MSG   The Message, copyright © 1993, 1994, 1995, 1996, 2000, 2001, 2002 by Eugene H. Peterson. Used by permission of NavPress. All rights reserved. Represented by Tyndale House Publishers, Inc.

NAB   The New American Bible, revised edition © 2010, 1991, 1986, 1970 Confraternity of Christian Doctrine, Washington, D.C., used by permission of the copyright owner. All Rights Reserved.

NCV   The Holy Bible, New Century Version®. Copyright © 2005 by Thomas Nelson, Inc.

NET   New English Translation Bible® copyright ©1996–2017 All rights reserved. Build 30170414 by Biblical Studies Press, L.L.C.

NKJV   The New King James Version®. Copyright © 1982 by Thomas Nelson. Used by permission. All rights reserved.

NLT   The Holy Bible, New Living Translation, copyright © 1996, 2004, 2007, 2013. Used by permission of Tyndale House Publishers, Inc., Carol Stream, Illinois 60188. All rights reserved.

NRSV   The New Revised Standard Version Updated Edition. Copyright © 2021 National Council of Churches of Christ in the United States of America. Used by permission. All rights reserved worldwide.

TLB   The Living Bible copyright © 1971 by Tyndale House Foundation. Used by permission of Tyndale House Publishers Inc., Carol Stream, Illinois 60188. All rights reserved.

TPT   The Passion Translation®. Copyright © 2017, 2018, 2020 by Passion & Fire Ministries, Inc. Used by permission. All rights reserved. thePassionTranslation.com

notes

1. Henri Nouwen, *Jesus: A gospel* (Orbis Books, 2001), p. v.
2. Michel Quoist, *Prayers of Life* (Gill and Son, 1963), p. 93.
3. Nouwen, *Jesus*, p. 5.
4. David Benner, *Sacred Companions: The gift of spiritual friendship and direction* (IVP, 2002), p. 138.
5. Nouwen, *Jesus*, p. 5.
6. Tim Keller, 'All of life is repentance', *Redeemer Report*, November 2004, p. 1.
7. *diabolos* – properly, a slanderer; a false accuser; unjustly criticising to hurt (malign) and condemn to sever a relationship.
8. The eagle-eyed will notice that Mark mentions John's imprisonment, which seems to take place later. It may be that John was arrested more than once or simply that he is taking liberties with the time scale for his own purposes. We have chosen to use Mark's words here because they are concise and clearly indicate the starting point of the ministry of Jesus and his emphasis on the kingdom.
9. This reflection was influenced by Michael K. Marsh, 'Wine time', **interruptingthesilence.com/2013/01/20/wine-time-a-sermon-on-john-21-11**
10. John places the clearing of the temple at the start of the ministry of Jesus, while the other gospel writers place it towards the end. There may have been two similar events or John may have placed it here for editorial reasons. He is less concerned with historical accuracy than with meaning and significance.
11. John's favourite word for 'miracle', a sign pointed to the character of the one performing the miracle.
12. From the chorus of the most popular song from the 2013 Disney movie *Frozen*.
13. N.T. Wright, *Simply Jesus* (Harper Collins, 2011), p. 76.
14. Ruth Haley Barton, *Strengthening the Soul of Your Leadership: Seeking God in the crucible of ministry* (IVP, 2018), p. 124.
15. **thegracecommentary.com/luke-5** (accessed 16 May 2023).
16. Tom Wright, *Matthew for Everyone – Part 1* (SPCK, 2004), p. 66.
17. It seems impossible to say if Jesus was anointed once, twice or even three times, as the gospel writers each give us different accounts, with similarities and discrepancies. Luke places the event early in the ministry of Jesus; the others place it nearer his death. John attributes the anointing to Mary at her home in Bethany; the others to 'a sinful woman' at the house of Simon the leper. For simplicity's sake, and because it is such a significant event, we have included it at three different times – here, and on Day 248 (John 12:1–11) and Day 283 (Matthew 26:6–13; Mark 14:3–9).
18. Matthew uses the alternative phrase 'kingdom of heaven' in his gospel.
19. R.T. France, *Matthew*, Tyndale New Testament Commentaries (IVP, 1985), p. 172.
20. David Ford, *The Gospel of John: A theological commentary* (Baker Academic, 2021), p. 153.
21. Ford, *The Gospel of John*, p. 153.
22. Tom Wright, *John for Everyone – Part 1* (SPCK, 2002), p. 83.
23. Mags Duggan, *A Better Song to Sing: Finding life again through the invitations of Jesus* (BRF, 2020), p. 24.
24. John Stott, *The Radical Disciple* (IVP, 2010), p. 109.

25 Ford, *The Gospel of John*, p. 165.
26 C.S. Lewis, *Mere Christianity* (MacMillan Publishing, 1952), p. 56.
27 '"Written in heaven" carries the connotation of being enrolled in the citizen-lists of a city.' David Gooding, *According to Luke* (Myrtelfield Trust, 1987), p.200.
28 John Ortberg, *Grace: An invitation to a way of life* (Zondervan, 2000), p. 11.
29 Anne Lamott, *Traveling Mercies: Some thoughts on faith* (Anchor, 2000), p. 75.
30 Ford, *The Gospel of John*, pp. 219, 221.
31 Tom Wright *John for Everyone – Part 2* (SPCK, 2002), p. 7.
32 Duggan, *A Better Song to Sing*, pp. 36–37. See chapter 2 for an excellent fuller exploration of this theme.
33 See the note on Day 108; Luke 7:36–50.
34 Bruce Milne, *The Message of John* (IVP, 1993), p. 174.
35 Michael Green, *The Message of Matthew* (IVP, 2000), p. 224.
36 Green, *The Message of Matthew*, p. 234.
37 Green, *The Message of Matthew*, p. 272.
38 Brennan Manning, *Abba's Child: The cry of the heart for intimate belonging* (Nav Press, 1994), p. 59.
39 David Benner, *Surrender to Love: Discovering the heart of Christian spirituality* (IVP, 2003), p. 64.
40 Milne, *The Message of John*, p. 229.
41 Alex B. Aronis, *Developing Intimacy with God* (Union Church of Manilla, 2002), p. 139.
42 Green, *The Message of Matthew*, p. 287.
43 Leon Morris, *Luke*, Tyndale New Testament Commentary (IVP, 1974), p. 350.
44 William Barclay, *The Gospel of Mark* (The Saint Andrew Press, 1954), p. 377.
45 Green, *The Message of Matthew*, p. 313.
46 Mark Brickman, *Borderlands: Navigating the adventure of spiritual growth* (IVP, 2018), p. 104.

bibliography

Commentaries

Matthew
R.T. France, *Matthew*, Tyndale New Testament Commentaries (IVP, 1985)
Martin Goldsmith, *Matthew and Mission* (Paternoster Press, 2001)
Michael Green, *The Message of Matthew* (IVP, 2000)
Craig Keener, *Matthew*, NTCS (IVP, 1997)
Robert Mounce, *Matthew*, NIBC (Paternoster Press, 1995)
Andrew Page, *The Matthew Experiment* (VTR Publications, 2018)
Charles Price, *Matthew* (Christian Focus, 2000)
Warren Wiersbe, *Matthew: Be loyal* (Scripture Press, 1988)
Tom Wright, *Matthew for Everyone – Part 1 & 2* (SPCK, 2004)

Mark
Donald English, *The Message of Mark* (IVP, 1992)
Tom Wright, *Lent for Everyone – Mark* (SPCK, 2012)

Luke
David Gooding, *According to Luke* (Myrtelfield Trust, 1987)
Leon Morris, *Luke*, Tyndale New Testament Commentaries (IVP, 1988)
Andrew Page, *The Luke Experiment* (VTR Publications, 2022)
Michael Wilcock, *The Message of Luke* (IVP, 1997)
Tom Wright, *Luke for Everyone* (SPCK, 2001)

John
David Ford, *The Gospel of John* (Baker Academic, 2021)
Andrew Page, *The John Experiment* (VTR Publications, 2017)
Bruce Milne, *The Message of John* (IVP, 1993)
Tom Wright, *John for Everyone – Part 1 & 2* (SPCK, 2002)

The life of Christ

A.B. Bruce, *The Training of the Twelve* (Keats Publishing, 1979)
Donald Guthrie, *A Shorter Life of Christ* (Zondervan, 1970)
Peter Hannan, *Nine Portraits of Jesus* (Columba Press, 2009)
Any-Jill Levine, *Short Stories by Jesus* (Harper One, 2015)
Steve Maltz, *Jesus: Life and times* (Malcolm Down, 2022)

Henri Nouwen, *Jesus: A gospel* (Orbis Books, 2001)
Dane Ortlund, *Gentle and Lowly* (Crossway, 2020)
Adrian Plass, *Jesus: Safe, tender, extreme* (Zondervan, 2006)
Simon Ponsonby, *Amazed by Jesus* (Muddy Pearl, 2020)
J.R. Porter, *Jesus Christ* (Duncan Baird, 2007)
Ann Sprangler and Lois Tverberg, *Sitting at the Feet of the Rabbi* (Zondervan, 2018)
N.T. Wright, *Simply Jesus* (Harper Collins, 2011)

Chronology

Orville Daniel, *A Harmony of the Four Gospels* (Baker, 1986)
Robert Thomas and Stanley Gundy, *The NIV Harmony of the Gospels* (Harper One, 1988)
Burton Throckmorton, *Gospel Parallels* (Thomas Nelson, 1992)

about the authors

Tony Horsfall is a writer, retreat leader and mentor based in Bournemouth. He is the author of several books published by BRF as well as a regular contributor to *New Daylight*. His passion is to see God's people deepen in their relationship with him and so be more effective in their service.

Mags Duggan is passionate about helping people grow in their experience of God's personal, life-changing love for them. It's a passion which energised her many years as a missionary in Asia, and then as a lecturer at a missions training college in the UK. Today, this passion is expressed in her ministry as a retreat leader, writer and soul friend.

John Ayrton lives in Southampton with his wife, Mary, where they're involved in church-based cross-cultural ministry. They also pastorally support cross-cultural workers in Eurasia with Interserve. John worked with them for 20 years before becoming a pastor in 2007, and loves to walk with others, following Jesus together in discipleship and mission.

Jenny Brown loves to walk alongside others, encouraging them to dig into the Bible and to grow into the person God created them to be. Having previously served with IFES in Uganda and Russia and with All Souls Church in London, she currently works with Friends International, supporting and training staff, and is a volunteer lay minister.

Melinda Hendry works for Living Leadership, with a focus on cultivating spiritually healthy leaders. Previously she was a senior minister at All Souls, Langham Place. Having studied spiritual formation at Gordon Conwell Seminary, she is also a retreat leader and is training as a spiritual director. She is married to Ross and lives in London.

Steve Aisthorpe is the director of Kilmalieu, a centre of the Abernethy Trust on the west coast of Scotland, a place of prayer, hospitality, adventure and nature. He is a researcher, a coach, the author of *The Invisible Church* and *Rewilding the Church* and a regular contributor to *New Daylight*.

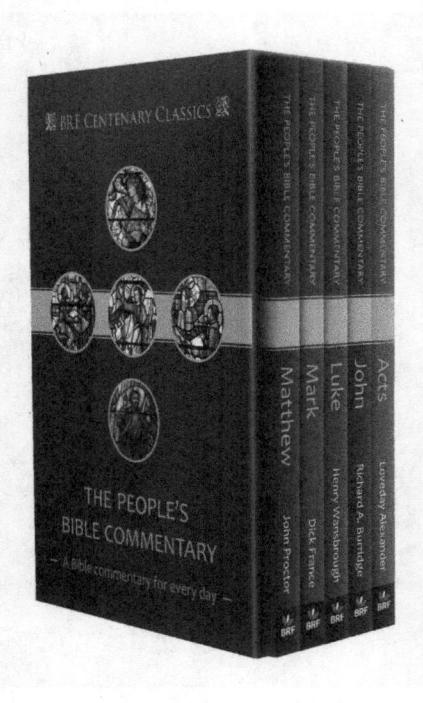

The People's Bible Commentary series presents scholarly insights in straightforward terms, aiming to instruct the head but also to warm the heart, and pointing to how the truths received can be applied personally. A special boxed set edition brings together five best-loved titles in the series to mark BRF's centenary. Matthew's gospel is clear, organised and practical, giving prominence to Jesus' teaching about lifestyle and relationships. Mark's gospel is the shortest of the four first-century books which share the story of Jesus of Nazareth, and the most vividly told. Luke's gospel stresses how acceptance of Jesus' message means a complete reversal of worldly standards of success. John's gospel is a sublime masterpiece that has fascinated theologians and mystics for centuries. Acts is the story of the birth of the church and the beginnings of its journey around the world.

The People's Bible Commentary: Matthew, Mark, Luke, John, Acts
A Bible commentary for every day
John Proctor, Dick France, Henry Wansbrough, Richard Burridge, Loveday Alexander
978 1 80039 093 5   £39.99

brfonline.org.uk

The Bible is at the heart of BRF's work, and this special anniversary collection is a celebration of the Bible for BRF's centenary year. Bringing together a fantastically wide-ranging writing team of authors, supporters and well-wishers from all areas of BRF's work, this resource is designed to help us go deeper into the story of the Bible and reflect on how we can share it in our everyday lives.

The BRF Book of 365 Bible Reflections
with contributions from BRF authors, supporters and well-wishers
978 1 80039 100 0 £14.99

brfonline.org.uk

Prayer is at the heart of BRF's work, and this special illustrated anniversary collection is a celebration of prayer for BRF's centenary year. It can be used in a range of different settings, from individual devotions to corporate worship. Including sections on prayers of preparation, seasonal prayers, and themed prayers for special times and hard times, it is the perfect daily companion to resource your spiritual journey.

The BRF Book of 100 Prayers
Resourcing your spiritual journey
Martyn Payne
978 1 80039 147 5 £12.99

brfonline.org.uk

Daily inspiration

Bible reading notes to sustain, comfort, inform and challenge

If you have enjoyed these daily reflections, you might like to continue your journey through the Bible with the help of our popular Bible reading notes. There are five series to choose from, each with a different style and focus, but all designed to encourage daily Bible reading, reflection and prayer. There's almost certainly one that's perfect for you.

New Daylight

Our most popular series, *New Daylight*, is for everyone on their daily walk with God. Enjoy getting to know the writers, from well-loved regulars to exciting new voices. *New Daylight* has everything you need in one pocket-sized volume, including full Bible reading, reflection and prayer. There's also a large-format deluxe edition.

Day by Day with God

This series is specifically written for women, to help readers root their lives ever more firmly in the Bible. All the contributors are women and write from a woman's perspective. Whatever your current situation in life, you will be inspired and encouraged by these notes.

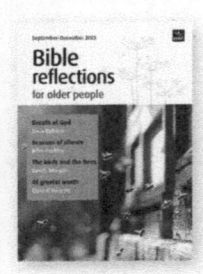

Bible Reflections for Older People

These notes grew out of our Anna Chaplaincy ministry and are written by older people, for older people. Each issue contains 40 undated reflections, written to bring comfort and encouragement, and a magazine section containing interviews, features, poems and a welcome letter from Anna Chaplaincy founder and pioneer, Debbie Thrower.

The Upper Room

'Where the world meets to pray' is a lovely description of *The Upper Room*. Uniquely, the readers of this series are also the writers, with contributions gathered from around the world. It has a worldwide readership of some three million, with over 70 different editions in 40 languages, and BRF is privileged to publish the UK edition.

Guidelines

Guidelines is our most serious and theological series and is popular amongst ministers, leaders and students. Each issue offers four months of in-depth Bible study written by leading scholars. Contributors are drawn from around the world, as well as the UK, and represent a stimulating and thought-provoking breadth of Christian tradition.

Bible reading apps

For readers on the move, we have iOS and Android app editions of *Guidelines*, *New Daylight* and *Day by Day with God*.

Reader feedback

'I want to express my – daily! – thanks for such inspirational writers and content... As I have several friends who also take part, I know my thanks are on behalf of many people who have found the notes a source of strength and support during challenging times.'

'My wife and I have been taking the BRF notes for many years now, and use them when we say the morning Office as part of our daily reading. We get so much out of them, and hope to continue to do so for many years to come.'

'These Bible study notes were such a support during lockdown when our church was shut and all I could get was a weekly service on television or radio. Thank you so much for all the work you and the writers do.'

For more information on all our Bible reading notes, go to
brfonline.org.uk/our-notes

BRF *Enabling all ages to grow in faith*

Anna Chaplaincy
Living Faith
Messy Church
Parenting for Faith

BRF is a Christian charity that resources individuals and churches. Our vision is to enable people of all ages to grow in faith and understanding of the Bible and to see more people equipped to exercise their gifts in leadership and ministry.

To find out more about our work, visit

brf.org.uk